IRAN CONTRA

S&L

THE GULF WAR

All these events cost America an unprecedented amount of money, reputation and, in the case of the Gulf War, American lives. In the case of the S&L Crisis, the unfortunate consequences brought this country to the brink of financial ruin.

Many feel that George Bush, as a key player in the decisions surrounding these events, should have some accountability for the negative fallout. Yet, it seems that the American public has been sold a bill of pork rinds and fishing trips in its stead.

Read for yourself and decide whether former CIA Director George Bush, veteran in the ranks of secret activities and secret agendas, has kept damaging information from the media through his extensive political connections.

THE CRIMES OF A PRESIDENT

New Revelations on
Conspiracy & Cover-Up
in the Bush & Reagan
Administrations

Joel Bainerman

A division of Shapolsky Publishers, Inc.

The Crimes of a President

S.P.I. BOOKS

A division of Shapolsky Publishers, Inc.

Copyright © 1992 by Joel Bainerman

For any additional information, contact:
S.P.I. BOOKS/Shapolsky Publishers, Inc.
136 West 22nd Street
New York, NY 10011
(212) 633-2022
FAX (212) 633-2123

ISBN: 1-56171-188-8

10 9 8 7 6 5 4 3 2 1

Printed and bound in the United States of America

Dedication

This book is dedicated to the profession of investigative journalism. Although it has become the orphan of the mainstream press and is practiced by only a small group of writers, it can play a vital role in protecting democratic societies from the threat of dictatorial rule. While senators and congressmen may be representatives of the people, the sole constituency of the investigative journalist is the truth.

Contents

THE
CRIMES
OF A
PRESIDENT

Introduction

"Secrecy has spread in Washington in the last 10 years, concealing much of what government does. The touted American system of constitutional checks and balances is no longer working as it was meant to. Freebooters like Casey and North can exercise power without responsibility, without accountability. They can sup with the devil — and be found out only much later, and by accident."

Anthony Lewis, *The New York Times*,
April 22nd, 1991

In 1989 I set out to write a book about Israel's involvement in the Iran-Contra Affair. My investigation led me to the mysterious death in Mexico of Israeli counter-terrorism official Amiram Nir in December 1988. There were many rumors at the time that Nir was "bumped off" by the CIA, because he was set to go public with what he knew of then-Vice President George Bush's dirty dealings with Panamanian dictator Manuel Noriega.

Eventually I discovered that the real story wasn't Israel's involvement in Iran-Contra, but President Bush's. Yet the more research I did, the more confused I got. While I thought I was fairly knowledgeable on American foreign policy, particularly in how it relates to the Middle East, I in fact discovered I knew little of the actual truth. Events which I thought I understood turned out to be nothing more than streams of "disinformation" designed to deceive the American public. Secret agendas and covert operations had replaced traditional forms of statecraft.

This came as quite a shock to someone who had supported the conservative agenda of the Reagan years. As my knowledge of these covert actions increased, I was no longer sure that the U.S. government was still the "good guys." Or if the Administration was truly interested in global peace and democracy and if the White House actually respected the independence of the judicial system. None of what I was discovering was compatible with what I *thought* America stood for.

I then set out to understand what was the driving ideological force behind the Bush Administration's policies. I figured if I knew what moved the President, the rest of the pieces of the puzzle would fall into place.

And did they ever. The more I learned of Bush's past, the more the present made sense. For instance, although he is often portrayed as bland and having no identifiable beliefs, President Bush does indeed have a particular ideology. It is a unique brand of imperialistic thinking stemming from his Freemasonry roots which contends that intervention into the domestic affairs of other countries is permissible if it is in the pursuit of global domination. This worldview is part of the "New World Order" the President talks about. While most people think he is referring to a morally based, idealistic concept of a more peaceful planet, he has something very different in mind.

Until embarking on my research, I never realized how important secrecy was to Vice President and President Bush. Nearly all of his foreign policies are carried out covertly, behind the backs of Congress and the American people. This obsession with secrecy is due to his past and present ties to the CIA and his membership in secret societies such as Skull and Bones and the Freemasons.

I wondered, "Are most American voters aware of Bush's ties to these organizations? What do Freemasons believe? What is their agenda?"

Another aspect of Bush's political life which astounded me was his ability to remain unscathed by any White House scandal. When he was Vice President his office was constantly being tied to the illegal effort to supply the Nicaraguan Contras. Yet Bush always denied he was personally involved. The Reagan-Bush Administration came up with something called "plausible deniability"; when asked about whether they or any other White House officials were involved in Iran-Contra, they could simply answer: "No." Nobody ever challenged these responses.

Yet consider this: Is it possible that although the Reagan Administration lobbied Congress for aid to support the Contras, the White House *didn't* direct the secret supply effort to the Contras? Could it be that private individuals were operating and financing this secret operation to arm the Nicaraguan rebels, but the White House was not aware of it? Or if it was, did nothing to stop it?

Could a lone Lt. Colonel Oliver North in the National Security Council have decided on his own to arm the Contras and trade arms for hostages without the Office of the Vice President being aware of it? Could it have happened that Bush disagreed with the operation but North and former CIA Director William Casey went ahead with it anyway, behind his back? Or that Casey and North kept the details from him so the Vice President would be able to tell an honest lie? Could the second-highest elected official in the U.S. government not be aware of the policies being carried out in the governing institutions he presided over?

Crimes of a President contains no smoking gun linking Bush directly to any White House scandal. I maintain no contacts in the intelligence community nor have I obtained any top-secret CIA documents. Nearly all of the content in this book was obtained by meeting investigative journalists and gathering materials from their published sources. All I did was to put it all together under one roof so it can be viewed in one glance. Let the reader be the judge. Has George Bush told the American people all he knows about Iran-Contra and other White House scandals? Has he manipulated justice and carried out policies in secret behind the backs of Congress and the American people?

If the American public does not wake up soon, it may find itself leading the world into a "New World Order" based on the teachings and aims of the American branch of Freemasonry. Bush and his covert operators have rigged the system so that whoever you vote for, you are voting for them.

Even as I write these words before the 1992 election, we shouldn't make the mistake of believing that if Democratic presidential candiate Bill Clinton wins we will have thrown the "one world order"/ global-domination crowd out. Bush and his Masonry objectives won't suddenly disappear. Quayle is already well groomed for 1996.

I have assembled the information contained in this book from a small group of dedicated people who still believe that a corrupt government is wrong and should be exposed. Together, we have for the first time documented the frightening influence George Bush has had on American society. Yet I'm sure *Crimes of a President* merely scratches the surface.

Read this book carefully and then give it to someone else. It was written as a warning: Conspiracy theories don't necessarily have to be wildly concocted tales fabricated by convicted arms dealers and drug dealers and leftist journalists out to smear the White House. That's what the White House wants you to believe.

Wake up, America! What you see isn't at all what you

are getting. George Bush has been hoodwinking you for the past twelve years and will continue to do so unless you take a serious look at the President's ideological roots. Bush's Freemasonry ties and New World Order ideology are a very serious threat to freedom of thought as we know it.

Joel Bainerman
Beit Shemesh, Israel
October 1992

CHAPTER 1

The Bush Illusion

How does President Bush do it? How did he implement his secret agendas, lie about his role in Iran-Contra, sucker Saddam Hussein and the American people into the Gulf War, with nobody catching on?

The answer lies in Bush's ideological underpinnings on how the world should be run.

Bush's talk of a "New World Order" isn't so new at all. It comes straight from the ideology of the Skull and Bones society, which believes that its members have a strategic and moral obligation (i.e., right) to control the events of the world. Their goal is to restore the "greatness of America" in world affairs and they see themselves as a sort of distinguished WASP caste, a modern-day version of the Roman warrior.

The Order of Skull and Bones, one of seven secret elite fraternal societies based at Yale University in New Haven, Connecticut, allows only 15 males in their junior year to join. Potential selectees must be white, male and wealthy. Non-WASPS are excluded. If a woman were ever allowed into the Skull and Bones meeting place, the clubhouse would have to be bulldozed (*Esquire*, September 1977).

Bonesmen, as they are called, believe in the notion of "constructive chaos," which justifies covert actions to "maintain order." To confuse the public they employ ambiguity and secrecy, i.e., disinformation. Thus the foreign policies of Bonesmen who hold public office are almost always carried out via a secret agenda through the instrument of covert operations.

Anthony Sutton, an historian who has written a book on the Order, says that since its founding it has taken on more occult and ritualistic trappings and that it is secretly known among its members as the "Brotherhood of Death." Others claim the society's Germanic origins are reflected in the building on the Yale campus that the secret order uses, which is said to contain remnants of Hitler's private collection of silver.

The 15 new members selected each year go through a formal initiation ceremony. The senior members of the Order come to their door, knock, tap the potential member on the shoulder and ask: "Skull and Bones: Do you accept?" If the candidate accepts, a message wrapped with a black ribbon sealed by black wax with the skull and crossbones emblem is handed to the inductee. This will tell him when and where to meet on initiate night.

According to a 1940 Skull and Bones document, the initiating ceremony consists of the potential member being placed in a coffin, as he is chanted over and reborn into the society. He is then removed from the coffin and given a robe with symbols on it. A bone with his name on it will be tossed into the bone heap at the start of every meeting.

Historically, Bonesmen have had a tremendous influence on American foreign policy. Alphonso Taft, a co-founder of Skull and Bones, was Secretary of War in 1876 and Attorney General in 1876-1877. He brought pressure on President William McKinley to enter the war against Spain to "liberate" Cuba and seize the Philippines. When McKinley was assassinated in Buffalo, New York, Bonesman Teddy Roosevelt moved into the White House and surrounded himself with fellow Bonesmen such as William Howard Taft, who himself would be elected President in 1908 (*Covert Action*, No. 33, Winter 1990).

Other Bonesmen include: Robert Taft, Speaker of the

House in 1921-1926 and then a Senator from Ohio, 1938-1950; Robert Lovett, Assistant Secretary of War 1941-1945, Deputy Secretary of Defense, and Secretary of Defense in 1950; Averell Harriman, U.S. Ambassador to the Soviet Union, 1943-1946, Governor of New York and then Under Secretary of State for Asia, 1961-1963; General George Marshall, Chief of Staff during World War II who would later serve as Harry Truman's Secretary of State; William Bundy, Stimson's special assistant at the War Department (one of Bundy's sons, McGorge, was President Kennedy's and Johnson's National Security Advisor; the other, William, was a CIA official and served in the Departments of State and Defense); William F. Buckley, Jr., the founder of the *National Review*, and his brother James, who served, 1981-1982, in the Reagan White House as Under Secretary of State for Security Assistance, Science and Technology (*Covert Action*, No. 33, Winter 1990). Along with George Bush, highly placed Bonesmen now serving in the government include James Lilley, U.S. Ambassador to Beijing, and David Boren, chairman of the Senate Intelligence Committee, a Democrat from Oklahoma.

Godfrey Hodgson, foreign editor of *The Independent* of London and author of *The Colonel: The Life and Wars of Henry Stimson 1867-1950* (1990), says that George Bush's mentor was Bonesman Henry Stimson, who was Secretary of State under Hoover and served in the Roosevelt and Truman cabinets. "Stimson contributed enormously to Bush's political development," writes Hodgson. "It was the "most important educational experience in his life" (*The Nation*, January 21st, 1991).

Early Bonesmen were internationalists (i.e., imperialists) who believed the U.S. would play a great role in the world's destiny. Stimson thought it was imperative for America to dominate the Pacific Ocean and Far East. It was this imperialistic ideology which encouraged President McKinley to enter the Spanish-American War.

Stimson served under six presidents: Theodore Roosevelt, William Howard Taft, Woodrow Wilson, Calvin Coolidge, Franklin Roosevelt and Harry Truman. He oversaw the Manhattan Project and personally decided to use atomic weapons against Japan and formulated Herbert Hoover's military and economic restrictions against postwar Japan.

Bush was brought up in the Stimson tradition that the U.S. was now (1890 to 1950) a great power. He learned from Stimson, according to Hodgson, that "the task of the leader is not to negotiate or prevaricate, but rather to stay firm, draw a line in the sand, and, if that line is crossed, to fight" (*The Nation*).

Stimson believed that America needed to enter into a military confrontation every thirty years or so. This, he contended, enables a nation to rally behind the flag and gives it a common cause. In one fell swoop the failures of past decades can be wiped clean. The Gulf War served that purpose for President Bush.

Armed with the Skull and Bones ideology, Bush needed a vehicle in the Reagan-Bush White House to carry out its covert foreign policy. That instrument was "The Vice President's Task Force on Combating Terrorism," followed by the National Security Decision Directive Number 3, which gave Bush responsibility for the "Crisis Management Committee" in the Cabinet (*New York Times*, April 12th, 1981). Then came the "The Terrorist Incident Working Group," created to bring back hostages held in Lebanon, and finally the "Operations Sub-Group" and the "Restricted Terrorist Incidents Working Group."

By establishing a special apparatus, the Vice President's Task Force on Combating Terrorism, Bush and Casey created a network which was able to bypass normal channels and initiate policies that might have been opposed by other White House officials such as Secretary of State Shultz and Secretary of Defense Weinberger (*Covert Action*, No. 33, Winter

1990).

The members of the Task Force are: Robert Oakley, then director of the State's Department Office to Combat Terrorism, Charles Allen, Robert Earl, and middle-level operatives at the CIA such as Duane Clarride, Ray Clines, and Charles Allen, as well as Noel Koch from the Defense Department, Lt. General John Moellering from the Joint Chiefs of Staff, Executive Assistant of the FBI Oliver Revell, Lt. General Sam Wilson and Lt. General Harold Aaron, both former Directors of the Defense Intelligence Agency, General Richard Stillwell, former CIA Chief of Covert Operations in the Far East, and Deputy Director of the CIA Robert Gates. (It's interesting to note that despite Bush leading the Task Force on Combatting Terrorism, the great threat of terrorism which the American people heard so much about during the Reagan Administration seems to have disappeared in the Bush White House.)

Members of the Task Force used their counterterrorism channels to thwart official U.S. policy and to conceal their activities from their superiors. They were the operatives who moved the policies from the Task Force Senior Review Group and executed them along with Oliver North through the Operations Sub-Group (*Covert Action*, No. 33, Winter 1990). They were Bush's secret team of covert operators.

"Probably the worst thing for society is to have a head of state who is also a former covert operator," says former CIA operative Victor Marchetti. "During these times the secret services get out of control."

THE REAGAN-BUSH WHITE HOUSE: A NEW ERA IN SECRET GOVERNMENT

As early as March 1981 the Reagan-Bush Administration paved the way for a new wave of covert operations. After Watergate, Presidents Ford and Carter tried to issue executive orders to curb the CIA's activities, particularly ones which involved the violation of the civil liberties of American citizens. Yet a blue ribbon commission established in 1975 headed by Vice President Nelson Rockefeller, and coincidentally with Ronald Reagan as a private citizen as a member, concluded that "Presidents should refrain from directing the CIA to perform what are essentially internal security tasks."

A proposal put forth by the Bush-Reagan Administration as early as March 23rd, 1981, drafted by mid-level career agents, permitted the agency to undertake covert operations within the U.S. and to spy on American citizens. The new order no longer required the CIA to collect information by the "least intrusive means possible," thus enabling searches without warrants, surreptitious entries, and infiltration of political organizations (*Time*, March 23rd, 1981).

The push for the executive order was made under the guise of combating terrorism. In the early meetings of the National Security Council, it was argued that limits put on the CIA prevented the agency from conducting surveillance on suspected terrorists once they had entered the country. (How many terrorist attacks took place in the United States during the 1970s?)

Some members of Congress didn't like the new regulations. Don Edwards, then chairman of the House Civil and Constitutional Rights Subcommittee, said the draft order would "put the CIA back in the business of domestic spying" (*Time*, March 23rd, 1981).

The Bush-Reagan Administration used another technique to create the political framework for its string of secret agendas and covert operations. Writing in June 1989 in *The Nation*, Eve Pell, a staff reporter at the Center for Investigative Reporting in San Francisco, describes how secret presidential decrees and National Security Decision Directives (NSDD) propelled America into some of the controversial events of the past decade. President Reagan issued nearly

300 NSDDs. It was an NSDD that enabled the CIA to begin arming Contra soldiers, and that led to the invasion of Grenada in 1983.

An NSDD is different than an executive order or presidential finding, as the latter are made known to the the House and Senate Intelligence committees, whereas NSDDs do not have to be revealed to any other branch of government. Of the 300 NSDDs issued by Reagan, less than fifty have been declassified in whole or in part by the National Security Council, the government body which decides if an NSDD will be made public. In other words, only 15 percent of the most important policy decisions made during the Bush-Reagan White House are known to the American people.

Allan Adler, a former legislative counsel to the American Civil Liberties Union, said the Reagan-Bush Administration "had a pronounced proclivity for using NSDDs, apparently because it didn't have to make them public." Anna Nelson, an historian at Tulane University, says that the Reagan White House was "extraordinary in its abuse of the process." "The original National Security Council documents were broad policy papers, with agency implementation," she also explained. "Some of Reagan's NSDDs bypassed even normal agency channels, as well as Congress. The arrogance of this arrangement is incredible."

Eve Pell argues that during the Reagan Administration, the NSDDs were the backbone of the hidden government, issued to evade congressional scrutiny and on certain occasions ordering actions which stand contrary to what the stated policy of the government was.

NSDD Number 77 is a good example of how Bush and Reagan employed NSDDs to serve secret agenda goals. It allowed the National Security Council to coordinate interagency efforts for what was called the "Management of Public Diplomacy Relative to National Security." This directive served as a the basis for "public diplomacy activities" (i.e., propaganda) by enabling "organizational support for foreign governments and private groups to encourage the growth of democratic political institutions and practices." In reality, the directive created propaganda ministries in the National Security Council, the State Department and the White House. The General Accounting Office believed these activities violated the law banning "covert propaganda" within the U.S.

In 1987, then head of the House Government Operations Committee Jack Brooks asked National Security advisor Frank Carlucci for a list of all the NSDDs issued by the Reagan Administration since 1981. Carlucci refused and called into the question the constitutionality of the request. Speaker of the House Jim Wright, after being denied access to the same list, claimed "Congress cannot react responsibly to new dictates for national policy set in operation by the executive branch behind closed doors."

Brooks was unable to pass a bill requiring that the Speaker of the Senate be informed of any new NSDDs. At the hearing on that bill, Representative Louis Stokes asked "Is the secret policy of the United States the same as the public policy of the United States . . . with respect to very sensitive matters such as terrorism and paramilitary covert actions?"

GEORGE BUSH, DONALD GREGG, AND IRAN-CONTRA—WHAT DID THEY KNOW?

George Bush would have preferred that all of the policies and covert operations he initiated remain secret. When they didn't, he and his staff simply denied their existence, or their involvement in them. To set the historical record straight, it's important to look at George Bush's entire repertoire of official responses to all of the scandals which came under the umbrella of what became commonly known as the "Iran-Contra Affair."

Bush insisted that he was "out of the loop" on all matters

relating to Iran-Contra. He came to understand the "hidden dimensions" of the scandal only in December 1986 after his National Security Advisor, Donald Gregg, briefed him. This was nearly a month after Attorney General Edwin Meese disclosed the diversion of arms sales profits to the Contras. "Not until that briefing," Bush says, "did I fully appreciate how the initiative was actually implemented."

What is Bush trying to tell us? That secret, covert operations are going on and the highest elected officials in the country are not informed of them? That's either a silent coup, or an extremely poor grasp on national affairs by the President and Vice President.

Logic would dictate that Bush would have had to know what was going on. He admitted he attended a meeting on August 6th, 1985, when former National Security Advisor Robert McFarlane outlined the deal to trade U.S. arms for American hostages held by the Iranians. On January 6th, 1986, President Reagan authorized the sale of TOW missiles to win the release of the American hostages. The next morning all of the President's advisors gathered in the Oval Office as Secretary of State George Shultz and Secretary of Defense Caspar Weinberger expressed their opposition. Shultz told the Tower Commission that by the end of the meeting it was clear that the President and the Vice President disagreed with him (Schultz). A few weeks later, National Security Advisor John Poindexter sent a computer message to North which acknowledged high-level opposition to his policies, but concluded: "President and V.P. are solid in taking the position that we have to try."

What was Bush's response to this meeting? "I may have been out of the room at the time and didn't recall the two Secretaries' strenuous opposition." Bush claims that if he had heard them he would have "moved to reconsider the whole project."

By his own response, at the very least Bush knew there

was a "project." He would like the American people to believe that while one of the most controversial issues of the Reagan White House's foreign policy agenda was being discussed and analyzed by the President's top advisors, George was out making a wee-wee.

Amiram Nir, Israel's advisor on terrorism to former Prime Minister Shimon Peres, met Bush in the King David Hotel in Jerusalem on July 29th, 1986. According to notes taken by Craig Fuller, Bush's aide, Nir outlined for Bush efforts taken throughout the past year "to gain the release of the hostages, and that a decision still had to be made whether the arms desired by the Iranians would be delivered in separate shipments or for each hostage as they are released." "We are dealing with the most radical elements," Nir told Bush, according to the memorandum which was published in the Tower Commission Report, despite Reagan administration officials efforts to quash it.

President Bush said that "he couldn't remember much about the briefing, nor did he fully understand what Nir was saying at the time." (Was Nir speaking in Hebrew?) He said, "I didn't know what he was referring to when he was talking about radicals, nor did I ask."

Why then didn't the VP say to himself, "Hey, if these activities are being carried out by a foreign government and involve the sale of American-made weapons to secure the release of U.S. citizens, I need to know all the details," and then ask Nir for a full explanation of the events?" If he didn't like what he was hearing, why didn't he demand the entire operation be halted? If Bush had no idea what Nir was talking about, why was he meeting him? What did his advisors who arranged the meeting with Nir brief Bush on, that was going to be discussed, if not arms for hostages?

In another comment Bush responded, "I listened to him [Nir] and there was not a big exchange in all of this. I did not know all the details. I didn't know what he was referring to when he was talking about "radicals." Asked why he didn't raise questions on the initiative, Bush responded by saying he felt "uncomfortable" at the meeting and thought it was a "listening session" (*Washington Post*, October 21st, 1988).

What does that mean? That Bush felt "uncomfortable" speaking to Nir about a secret effort to release U.S. hostages, or about selling American weapons to a country that supposedly America hates and considers a terrorist threat. What does he mean by a "listening session"? Listening to what? Nir's views on Third World economic development? When did Bush believe it was going to become a "doing session"?

On the campaign trail in July 1988, Bush said, "Nir presented him with only a tiny piece of a very complicated puzzle." Does that mean Nir told gave him details of the arms for hostages deal but George couldn't complete the "puzzle"?

Bush is asking the American people to believe that the Vice President of the United States takes time out of a busy two-day state visit to meet with Israel's official counterterrorism expert, a subject which Bush heads a high-level inter-agency group on in the White House. But when they speak, he has no interest in what Nir is saying. He doesn't bother to ask Nir to clarify his words or thoughts, instead just sits and listens, but hasn't a clue to what Nir is talking about because Bush knows nothing of any efforts to free any hostages. Bush then stands up, shakes his head because he hasn't understood a word this person has told him, announces that he doesn't want to hear any more, and walks out of the room.

DID BUSH KNOW OF THE OPERATION TO SUPPLY THE CONTRAS?

Bush's official response to what he knew of the secret effort to supply the Nicaraguan Contras is more complicated. Here, his National Security Advisor, Donald Gregg, saves his boss from having to answer any questions by insisting that Bush didn't know about any of these initiatives. He claims he didn't tell Bush about any of these activities because "he didn't think it was Vice Presidential" enough for Bush to know. Thus, Bush never knew.

Is such a contention believable? Is it possible that the Vice President's chief aide was fully informed of all activities to arm and train the Contras, but his boss, the Vice President, wasn't? Why would Gregg want to keep these important security matters secret from his boss? Deniability? Did Bush tell Gregg, "Since Congress won't let us support the Contras, you have to find a way to keep them supplied with weapons. Do whatever you have to do, just don't tell me about it so I will be able to claim I didn't know"? If so, this means that at the very least Bush knew about the existence of these secret operations and is guilty of violating a congressional ban.

Efforts by the Vice President's Office to supply the Contras begins in the summer of 1982 when Bush and Casey met and came up with the Black Eagle Operation, a plan to ship weapons to the Contras through San Antonio, Texas, to Panama and then on to El Salvador (*Rolling Stone*, November 3rd, 1988). According to a retired army covert operative assigned to the operation, Bush agreed to use his office as a cover as Gregg coordinated financial and operational details. "Bush and Gregg were the asbestos wall," says the retired military man. "You had to burn through them to get to Casey" (*Rolling Stone*, November 3rd, 1988).

A memo dated March 17th, 1983, written by Gregg to then-National Security Advisor Bud McFarlane, described how former CIA operative Felix Rodriguez, who served under Donald Gregg in Vietnam, had devised a military plan called "Pink Team" to launch mobile air strikes with "minimum U.S. participation" against leftist rebels in Central America. The plan was never implemented, but Rodriguez was soon after recruited full-time into the effort to resupply the Contras.

When asked, after he gave sworn testimony to Iran-Contra investigators, why he had failed to mention this secret memo, Gregg replied, "One, I didn't think of it. Two, it had nothing to do with the questions being asked of me." In those same hearings, he testified: "We [Bush and Gregg] never discussed the Contras. We had no responsibility for it; we had no expertise in it." Also in 1983 the Vice President's Office dispatched Gustavo Villoldo, former CIA agent in Honduras and Bay of Pigs veteran, to work as a combat advisor and to establish an arms supply line to the Contras. According to former intelligence agents who claim they worked with the VP's office, Villoldo was one of several individuals recruited by Gregg to work outside normal CIA channels (*The Progressive*, May 1987).

In November 1983 the National Security Council (which Bush was a member of) needed to find more weapons for the Contras. One of North's memos stated that Bush had been asked to "concur on these [weapons] increases in each previous case" (*Rolling Stone*, November 3rd, 1988).

In an eleven-point memo to his boss on September 18th, 1984, entitled "Funding for the Contras" and made available to Iran-Contra investigators, Gregg discussed military and political aspects of the Contra war. He told Bush, "In response to your question, Dewey Clarridge supplied the following information: A very tough estimate would be that they [the Contras] have received about $1.5 million [from private sources]. This is based on what we know of Contra purchases of gasoline, ammunition, etc." (*The Progressive*, March 1987).

For ten months in 1985 an operation known as the "Arms Supermarket" supplied the Contras. It consisted of private arms merchants tied to the CIA, as well as the intelligence arms of the Honduras military, and was financed in part with money from the Medellín cocaine cartel (*Rolling Stone*, November 3rd, 1988).

In April 1988 the Senate Foreign Relations Subcommittee on Narcotics, Terrorism and International Operations, headed by Senator John Kerry, heard testimony from Richard Brenneke, who worked for the CIA on the project. Brenneke said Gregg was the Washington contact for the operation and that he (Brenneke) made numerous purchases of arms manufactured in the Eastern Bloc. Brenneke further claimed Noriega granted transit privileges for the flights and took his cut of the profits.

Bush responded to allegations that his office was involved in the operation by personally accusing Senator Kerry of allowing "slanderous" allegations to leak from his committee, and insisted that the newsmagazine *Newsweek*, which published details of the operation, was printing "garbage." Despite the fact that Brenneke was not charged with any crime, Bush said, "The guy whom they are quoting is the guy who is trying to save his own neck (*Washington Post*, May 17th, 1988).

Another incident Bush denied involvement in was whether he had offered a *quid pro quo* to Honduran President Roberto Suazo Córdova in return for his help in training the Contras. A memo written by John Poindexer on February 20th, 1985, reads: "We want the VP [Bush] to discuss these matters with Suazo" (*Time*, May 15th, 1989).

Bush paid a visit to Tegucigalpa on March 16th, 1985, and met with President Roberto Suazo Córdova, promising him that the U.S. would increase military and economic aid in return for his help in aiding the Contras. Bush assured the Honduran government that it could expect to be rewarded if it continued to harbor Contra camps on its territory and supply military goods to the rebels. This was at the point when Córdova was threatening to close down the camps and stop all arms shipments.

That *quid pro quo* was approved the previous month at a meeting of the Special Interagency Crisis-Planning group

Bush headed (*Time*, April 17, 1989). While aid began almost immediately after Bush's visit, as did Honduran support for the Contras, Bush would still contend at a photo session after he had become President that "the word of the President of the United States, George Bush, is, There was no *quid pro quo*. No implication, no *quid pro quo*, direct or indirect, from me to the President of Honduras. There has been much needless, mindless speculation about my word of honor, and I've answered it now, definitely" (*Time*, May 15th, 1989). (No, George, you didn't answer it. You simply denied it.) But if it wasn't a *quid pro quo* and Bush didn't discuss Contra business with Suazo Córdova, what was so important that the VP had to make a personal trip to Honduras? A tourist exchange?

Also in 1985 Gregg sent Felix Rodriguez to El Salvador to aid the Contra resupply effort. General Paul Gorman, then head of U.S. military forces in Central America, wrote a memo to the U.S. ambassador in El Salvador. In it he said: "Rodriquez is operating as a private citizen but his acquaintanceship to the VP is real enough, going back to the latter days of DCI [Director of Central Intelligence]" (*The Progressive*, March 1989).

While Gorman knew the purpose behind Rodriquez's presence in El Salvador, Gregg claimed he didn't, contesting that all he knew was that Rodriguez was sent to El Salvador "to deal with insurgency." When asked why Rodriguez would tell his plans to Gorman but not to Gregg, Gregg replied, "Felix doesn't tell me everything he does. I just had never heard of it" (*The Progressive*, March 1987).

Gregg, however, does admit he met with Felix Rodriguez, but said they never discussed the Contras. He maintained that Rodriguez didn't mention his work with the Contras because he knew "that was not my interest." Gregg is saying Rodriguez may have been working on an operation to supply the Contras, but it wasn't on behalf of the Vice President's

Office. That it must have been a private initiative by Rodriguez which was not sanctioned by the U.S. government; therefore it would not "be in Gregg's interest."

Bush's ties to Rodriguez and Latin American drug lords were confirmed by Ramón Milián Rodríguez, a financier for the Medellín drug cartel who is currently serving a 43-year prison sentence. Rodríguez testified before a Senate investigation into ties between the Contras and drug traffickers. He told the PBS documentary program *Frontline*: "Guns, Drugs, and the CIA" that he received a request for $10 million from Felix Rodriguez to finance Contra support: "The request for the contribution made a lot more sense because Felix was reporting to George Bush. If Felix had come to me and said I'm reporting to anyone else, let's say, you know, Oliver North, I might have been more skeptical. I didn't know who Oliver North was and I didn't know his background. But if you have a CIA, or what you consider to be a CIA-man, coming to you saying, 'I want to fight this war, we're out of funds, can you help us out? I'm reporting directly to Bush on it,' I mean it's very real, very believable, here you have a CIA guy reporting to his old boss."

For two guys who rose to the highest levels of the political echelons in the United States, Gregg and Bush sure have bad memories. In Oliver North's notebooks there is an entry from September 10th, 1985, which discusses a meeting he had with Donald Gregg and the chief of the U.S. military advisory group in El Salvador, Colonel James Steele. The three discussed "logistic support" for the Contras. When asked about the meeting, Gregg simply said: "I don't think that meeting ever took place" (*Newsweek*, May 23rd, 1986). A handwritten note from November 1985 from George Bush to Oliver North thanked North for his "dedication and tireless work with the hostage thing and with Central America." When asked later about the note, Bush said "he didn't recall why he sent it." (What other reason could Bush have had to send it other than to thank North for his efforts? Does Bush not remember anything to do with "the hostage thing" or "Central America"? What would happen to a doctor who told the jury during a malpractice suit against him that "he forgot" to tell his patient there would be side effects to the drug he prescribed for him? Why can a doctor be sued for malpractice of his profession but a national leader can just say he forgot, and no further investigation is required?)

In a April 1986 meeting on supplying the Contras, Rodriguez complained to Gregg that North's men were skimming profit from the arms sales. When asked about this meeting, Gregg said he didn't tell Bush about Rodriguez's complaints because it wasn't "Vice-Presidental." Gregg's response indicates that he knew about the operation to arm the Contras, from at least April 1986 onwards. It could also be inferred that Bush knew, but that Gregg didn't want to inform him of Rodriguez's complaints.

Gregg's aide Colonel Samuel Watson wrote two memos before attending a May 1986 meeting with Bush and Gregg which briefed Bush on "the status of the war in El Salvador and resupply of the Contras." When asked how it was, when he had already denied knowing anything about supplying the Contras, that the meeting apparently discussed those very topics, Gregg admitted he was "baffled as to how that agenda item appears. . . . It was possible that it was a garbled reference to resupply of copters instead of resupply of Contras," he explained (UPI, May 13th, 1989).

When Colonel Watson was asked by Iran-Contra investigators of the role of the Vice President's Office in the Contra effort, he answered: "I've taken it as assumed that it was my duty that anything to do with Nicaragua or Central America that came through the Office of the Vice President was of interest to us because the Vice President is a principal of the National Security Council. Dealing with the Contras would be among my responsibilities." Contra leader Eden

Pastora said in a sworn deposition in July 1987 that Bush was in the "Contra resupply chain of command" (*The Nation*, January 23rd, 1988).

In August 1986 Gregg had a meeting with Rodriguez at which he was told about a scheme to "swap weapons for dollars to get aid for the Contras." When asked about his own hand-written notes on the meeting, Gregg claimed he "didn't know what that line meant," and that "he didn't tell his boss about the meeting because it wasn't Vice-Presidential material." (Probably the most vital national security issue of the day, but Gregg didn't think it was important enough to disturb Bush over.)

At his confirmation hearing for ambassador to South Korea in 1989, Senator Alan Cranston, then chairman of the Foreign Relations Subcommittee on East Asian and Pacific Affairs, became fed up with Gregg's constant denials about the Contra resupply effort, and eventually shouted at him: "Your career training in establishing secrecy and deniability for covert operations and your decades-old friendship with Felix Rodriguez apparently led you to believe that you could serve the national interest by sponsoring a freelance operation out of the Vice President's Office" (*New York Times*, May 13th, 1989).

When Cranston remarked how it could be possible that Gregg didn't know that Rodriguez was involved with an operation to supply the Contras, Gregg replied that Oliver North and Rodriguez must have been "conspiring against him." When North testified at his trial that it was Gregg who introduced him to Rodriguez, Gregg said North's statements were "just not true" (*Los Angeles Times*, May 13th 1989).

Even after Eugene Hasenfus, who was flying arms to the Contras on one of Secord's C-123 planes, was shot down on October 5th, 1986, over southern Nicaragua, Gregg said he still didn't tell Bush about the operation. (Apparently, the Vice President didn't have a minute free on his busy calendar to deal with such mundane affairs.)

Asked about the reports of the downed plane's ties to the VP's office, that the first telephone call Hasenfus made was to the Vice President's staff, Bush said: "It's absolutely, totally untrue. I can deny it unequivocally" (*The Progressive*, May 1987). When *Newsweek* queried him on February 8th, 1988, about the incident, Bush replied: "I am told that Colonel Watson canvassed appropriate officials in the U.S. government and was informed that the missing airplane did not belong to the U.S. government, was not on a U.S. government operation and that the missing person was not a U.S. government employee. Based on the definitive statements from responsible officials, Colonel Watson set aside the fragmentary information Mr. Rodriguez had given him and took the word of the U.S. officials that there was no U.S. government connection."

In plain English, Bush is saying that the entire effort to resupply the Contras was a totally private affair, with no connection or knowledge whatsoever by the White House.

When press reports of telephone records from Rodriguez's safe in San Salvador showed a number of calls to the White House and Gregg's home, on December 15th, 1986, Bush's office acknowledged that Gregg and Rodriquez had discussed Contra aid, and that Colonel Watson had been called by Rodriguez and told the Hasenfus flight was missing— a full day before the downing was announced by the Nicaraguan government" (*The Progressive*, May 1987). A statement released by the Vice President's Office said that "Gregg and his staff maintained periodic communications with Felix Rodriguez, but were never involved in directing, coordinating, or approving military aid to the Contras in Nicaragua" (*The Progressive*, May 1987). The Vice President insisted that these contacts concerned El Salvador, not the Contras.

When interviewed on the CBS news program *60 Minutes* in March 1987, the Vice President replied that these statements had "stood the test of time." Asked about media reports of his involvement to supply the Contras, Bush countered: "There is this insidious suggestion that I was conducting an operation. It's untrue, unfair, and totally wrong. I met with Max Gomez [Rodriguez's alias] three times and never discussed Nicaragua with him. . . . There was no linkage to any operation, yet it keeps coming up. There are all kinds of weirdos coming out of the woodwork on this thing." Bush was asked whether or not Donald Gregg "lied" when he denied discussing the Contras with Rodriguez. Bush said no, and that Gregg merely "forgot." "He's not a liar. If I thought he was a liar, he wouldn't be working for me," the then-Vice President added.

When asked if "in retrospect, do you wish Mr. Gregg had told you about it [North's role in the resupply effort] in August 1986," Bush remarked: "Yes, particularly knowing what I know now."

Which means Gregg must be a liar because he didn't tell the Vice President everything in August 1986, or in April 1986 when Rodriguez complained to him about the profits being skimmed. Yet Bush wasn't at all angry at his chief aide for hiding important information from him, and instead of punishing him, appointed him ambassador to South Korea.

In his autobiography, *Looking Forward* (1987), Bush denies knowing about North's "secret operations" before November 1986.

In a 1988 interview with *Newsweek*, when Bush was asked, "When did you first learn of North's role in the Contra operation?" he answered, "What I know of Mr. North's role in the Contra-resupply effort has come from the information made public during the investigations."

Bush is asking us to believe that he chaired the Task Force on Combating Terrorism which served as a springboard for North's activities, and the Committee on Crisis Pre-Planning and the National Security Planning Group, but knew nothing of North's activities. He is asking us to believe that Oliver North ran the entire resupply operation on his own, without the knowledge of any of his superiors, as a rogue operation, and then when brought to trial tried to drag these other men's names and reputations through the mud. That he only learned of Oliver North's role in the entire Contra-resupply effort from information made public during the investigations. In other words, the Vice President of the United States had no more knowledge or intelligence about Oliver North's secret agendas and covert operations than any average American receiving his news from ABC and *Time* magazine and NBC?

In what must be the ultimate in hypocrisy, during the election campaign of 1988 Bush said that the whole issue of Iran-Contra was "old news." "You get sick and tired of saying, I've told the truth."

What became of the Contra connection after Iran-Contra became public? One covert operation which the Bush White House was likely behind is the secret effort to fund the 1990 campaign of Violeta Chamorro and the National Opposition Union (UNO), the main opposition to the Sandinista candidate, President Daniel Ortega.

In the eight months before the February 25th, 1990, vote, the CIA managed a covert operation which sent more than $600,000 to more than a 100 Miami-based Contra leaders so they could return to Nicaragua (*Newsweek*, October 21st, 1991). Although Congress approved $9 million to be spent on the Nicaraguan election, it banned covert CIA financial support for the UNO.

When asked about the payments, Administration officials claimed the payments were simply expenses for helping 100 or so Contra leaders return home. However, one White House official acknowledged, "We were spending this money for them to go back and work in the Chamorro campaign. They knew what they were supposed to do" (*Newsweek*, October 21st, 1991).

The payments may have been a continuation of the money supplied to Contra leaders throughout the 1980s as part of the White House's plan to destabilize Nicaragua. To do this, the CIA created a Nicaraguan Exile Relocation Program (NERP), which dispensed the money between July 1989 and February 1990.

BUSH AND NORIEGA: HOW WELL DID THEY KNOW EACH OTHER?

The extent of George Bush's ties to former Panamanian dictator Manuel Noriega is important in order to determine what the President knew of the secret operation to arm the Contras and whether Contra leaders received money or helped narcotics traffickers import drugs into the U.S.

Panama General Manuel Noriega's ties to the U.S. intelligence service goes back to 1960, when as a young cadet at a Peruvian military academy he provided information on leftist students to the Defense Intelligence Agency.

When Bush became head of the CIA in 1976, he thwarted an army investigation into Noriega's activities code-named "Canton Song" because he feared it would cause further damage to an already discredited CIA. Noriega, then Panama's chief of intelligence, was buying reel-to-reel audiotapes from the Army's 470th Military Intelligence Group. When Noriega discovered a U.S. wiretap operation against Panamanian officials involved in Canal Treaty negotiations, he bought copies of the tapes for his boss, Ómar Torrijos. Instead of prosecuting Noriega, as the head of the National Security Agency wanted, Bush not only didn't punish either him or the officers, he decided to continue paying Noriega an annual sum of $110,000 for his work on behalf of the agency (Frederick Kempe, *Divorcing the Dictator*, Putnam's, as reported in *Newsweek*, November 15th, 1990).

Bush met Noriega in Washington in December 1976. He denied it at first, then acknowledged the meeting took place, but, in what has become somewhat of a George Bush trademark, remembers nothing of what transpired. Other guests at the lunch say it was the third meeting between the two since Bush became CIA director.

Although CIA Director (under Jimmy Carter) Stansfield Turner took Noriega off the payroll of the CIA, by 1981 he was back on.

In December 1983 Bush flew to Panama to meet with Noriega. A Bush spokesperson claims the meeting was a "privileged" talk (whatever that means). Bush told reporters: "What I talked to the Panamanians about was doing what they could to get their banks out of laundering money for the narcotics traffic" (*Washington Post*, May 8th, 1988). Former U.S. ambassador to Panama Everett Briggs, who also attended the meeting, said that Bush may have sought diplomatic support (for the Contras) but never requested military help. (Of all countries, why would the U.S. need to solicit diplomatic support from Panama?) (*Newsweek*, January 15th, 1990). Noriega interpreted this visit as an appeal for help in arming and training the Contras.

José Blandón, a former Panamanian diplomat who was Noriega's top political aide, testified before a Senate investigating committee in February 1988. He says of the same meeting that both Gregg and Bush asked for and got Noriega's commitment to "help secretly arm, train and finance the Contras, which was to begin in early 1984." Gregg denied the meeting ever took place (*Newsweek*, October 31st, 1988).

Further proof of Bush's knowledge of Noriega's support for the Contras was presented at Oliver North's trial in 1989, where it was revealed that a Southern Front Resistance leader had "received $100,000 from Panamanian Defense Forces Chief Noriega in July 1984." Bush, it was claimed, received copies of these documents, which showed Noriega's financial assistance for the Contras (*Newsweek*, January 15th, 1990).

Bush has always pleaded ignorance about Noriega's drug-dealing activities. Yet many of the operatives in Black Eagle, one of the Contra resupply operations Bush and Casey devised in 1982, claim that Noriega played a major role in the operation by providing his country's airfields and front companies, as well as allowing Contras to be trained in Panama. In return, he was given the green light to smuggle cocaine and marijuana into the U.S. on behalf of the Colombian cocaine cartel. According to one retired covert operative, one percent of the gross income generated by the drug traffic was set aside to buy additional weapons for the Contras.

Blandón confirms that the CIA and North used Noriega to funnel guns and money to the Contras, and Panama as a training base. He also claims that Noriega's right-hand man, Mike Harari, told him that Casey and Bush were involved in these operations. "Harari told Noriega in front of me that Bush was very grateful for the help Noriega was providing," Blandón testified.

An Argentine arms dealer who was brought into the operation by Noriega, Jorge Krupnik, told Blandón that everything in the operation had the full backing of Bush and Gregg, including the drug trafficking. Gregg denies meeting Harari or being involved with him (*Newsweek*, January 15th, 1990). Noriega meanwhile gathered a dossier on the role of Bush in the operation, which he referred to when he told a former aide, Colonel Roberto Díaz Herrera, "I've got Bush by the balls," and that he knew things that "could affect the elections of the U.S."

Although Blandón was very credible, there was an immediate attempt by the CIA and Defense Department to discredit him, calling him an "untrustworthy leftist."

"Blandón was the first guy who wasn't a sleazeball who offered evidence against Noriega," says a former Senate Foreign Relations Committee staffer. "He was able to corroborate the testimony we'd been getting from convicted drug dealers, but more important, he was able to put it into a larger context" (*New York*, January 15th, 1990).

It's not as if the administration never realized or discovered what was happening. They tried to block any investigation which might implicate U.S. government officials in any way with Noriega's drug trafficking. Blandón testified that the White House knew Noriega was involved in drug trafficking since the early days of the Administration, but because of the support Noriega gave the Contras, it ignored it.

In the spring of 1988, when the General Accounting Office (GAO), the investigative branch of Congress, opened an investigation, using Panama as a case study of how drug trafficking by foreign officials influences U.S. foreign policy decisions, the White House ordered the State Department, the Pentagon, the CIA and the Drug Enforcement Administration not to cooperate. According to a UPI report on August 18th, 1988, on the stonewall effort, "Democrats and investigators said the White House order was aimed at preventing potentially embarrassing discoveries from rocking the presidential campaign of Republican Vice President George Bush." In August 1988 the White House said that the Justice Department had decided that "the subject matter of the request is beyond the GAO's statutory authority" (*Common Cause*, September/October 1988).

The report might very well have revealed George Bush's knowledge of the United States' ties with Noriega. Yet the White House, specifically the National Security Council (NSC), intervened. GAO investigators discovered that officials of the State Department, Justice Department, Customs Service and Drug Enforcement Agency were told they couldn't assist the probe until the NSC agreed (*Washington Post*, March 12th, 1989). According to a chronology of one of the GAO investigators, the State and Justice officials were instructed by the NSC "not to deal with us until [the] NSC had developed operational guidelines on what to do and what not to do on this assignment" *(Washington Post*, March 21st, 1989).

Nancy Kingsbury, who at that time was a senior official in the GAP's National Security and International Affairs Divison, commented on the NSC's coordinating activities, "The NSC would not ordinarily have played that kind of role" (*Washington Post*, March 21st, 1989).

The White House effort to protect Noriega may also been because of the useful role the Panamanian dictator played in the Reagan-Bush Administration's Central American foreign policy. One former national security assistant to President Ronald Reagan claims the U.S. government "conspired" for years to protect Panamanian General Manuel Noriega and "willfully ignored" evidence of his narcotics activities because he had agreed to help the Contras.

Norman Bailey, who served as a director of planning on the National Security Counsel staff and was a former special assistant to President Reagan for national security affairs, doesn't believe Reagan Administration officials when they say they didn't have enough solid evidence of Noriega's narcotics activities to indict him in February 1988, more than eighteen months before President Bush sent U.S. troops into Panama to ouster Noriega.

In September 1988, Admiral Daniel Murphy, Bush's top drug aide, declared: "I never saw any intelligence suggesting General Noriega's involvement in the drug trade. In fact, we always held up Panama as the model in terms of cooperation with the United States in the war on drugs" (*Convergence*, Christic Institute, Fall 1991).

Bailey disagrees. Testifying before the House Select Committee on Narcotics Abuse and Control in March 1988, he said, "Black and white evidence about Noriega's narcotics activities has been available since at least the mid-1970s. It could have been read by "any authorized official of the U.S. government with appropriate security clearances" (*Common*

Cause, September/October 1988).

The question is: To what extent was the Reagan-Bush Administration's policy on drug trafficking influenced by the help they were getting from people like Noriega?

Senator Kerry says the congressional hearings he chaired showed that "stopping drug trafficking to the U.S. has been a secondary U.S. foreign policy objective. It has been sacrificed repeatedly for other political goals" (*Common Cause*, September/October 1988).

Francis McNeil, a former senior Deputy Assistant Secretary of State for intelligence and research, told the Senate in April 1988 that "some government officials looked away when they thought vigorous pursuit of narcotics trafficking conflicted with national security priorities."

Another question which arises is: Because of the Administration's commitment to the Contra effort, and due to the ties Contra supporters had with narcotics traffickers, was the White House's commitment to keeping dangerous drugs out of the U.S. compromised?

As Vice President, George Bush headed two main administration initiatives to coordinate drug investigations: the South Florida Task Force and the National Narcotics Border Interdiction System (NNBIS). Despite their being created as a clearinghouse for intelligence, former DEA Administrator Francis Mullen and the GAO criticized the two groups for not doing that, but instead establishing an intelligence network which bypassed DEA contacts and "threatened to fragment the narcotics intelligence data base."

In 1987 the GAO said of NNBIS: "Seizures are small compared to the amounts of drugs successfully smuggled into the U.S."

Mullen claimed that these two groups were inflating drug-seizures statistics and that the public was being misled about the two organizatons' successes. "If NNBIS continues unchecked it will discredit other federal drug programs and become the adminstration's Achilles heel for drug law enforcement," he warned.

Supporting the Contras also blinded other moral fibers of the Reagan-Bush White House. In 1984, Honduran General José Buesco, a supporter of the Contras, was labeled by the Justice Department as an international terrorist, and was indicted in connection with a plot to kill President of Honduras Roberto Suazo Córdova, which was to be financed with profits from cocaine smuggling.

Senior administration officials, including Oliver North, Assistant Secretary of State Elliot Abrams, and former National Security Advisor John Poindexter, tried to get leniency for Buesco due to his role in helping set up Contra camps on Honduras' border with Nicaragua. When the plot to kill Suazo Córdova was discovered, Buesco agreed to come to the U.S. to face charges, but officials from the Department of Defense and the CIA started asking for leniency, a full pardon, sentence reduction or deportation. On September 17th, 1986, North sent a message to Poindexter stating that the administration should help Buesco because if not, "he will break his longstanding silence about the Nicaraguan resistance and other sensitive operations."

The Justice Department, particularly Deputy Assistant Attorney General Mark Richard, opposed leniency for Buesco. Richard would later testify to the Iran-Contra Committee that Abrams insisted "we should do what we can to accommodate this man." The Justice Department still refused, and Buesco eventually pleaded guilty to two felony charges in the attempted assassination plot and was sentenced to two five-year jail terms.

McNeil believes that is wasn't only Buesco's support for the Contras that encouraged the Administration to help him, but also what North told Poindexter in a memo was "songs nobody wants to hear."

Hoping perhaps that George Bush was listening at the

time, McNeil told the Senate subcommittee: "We're certainly going to have to stop giving these signals that if you have a military or intelligence relationship with the U.S., it's a license to commit major crimes in this country."

CONCLUSION

How did Bush get away with it?

For starters, disinformation became a very powerful and influential tool in the Reagan years, particularly when it was used against an unknowing public.

A major part of this disinformation effort was to manipulate the public with the "kick ass" image of the Reagan-Bush White House. With the use of key phrases such as "counterterrorism," "anti-terrorism," "the war on terrorism," and "the Russians are behind all acts of international terrorism," the Reagan Administration was seen as highly committed, morally upstanding national leaders so they gained the confidence of the American public. This reservoir of integrity the Administration created stood up well to the allegations made against Reagan's or Bush's knowledge of involvement in Iran-Contra. When Irangate first broke, most Americans really didn't think the President knew because it was difficult to conceive of Ronald Reagan lying about anything. With the entire question being whether Reagan did or did not know of the diversion of profits from arms sales to Iran to buy arms for the Contras, Bush was let off the hook.

The question of George Bush's guilt in Iran-Contra comes down to two possibilities: either he knew everything, or, while all the efforts to resupply the Contras were happening, he was kept in the dark by Gregg and was absent from all meetings where arms-for-hostages were discussed.

Could it be that Gregg knew everything but kept it from the Vice President? That despite all the committees which bore the Vice President's name, he didn't attend the meetings and had no interest or knowledge of what policies transpired there?

Could it be that a lone Lt. Colonel in the National Security Council could carry out a private foreign policy by arming and financing the Contras without anyone in the White House knowing about it or finding out? And if so, and the Vice President or his National Security Advisor didn't discover these activities, what does that say about their level of competence?

Of course George Bush knew everything. How could he not have known?

In fact, far from being a wimp, George Bush ran the White House. Says former Army investigator Gene Wheaton: "Ronald Reagan may have been President but George Bush was in charge. Weinberger and Schultz were no match for a covert operator like him."

Bush was smart. He figured out that to implement his secret agendas all he had to do was arrange it so he was appointed chairman of all the important White House committees: the President's Task Force on Narcotics, Terrorism, Deregulation of the Savings and Loans and Airlines Industry. This meant he could appoint the key people to work on these inter-agency committees to establish policy and Bush's covert agendas.

The scary part of all this is that Bush seems to be invincible. No one can pin him down and corner him by saying: "Of course you know about these secret agendas and covert operations. You were there. Stop treating us like a bunch of imbeciles and explain to us how if these covert operations were going on all around you, how could it be that you, the Vice President, didn't know about them?"

No one did that. Not Congress. Nor the press. Nor any of the presidential contenders in 1988 and 1992. Like any good covert operator, Bush has a brilliant cover. About the only thing the American people know about their President is that he jogs, fishes, and has a dog.

They called Reagan the Teflon President. Bush has him beat by a mile.

CHAPTER 2

Vice President Quayle's Role in President Bush's Secret Agenda

When Dan Quayle was chosen as George Bush's vice-presidential candidate most people had never heard of him. Some speculated that he was "impeachment insurance" for Bush in case Iran-Contra blew up in his face if he was elected President. Others claimed that it was to satisfy the conservative wing of the Republican Party.

While the media labeled Quayle as an "idiot" and the public views him as a dummy, incapable of sophisticated thinking, Bush knew otherwise. He chose Quayle because of the ability of Quayle to carry out covert operations, such as the key role he played in the secret effort to supply the Contras during the Reagan White House.

To carry out his secret agendas Bush has to control key committees in the House and Senate, such as Finance, Intelligence, and Armed Forces, and command the loyalty of legislative assistants to congressmen and senators. Senator Quayle served the then-Vice President Bush well in the Senate as an integral part of the Secret Team. He was the Vice President's point man for the Contras, soothing Congress' mind over the nasty rumors it was hearing about the Contras' ties to drug dealers and unscrupulous mercenary groups. When money is spent, congressmen and senators have to be informed. When "humanitarian aid" for the Contras was granted by Congress, Quayle did the explaining.

In the summer of 1991 I got to know William Northrup,

the Israeli arms dealer who was arrested in Bermuda in 1986 for selling arms to Iran. Before leaving for the States in September, he told me to try and get out to California and meet Gene Wheaton. "Gene's a good man," he assured me.

Wheaton had been investigating Reagan-Bush covert operations since the early 1980s and had seen from the inside how these secret agendas operated. In addition to his 25 years' experience as a criminal investigator for the U.S. Army, he had designed security systems for airports in the Middle East and served as an anti-smuggling narcotics advisor to the Shah.

By that time I had interviewed covert operators like Richard Secord, and Iran-Contra players such as Yaacov Nimrodi. Now I had someone who looked at the world of covert operations from the perspective of an investigator. Unlike intelligence agents, Wheaton didn't thrive on lies and deceit. Judging from his very modest home, he obviously wasn't in it for the money.

In 1985 Wheaton was vice president of a small cargo airline company that Oliver North's network wanted to use to haul arms to the Contras and rebels elsewhere, such as in Afghanistan. Wheaton had the expertise the secret team wanted, so they set out to recruit him. While Wheaton may have fit their political profile, he was conservative and right-wing; he was a cop, not an intelligence agent. He was brought into the center circle, where he stayed long enough to learn about the White House's ties to drug runners, the massive arms transfers to rebel groups, the mountains of falsified documentation and miscarriages of justice.

"I had no objection to the covert end of it, as long as it was legal," says Wheaton. "It wasn't. Whenever I asked about the legality of a certain operation I was told, 'It's all right, this is a vital national security issue.' I talked myself out of the inner circle but I was in it long enough to get to know the players and their method of operation. The government officials I met in the Pentagon called supporting the private covert operator 'intelligence support activity.' These covert operators trampled on our Constitution and made a mockery of our judicial system. They aren't motivated strictly by anti-communism, power, or money, but by the adrenaline that stems from being able to create chaos. They would gladly destabilize a democratic ally of America just so they can go back in and save it."

Wheaton explains that the origins of Oliver North's network was in the mid-1970s. There were, he says, literally tens of thousands of ex-covert operators and former Air America "employees" running around loose in the U.S. These weren't the kind of guys to lay back and run 7-11 stores, so they set up an array of covert airlines using the assets of Air America, the former CIA proprietary airline which had helped fly heroin out of Burma and Laos.

When Air America was liquidated it created scores of smaller airlines, including Global, Capital, and Southern Cross. All tolled, these companies employed over 15,000 people. The subsidiary companies of Air America, Southern Air Transport, Continental Air Services, and Air Asia were also broken up. This meant this secret team was able to supply pilots and mechanics, logistics and control people for future, privatized covert operations.

The 800 or so covert operators who got thrown out of the CIA by Jimmy Carter in 1977 allied themselves with the conservative element of the Republican Party. Their goal was to get George Bush elected to either president or Vice President. They didn't care which one it was, as long as their man got into the White House. They rallied around Bush and worked like a political action committee. They put their unique talents into action. They were going to do in America what they had done throughout the 1960s and 1970s in Africa and South and Central America: rig elections and overthrow governments.

One aspect of the covert operators' activities was the "October Surprise" theory, which claims members of Reagan's 1980 campaign team, including George Bush and William Casey, made a deal with Iranian leaders not to release the 52 American hostages they were holding until after the November presidential election.

Wheaton claims Quayle was brought "into the game," Bush and Casey's network of the Secret Team, early on. He believes that a major source of Quayle's political power in his home state of Indiana comes from an old friend of William Casey's, Beurt SerVaas, who was on the executive board of the Veterans of the OSS, the predecessor organization of the CIA. SerVaas's daughter is married to what Wheaton describes as an "off-the-books" French intelligence asset, Bernard Marie. Wheaton says that he introduced Marie to Defense Intelligence Agency officials who were part of the Reagan-Bush White House's secret arms deals with Iran in the early 1980s.

"Quayle is being groomed," says Wheaton. "Quayle was a true believer and they wanted to bring him up through the ranks. It wasn't easy for Bush and Casey to find people who would go along with their far right-wing philosophy, who at the same time were articulate and presentable." Quayle's "smoking gun" was Robert Owen and Owen's ties were to John Hull, a native of Indiana who owned and managed 8000 acres of land in northern Costa Rica 30 miles from the Nicaraguan border. The CIA and Oliver North used Hull's ranch as a supply depot to move weapons to the Contras. Hull used American government protection to fly drugs from there into the U.S., sometimes on the very same planes.

Wheaton points to a October 15th, 1980, "Memorandum for the Record," written by then-Assistant Secretary of State Harold Saunders, stating that "Bob Owen had been made privy to the details of a pre-1980 election arms-for-hostages offer made by Iranian arms dealer Houshang Lavi to President Carter's State Department and the CIA. In her 1989 book, *October Surprise*, author Barbara Honegger cites an unnamed source that claims Owen, Dan Quayle's legislative aide, covertly "worked" (i.e., reported to) for Donald Gregg in October 1980 when Gregg was still serving in Carter's National Security Council. (When Bush became Vice President, Gregg was appointed his National Security Advisor. Gregg is assumed to have played a major role in the "October Surprise" operation.)

If Owen knew about the 1980 deal, then it's likely that Quayle also knew, and therefore he would be privy to many of the Reagan-Bush White House's deepest secrets and covert agendas.

John Hull visited Washington in July 1983 to convince Congress that Contra leader Eden Pastora should not be supported, claiming he was being controlled by the Sandinistan government. Pastora and Hull both visited Quayle and his legislative assistant, Robert Owen. Owen arranged for other congressional aides to talk to the visitors too, such as Vaughn Forrest, an administrative assistant for Representative Bill McCollum (R-Florida), and also introduced Hull to Oliver North.

In November 1983 Owen began working for Gray and Co., a powerful Washington, D.C., public relations and lobbying firm known for its close ties to the Administration and U.S. intelligence bodies.

In April 1984 Contra leader Adolfo Calero, head of the Nicaraguan Democratic Front, the largest Contra group, asked Gray and Co. to represent the Contras. Owen was given the assignment and came up with plans to raise money in the U.S. through non-profit organizations and companies to purchase weapons for the Contras.

One of Owen's tasks was to garner information on the financial and military needs of the Contras and pass this on to North. He reported to North that more that $1 million a month would be needed to just to keep the level of resistance at its current level, and $1.5 million if it were to increase.

In July 1984 Owen procured South African arms for the Contras. In late October he returned to Central America, met with Calero and Hull, and made an arrangement whereby he would receive $2,500 a month plus expenses from Calero, and Hull would get $10,000 a month in return for his assistance on the southern front.

In summer or fall 1985 Owen served as a courier for North, delivering Swiss bank account numbers to representatives of the Taiwan government in Washington so they could make "Contra contributions." In February 1985 he went to Central America with a letter from North assuring Calero that he would soon receive $20 million. Owen knew what type of people he was dealing with and of some Contra leaders' ties to drug runners. Oliver North was also informed. On April 1st, 1985, Owen described to North Costa Rican rebel leader José Robelo's "potential involvement in drug running." Owen told North that another Contra leader, Sebastián González, was "now involved in drug running out of Panama." North wrote during an August 9th, 1985, meeting with Owen that the "DC-6 which is being used for runs out of New Orleans is probably being used for drug runs into U.S." On February, 10th, 1986, Owen informed North that another Contra plane, a DC-4, was "used at one time to run drugs, and part of the crew had criminal records. Nice group the Boys [the CIA] chose," Owen added.

In January 1985 Owen founded the Institute for Democracy, Education, and Assistance (IDEA). IDEA received a $230,000 grant from the State Department's Nicaraguan Humanitarian Assistance Office (NHAO), which was in fact nothing more than a scheme to deliver both lethal and non-lethal aid to the Contras.

Over the next few years, four companies which were also used by Hull to smuggle Colombian cocaine to the U.S. from his ranch, received more than $800,000 of State Department funds under this program. Frigorificos de Puntareñas, a Costa Rican shrimp company, had cocaine shipped from Hull's ranch to Costa Rican ports packed in frozen shrimp and delivered to Miami and Gulf ports (*Out of Control*, page 157). In February 1986 Oliver North chose Vortex Aircraft Sales and Leasing to fly the so-called humanitarian assistance to the Contras. At the same time, that company's vice president, Michael Palmer, a fomer Delta Airlines pilot turned drug smuggler, was under indictment for marijuana trafficking (*The Nation*, August 29th, 1987).

Other companies which received Contra "humanitarian aid" included Setco, which was controlled by a billionaire drug lord currently serving a life sentence in a Federal prison for the torture-murder of a Drug Enforcement Agency agent. According to an FBI report, another company, Diacsa, served as a central distribution point for cocaine trafficking and money laundering (Senate Foreign Relations Subcommittee on Narcotics, Terrorism and International Organizations, April 1989).

Owen's ties to Calero are confirmed by Joseph Adams, a former Marine Corps intelligence officer, who trained with the elite Delta Force unit of the U.S. Army. Adams was the security chief and consultant to Calero from the fall of 1984 to the spring of 1986. He lead a team of American mercenaries and a Pentagon intelligence agent on a two-month combat mission inside Nicaragua called "Operation Pegasus."

Adams says that Calero met Owen on a number of occasions. "Rob Owen was Adolfo's contact," Adams says. "I met with Owen several times with Adolfo. Rob was reporting to Adolfo on the Southern Front activities." Adams remembers at least a dozen such meetings in 1984 and 1985 (*The Progressive*, March 1987).

While being interviewed by the CBS News program *West 57th St.*, Jack Terrel, a military commander for a private American group that supplied trainers for the Contras and who was a key witness for Senator Kerry's Senate investigation of the Contras' ties to drug trafficking, said he met twice with John Hull and Robert Owen and that Owen was the go-between between Costa Rica and the White House, and the "bag man" for Oliver North.

Said Terrel: "Owen told me, 'I take a $10,000 a month to John Hull from the National Security Council for these types of operations, and, if we need more money, that's no problem' " (*West 57th St.*, June 25th, 1986). When John Hull was asked by CBS News if he knew Owen, he replied: "I've met Rob on several occasions. I have no business dealings with Rob." When asked what he did for living, Hull said; "I have no idea."

Mike Wallace of CBS News asked Terrel if he had ever heard about Hull's drug smuggling, to which Terrel answered, "We've got a cancer here; it's like Watergate. It's not going away."

U.S. investigative bodies were simply not interested in hearing about John Hull's deeds. "We sent stuff to all the committees," says Tony Avrigan, who together with his wife and fellow journalist Martha Honey, filed suit along with the Christic Institute in a Federal court in Miami charging Calero and officials in the American government with planning the May 30th, 1984, La Penca, Nicaragua, bombing at a press conference held by Contra leader Eden Pastora. "We made everything available to them" (*The Progressive*, March 1990).

The Iran-Contra investigating committees sent Thomas Polgar, a former CIA station chief in Vietnam, to Costa Rica to investigate charges that Hull was involved in drug dealing. He too wasn't too interested in getting at the truth.

"Polgar didn't want to hear anything specific—dates, evidence, sources," said Beth Hawkins, a journalist who worked for the *Tico Times*, in San José. "His questions were subjective, what we thought about Pastora and Hull" (*The Progressive*, March 1990).

Avrigan remarks on the difference between the U.S. government's treatment of John Hull and that of Manuel Noriega in its efforts to bring drug dealers to justice. "It just shows very clearly that in the eyes of the United States, Noriega only became a drug dealer when he stopped taking orders from the CIA. Drug traffickers who continue to take orders from the CIA are protected" (*The Progressive*, March 1990).

There is also ample proof that the U.S. government not only rejected allegations of Contra involvement in drug tracking, but also tipped off these smugglers when they had become targets of an investigation.

Journalist Jonathan Kwitny says Hull acknowledged to him that he was warned in early 1985 by a NSC source of a potential investigation. After discussing the matter with the U.S. Embassy in Costa Rica, he declined to talk with Justice Department officials (*The Nation*, August 29th, 1987). Kwitny investigated other charges that the NSC tipped off drug dealers of pending investigations. He says an American filmmaker, Lawrence Spivy, who in early 1985 had worked with the Contra supply operation, saw FBI memos from Miami about North's Office ties to drug smugglers.

The U.S. government not only tolerated drug dealers like Hull and informed them of any investigation of their activities, they also assisted them by intervening on their behalf when they got caught.

Costa Rican prosecutor Jorge Chavarria Guzmán had unsuccessfuly tried to charge Hull for his role in the 1984 La Penca bombing. Guzmán claims that Robert Owen had foreknowledge of the bombing.

When Hull eventually was arrested for drug trafficking, the U.S. Embassy in Costa Rica, officials of the Bush Administration, and no less than 19 legislators petitioned Costa Rican President Oscar Arias to have him released (*The Progressive*, April 1989).

In a January 26th, 1989, letter, Lee Hamilton, co-chairman of the House committee that investigated the Iran-Contra scandals, wrote, "It is our hope that Mr. Hull's case will be concluded promptly and that it will be handled in a manner that will not complicate U.S.-Costa Rican relations. We understand that his arrest occurred under unusual circumstances. We urge you to investigate Mr. Hull's case to ensure that the charges against him have been brought with just cause and to ensure that his rights under Costa Rican law and under the Universal Declaration of Human Rights are protected" (*The Progressive*, March 1990).

President Arias wrote Hamilton back, reminding him that it was up to the courts, not himself, to judge Hull's case. "It pains me," he responded, "that you insinuate that the exemplary relations between your country and mine could deteriorate because our legal system is fighting against drug trafficking, no matter how powerful the people who participate in it, or what external backing they might have" (*The Progressive*, March 1990).

Hull jumped bail in August 1989 and fled to the United States. He charged that the murder allegations were because the "the government down there [Costa Rica] is infiltrated and manipulated by communists headed up by the Christic Institute" (*The Progressive*, March 1990).

It may be difficult for most people to comprehend that the American government employs drug dealers in its foreign policy pursuits. Yet unless everyone in this story is lying in order to defame the White House, or John Hull, or Robert Owen, then this is exactly what happened.

Quayle could argue that he knew nothing of this because it began after Owen left the position as his legislative assistant. Yet the question remains: Why was Owen chosen for the task in the first place? At least in 1983, Owen, when he was still working for Quayle, knew Hull, and introduced him around Washington on behalf of Quayle's Office to key senators and congressional supporters of the Contras. Did Owen know then that Hull was involved in drugs? Did Quayle?

As a footnote to the Bush-Quayle Administration, the two may never have even been elected to the White House had it not been for their campaign team's manipulation of justice just prior to the 1988 election. In late October 1988, a request was made on behalf of the Bush-Quayle campaign via the Justice Department to an official of the Bureau of Prisons to silence Brett C. Kimberlin, a prisoner who claimed that he had once sold drugs to Dan Quayle.

Kimberlin asserts he tried to come forward four days before the 1988 election to tell his story but was ordered into solitary confinement by the director of the Bureau of Prisons in Washington. A press conference that had been planned by authorities at the Federal Correctional Institution in El Reno, Oklahoma, was canceled after a Bush-Quayle campaign official complained about it to the Justice Department (*New York Times*, May 3rd, 1992).

In 1990 Kimberlin filed a lawsuit claiming that canceling the press conference and putting him into solitary confinement violated his First Amendment rights. Kimberlin was released from solitary confinement six days after the election.

According to a Justice Department memo the Bureau of Prisons Director, J. Michael Quinlan, revealed he put Kimberlin in solitary confinement because of a request of Loye W. Miller, Jr., the Justice Department's Director of Public Affairs. Miller had received a complaint from Mark Goodin, an aide to Lee Atwater, then the chairman of the Republican National

Committee, about the news conference Kimberlin planned to hold. The news conference was to be held to satisfy the many requests the prison was receiving from news organizations about Kimerlin's claims after National Public Radio and NBC News took an interest in the story.

In a memo Quinlan wrote ten months after the incident to Francis A. Keating, an Associate Attorney General at the Justice Department, he says the decision to incarcerate Kimberlin was taken after he heard from Miller that Kimberlin's life was in danger; he claimed that he had heard this from Nina Totenberg, a reporter with National Public Radio. Totenberg denies that she suggested Kimberlin's life was in any danger, nor does Kimberlin remember saving any such thing. When prison officials investigated the matter, they concluded that his life was never in danger.

Kimberlin's accusations were never heard.

The cover-ups and corruption of the Bush White House began even before George Bush took office.

CHAPTER 3

Oliver North:
A Bush Illusion

The crimes of Irangate were far more serious than Watergate since the White House circumvented laws passed by Congress and violated the Constitution. It also privatized foreign policy. Yet the American public never really took Iran-Contra seriously. After a relatively short period of time the scandal had lost the attention of the media and hence the American people. Why?

North was charged with altering, concealing, and destroying National Security Council documents, obstructing a congressional investigation, and lying to Congress. He was liable for a $750,000 fine and up to ten years in prison. In the end he had to pay $150,000 and was sentenced to two years' probation and 1200 hours in community service at a drug program.

Never mind the irony that after financing the Contra resupply operation with proceeds of drug profits and facilitating the importation of kilos of narcotics into the U.S., North was going to stand before teen-agers and lecture them on the grave dangers of snorting cocaine. Rather than being shamed in front of the entire country, Oliver North became an American folk hero. Why? How?

North was perceived as a patriot driven by the highest ideals of nationalism. The President himself started the ball rolling by calling North "a national hero." Next came "Ollie Mania." Then there were the Ollie T-shirts and Ollie dolls. Despite the grave crimes he was charged with, a *Time*/CNN poll in May 1989 during his trial revealed that there was widespread sentiment against sending him to prison. The majority wanted Bush to pardon him.

It would be his testimony before the televised Iran-Contra committee hearings from July 7th to 14th, 1987, that would serve North best. As Daniel Schorr, a veteran of twenty-five years of covering congressional inquiries and winner of three Emmy Awards for his coverage of the Watergate Hearings, would say: "Verdict by television can be a fickle thing" (*Taking the Stand*, 1987).

Schorr explains that after five days, John Dean, the former White House Counsel who testified before Senator Sam Ervin's Watergate committee, became a media hero. Yet that would be "nothing that remotely rivaled the 'Ollie North phenomenon'—the wave of popular approval and adulation that he [North] generated by his testimony" (*Taking the Stand*).

North was presented as the underdog the American people just love to rally behind. The immorality or illegality of his deeds weren't important. A nation of television viewers saw a proud, strong Marine in a fully decorated uniform on their screens. It wasn't difficult for them to believe that he had been unjustly thrown to the wolves. For the majority of the American public, this image of Ollie North became Iran-Contra in a nutshell for them.

"This could not be dismissed as simply a 'media event,'" says Schorr. "It was a triumph of projected personality over complicated issues, reminiscent of the simple evocation of patriotism that has made President Reagan so successful a political figure."

One aspect of the phenomenon has never been looked into. Who initiated the campaign to send telegrams and raise money to help pay his defense? What started the mass marketing of Ollie dolls and T-shirts? Was this simply a spontaneous outburst of patriotic fever by an American public dying to rally around the flag? Was it Oliver North on his own versus the rest of the Administration? Or was he (with the help of others) then, and still today, creating an image for himself as being the fall guy?

The Bush-Reagan White House must have realized that, after Watergate, damage control was to be the first order of the day. Their strategy had four basic tenets: 1) There had to be someone, an image even, to be in the public's eye for the media to focus on and believe was guilty of something. 2) The person chosen had to be a soldier, prepared to take the heat, but always assured that he was going to come out on top. He also had to have a personal stake in the overall success of the campaign to manipulate the public's perception of events—in other words, someone who was liable to go to jail for his participation in the crimes. 3) It wouldn't have been believable if the person chosen for the media and public to focus on as the guilty party pleaded innocent of all charges; if so, the public would have asked: "Well, who *is* responsible then?" 4) Once that person was charged with a crime, and all focus was on him, then a few simple legal tricks and help from the Administration, particularly the Attorney General, would be enough to keep that person out of jail.

A diversion was needed to take the focus away from all other White House covert operations and secret agendas. That diversion would be the question of whether the President did or did not know that profits from arms sales to Iran were being used to buy arms for the Contras. This would be the major crime at stake.

Between this and the question of whether Ollie North was or was not a patriot would be enough to occupy the attention span of the American public. Nobody would have the time or energy to look into what George Bush or anyone else knew.

At North's trial in May 1989 a new technique was introduced, known as "legal blackmail." The maneuver was particularly effective because the public was led to believe that the judicial process had tried its best for a conviction. For legal blackmail to work, all that has to happen is that the defense lawyers stand before the judge and say they need key documents to prove the innocence of a client. The Administration or Justice Department would refuse to release these documents, citing reasons of national security. That's it. Case dismissed. Thus the superiors of those charged with the crimes decide what the court will hear as evidence.

The courts, in a sense, were hijacked by the White House. The tactic worked like a charm. After a two-year investigation at a cost of nearly $13 million, Special Prosecutor Lawrence Walsh asked U.S. District Court Judge Gerhard Gesell to drop the most serious charges against North of conspiracy and theft of government property. Walsh cited as his reasons: "A continuing problem in the case has been the protection of national-security information in light of this defendant's insistence on disclosing large quantities of such information at trial" (*Time*, January 16th, 1989).

"Legal blackmail" worked again in 1990 when José Fernandez, the ex-CIA station chief in Costa Rica, was indicted for lying about Oliver North's secret supply network to Congress. These charges were dropped when Attorney General Richard Thornburgh refused to release classified information for Fernandez's defense (*Newsweek*, February 12th, 1990).

After having been singled out as the fall guy, wouldn't North have been a bit angry over his superiors' sacrificing him? If North was indeed bitter that he had, as he claimed at his trial, "felt like a pawn in a chess game being played by giants" (*Time*, April 17th, 1989), why did he go after the former president and not the current one?

In his book *Under Fire*, published in October 1991, North focused all eyes on President Reagan. Both in the book and in the series of interviews he gave to the ABC News program *Nightline*, North revealed that on November 25th, 1986, he got a call from President Reagan, who allegedly told him: "Ollie, you have to understand, I just didn't know" (*Time*,

October 28th, 1991).

On December 11th, 1986, North and his lawyer, Brendan Sullivan, were paid a visit by H. Ross Perot, the Texas billionaire. Perot, who had a special relationship to the White House, had two of his employees rescued from Iran in a daring escape that was later made into a mini-TV series, "On Wings of Eagles." Ollie claims Perot told him and Sullivan: "Look, why doesn't Ollie just end this thing and explain to the FBI that the President didn't know? If he goes to jail, I'll take care of his family and I'll be happy to give him a job when he gets out."

When *Nightline* questioned him about the offer, Perot denied the meeting ever took place.

On December 17th, 1986, a military aide to Vice President Bush visited North and suggested that he waive his Fifth Amendment rights and absolve the President of responsibility.

By framing the debate in terms of "Did the President know," North is presenting a red herring, a diversion. The real issue should have been "What did the Vice President know?" By insisting that Reagan knew everything, North is telling the American people: "Relax, Irangate is now solved. Reagan knew everything; therefore we got to the bottom of the scandal."

How did Iran-Contra become known as Iran-Contra? There really was no connection between the two operations other than a few million dollars that were diverted.

It was the Administration itself, former Attorney General Edwin Meese in particular, who created the connection by announcing publicly that money earned from the Iran affair had been transferred to the Contras. That is where the Contra in Iran-Contra came from. There was no evidence of any purchase of arms for the Contras using money earned from the sale of arms to Iran before Meese informed reporters of it. The diversion certainly wasn't part of the story which was leaked to a Beirut newspaper of Bud McFarlane's May 1986 secret trip to Teheran.

When Meese announced on November 25th, 1986, that $4 million had been diverted to the Contras by Israel (as if Israel would have had this great, dire ideological desire to ensure that the Contras were properly funded), it merely served to emphasize the diversion in the public's mind. This wouldn't be the only attempt by the Administration to pin Iran-Contra on Israel. During his confirmation hearings to become CIA Director in September 1991, Robert Gates said that the misinformation on Iran that justified the arm sales while he was Deputy CIA Director came from Israel.

Once Iran-Contra became public it was definitely in the interest of the Administration to link the support for the Contras and the arms sales to Iran because then the debate would revolve around the issue of whether the President did or did not know of these diversions. And in fact, lo and behold, on November 21st Attorney General Meese discovered a very important memo that hadn't shared the fate of other memos which went to the shredders and burn bags by way of Oliver North. It was dated April 4th, 1986, and read: "The residual funds from this transaction are allocated as follows: $2 million will be used to purchase replacement TOWs for the original 508 sold by Israel to Iran for the release of Benjamin Weir. $12 million will be used to purchase critically needed supplies for the Nicaraguan Democratic Resistance Forces." The memo recommended to John Poindexter that the President "approve the structure depicted." The space for presidential "Approve" or "Disapprove" was left blank (Iran-Contra Hearings, Vol. 1, Appendix, p. 537).

There it is, folks. Iran-Contra is about whether the President did or did not approve this diversion. Since the space was left blank, we'll never know if he had forgotten to sign it, or he was against the initiative but North carried it out anyway behind his back.

Along with Bush, Meese was never questioned on his role

in Iran-Contra. At that press conference, he announced: "The only person in the U.S. government that knew precisely about this [the diversions of profits from the arms sales to Iran had been diverted to the Contras], the only person, was Lieut. Colonel North."

Meese was the first White House official to try to tell the American public that North alone had been responsible for these scandalous actions. It is ironic that it would be Meese who would be in charge of looking into North's alleged illegal actions. The most scandal-ridden member of the Reagan Administration, holding no less a post that of the Attorney General, would be in charge of exposing North's illegal actions.

During research for this book I interviewed Ed Meese, who is now a fellow at the Heritage Foundation in Washington. When I returned to Israel and listened and re-listened to the tape recording I had made of our discussion, I realized that George Bush and Donald Gregg were not alone in their "denial" approach to journalists' questions of their role in White House scandals. It didn't matter what event I asked the former Attorney General to comment on, his response was always the same: "I don't quite remember the events leading up to that incident," or, "I don't think I was consulted about that," or, "No, that didn't go through my office," or, "You as a journalist would probably know more about that than I would."

There was no attempt at justifying any of the actions the Administration took. He simply denied knowing about any of the scandals. This was the same tactic Bush, Gregg, and Robert Gates would use in their defense. The sad part about it is that although some people immediately realize these men are lying, the majority give them the benefit of the doubt because they are national leaders. This is perhaps the theme of the entire Iran-Contra story: the betrayal of trust the public has put in its political leadership to carry out their duties with honor and respect for the positions they hold.

OLLIE FIGHTS BACK

Considering the ordeal he had been through, the timing of North's "going public" with his book and appearances on *Nightline* in October 1991 was unusual. Said *Time* magazine: "The judicial process, the hearings, the hounding by the press, his trial and conviction—a siege relieved only five weeks ago by his 'exoneration'—placed heavy burdens on North and his family" (October 28th, 1991). North says that during that process he would "wake up and find myself in Machiavelli's palace."

It was it all behind him now. Only a month or so before his book came out, Special Prosecutor Lawrence Walsh asked Judge Gesell to drop all charges because he would be unable to show that North's trial had not been tainted by the testimony he gave under immunity to the congressional Iran-Contra committee. Of course, the book project was well underway before North was finally cleared of all charges.

What made North decide to publish a book about Iran-Contra when it was finally all behind him? Yet, the first thing North did after finally overcoming the ordeal of Iran-Contra was to write a book about Iran-Contra and thrust his name back into the scandal.

Indeed, North was very selective in the book as to who got blamed. In his 42-page "admission of facts," read to the jury before North took the stand in his trial, he stated that not only he but Reagan, Schultz, Casey, and Bush knew of the efforts to sell arms to Iran and to arm the Contras. Yet why is Bush's role in Iran-Contra virtually absent from his book?

North challenged the claim that he was merely being selective in his version of events. Yet while Bill Casey is dead and Reagan is no longer in office, North says precious little about George Bush and Robert Gates. He says that although phone records revealed hundreds of contacts between his office and Casey, he had no direct knowledge of any incriminating involvement of Bush or Gates (*Time*, October 28th, 1991).

Bush was a member of the National Security Council and Gates was third in command at the CIA and both were deeply involved in the Contra supply operation. Yet North had not even a single memo implicating either one of them in the scandal. He had the goods on a dead former CIA Director, a former President, and claims that Schultz and Weinberger knew everything, but miraculously he wrote nothing about the current President or the current director of the CIA. (What a lucky break for George and Bob.)

North was supposedly going public with his story, his version of the events. He was now going to tell everyone he was just following orders and had been set up as the fall guy, while everyone else knew everything. Then it might be assumed that he would also be angry and bitter that only *he* took a fall. Now he had his chance to at least say something about Bush's role in Iran-Contra, but instead, bent over backwards to save the President's skin. If North had been truly been angry at those who "betrayed him in the global fight against terrorism and communism" (*Time*, October 28th, 1991), he would have gone after everybody—the higher up the better.

Even the American public thought Bush was involved in some way with Iran-Contra. A Gallup Poll of 500 adults on May 5th, 1989, revealed that 63 percent thought that because of evidence at North's trial President Bush was more involved in the Iran-Contra Affair than he has said. Nearly 55 percent thought he should tell more about this role in the affair. Didn't North have any suspicions about Bush's role? Something?

Probably the most explosive piece of evidence that North introduced in his book, which he produced during his interview on *Nightline*, was an audiotape supposedly between two employees in two different Manhattan offices of New York's

Citibank. Record on June 17th, 1987, three weeks before North testified at the congressional hearings, it supposedly proved that the President was hiding something. Throughout the conversation, in the background, was another dialogue, between two men on the issue of what the President knew. Once again, the smoking gun points directly to Reagan.

The conversation went like this:

Voice A: Yeah, there's a smoking gun in the closet. Reagan knows.

Voice B: Listen ...

Voice A: I told the committee. There was no ... I told the committee there was ... I had nothing to do with those papers. Ollie North knows about it. Reagan knows ... Reagan knows about i ...

Voice B: Listen, he ain't testifying.

Voice A: ... and the ... and the other, the other people involved do know about that.

Voice B: (unintelligible)

Voice A: Well, you have to go the committee. You have to go to the committee.

Voice B: Listen ...

Voice A: Somebody's got to bring this up, I think someone ought to go; somebody's got to be responsible for this. Reagan knows. Reagan has all the memos.

Voice B: He's got all the memos. I thought he tore all the stuff up.

Voice A: No. He's got all the memos, and there are copies.

Voice B: Didn't you burn that stuff?

Voice A: No

Voice B: Oh, jeez. I warned you about that.

Voice A: Nobody ... no

Voice B: It's going to hit the papers like crazy.

Voice A: Nobody told me to.

Voice B: (unintelligible).

Voice A: No.

Voice B: What about your secretary? She couldn't get the stuff copied?

Voice A: Not all of it.

Voice B: (unintelligible) about Reagan (unintelligible).

Voice A: Well ... I'm getting out of this thing, and if somebody comes to me, I'm blowing the cover.

Voice B: I'll tell you, if I go down, I'm taking you with me.

Voice A: Well, me too.

Voice B: You and your ... secretary ... (unintelligible).

Voice A: I'd better call you back. I think we're tapped

Voice B: I think so.

Voice A: All right. Bye.

This sounds like a staged conversation. Does Citibank routinely record every employee's calls? Why, all of a sudden, did Voice A believe the phone was being tapped?

Nothing is known about the people behind the voices on the tape. North says the bank gave the tape to the FBI, and that a member of North's legal team found it in a pile of potential evidence that was provided to them by the prosecution. It's not known when the tape was discovered, by whom at Citibank, or how it made its way to the prosecutor. North says he and his lawyer took the tape to the White House and on July 28th, 1988, met with Arthur B. Culvahouse, the President's counsel. North's attorney, Brendan Sullivan, claims he asked to interview Reagan about the tape but the request was denied (*Time*, October 28th, 1991).

This seems to be a hell of a smoking gun, equivalent to Nixon's June 3rd tape, yet the prosecution is so carefree with it they simply toss it into a pile of paper and documents that they are going to show North's lawyers. Don't they wonder about it and take it to the White House to clarify it? If it was taped on June 17th, 1987, three weeks before North testified in front of Congress, why did the Iran-Contra Congressional Committee not hear it? If it was authentic, this is one tape that North's lawyers would have certainly leaked to the press during his court trial. Even if he was unable to introduce it as evidence, it would certainly back up his claim in the minds of the public that the President knew about the diversion. Yet the first time we hear about its existence is through North, after his trial.

Time magazine called the taped conversation "a coincidence almost too bizarre to believe." It certainly was. It seems the tape had one clear objective: to reinforce the idea in the American public's mind that Iran-Contra was about whether the President knew about the "diversion."

POST IRAN-CONTRA OLIVER NORTH

One would think that after all Ollie has been through, his anguish over being the fall guy for the Reagan Administration, his legal battles and their cost, the toll it took on his family, he would want nothing to do with conservative politics or the Republican agenda.

Not so. North is now the driving force behind the Freedom Alliance, a not-for-profit foundation that espouses "traditional American values" and "spreads the political gospel" through a monthly newsletter and daily radio broadcasts by Ollie syndicated to nearly 300 stations in the United States. North also writes a weekly column published in more than a dozen newspapers from the *Dallas Times-Herald* to the *Crockett Times* of Alamo, Tennessee (*Time*, October 28th, 1991). The Freedom Alliance is involved in many different activities; for instance, during the Gulf War it shipped $2.7 million worth of gift packages to U.S. troops in Saudi Arabia (*Time*, October 28th, 1991).

What's North's attraction? According to Mark Merritt, an official at the Freedom Alliance, it's because "Ollie is popular among people who see him as a guy who got slammed by Big Government" (*Time*, October 28th, 1991). Could be, but for a guy who got "slammed by Big Government," North isn't doing too badly. Despite being stripped of his annual military pension of $23,000, he commands $25,000 a night on the lecture circuit.

Although his most recent commercial venture is said to be aboveboard, there's room for speculation. North is chairman of Guardian Technologies International, a company which manufactures bulletproof vests made from Spectra, a lightweight fiber which is supposed to be more efficient that the current material, Kevlar. The company, which has annual sales of $1 million, sells primarily to law enforcement agencies in the U.S. and abroad.

What does an ex-Lt. Colonel know about marketing bulletproof vests? Not much, but his primary function is to travel around the U.S and the world meeting local police chiefs and law enforcement officials. He is no doubt a front for intelligence recruitment. In fact, North's partner in Guardian Technologies is none other than former CIA station chief in Costa Rica, José Fernandez.

What's the bottom line on Oliver North?

To begin with, regardless of how the media portrayed it, he didn't get shafted by "Big Government," nor did he "take the rap." He merely followed orders. Bush and his cadre of media specialists must have realized that the last thing they needed was another squealer like former White House Counsel John Dean: someone who would be designated as the fall guy, but after taking the rap became disgruntled, and, in return for immunity (although Dean only received limited immunity and was sent to prison) from prosecution, told all he knew. There would be no plea bargaining in this scandal.

Bush's team of media manipulators probably told North: "Don't worry, we'll make sure the congressional investigative committees don't get near the truth. We'll manipulate the media so the American public thinks you are a hero, a patriot who is being unjustly singled out. We'll manipulate the judicial process so that you can argue for a mistrial on the basis of testimony you previously gave to Congress. You'll claim you can't prepare a proper defense without documents we'll claim contain too many national security secrets to be released. When your trials ends you'll go on the speaking circuit, we'll create a foundation for you, you'll write articles in newspapers. Then we'll give you a front as head of a company so you can go around the world and make contracts for the CIA. We'll make you a hero. You'll be popular and rich and everyone will love you."

In this book, what was North telling the American people? That the entire operation of Iran-Contra wasn't really such a bad idea, although maybe it went a bit too far. That he was a brave soldier and merely followed orders. This served to smother any anger the public might have had over the White House's illegal acts.

Oliver North was simply another Bush-Reagan White House illusion. The objective behind the exercise was to have the entire country riveted on him. This was a diversion because if the public wasn't concentrating on him, it would have started looking at others in the Administration, particularly President Bush. If North hadn't been on trial, Bush would have been. The public could not have stood for two trials. In a sense, North defused Iran-Contra. His mission was to dull the senses of an American public known for its extremely short attention span.

The proof is in the pudding. The diversion(s) worked like a charm. The public took North's side of the story as the truth. After Ollie, by late 1989, the American public had no more tolerance for Iran-Contra. George Bush sailed into the White House. Iran-Contra was not even an election issue for Bush.

The tragedy in all this is that today many, perhaps even the majority of, Americans believe Meese's initial contention that a lone colonel in the National Security Council operated a private foreign policy that planned and carried out all the events of Iran-Contra, and that the buck stopped at Ollie. Yet at his trial, Ollie himself said that this wasn't so, that everyone in the Administration was involved and that he was just following orders.

How come few people (if any) caught the contradiction?

Because the American people were not perceiving reality. They were being manipulated by "a Bush illusion."

CHAPTER 4

George Bush and the Secret Team of Covert Operators

WAS THE REAGAN-BUSH WHITE HOUSE IN CAHOOTS WITH DRUG LORDS?

Did the Reagan-Bush White House do business with drug traffickers? This question not only applies to the Presidencies of George Bush and Ronald Reagan, but to every single administration since the end of World War II.

The Christic Institute and its founder, Daniel Sheehan, deserves special credit for its work in exposing the CIA's ties to drug lords, particularly during the Reagan years. Founded in 1980 as a non-profit, public-interest law firm and public policy center, the Christic Institute had previously prosecuted some of the most celebrated public-interest lawsuits of the decade, including the Karen Silkwood case as well as the Greensboro Massacre suit against the American Nazi Party and the Ku Klux Klan.

During one of my trips to Washington I finally got a chance to meet Sheehan. Although situated only a few blocks from Washington's Union Station, it seemed only right that a non-profit organization fighting against the tremendous odds of battling covert operators would be housed in a rundown, near-slum neighborhood of the nation's capital.

Although we had just a short time together because I was flying back to Israel that evening, Sheehan struck me as being one of the very few people in the United States who grasped most of the complexities of the story of how the CIA had become involved with drug traffickers. The way he rattled off the names and events, he could probably have repeated them in his sleep.

Sheehan claims that there existed a conspiratorial "secret team" of covert operators which carried out its own, private foreign policy much of it funded by proceeds from the international drug trade. The 29 defendants named in a suit instituted by the Christic Institute in Florida included Lt. Colonel Oliver North, retired major generals Richard Secord and John Singlaub, former CIA intelligence officers Theodore Shackley and Thomas Clines, financier Albert Hakim, Robert Owen, a former aide to Vice President Quayle, Contra rebel leader Adolfo Calero, mercenary Thomas Posey, and drug dealers John Hall and Jorge Ochoa.

"We assembled evidence that the Contra resupply network orchestrated criminal covert operations, including secret wars, assassination programs and illicit arms deals. It financed these activities, in part, through the smuggling and sale of tons of cocaine and other illegal drugs into the United States," says Sheehan. "Since the Congress, the Reagan-Bush White House's Justice Department, and the Judiciary had, for the most part, turned a blind eye to these allegations, we took our evidence directly to the American public. The public needs to know and has a right to know of covert and illegal activities undertaken by private citizens in the name of U.S. foreign policy and 'national security.' "

In the lawsuit, the institute used the RICO statutes, passed in 1970 to bring Mafia bosses to justice (the statutes enable a member of a conspiracy to be held accountable for crimes committed by those under his orders). The institute was able to formally charge the Reagan-Bush Secret Team as a result of the 1984 bombing of a press conference in La Penca, Nicaragua. During the early part of 1984, after the Boland Amendments were passed, Oliver North came up with a new plan to secretly circumvent the congressional ban on Contra military aid. The idea was to take away the responsibility of arming and training them from the CIA and transfer it to a "private" network controlled directly by him from the White House. This meant uniting the various Contra forces into one effective fighting force.

One of the Contra leaders, Eden Pastora of the ARDE organization based in Costa Rica, refused a CIA ultimatum to ally his group with the larger Contra group the administration was supporting, the FDN. He was told by the CIA to "unite with the FDN or suffer the consequences."

At a press conference where Pastora was to announce that he was not going to accede to these demands, a bomb exploded, killing eight people and injuring many others. The White House obviously wouldn't take no for an answer.

Sheehan alleges that the explosion was arranged by Hull, a drug trafficker who helped Oliver North's Contra supply operation, and Felipe Vidal, another narcotics smuggler who worked with Hull. At a crucial December 1984 meeting at the Shamrock Hilton Hotel in Houston, Texas, attended by Hull and Owen, Jack Terrell, another participant in North's supply network, claims Hull told him "Pastora had to be killed" (*The Progressive*, March 1990).

The CIA helped cover up the bombing through extensive use of disinformation within Costa Rica. A Costa Rican government report revealed that in 1984 CIA agent Dimitrius Papas trained an elite 15-member group of Costa Rican intelligence agents known as "the Babies" to organize a network of illegal telephone taps and a slush fund for payoffs to Costa Rican leaders (*The Progressive*, March 1990; *Newsweek*, February 12th, 1990).

During the course of preparing for the suit, Sheehan met Paul Hoven, a Vietnam veteran who led a group called "Project on Military Procurement" in support of military reform in the purchasing and development of weapons (*Out of Control: The*

Story of the Reagan Administration's Secret War in Nicaragua, the Illegal Arms Pipeline, and the Contra Drug Connection, 1987). Hoven introduced Sheehan to a retired military intelligence officer who had first hand knowledge about a group of former CIA senior officials who formed a "secret team" to undertake covert operations on a commercial basis. Operating independently of the U.S. government, some members were even involved in CIA-sanctioned assassination plots as far back as the Kennedy era. The former intelligence officer told Sheehan he came in contact with the secret team when he tried to acquire semi-covert mercenary work in Central America and Iran.

This convinced Sheehan that a secret team did exist and that his institute had do something to stop them.

He knew who the criminals were. When he found his victims, two American journalists based in Costa Rica, Tony Avigran and Martha Honey, who were injured in the blast, he set the legal work in motion. The institute's lawsuit was filed on May 29th, 1986, in the U.S. District Court of Southern Florida. The racketeering charges described a complex criminal enterprise, including former United States military and intelligence officers, mercenaries, businessmen, and drug dealers, who conspired to covertly organize military aid to the Contra forces. The Court Declaration charted the racketeering activities from 1959 through 1987, and divided them into geographical locations: Cuba, Southeast Asia, Iran, Afghanistan, and Nicaragua.

CUBA

In Cuba, Sheehan's account of the Secret Team's activities begins in the late 1950s and early 1960s with a plan to overthrow Cuban dictator Fidel Castro, which violated the United States' Neutrality Act. Expatriate Cubans were recruited and sent to one of two secret military training bases established for this purpose—one in the south of Miami, Florida, and the other, named Camp Trax, in Retalhuleu, Guatemala (*Inside the Shadow Government*, 1988).

The force later became known as the 2506 Brigade. The purpose of their missions was to allow the expatriate Cubans to re-enter Cuba covertly and establish a center of guerrilla resistance to the Cuban government and to disrupt the new economy. A later plan included the assassination of Fidel Castro (*Report of the Select Committee to Study Governmental Operations with Respect to Intelligence Activities, Alleged Assassination Plots Involving Foreign Leaders*, 94th Congress, 1975). This would have paved the way for former President Fulgencio Batista's return to power as well as the narcotics and gambling activities run by such underworld figures as Meyer Lansky and Santo Trafficante, Jr.

The low-profile, guerrilla-infiltration assassination strategy, code-named Operation 40, was replaced with a plan for a full-scale military invasion of Cuba, to be staged at the Bay of Pigs in April 1962. After that invasion failed, from 1962 to 1965 Theodore Shackley headed a program of raids and sabotage against Cuba. Working under Shackley was Thomas Clines, Rafael Quintero, Luis Posada Carriles, Rafaël and Raúl Villaverde, Frank Sturgis (who would later be one of the famous Watergate burglars), Felix Rodriguez and Edwin Wilson. This operation, called JM/WAVE, was eventually closed down in 1965, when several of its participants became involved with smuggling narcotics from Cuba into the United States (*New York Times*, January 4th, 1975).

SOUTHEAST ASIA

When the JM/WAVE project ended, Shackley and Clines, Rodriguez, Wilson, and Quintero left for Laos in Southeast Asia. Shackley was chief of the CIA's station in Vientiane until 1969, while Clines was under Shackley's direction as the base chief in Long Tieng (*The Ravens: The Men Who Flew in America's Secret War in Laos*, 1987).

The goal of these two covert operators was to organize, direct, and fund an army of Hmong tribesmen (historically, opium poppy farmers) on bases in northern Laos to fight the Communist Pathet Lao insurgent forces. The leader of this secret army was general Vang Pao, who was also a major opium supplier. In 1960 a civil war broke out when General Phoumi Nosavan's right-wing government was overthrown by a group of army officers, together with former Prime Minister Souvanna Phouma and leftist leader Pathet Lao. Nosavan recruited Pao to take control over northeastern Laos with Shackley and Clines providing air support. In return for fighting the Communists, Shackley, Clines and Richard Secord helped Pao control Laos' opium trade by sabotaging competitors. Secord oversaw and authorized the transport of raw opium by Pao's tribesmen in paramilitary aircraft from the mountain opium fields to processing centers. Eventually, Vang Pao had a monopoly over the heroin trade in Laos (*Inside the Shadow Government*).

Six air bases were built in Thailand and Long Tieng in northern Laos as well as landing strips for Air America planes throughout Hmong-controlled territory (David Truong, *Running Drugs and Secret Wars, Covert Action* Information Bulletin No. 28, Summer 1987). In 1967 Shackley and Clines helped Vang Pao attain financial backing to form his own airline, Zieng Khouang Air Transport Co., to transport opium and heroin between Long Tieng and Vientiane. In 1968, Shackley and Clines arranged a meeting in Saigon between Mafia chief Santo Trafficante, Jr., and Vang Pao to establish a heroin-smuggling operation from Southeast Asia to the United States (*The Politics of Heroin*, 1972).

Ron Rickenbach was a former official with the U.S Agency for International Development who served in Laos from 1962 to 1969. "Early on," he wrote, "I think that we all believed that what we were doing was in the best interest of America, that we were in fact perhaps involved in some not so desirable aspects of the drug traffic, however we believed strongly in the beginning that we were there for a just cause. These people were willing to take up arms. We needed to stop the Red threat" (PBS documentary *"Frontline: "Guns, Drugs and the CIA,"* May 1989).

Although Richard Secord claims that "there was no commercial trade in opium going on," Rickenbach says: "I was in the areas where opium was transshipped, I personally was witness to opium being placed on aircraft, American aircraft. I witnessed it being taken off smaller aircraft that were coming in from outlying areas."

Former Air America pilot Neil Hanses adds, "Yes, I've seen the sticky bricks come on board and no one was challenging their right to carry it."

Another smuggling route had the opium being traded for guns before being loaded onto planes operated by the French Corsican drug syndicates and dropped into the Gulf of Siam. It would later be picked up by fishing boats and taken to ports in South Vietnam.

As part of their covert operation, with training by Quintero and Rodriguez, Vang Pao is reported to have killed rival opium warlords, civilian functionaries, and supporters of the Pathet Lao (*Inside the Shadow Government*). These actions were continuing when in 1969 Clines and Shackley were posted to Saigon, where they are alleged to have directed "Operation Phoenix" to "neutralize" non-combatant Vietnamese civilians suspected of collaborating with the National Liberation Front. Former CIA director William Colby would later testify at a 1971 Senate hearing that "Operation Phoenix" killed 20,587 Vietnamese and imprisoned another 28,978 between August 1968 and May 1971 (Fred Branfman, *South Vietnam's Police and Prison System: The U.S. Connection*, Free Press, 1978).

Alfred McCoy, a professor of history at the University of Wisconsin, wrote the monumental work on the subject of the CIA's involvement in the drug trade: *The Politics of Heroin in South East Asia* . In 1991 he followed it up with *The Politics of Heroin: CIA Complicity in the Global Drug Trade*.

McCoy has specialized in the area of the CIA's historic ties to the international drug trade. He asserts that the organization's involvement in the Asian drug trade actually dates back to the late 1940s, after the People's Republic of China was proclaimed by Mao Tse-tung. The CIA allied itself with Kuomintang forces that had fled to the Shan states of northern Burma to carry out sabotage against China. They supported themselves via the opium trade by sending caravans of the drug to Laos for sale.

"Whenever the CIA supports a rebel faction in a regional dispute, that faction's involvement in the drug trade increases," McCoy claims. "Just as CIA support for National Chinese troops in the Shan states increased Burma's opium crop in the 1950s, so too did the agency's aid to the mujahideen guerrillas in the 1980s expand opium production in Afghanistan" (*The Progressive*, July 1991).

Victor Marchetti, who worked for the CIA for 14 years and served as executive assistant to the deputy director under Richard Helms until 1969, is probably the leading critic today of the CIA's "covert" activities. Having seen how things work from the inside, in 1975 he wrote *The CIA and the Cult of Intelligence*, the first book to expose the workings of the U.S. organization. The book has become somewhat of a classic in certain circles. On April 18th, 1972, Marchetti became the first American writer to be served with an official censorship order issued by a court of the United States forbidding him to disclose any information about the CIA. The verdict was eventually overturned.

"I guess people like the book," Marchetti told me one morning at a coffee shop in the National Press Building in Washington. "Every once in a while I get a royalty check for a few hundred dollars from my publishers."

Marchetti was a Soviet military specialist and at one point

was probably the U.S. government's leading expert on Soviet military aid to the countries of the Third World. He left the CIA and wrote about its shortcomings. He felt the agency was incapable of reforming itself and that Presidents had no interest in changing it because they viewed it as a private asset.

Out of all the people I interviewed for this book, Marchetti was perhaps the most insightful. He spoke about covert operations and secret agendas of the Bush-Reagan White Houses the way most people would about yesterday's football scores.

"It shouldn't surprise anyone that the history of the CIA runs parallel to criminal and drug operations throughout the world," he says. "The connection stretches back to the predecessor organization of the CIA, the OSS [Office of Strategic Services], and its involvement with the Italian Mafia, the Cosa Nostra, in Sicily and Southern Italy. When the OSS was fighting communists in France they 'mingled' with the Corsican brotherhood, who were heavily into drugs at that time."

Many of these contacts were formulated in the late 1940's when the OSS worked covertly to replace the leftist leaders of the Marseilles dock union, after it was thought that the union might interfere with American shipping in a crisis (*The Nation*, August 29th, 1987).

Exploiting the drug trade amplifies the operational capacity of covert operations for the CIA. When the CIA decides to enter a region to combat a communist force or country, the purpose is to seek out allies and assets which are effective and won't squeal. The CIA's allies' involvement with narcotics enhances their operational capacity because they are fully integrated into the household economies of the region and monopolize what is usually the largest cash crop in that country. Any group which controls such a lucrative trade commands extraordinary political power that is extremely useful to the CIA. Powerful drug warlords can mobilize people to die. No amount of money in the world can buy this operational capacity.

Says Alfred McCoy: "In the mountain ranges along the southern rim of Asia—whether in Afghanistan, Burma, or Laos—opium is the main currency of external trade and thus is a key source of political power. Since operations involve alliances with local power brokers who serve as the CIA's commanders, the agency, perhaps unwillingly or unwittingly, has repeatedly found its covert operations enmeshed with Asia's heroin trade. By investing a local ally such as Hekmatyar or Vang Pao with the authority of its alliance, the CIA draws the ally under the mantle of its protection. So armed, a tribal leader, now less vulnerable to arrest and prosecution, can use his American alliance to expand his share of the local opium trade" (*The Politics of Heroin*, 1991).

Marchetti agrees: "Drug dealers are in a position to know things, to get things done. They have muscle and no qualms about using it. This is attractive to the covert operators."

NUGAN HAND BANK

Covert operations, like any other type of operation, need financing and the use of financial instruments. Just as BCCI served a useful purpose for many countries' and dictators' illicit activities, back in the mid-1970s the Secret Team decided it needed to control its own bank for covert operations.

Daniel Sheehan gathered information which suggests Clines, Secord, Shackley, and Quintero siphoned off a percentage of the funds derived from the opium profits of Vang Pao to a secret bank account at the Nugan Hand Bank in Sydney, Australia.

The Nugan Bank was founded in 1976 by Francis John Nugan and Michael Jon Hand. Hand was a member of the U.S. Special Forces in Laos, a former Green Beret and a CIA agent. Shortly after its establishment the bank boasted deposits of $25 million. Its board of directors was impressive.

The President of the Nugan Hand Bank was Admiral Earl F. Yates, former Chief of Staff for Strategic Planning of U.S. Forces in Asia and the Pacific. The President of Nugan Hand Bank Hawaii was General Edwin F. Black, commander of U.S. troops in Thailand during the Vietnam War and then-Assistant Army Chief of Staff for the Pacific. Nugan Hand's representative in Saudi Arabia was Bernie Houghton, a U.S. Naval Intelligence agent.

Another director of Nugan Hand Bank was Dale Holmgree, a former employee of Civil Air Transport, which later became the CIA's proprietary company, Air America (the airline run by the CIA that transported opium out of the Golden Triangle to Saigon, Hong Kong, and Bangkok). George Farris, a Green Beret and CIA operative in Vietnam, ran the Washington, D.C., office of Nugan Hand Bank. General LeRoy J. Manor, former Chief of Staff for the U.S. Pacific Command, was Nugan Hand's man in Manila. The bank's legal counsel was William Colby, a former director of the CIA.

The Board of Directors for the parent company that preceded the establishment of the Nugan Hand Bank, were Grant Walters, Robert Peterson, David M. Houton, and Spencer Smith, all of whom listed their address as C/O Air America, Army Post Office, San Francisco, California (*Canadian Dimension*, September 1987).

Despite having established branches throughout the world, the Nugan Hand Bank rarely conducted any banking activities. In fact, the bank was a mini-BCCI, its reach spanning six continents, and was involved in drug operations, laundering money, tax evasion, and investor fraud operations. Not only did it serve as a transaction center for the profits the CIA earned from the Southeast Asian drug trade, but it also funneled money to South African-backed forces fighting in Angola.

The bank made the headlines of Australia in 1980 when Frank Nugan was found dead from a gunshot wound in his

Mercedes-Benz on January 27th of that year. In his trousers police found the business card of Nugan Hand's lawyer, William Colby, with the details of Colby's upcoming trip to the Far East. Inside his briefcase were the names of prominent Australian politicians and business personalities with dollar amounts handwritten in the five and six figures (*Mother Jones*, August/September 1987).

The circumstances behind how Hand met Frank Nugan, a local lawyer and heir to a food-processing fortune, have never been properly clarified. Under oath, at the inquest, Hand claimed he couldn't remember.

The bank grew and had offices or affiliates in 13 countries. According to Jonathan Kwitny, whose book *Dope, Dirty Money, and the CIA: Crimes of Patriots* (1987) documented the scandal, the bank did little banking. However, over its seven-year existence it amassed large sums moving, collecting, and disbursing money. As soon as investigators began looking into the affairs of the bank in 1980, it was declared insolvent. Kwitny discovered that in the immediate days after his death, Nugan's house was taken over by Hand, Yates and Houghton, as company files were packed in "cartons, sorted, or fed to a shredder" (*Mother Jones*, August/September 1987). Its branch in Chiang Mai, Thailand, writes Kwitny, was the most mysterious of all of Nugan Hand's activities. Why was a supposedly legitimate bank opening an office in Chiang Mai, a region awash in the opium-growing trade?

After much investigative work, Kwitny discovered that the Chiang Mai branch of the Nugan Hand Bank was on the same floor in what he believed to be the same suite as the United States Drug Enforcement Agency office. When asked, the DEA wouldn't offer an explanation. Kwitny found that every which way he turned he was stonewalled.

He finally hit pay dirt when he tracked down Neil Evans, an Australian who was selected by Hand to run the Thailand branch. Evans reported to Kwitny that during his seven-month stint, Hand told him to deposit $2.6 million from six major drug dealers. Another employee at the Bangkok office said, "There was nothing there but drug money." (Before releasing it to the public, the Joint Task Force on Drug Trafficking, an investigation commissioned by the Australian government, deleted ten pages on Nugan Hand's Thailand activities from its report.)

The bank collapsed, owing some $50 million. None of the deposits were secured because they were used for illegal activities. These included defrauding American military personnel in Saudi Arabia out of nearly $10 million. The bank sent out "investment counselors" to installations where Americans were working in Saudi Arabia and told them to invest their salaries in Nugan Hand's Hong Kong branch in secured government bonds.

The Australian government eventually investigated the collapse of the bank and found that millions of dollars were missing and unaccounted for. It discovered that the main depositors of the bank were connected with the narcotics trade in the Middle East and Asia, and that the CIA was using Nugan Hand to finance a variety of covert operations. Government investigations revealed ties between Nugan Hand and the world's largest heroin syndicates. The reports said that the Bank was linked to at least 26 separate individuals or groups known to be associated with drug trafficking."

In 1983 the Australian Joint Task Force on Drug Trafficking released a report on Nugan Hand's activities to Parliament which said Shackley, Secord, Clines, Quintero, and Wilson were people whose background "is relevant to a proper understanding of the activities of the Nugan Hand group and the people associated with that group."

The investigations also detailed Nugan Hand's involvement in the sale of an electronic spy ship to Iran and arms shipments to South African-backed forces in Angola which were being supported by the CIA. These operations were run by Edwin Wilson, a career CIA officer who in 1983 began serving a 52-year prison sentence for selling tons of weapons and training expertise to Libya. Wilson claims he was set up to cheat him out of his fair share of the profits of the Secret Team's covert operations.

Confirming Nugan Hand's illicit activities and spilling a few beans of his own, in 1983 Wilson's business partner, Frank Terpil, told journalist Jim Hougan:

"The significance of Miami is the drug syndicate. That's the base. Shackley, Clines, the Villaverde brothers, Chi Chi, Rodriquez—all the people that I hired to terminate other people, from the Agency—are there. Who's the boss of Clines? Shackley. Where do they come from? Laos. Where did the money come from? Nugan Hand. The whole goddamned thing has been moved down there. ... Clines was running drugs ... The pilot of the plane in Asia was Dick Secord, a captain in the Air Force. ... What was on the plane? Gold! Ten million bucks at a time, in gold. He was going to the Golden Triangle to pay off warlords. The drug loans. ... Now what do you do with all the opium? You reinvest it in your own operation. Billions of dollars—not millions—billions of dollars" (*Covert Action*, Information Bulletin, Summer 1987).

None of those involved in the scandal have ever been convicted of any crimes as all eventually fled Australia.

Marchetti says that Nugan Hand is a good example of a unique type of covert operation: an independent group of people with ties to the CIA are in business for themselves, but at the same time carry out tasks for the CIA. The group is in a position to do the agency special favors, such as laundering money or providing cover for secret operations. The agency, in turn, will use its influence to throw business the company's way or to offer the company protection from criminal investigation" (*Mother Jones*, August/September 1987).

In light of the scandal, Kwitny concludes that "the license

to commit crimes in the name of national security has been granted too often and too lightly." He asks some very relevant questions the American people should also ponder: When agents of the U.S. steal, when they get involved in drug deals, how far should the patriotic cloak granted by national policy stretch to cover them? Does it cover an agent who lines his pockets in side deals while working in the name of national security? (*Mother Jones*, August/September 1987).

IRAN

After the fall of Saigon in April 1975, the focus of operations for the Secret Team moved to the Middle East. Shackley was now in Washington as CIA Associate Deputy Director in the Directorate of Operations. Clines was in Washington as head of CIA operations training. Richard Secord was appointed chief of the U.S. Air Force's Military Assistance Advisory Group, which represented U.S. defense contractors selling arms to the Shah's army and training them in the use of this new military equipment. The secret team was also advising the Shah on how to use sophisticated communications equipment so his secret police force, SAVAK, could contain the regime's adversaries and political opponents.

One major military contract the group maintained during this time was Rockwell International IBEX's electronic and photographic surveillance project for intelligence gathering, not only in Iran but in the entire region, including the then-Soviet Union. On August 28th, 1976, three of the top managers of the project were shot dead while driving through Teheran. Officials blamed Libyan-trained Islamic Marxist guerrillas (*Washington Post*, August 29th, 30th, 1976), but Gene Wheaton, a longtime U.S. military investigator and former IBEX Director of Security, says that these people were killed to cover up a scam which skimmed profits from the IBEX project.

From the start, IBEX was plagued with corruption. According to a report in the *Washington Post*, a month before the assassinations, U.S. ambassador to Iran Richard Helms and a former CIA head, sent a handwritten letter to then-CIA Director George Bush complaining about the project and urging him to investigate allegations of corruption (*The Nation*, August 27th, 1988).

Wheaton discovered that Secord, Clines, Quintero, and Albert Hakim had a "historical record of skimming off of military projects, taking kickbacks" and that they had laundered large amounts of payoffs for military programs in the Middle East through Swiss bank accounts. Gene Wheaton testified in a deposition for the Christic Institute that the three Rockwell men "were murdered to cover misdeeds on the project, a project where Albert Hakim served as the bag man and that this was part of the Ed Wilson network." He claims that John Harper, who served as head of security for the project from November 1976 to May 1977, was told by Frank Terpil after the murders that the "Rockwell matter" had been taken care of.

AFGHANISTAN

In May 1980 Dr. David Musto, a Yale University psychiatrist and White House advisor on drugs, discovered that the CIA and other intelligence agencies denied the White House Strategy Council on Drug Abuse he was heading access to all classified information on drugs. He warned then that what happened in Laos would occur in Afghanistan. Another White House Drug Council Member, Dr. Joyce Lowinson, writing the *New York Times*, accurately questioned: "Are we erring in befriending these tribes (Afghanistan and Pakistan rebel tribesmen) as we did in Laos when Air America helped transport crude opium from certain tribal areas?"

They were both right. After President Carter began shipping arms to the mujahideen guerrillas in December 1979, drug-related deaths in New York City rose by 77 percent (*The Progressive*, July 1991). By 1982, Southern Asia, although never before a source, supplied 60 percent of the U.S. heroin market.

University of Wisconsin professor Alfred McCoy says that during the more than ten years of CIA covert support for the mujahideen resistance, the Bush-Reagan Administration and the mainstream media said almost nothing about the involvement of leading Afghan guerrillas and Pakistan military in the heroin traffic.

McCoy tracks the relationship between the CIA and the narcotics trade in Afghanistan and Pakistan to a May 1979 meeting at Peshawar in Pakistan's Northwest Frontier province between a CIA envoy and Afghan resistance leaders chosen by Pakistan's ISI (Inter Service Intelligence). The ISI was said to offer an alliance with its own Afghan client, Gulbuddin Hekmatyar, leader of the small Hezbi-i Islamic group, rather than a broad spectrum of resistance leaders (*The Progressive*, July 1991).

It's never been fully explained why, but when Reagan and Bush took office Pakistan-U.S. relations soared. More than $3 billion in U.S. aid, including F-16 fighter jets, flowed to General Zia's army. In return, Zia allowed the CIA to open an electronic intelligence station in northern Pakistan aimed at the Soviet Union. This enabled U.S. spy flights over the Indian Ocean from Pakistani air bases near the Persian Gulf.

With CIA and Pakistani support, Hekmatyar became Afghanistan's leading drug trafficker. In May 1990, the *Washington Post* published a series of articles explaining how the United States had ignored Afghan complaints of heroin trafficking by Hekmatyar. The newspaper reported that Hekmatyar commanders close to the ISI ran laboratories in southwest Pakistan and that ISI cooperated in its heroin operations.

McCoy says that during the time the mujahideen were being supported by the CIA, their opium harvest doubled to 575 tons. Once these mujahideen elements brought the opium across the border, they sold it to Pakistani heroin refineries operating under the Pakistani government's protection (*The Progressive*, July 1991).

In September 1985 the Pakistani newspaper *The Herald* reported: "The drug is carried in National Logistics Cell [part of the Pakistani Army] trucks, which come sealed from the Northwest Frontier and are never checked by the police."

Drug Enforcement Agency officials admitted that the shipment of CIA weapons into Pakistan played a key role in allowing the trade in heroin to flourish. No heroin was refined in Pakistan before 1979 but now Pakistan produces and exports "more heroin than the rest of the world combined," one agent told the *Philadelphia Inquirer* (February 28th, 1988).

The free flow of heroin had a devastating effect on the Pakistani people. Addiction rose to 5000 in 1980, to 70,000 in 1983, and to more than 1.3 million by 1985. At more than $10 million in sales made each year from the sale of heroin, it was larger than Pakistan's governmental budget and equal to more than one quarter of the gross national product.

When investigative journalist Larry Lifschultz began looking into the ties between General Zia and the Afghan drug trade, he discovered that European and Interpol police investigations of the major heroin traffickers had been aborted at the highest levels of the Pakistani government. The U.S. Drug Enforcement Agency itself had 17 agents working out of the U.S. Embassy in Islamabad and compiled reports on 40 narcotics dealers in Pakistan. Yet not a single major syndicate was investigated by Pakistani police.

Typical of the misinformation that had blocked U.S. action against Pakistan's heroin trade, the State Department's semi-annual narcotics review in September 1988 called General Zia "a strong supporter of anti-narcotics activities in Pakistan."

"Once the CIA has invested its prestige in one of these opium warlords, it cannot afford to comprise a major covert action with an investigation," McCoy points out. "Respecting the national security imperatives of CIA operations, the DEA keeps its distance from agency assets, even when they are the major drug lords" (*The Progressive*, July 1991).

NICARAGUA

The Secret Team's activities can be connected from Cuba, to Laos, through Iran, and to Nicaragua. It was the same network, the same people, and the same set of covert operators. The reasons the CIA became entangled with drug traffic in Central America were the same as they were in Burma and Laos.

Victor Marchetti contends that the CIA got involved with the Kuomintang drug runners in Burma because they, too, were resisting the drift towards communism there. The same thing happened in Southeast Asia, and in the 1980s in Latin America.

"Some of the very people who are the best sources of information, who are capable of accomplishing important tasks to stifle communist movements, happen to inhabit the criminal world," he says. "The CIA keeps getting involved with these kinds of people, not for 'drug purposes' or for personal gain, although that has become a major part of it, but to achieve the higher ideological goal of fighting communism" (*Frontline*, May 1989).

The use of drug profits to finance the Contra war was confirmed in April 1989 by the Senate Foreign Relations Subcommittee on Narcotics and Terrorism. Chaired by Senator John Kerry of Massachusetts, the investigation discovered that, through a web of business relationships with Latin American drug cartels, the Contras were supplied with "cash, weapons, planes, pilots, and air supply services." The subcommittee found that senior officials in the Reagan-Bush White House were fully aware that the Contras were shipping drugs into the United States, but did nothing to stop it.

"The logic of having drug money pay for the pressing needs

of the Contras appealed to a number of people who became involved in the covert war," the report of the Subcommittee stated. "Indeed, senior U.S. policy makers were not immune to the idea that drug money was a perfect solution to the Contras' funding problems."

Daniel Sheehan says that evidence of drug trafficking by the Contras and their supporters centers on three related allegations: that a major "guns-for-drugs" operation existed between North, Central, and South America and that helped finance the Contra war; that the Contra leadership received direct funding from major drug dealers; and that some of the Contra leaders themselves have been directly involved in drug trafficking.

Some of these allegations come from less than ideal sources. For instance, Pilot George Morales says after he was indicted in the spring of 1984 for drug trafficking that he was approached by Contra leaders offering him "a deal." If he set up a Contra drug-smuggling operation, his indictment would be "taken care of by people in Vice President Bush's office." He agreed, and flew weapons to John Hull's ranch (a liaison to the Contras) and returned with narcotics (CBS's *West 57th St.*, April 6th, 1987). Morales said his planes landed at Hull's ranch in Costa Rica.

Gary Betzner, one of Morales' pilots, said he himself took two tons of small-aircraft weapons and returned to Florida with a thousand kilos of cocaine (*Out of Control*). In March 1986 another pilot, Michael Tolliver, flew 28,000 pounds of weapons to Honduras and returned to South Florida with 25,360 pounds of marijuana (*Newsday*, April 6th, 1987). "I smuggled my share of illegal substances, but I also smuggled my share of weapons to the Contras in exchange, with the full knowledge and assistance of the DEA Drug Enforcement Agency and the CIA," Betzner claims (*Newsweek*, January 26th, 1987).

The cocaine originated from Pablo Escobar and Jorge

Ochoa, Colombian drug traffickers who worked with the Medellín cocaine cartel. The drugs were shipped to John Hull's ranch and then sent on to the U.S. Two Cuban Americans, Felipe Vidal and René Corvo, arranged the money transfers. Hull, Vidal, Ochoa, Escobar, and Corvo were defendants in the Christic Institute's lawsuit.

Ramón Milián Rodríguez, chief accountant of the Colombian Medellín cocaine cartel, who is currently serving a 43-year prison sentence for money laundering, told CBS News and the Senate Foreign Relations Subcommittee that he personally arranged to have $10 million of Colombian drug money funneled to the Contras from late 1982 through 1985. "The cartel figured it was buying a little friendship," Milián Rodríguez told congressional investigators. "What the hell is 10 million bucks? They thought they were going to buy some goodwill and take a little heat off them" (*Newsday*, June 28th, 1987).

When Congress cut off funding for the Contras in 1984, replacement funds had to be found. Milián Rodriguez testified that although he had been laundering foreign payments for the CIA up through 1982, the CIA turned to him again (*Frontline*). He says he used Cuban-controlled front companies in Miami to funnel the money to the Contras, and that the money pipeline to the Contras was arranged by CIA veteran Felix Rodriguez, who would call him and tell him where to drop the money (*Out of Control*).

"To have people like me in place, that can be used, is marvelous for them," Milián Rodríguez points out. "The agency, and quite rightly so, has things that they have to do which they can never admit to an oversight committee, and the only way they can fund these things is through drug money or through illicit money that they can get their hands on in some way (*Frontline*). Adds General Paul Gorman, the commander of the U.S. Southern Command in Panama from 1982 to 1985: "If one wants to organize an armed resistance or an armed undertaking for any purpose, the best place to get the money, the easy place to get the guns are in the drug world."

Probably the most disturbing aspect of the entire connection of drugs to the Bush-Reagan White House's Contra supply effort is the way Congress dealt with the issue. For instance, on July 23rd, 1987, Senate and House Select Committee investigator for the Iran-Contra Affair Robert Bermingham sent a memo to Co-Chairman Senator Daniel Inouye and Congressman Lee Hamilton, requesting them to issue a statement stating that the investigative staff found no direct evidence of Contra involvement in drug trafficking. Yet Bermingham hadn't even consulted with the investigator on the Senate Foreign Relations Committee looking into the Contra-drug link (*Boston Globe*, July 29th, 1987).

To their credit, some politicians, like Senator John Kerry, did try to investigate the matter. He learned that not everyone was as earnest as he was in getting at the truth. He discovered that Richard Messick, a Republican staff member of the committee, was believed to be passing documents and information to the Justice Department (*Village Voice*, July 14th, 1987). Messick was also found to be relaying misinformation from the Justice Department to discredit witnesses before the committee.

The Christic Institute was the only investigation that got even as far as the courts. Yet its lawsuit was eventually dismissed by a Miami judge—as Sheehan believes, because of intervention by the Justice Department in the judicial process.

Prior to this decision David Corn wrote an article in *The Nation* (July 2nd, 1988) entitled "Is There Really a 'Secret Team'?" which put the entire affair into perspective. Corn was critical of the effort by the Christic Institute. He thought Sheehan was trying to do too much: to make a legal point, as well as to educate the American people of the evils of the national security apparatus in order to rally public opposition to it. "These various aims," he writes, "though, can collide with one another. The reliance of a Secret Team may work fine given the confines of a RICO suit. Outside, however, it may undermine the Christic Institute's broader public education campaign, which aims to raise questions about the national security state and U.S. foreign policy as a whole."

Corn argues that by ascribing the events in the affidavits as the work of a "Secret Team," it lets the CIA, the Pentagon, the State Department, and various Administrations off the hook. For instance, the secret war in Laos was a massive, and official, CIA operation with the support of a full range of U.S. government agencies. It wasn't carried out exclusively by a "secret team" of covert operators.

Edith Holleman, a Christic Institute lawyer, says that these actions should be considered nongovernmental because those involved were acting above and beyond their authority, even if they were employed by the U.S. government. She believes journalists are making the mistake of not seeing the case as a legal finding. "Lawsuits," she adds, "are not history books. They're only parts of history books. To suggest that these events reflected a pattern of government action is to look at it from a political scientist or historical perspective. Are the courtrooms the place to decide the crucial issues of political analyses?"

Corn wondered whether the individuals in the Secret Team were (are) acting on behalf of themselves, or the "enterprise"—the term which the Christic Institute eventually began using after it was brought out in the Iran-Contra hearings—or were semi-official agents of the CIA.

"With its advocacy of the Secret Team theory," Corn writes, "the Christic Institute has painted itself into a corner. If all these ventures are the handiwork of a few rogues, there is no reason to worry about the national security system at large. What's the remedy for a few bad apples? Better screening of personnel. . . . If anything like the Secret Team exists, the issue is the system that spawned it." Corn believes that the guilty party is not the Secret Team, but rather decisions made by Presidents and Vice Presidents, in most cases, supported by the entire national security bureaucracy, to employ the Secret Team (*The Nation*, January 27th, 1992). The question is whether the system that spawned it can stamp it out?

A more important question is whether George Bush knew that his office, through his National Security Advisor, Donald Gregg, was associated with and jointly carried out operations together with elements of Latin America's drug cartel? If so, what does that say about the Reagan-Bush Administration's so-called "war against drugs"?

CHAPTER 5

How Many Weapons Did the Reagan-Bush Administration Really Sell to Iran?

The Reagan-Bush White House's policy towards the Iran-Iraq War remained hidden from the American public for more than a decade. There were no columnists asking piercing questions. No allegations. No public debate. It worked so well it could serve as a model for future covert operators on how to successfully carry out a secret agenda.

The goal of any secret agenda is to hide the real aims of policies from the American people. To do this, the public has to be manipulated to accept a perceived policy as reality so the covert policy can be carried out. Former CIA agent Victor Marchetti says that the key to covert operations is to keep your own public from knowing what's going on.

"If they did, then the debate over whether the government should or should not be doing that particular strategy becomes public," he says. "If they know about it the public can ask whether the White House is doing a good job or not. The reason why the Reagan Administration kept so much of its foreign policy secret was so that it couldn't be be criticized or judged."

Such was the case of the Bush-Reagan White House's official stance during the Iran-Iraq War. For eight years, officially, the American people were being told that the White House was neutral and not selling weapons to either side.

That was a lie. The U.S. government sold billions of

dollars' worth of arms to Iraq, which, according to U.S. law, was illegal as Congress was not notified. If more than $14 million worth of weapons are sold to a foreign country, it is a violation of the Arms Export Munitions Control Act if Congress is not informed. During the Iran-Iraq War the Bush-Reagan Administration was the greatest single violator of that law.

Bush wanted the American public to perceive that the Reagan Administration was "tough on terrorism"; thus in May 1983, the White House came up with Operation Staunch, the so-called arms embargo against Iran for its support of international terrorism. The U.S. urged all countries, particularly its NATO allies, not to sell weapons to Iran. As the Iranian army was supplied with an American order of battle under the Shah, the lack of American-made weapons systems and spare parts was supposed to have crippled Iran's military capability. But in fact, Operation Staunch was a lie. America sold billions of dollars' worth of arms to Iran.

The Administration also told the American people that it was not selling arms or diplomatically supporting Iraq because of Saddam Hussein's atrocious record on human rights. That was also a lie. The Bush-Reagan White House supplied Saddam's army with everything from military uniforms to attack helicopters.

Why did the Bush-Reagan White House tell the public it wasn't selling arms to Iran or Iraq when it was? Because arms sales play an important role in funding and furthering secret agendas. In order for these covert operations to remain covert, they have to be funded by black money, not funds that are allocated through official budgets and thus have to be accounted for. As covert weapons sales are hidden from any governing agency, these proceeds can be spent on whatever the sellers of the weapons wish. Yet the Bush-Reagan Administration sold arms to Iran and Iraq not solely to make money to fund covert operations. They did so to further the

White House's geopolitical goals that it didn't want to be made public.

Says Marchetti: "There's no reason to believe that the Americans didn't want the same thing Israelis did: to keep the war going. There were people in the White House and Pentagon arguing for both sides. Someone must have said, "Let's support them both and keep them fighting and sell arms to both of them." Many people in the Pentagon had personal ties to those in Iran who worked under the Shah in the military so it was perfectly logical for the Pentagon to be sending material via the NATO stores to Iran.

Just as George Bush's Skull and Bones imperialistic ideology feeds on domestic confusion, it needs chaos abroad to step in to manipulate events in a particular region.

Intelligence information is an extremely powerful weapon in the hands of those intending to deceive. Even the countries that are being supported by the Americans covertly wind up "confused." How else can the Administration's policy towards sharing intelligence data, particularly satellite photos, to both sides in the war be explained?

While the Gulf War was on its last legs, American intelligence sources were becoming bewildered with this approach and they began leaking the details of these operations to the press. The *New York Times* quoted intelligence officials as saying that both Iran and Iraq were given "deliberately distorted or inaccurate intelligence data." These sources claimed that some information derived from satellite photography that was shared with Iraq was altered to make it misleading or incomplete, for example, the images were cropped to leave out important details" (*New York Times*, January 12th, 1987).

An administration official revealed that covert operations aimed at Iran and Iraq were often in conflict, both with each other and with the diplomatic goals being pursued through the State Department. When asked what the overall American policy in the region was, one of them who took part in these operations replied: "You had to have been there" (*New York Times*, January 12th, 1987).

Most Americans weren't there. With the effective use of such mirrors as "Operation Staunch" and the manipulation of the media with terms such as "anti-terrorism," the American public was being told one thing while the Administration was doing something completely different—carrying out a secret agenda.

U.S. ARMS SALES TO IRAN

During most of the 1980s Iran and Iraq were the most lucrative arms markets. Iran was the largest black market for weapons. Kenneth Timmerman, an expert on arms sales to Iran and Iraq, contends that markups were often up to ten times the normal selling price (*The Nation*, July 18-25th, 1987).

In August 1987, the director of the Stockholm International Peace Research Institute, Walter Stuetzle, revealed that "The arms export business to the Gulf is booming. In 1984 only 40 countries delivered to both Iran and Iraq, today that number has risen to 53" (Reuters, August 4th, 1987). Stuetzle pointed out that despite "Operation Staunch," Algeria, Argentina, Canada, Kenya, Denmark, Finland, Israel, South Korea, Libya, Mexico, Taiwan, Singapore, Syria Turkey, Vietnam, and Yemen were all supplying Iran with arms.

How much of this market belonged to the American government?

Of late, much has been written of arms sales made by Israel with U.S. approval after January 1981 as part of the "October Surprise" deal. The arrangement that William Casey, then head of Reagan's campaign team, allegedly made with the Iranians was to ensure that Iran would not release the 52 American hostages held captive by Khomeini's revolutionary guards since November 4th, 1979. In the book *October Surprise*, by Barbara Honneger, and in Gary Sick's book, *October Surprise: America's Hostages in Iran and the Election of*

Ronald Reagan, these arms sales are thoroughly documented.

If the "October Surprise" theory is eventually proven correct, and the arms sales by Israel to Iran on behalf of the U.S. are verified, then the next question to be asked is: What happened after December 1982? According to Avraham Tamir, then Director General of Israel's foreign ministry, the permission given by the Americans until then for Israel to sell U.S.-made weapons to Iran ceased (interview with Avraham Tamir by author, Tel Aviv, January 1992). It's likely that if a deal was made in 1980 to ensure a steady supply of U.S. arms to be delivered by way of Israel, by the end of 1982 someone in the White House must have figured out that there was no reason for Israel to make money selling to Iran American-made arms. The American government could do it, covertly, and at the same time earn money for covert operations, or, as William Casey used to like to refer to them, "off-the-shelf" covert operations.

Did America sell arms to Iran between 1981 and 1985? This question is paramount to determining whether "Operation Staunch" and the official policy of the White House was nothing but a deception that the American public bought—hook, line, and sinker. If so, it would be yet another secret agenda of the Bush-Reagan White House.

OPERATION DEMEVAND

Although it never made its way into the mainstream press, the alternative press—*The Nation*, the *Village Voice*, *The Progressive*, and *In These Times*—has given extensive coverage to "Operation Demevand." Named for a mountain range in Iran, this was a White House operation to sell massive amounts of arms to Iran, covertly and illegally.

Barbara Honegger, in her book *October Surprise*, gave one of the earliest reports on massive arms sales from the U.S. to Iran. Although many of sources remained anonymous, she has to be given a lot of credit for investigating a secret agenda that up to then had been virtually undetected. Her sources told her arms shipments began in 1981, and by 1986 more than $15 billion worth of arms had been redirected to Iran. She quotes Richard Muller, a former colonel in the Marine Reserves, as claiming that secret NATO military supplies stored in reforger stores throughout Europe were being drawn down and sold to Iran, as well as to rebel forces the administration was supporting in Angola, Afghanistan and Central America. The proceeds went to the Pentagon's "black budget" for covert activities.

There was one aspect of the operation that Honneger couldn't figure out. Why would the U.S. knowingly leave itself unable to defend itself against a conventional attack from Warsaw Pact countries? The rationale for the reforger stores was to give NATO additional time before a decision to use nuclear weapons would be made.

One of her sources, who was a former CIA official stationed in Germany for a number of years, finally answered that question for her. It was exactly that intention, to draw down the reforger stores; thus NATO commanders would then be forced to go nuclear. If the Soviets knew of this likelihood, it would serve to counter their more than two-to-one superiority in conventional forces. Thus the threat of using nuclear weapons, the source claimed, brought the Soviets to the Intermediate Nuclear Forces bargaining table.

The United States' allies would obviously refuse to go along with such a plan, but they didn't know because they were given falsified lists of the what was in the supply depots.

The source revealed the Soviets were "told" about the operation when in 1986 the U.S. traded an Eastern Bloc spy named Koecher, for Natan Sharansky. Koecher told his KGB bosses in Prague about the draw-down at the NATO stores.

Honneger's initial reports of official U.S. government complicity in arms sales to Iran were verified by other investigative journalists. ABC News' European correspondent

Pierre Salinger quoted Swedish arms dealer Sven Klang as saying that he was involved in arms shipments initiated by the Reagan-Bush Administration to deliver F-4 fighter jet engines to Iran in 1981 from NATO warehouses through the Belgium-based ASCO company.

A *Newsday* reporter discovered that in 1981 customs agents at the U.S. embassy in London told State Department officials that two Iranian-born arms dealers were shipping U.S. military equipment to Iran. The customs agents were ordered by State Department officials to drop their investigation. The newspaper also reported that British merchant marine captain Thomas Screech ran ships carrying 2000 U.S. aerial bomb fuses from Portugal to Bandar Abbas, Iran, in summer 1982, with cargo which originated in U.S. government ammunition plants. When Screech reported these deliveries to the U.S. embassy in London, the State Department told them to ignore him (Honegger, pages 195-96).

Operatives from one "Demevand operation" operating out of the U.S. Embassy in Paris claimed that profits of $400 million from these arms sales were used to supply weapons to U.S.-supported rebel groups in Nicaragua, Afghanistan, Angola, and Ethiopia.

Details of this arms pipeline was discovered in August 1985 when Lt. William Gillespie, 46, a missile expert, graduate of West Point, and a veteran of two tours of Vietnam, was caught in a sting operation in Orlando, Florida (*Los Angeles Times,* August 2, 1985). From 1982, Gillespie worked on military projects with the U.S.'s NATO allies at the army materiel command in Alexandria, Virginia.

The group operated through European Defense Associates, a company set up by Colonel Ralph Borman, who was then chief of the Pentagon's Office of Defense Cooperation in Paris, entrusted with monitoring international shipment of arms to Iran under Operation Staunch. In one sale European Defense Associates was involved in, more than a billion dollars' worth of U.S.-made weapons, including tanks, missiles, submarines, and fighter jets, were to be transferred from U.S. stockpiles in Europe to Iran.

Along with Paul Cutter, who worked for the U.S. Information Agency in the Soviet Union in the mid-1960s and spent five years in jail, from 1976 to 1981, for importing rifles into Yugoslavia, and three others, Gillespie was arrested by undercover customs agents when the three tried to sell the agent more than $40 million in arms including Sidewinder, Sparrow, Harpoon, Phoenix, and French-made Exocet missiles. William Mott IV, an officer at the U.S. Embassy in London and founder of Spearhead Atlantic, did business with European Defense Associates and worked with Gillespie and Cutter (Honegger, pages 201-2).

Cutter originally kept quiet when he was sent to jail in 1985. He then discovered that Gillespie and the others didn't share the same fate. They were found innocent based on their testimony that Cutter was a government agent and thus they believed they were acting with government sanction. Cutter concluded that he was set up and began talking to the press, claiming: "We all worked under the umbrella of the U.S. Defense Department approval" (*New York Times*, December 5th, 1986). He said his operation alone sold at least $1.2 billion worth of military equipment to Iran from NATO supply depots in Europe.

Italy was another major transshipment point for U.S. arms to Iran. In November 1986, Italian Prime Minister Benito Craxi ordered an inquiry into reports that small Italian ports of Tuscania and Talamone were being used for arms shipments to Iran without the knowledge of the Italian government.

Official statements from the prime minister's office and Defense Minister Giovanni Spadolini said there had not even been tacit accord with the U.S. government on these shipments. Opposition legislators claimed that by October 1986 sixty ships full of arms had left the Italian port of Talamone

(*New York Times*, November 12th, 1986). As the Italian government had no record of these shipments, they were believed to have been taken out of the military supplies kept by the U.S. Army in Italy and sold covertly.

Italian judge Carlo Palermo eventually wrote a 6000-page report revealing that CIA headquarters and the U.S. Embassy in Rome, and U.S. military bases in Italy as well as U.S. naval forces based on Maddalena near Sardinia, were involved in the arms shipments.

George Bush has claimed he was "out of the loop" with regards to the affair. However, what neither he nor any other official of the Reagan Administration has ever been asked is whether there were efforts by the U.S. government to sell arms to Iran before Irangate broke. The Administration's official version of events is that sales of U.S. arms to Iran began only in the late summer of 1985 when Israel sold HAWK missiles to Iran. Then, from January 1986 until Irangate became public in November 1986, a series of arms shipments were made by way of Oliver North to Iran in return for the release of U.S. captives held hostage by Islamic extremist groups in Lebanon.

That is what the public was told Iran-Contra was all about; the U.S. never sold arms to Iran before 1985. It was a lie. Another illusion. Massive arms sales to Iran by the Reagan-Bush White House began almost immediately after President Reagan's inauguration.

Through another investigation he was involved with at the time, in 1984 Gene Wheaton, a former army criminal investigator, learned that planes operated by the Pan Aviation Company, owned by arms dealer Sarkis Sonokanahan, was flying arms into Iraq. That made sense, Wheaton thought, as it was the world's worst-kept secret in the intelligence world at the time that the CIA was arming Iraq. Then he discovered some of Pan Aviation's planes were being diverted and also flying arms into Iran.

"At first I thought Sonokanahan was cheating on the U.S. government," says Wheaton. "The logic escaped me that in 1984 we could be sanctioning arms sales to Iran at the highest levels of the government."

PAYING THE PRICE FOR OLIVER NORTH

Wheaton also served as the court-appointed investigator in the Durrani Case. Arif Durrani has testified that he witnessed massive sales of U.S. arms from NATO supply depots to Iran. Although Oliver North didn't go to jail, some people did, for doing exactly what North told them to do. One of them is Arif Durrani.

I first heard about Durrani from Larry Lifschultz in March 1991. Lifschultz was a former South Asia correspondent of the *Far Eastern Economic Review* and believed Durrani was wrongfully convicted. Lifschultz's investigation lasted more than a year and in the end he believed he had unlocked the details of an illicit world of arms trading linked to the Iran-Contra scandal. It was a side to the story that has never been told.

"I discovered that the scope and volume of arms illegally shipped to Iran from NATO stores and NATO suppliers was hundreds of times greater than the size of shipments revealed at the Iran-Contra hearings," says Lifschultz. "Durrani's own operation exported more than $750 million worth or arms to Iran" (*The Pamphleteer's Press*, East Haven, Conn., September 1991).

Durrani's story begins in the spring of 1986 when he was asked by the Israeli purchasing office in New York to meet with Manuel Jose Pires, a Portuguese arms salesman. Pires was working with Israel to locate more than 240 different parts which the Iranians were desperate for. Through Pires Durrani met senior officials of the U.S. government, including Oliver North. In September 1986 Durrani was asked by Pires to come to London to discuss future arms shipments with

Oliver North at the Hilton Hotel. North told them that although the parts are ready for shipment, there would be no problem with export licenses. He said: "You don't need them. It's all going to be authorized" (*The Pamphleteer's Press*, page 12).

On October 2nd, 1986, Durrani arranged a shipment of the HAWK parts to Belgium and falsely signed a declaration that he had all the required export licenses. The next day he was arrested by U.S. customs agents in Danbury, Connecticut, just weeks before the Iran-Contra scandal broke. During his trial in the spring of 1987, CIA and NSC officials came to Bridgeport, Connecticut, and denied under oath that Durrani was connected in any way to any U.S. government operation. The jury believed them and in mid-April 1987 sentenced the 41-year-old Pakistani national to ten years in prison and a $2 million fine.

The judge did not allow Durrani's lawyers to introduce as evidence any parts of the Tower Commission Report, which indicated that North was seeking HAWK parts that couldn't be procured within existing Israeli or American government inventories. Nor did he allow any classified government documents which might have supported Durrani's case. In sentencing him, Judge T. Gilroy Daly said that Durrani's "behavior might under other circumstances be considered by some as 'bordering on treason.' "

Lifschultz and his team realized that Pires was the key to proving Durrani's innocence. Looking into his, past they discovered he was a major player in Spanish arms sales to Iran using end-user certificates issued by the Brazilian Defense Ministry (*El Tiempo*, December, 26th, 1988). He also specialized in selling arms to embargoed countries such as South Africa.

They also discovered that Pires met with Assistant U.S. Attorney Holly Fitzsimmons and U.S. customs agents in February 1987, and although never having been indicted, turned over records of communications between him and

Durrani showing Pires had no connection with the U.S. government.

In Brussels, Lifschultz obtained a 400-page report of a Belgian special police investigation showing how Brussels had been used by black market arms traffickers. Brussels was Pires' main shipment point. One of these deals was for 10,000 TOW missiles to Iran via Israel in 1985.

Procuring 10,000 TOW missiles covertly is not an easy task. Only the U.S. and NATO's European inventories had such stocks available. The official Iran-Contra story tells of TOW missiles being sold to Iran from stocks in the U.S. and Israel.

Ken Timmerman, an expert in the international arms trade, reported in 1987 (*The Nation*, July 18th-25th, 1987) that a major smuggling operation involving TOW missiles from NATO stockpiles in the U.S. and Europe was carried on inside the sealed customs zone of Brussels' Zaventem International Airport. He quotes intelligence sources in France and West Germany as saying that General Bernard Rogers, then NATO's Commander in Chief and head of the U.S.-European command, ordered an internal investigation in 1986 of reports that TOW missiles from NATO warehouses in West Germany were diverted to Iran in 1985. He quotes a spokesperson for the Supreme Headquarters Allied Powers in Europe in Belgium as saying the investigation was "a political issue" and "the Pentagon has ordered us not to comment on it." The intelligence official said General Rogers was "furious to learn that NATO weapons were being sold to Iran without his knowledge."

Timmerman cites Belgian customs documents showing that "at least 3000 TOW missiles" were involved in a shell-game assembly operation. Chartered cargo planes arriving from military bases in the U.S. brought in the TOW warheads. Shortly after they taxied to a stop in the customs area, additional planes, carrying missile fuselages and motors from

NATO storehouses in Bavaria, would pull up alongside them. Since the warheads were never offloaded—and thus technically not imported into Belgium—no customs documents were required. The Belgian daily *Le Soir*, which surveyed the customs documents, concluded that the operation" had the benediction of the Pentagon" (*The Nation*, July 18-25th, 1987).

In the Tower Commission former National Security Advisor Robert McFarlane testified that he and David Kimche, Israel's Director General of the Foreign Ministry, discussed the request by Israel for the U.S. to replace at least 500 TOW missiles to replenish Israeli stocks. In the Belgian police file Lifschultz noticed an August 1st, 1985, sales contract between Kennard International of Panama and a Greek firm, for the sale of 5000 TOW missiles. The police investigators explained to Lifschultz that they believe Kennard International was a front company for the Israeli government to mask the sale of TOW missiles to the Greek firm which transferred the possession of the TOWs to Pires in Lisbon before they were shipped to Iran. The whole exercise was done to hide the actual origins of the supplier.

This means that the number of missiles Israel shipped to Iran, as part of the Shimon Peres/Yaacov Nimrodi/Al Schwimmer pipeline at the end of August and early September 1985 was 5000, not 500 as the public record indicates.

One source Lifschultz calls "Max" claimed to have personal knowledge of the sales. In an interview in Brussels on March 23rd, 1990, Max described for him North's travels in Europe during September and October 1986. During that period a close associate in his firm personally observed Pires and North together, and said that during 1986 North was telling everybody, "You are working for the U.S. government. You are working for the Boss. Don't worry. You will have no problems."

Willy de Greef, who directed Pires' office in Brussels for

three years, told Lifschultz that Manuel Pires told him he had met Oliver North in London twice and that they fixed everything for the TOW shipment to Iran. The Belgian police file revealed how in 1985 Pires used military bases in Addis Ababa, Ethiopia, to fly TOW missiles from Israel and Europe to Bandar Abbas in Iran. Pires used TransEuropean Airways, owned by George Mittleman, an Orthodox Jew in Belgium who earned his bread and butter flying Islamic pilgrimages to Mecca. It was the same charter airline used to fly Jews out of Ethiopia during "Operation Moses" in 1984. "The same planes which brought arms to Ethiopia en route to Iran left carrying Jews destined for Israel," Durrani claims.

Why did the U.S. government not bother to indict or further investigate Pires as a co-conspirator in the Durrani case? Lifschultz speculates that Pires "knows too much" and has a long history of clandestine associations which Israel and some Western governments could not afford to have aired in an open courtroom.

Three weeks after Durrani was sentenced, on July 9th, 1987, Pires visited Durrani at the Federal Correctional Institution in Phoenix, Arizona. Pires indicated to Durrani that their conversation was being recorded. He tried to get Durrani to talk about various aspects of their transactions. After Durrani accused Pires of not coming to his aid, Pires replied it was a mistake and that he never imagined he would be given a ten-year sentence. "It wasn't supposed to have happened that way," Pires said.

Durrani's lawyer, William Bloss, can't understand how Pires was able to receive permission to see Durrani as he is not a family member and it is customary for such visits to be proceeded by extensive background checks. He says: "There is no chance that a foreign national would just show up at a federal prison saying, "I want to see my friend," and the warden would say, 'Fine ... just go on in.' It is impossible." Durrani was told by personnel at the prison that the

Pires visit was arranged at the request of a lawyer, "the woman from Connecticut."

Wasn't Pires concerned he would be arrested if he traveled to the U.S.? Bloss speculates that a deal had been worked out giving him immunity from prosecution. Lifschultz spoke with a prison official who told him Pires met a U.S. customs agent and Assistant U.S. Attorney Holly Fitzsimmons in Phoenix and that Pires was working with the U.S. government on "matters which are classified."

In fact, Fitzsimmons did admit that she met Pires in Phoenix, but not that she arranged for him to visit Durrani. In an interview with Lifschultz, Fitzsimmons claimed it was not a coincidence that Pires, the customs agent Steven Arruda, and herself were in Phoenix all at the same time. However, since Pires had been a federal witness prior to the trial, she could not comment "as a matter of policy," nor would she admit that the U.S. Customs Office had arranged for Pires to see Durrani.

Lifschultz later discovered that Pires' visit was linked to a continuing U.S. Customs investigation about HAWK missile parts that agents had believed Durrani hid in some secret location in the U.S. and that Pires was in Phoenix as an informant for this investigation. The Customs Office tried to get Durrani to tell Pires where these parts were hidden.

"At the very least this means that the U.S. government was cooperating with Pires, for how long we don't know," says Lifschultz.

In a telephone interview in October 1990, Pires said that he had visited Durrani "officially . . . through legal channels," claiming Durrani owed him money from previous shipments. He denied meeting Fitzsimmons and U.S. customs agents. When Lifschultz told Pires that Fitzsimmons had admitted meeting Pires in Phoenix, Pires changed his story and said they had only spoken by telephone.

Considering Oliver North only had to pay a fine of

$150,000 and was sentenced to two years' probation and 1200 hours in community service at a drug program, Durrani got an unusually harsh sentence. The larger questions are whether arms sales to Iran were hundreds of times greater than the public has been told and if the Pentagon knew about and aided in the transfer of weapons from NATO supply depots to Iran? If so, then this generated profits in the hundreds of millions of dollars. How many covert operations they funded is anyone's guess.

THE OIL WEAPON

Manipulating the price of crude oil was a covert, secret agenda of the White House that was tied up with America's policies in the Iran-Iraq War.

The basis for that policy could be attributed to Edward Luttwak, a strategic thinker for the Georgetown Center for Strategic and International Studies, a Washington-based think-tank. In August 1980 he claimed that the control of oil prices was "the one and only problem Reagan has to take seriously that requires Alliance [NATO] cooperation" and that "it would be necessary to develop rapid intervention forces for oil security" (*In These Times*, January 21st, 1987).

A less militaristic approach would be merely to have the Saudis flood the market with overproduction, driving world oil prices down. This is widely believed to be the cause for the flood of oil and subsequent drop in prices in the mid-1980s.

One aspect of Irangate which has gone unreported is the role the price of oil played in the secret negotiations between the U.S. and Iranian leaders. In a 1986 article in the *Washington Post*, Edwin Rothschild, assistant director of the Citizen's Energy and Labor Coalition, a public interest organization that monitors U.S. government energy policy, claimed that in 1985 the Administration encouraged Saudi Arabia to enter into a "price war strategy" against Iran to lower the price of oil so Iran would not have the means to buy arms to battle Iraq. In October 1985 Saudi Arabia defied previous OPEC agreements and increased production of its oil wells. Before this, Iran's annual oil revenues were $25 billion. By mid-1986, they were down to $6 billion.

In February 1986 the Iranian leadership threatened Kuwait and Saudi Arabia with ground attacks after Iran's successful offense in the Fao Peninsula, a mere 25 miles from the Kuwaiti border. It's been claimed that National Security Advisor Admiral John Poindexter provided the Iranians with surveillance photographs detailing the Iraqi order of battle—ensuring an Iranian victory.

Then, in a complete reversal of policy, the White House might have pledged to Teheran a push for higher oil prices so that Iran had the financial means to continue its war with Iraq?

With a barrel of oil selling then for $9.10, Bush tried to convince Saudi Arabia not to pump more oil in the face of the glut. In April 1986, in what is widely believed to be an effort by America to pressure the Saudis into capping a few of their wells, Bush traveled to Saudi Arabia and told King Fahd in person that "U.S. interests and Saudi interests aren't identical with regard to oil prices," pointing to recent statistics showing rising unemployment in the U.S. energy industry, and that "as part of our national security interests, we need a strong domestic oil industry" (*Wall Street Journal,* April 7th, 1986). At an April 1st press conference, sounding more like a spokesman for OPEC rather than Vice President of the free-market, free-pricing advocate the United States, Bush averred: "I think it is essential that we talk about stability of world oil prices and that we just not have a continued free-fall like a parachutist jumping without a parachute."

While it is possible Bush may have made the trip to help out American oil producers, the concurrent events of Irangate need to be addressed. Four months later at an OPEC meeting in Geneva, Iran agreed to share in production cutbacks to boost the price of oil. That very same day, President Reagan signed a Presidential Order for the National Security Council to arrange a $6.5 million shipment of spare parts for Iran's HAWK anti-aircraft missiles. Subsequently, Iraq's air superiority ended.

As the Iran-Iraq War ended and with the U.S. presidential election approaching, Rothschild claims Bush manipulated the price of oil again, this time to keep it under $20 a barrel. He asserted: "Energy Secretary John Herrington was dispatched to Saudi Arabia last fall [1987] to trade weapons and "security" for a Saudi pledge to keep oil prices between $15-$18 per barrel to make sure that the summer before the presidential elections the price of oil wouldn't rise for American consumers" (*The Nation,* June 11th, 1988).

While the American public believed that it was Middle Eastern oil sheikdoms who were deciding what price they would have to pay to fill up their cars, that was only the perception, the illusion. It was George Bush's secret agendas and political ambitions that were determining the price at the pumps.

ANOTHER SIDE OF IRAN-CONTRA

While there have been many attempts to discredit former Israeli intelligence official Ari Ben-Menashe, both by journalists and the Israeli government, the question isn't what position Ben Menashe held or whether he was involved personally in all of the capers he claimed he was, but rather, the quality of his information. Too many people hastily discarded him as nothing but a charlatan. Nor does it really matter if he did or didn't or whether he learned about things from first- or secondhand sources. What is pertinent are the events he is describing. He's simply a mouthpiece, a window into a covert world. It is up to investigative journalists and congressional committees to verify them.

The first time I met Ben-Menashe, in March 1991, we spent the entire morning and a good part of the afternoon together, weaving in and out of ten years of secret agendas of the Reagan and Bush White Houses. Among them: how the current director of the CIA, Robert Gates, helped Iraq gain chemical weapons capabilities; the "October Surprise" allegations in which the Reagan campaign team purposely delayed the release of the 52 American hostages held in Iran; the INSLAW case, a Washington, D.C., computer company which had its prize software stolen by a crony of former Attorney General Edwin Meese.

Ben-Menashe asserted that Israeli and American arms sales to Iran and Iraq were far greater than publicly known, and that the Israeli government had earned $800 million in commissions on more than $80 billion worth of arms sold to Iran during the eight-year-long war. The money, he said, has accumulated in slush funds in several Latin American banks.

In April 1989 he was caught in a U.S. Customs sting operation and charged with conspiring to violate the Arms Export Control Act. He was trying to sell three Israeli-owned C-130 Hercules transport airplanes to Iran without the State Department approval needed to resell U.S.-made military goods. After a six-week trial in November 1990, however, he was acquitted.

Ben-Menashe asserts that from 1987 to 1989 he was a member of an elite Israeli intelligence unit that was run directly out of Prime Minister Yitzhak Shamir's Office under the direction of Shamir's media adviser Avi Pazner. The sale of the three C-130s, Ben-Menashe asserts, was part of an arms-for-hostages deal for the release of three Israeli soldiers held in Lebanon.

He also claims to have worked on a special team, called the Joint Israeli Defense Force Military Intelligence/Mossad Committee for Iran-Israel Relations, set up in November 1980 as part of the "October Surprise" deal to supply American-made arms through Israel to Iran. The operation was run jointly by the Mossad and Israeli military intelligence.

One series of events which Ben-Menashe described to me begins in early July 1987, when then-CIA Director Robert Gates met with Iranian Defense Minister Mohammed Hossein Jalali at the Vista Hotel in Kansas City, Missouri, to consummate an enormous weapons sale. He claims he was at that meeting representing Israel's interests. The deal was to be a "pass-through," meaning that the weapons would originate in the U.S. or that Washington would replace Israeli stocks of any weapons sold from its stockpile (*Israel Foreign Affairs*, October 2nd, 1991).

In other words, even after the Iran-Contra scandal was made public, both Israel and the U.S. were still selling arms to Iran.

Ben-Menashe's version was verified when on February 23rd, 1987, the U.S. Customs branch at the U.S. Embassy in Rome cabled Washington that it had learned of an Israeli effort to ship TOW missiles to Iran. The report said that "a foreign national is attempting to acquire in Italy an end-user certificate for the purchase of 10,000 TOW missiles." The sale was to have taken place in Switzerland.

Ben-Menashe said that in that deal Israel sold Iran a total of 12,000 U.S.-made TOW missiles in three batches of 4000 each. On November 8th, 1987, the *International Herald Tribune* reported that "Israel might have negotiated to sell up to $750 million in arms to Iran late last summer." The package was said to include U.S.-made TOW anti-tank missiles, Israeli-made Gabriel air-to-surface missiles, F-4 and F-5 aircraft engine parts, tanks and jeeps. The sale was executed through a third party based in Geneva, Switzerland.

During that summer, the Israelis held three meetings in Geneva with an Iranian delegation headed by Khomeini's son Ahmed, and which also included Parliament Chairman Hashemi

Rafsanjani (*La Suisse*, August 14th, 1987). The two-day meeting was held without the knowledge of Iran's ambassador to the UN or the local Counsel-General. The Iranians sent a cabinet-level committee to continue contacts with the Israelis and the Americans (*Middle East Insider*, August 17th, 1987). The two sides also discussed a plan for increasing Jewish emigration from Iran in return for Israeli arms. More than 25,000 Jews were to leave Iran over the next six months (*London Observer*, September 13th, 1987).

It is very unlikely that Israel would have been able to sell that amount of U.S.-made TOW missiles without the White House's full acknowledgment, perhaps even on behalf of Washington.

Larry Lifschultz, the journalist who has closely followed Arif Durrani's case, also found Ben-Menashe to be a very credible source on a little-known aspect of the Iran-Contra Affair.

Lifschultz discovered how in the mid-1980s Pakistan became a conduit for the sale of hundreds of millions of dollars' worth of U.S.-made arms to Iran and how the $2 billion supply line which was established by the White House to provide arms to the rebels in Afghanistan was exploited as a source of weapons for the Nicaraguan Contras and to fund covert operations (*Far Eastern Economic Review*, December 1991).

Ben-Menashe says that for more than three years an Israeli military logistics and advisory team was based in Pakistan which managed the secret arms pipeline to Iran. Lifschultz confirmed this story from two Pakistani intelligence sources who were involved in the operation and another one who worked for the National Logistics Cell, a special agency which was under the command of the Pakistani Army and which served as the main carrier of the weapons to Iran. Another source, a prominent figure in Pakistan's Shia community with close connections to Pakistan's Inter-Services Intelligence (ISI), also confirmed the incident.

A former Pakistani intelligence agent described the network as one of Islamabad's "biggest secrets" (*New Delhi Times*, November 24th, 1991).

One diversion involved $300 million worth of weapons which, although sent to Pakistan and paid for by Congress, the agent thought were going to the Afghan rebels. However, after arriving in Peshawar and after the paperwork showed that they had arrived at the intended destination, they were routed to Iran. The Iranian government paid $300 million cash for the weapons, which was deposited into a bank account in Luxembourg.

"This was the first major attempt to create additional funding for those people in the American intelligence community linked to the Contras," Ben-Menashe told Lifschultz.

The illegal diversion of U.S. government funds was not the first or the last. In 1987 allegations were made by the Federation for the American Afghan Action that only $390 million of the $1.09 billion of aid approved by Congress between 1980 and 1986 to support the Mujahideen rebels had actually reached them. The chairman of the group, Andrew Evia, said that between 1980 and 1984 of the $342 million appropriated by Congress, only $36 million of military aid arrived in Afghanistan. Evia believes that, overall, 70 percent of the assistance never even reached the rebel groups.

Yet it isn't even certain that the money was diverted to support the Contras in Central America.

Says Evia: "Maybe somebody wanted the money to go to the Nicaraguan Contras, but Contra leaders say even Ollie North's money didn't reach them. The question is where is the money? Where did $700 million go?" (*Sunday Times of India*, November 24th, 1991).

It went to fund covert operations which to this day have yet to be unearthed.

ONCE AGAIN: "OCTOBER SURPRISE"

No study of America's relationship with Iran would be complete without coming to terms with the "October Surprise" theory.

Conspiracy researchers had been knocking around the idea that there was a deal by the Reagan campaign team in 1980 to delay the release of the U.S. hostages in Iran since 1978. It wasn't until May 1991, when Gary Sick, a former member of the National Security Center for Persian Affairs in the Carter Administration and an adjunct professor of Middle East politics at Columbia University, wrote an Op-Ed in the *New York Times* that the theory gained mainstream exposure. Most of the investigative journalists trying to expose the "October Surprise" scandal thought that their time had finally come.

It was easy for the Administration to discredit journalists from leftist and progressive magazines, but Sick was credible. He had authored a 1985 book about the 1980 hostages crisis, entitled *All Fall Down*. After he began conducting research for a book on the Iran-Contra Affair and came across curious incidents and events which could neither be explained nor simply ignored, he concluded that before he could even begin to write about Iran-Contra he had to first resolve this question of whether an "October Surprise" did or did not occur.

I met Sick after his article appeared in the *New York Times*. It was just after I had interviewed Ari Ben-Menashe, the Israeli intelligence official who claimed personal knowledge of meetings in Paris in October 1980 where American, Iranian, and Israeli officials were to have met to work out the details of the agreement. This gave Sick and me an instant rapport. Anyone who has ever spoken with Ben-Menashe knows the only was to sort out what he says is to discuss his allegations with other journalists or researchers who have interviewed him. Sick and I agreed on one thing: Ben-menashe may be considered a crackpot by some, but his information is superb.

"I was amazed at the detail with which he described certain events," Sick said. "Sometimes he told me things that I couldn't believe were true. When I checked them out I discovered they were."

After Sick's book on the subject came out in October 1991, a number of mainstream publications published articles "proving" that there was no "October Surprise." Since some of the sources Sick used were either arms dealers or intelligence officials, they were deemed not credible, therefore, as their stories went. There was no "October Surprise." It was as if the mainstream press was saying, "Bush, Meese, and Allen would never lie to the American people, and of course there were no secret dealings or corruption in the Reagan White House."

Investigative journalist Christopher Hitchens believes that a few of these publications, such as *Newsweek* and *The New Republic*, might have dismissed the "October Surprise" conspiracy as "vindictive catch-up" for reasons of "professional pride" because they missed the story (*The Nation*, December 2nd, 1991).

In response to their claims of Sick's using "less than credible sources," Hitchens has reminded his colleagues: "You ask of a source not, 'Is he an honest, incorruptible man?' but 'Does his information check out?' " He points out that powerful people, like Edwin Meese, Richard Allen, George Bush, and Robert MacFarlane, despite their assumed role in covert or even illegal activities, are never called liars or frauds by *Time* or *Newsweek*.

But anyone who claims that "the Reagan people would never commit such a treasonous act" has never studied what those same people did once they got into the white House.

Since most mainstream journalists have been eager to throw the "crazy conspiracy theory" label at investigators, two main questions were never addressed: Despite the many attempts to interfere, are we to assume that the Reagan campaign kept a safe distance away from any of Carter's efforts to have the hostages released? And was it merely a coincidence that Donald Gregg, a member of the National

Security Council under Carter, was appointed National Security Advisor to Vice President Bush?

Still, there are a number of mysteries surrounding "October Surprise" that just don't make sense. Let's assume there was a prearranged deal: The Iranians hated Carter because he refused to extradite the Shah, and didn't want Carter to win the election. They made a deal with Reagan's campaign team not to release the hostages until after the election. Why, then, did they wait until the third week of January to release them? What did they have to gain by holding on to them after the election? If the Reagan campaign team did make a deal, didn't it realize that having the hostages released at literally the same moment as Reagan was being inaugurated would look just a bit too coincidental? Having them released in mid-November would certainly have made it look as if the Iranians had done Carter in.

If Reagan's team *did* make a deal, what kept them to the deal? Once the hostages were released, the Iranians had nothing to bargain with. Once Reagan was in office, any deals consummated before the election would have become irrelevant unless the Administration simply wanted to keep its word and live up to its side of the bargain.

In fact, that is exactly what happened. The Administration permitted Israel to sell U.S.-made arms to Iran as part of the "October Surprise" arrangement until the end of 1982. Avraham Tamir, former Director General of Israel's foreign ministry claims that by December 1982 the permission the U.S. had granted Israel ended. It was at this time that the U.S. began to support Iraq in the Iran-Iraq War, so it would be logical that the U.S. would want Israel to stop selling Iran arms.

It must have taken the Iranians a while to figure out what to do. Yet it was really quite simple. They had taken hostages before and the Americans sold them arms. So, in March 1984, they kidnap William Buckley, CIA station chief in Beirut, and afterwards other Americans. The story repeats itself: The

Iranians want arms; the Americans, their hostages back. The only difference is that this time there was no presidential election to manipulate.

What is important to students of covert operations is what the Reagan and Bush Administrations did after the 1980 presidential election. If it is eventually proven that a deal with the Iranians was made, it would be only the first in a long line of Reagan-Bush secret agendas.

CHAPTER 6

The Arming of Iraq

When President Bush announced in August 1990 that he was sending troops to the Persian Gulf to defend Saudi Arabia, the American public thought it was going to do battle with a vicious dictator. What they didn't realize was that it was their own government that created this monster.

The Bush-Reagan White House's policy towards Iraq is more complicated than it has been presented. With Iran the goal was to sell arms to replace NATO stocks, as well as to fund covert operations. With Iraq it is believed to have been a geopolitical goal: to ensure that Iran didn't win the Iran-Iraq War. The problem with this explanation is that it fails to take into account the fact that the effort to arm Saddam Hussein increased, in some areas dramatically, after Iran and Iraq agreed to a cease-fire in August 1988.

Although Frank Carlucci, who was Undersecretary of Defense under Caspar Weinberger in 1981 and 1982 and National Security Advisor in 1987, contends that there were some "broad exchanges of information with the Iraqis" and "any weapons the U.S. sold them didn't give them any enduring capability" (interview with author, November 21st, 1991), the American government supported Saddam Hussein throughout the Iran-Iraq War even after the war had ended, right up until the invasion of Kuwait in August 1990. This policy was never reported to Congress or made public to the American people. It was a covert operation.

The genesis of this relationship goes back to March 1982, when then-CIA Director William Casey is reported to have made a secret trip to Baghdad and arranged for Iraq to be removed from the State Department's list of nations supporting terrorism, a prerequisite for the subsequent restoration of diplomatic relations (*Commonweal,* June 14th, 1991). Casey met with his counterpart at Iraqi Intelligence, Barzan Hussein (Saddam's half brother), but failed to inform the House or Senate Committees on Intelligence of these meetings or that the U.S. was now sharing intelligence with Iraq (*New York Times,* January 26th, 1992). The direct intelligence link was run out of the American Embassy in Baghdad.

Recent press reports (*Los Angeles Times,* May 7th, 1992) reveal that George Bush himself acted as an intermediary in sending strategic military advice to Saddam Hussein. During a trip to the Mideast in August 1986, Bush relayed the message to Hussein via Egyptian President Hosni Mubarak. According to Adminstration officials who were familiar with the incident, Bush was said to have asked the Egyptian leader to tell Hussein to make better use of his air force against Iranian troops. Less than a month later, Iraq intensified its air campaign against Iran by attacking Iranian oil facilities.

While at the same time the U.S. was selling arms to Iran, it was providing Iraq with satellite intelligence photographs to assist Iraqi bombing raids on Iranian oilfields and power plants. "The information has been flowing to Iraq for nearly two years," American intelligence officials told the *Washington Post* in 1986. The officials claimed that "[William] Casey reportedly met twice this past fall [1986] with senior Iraqi officials to make sure the new channel for providing the intelligence was functioning well to initiate more attacks on Iranian installations." In early October, shortly after the Iraqis executed a surprise bombing raid on the Iranian oil terminal at Sirri Island, which Iran thought was safe from attack, Casey met with Tariq Aziz, the Iraqi Foreign Minister at the UN, to make sure he was happy with the flow of intelligence. Casey pledged the secret intelligence flow would continue (*Washington Post*, December 15th, 1986).

The *Sunday Times* of London reported that Iraq also received assistance from American AWACS operating from Saudi Arabia. "Since the beginning of the Iran-Iraq War, the Saudis have been passing information on Iran's military activities to Iraq, with the permission of the U.S. government" (*Sunday Times*, March 17th, 1985). "Over the course of battle, information on Iran's sea and land movements was relayed to Iraq regularly, every 12 hours, and even more frequently regarding the air movements."

U.S. military support for Saddam Hussein began shortly after Casey's secret trip to Iraq. By taking Iraq off the State Department's list of nations which support terrorism, it enabled the sale of so-called "dual use" items which, although ostensibly they would be sold for civilian purposes, would have a separate use for the battlefield.

Said one former senior State Department official: "The decision to help Iraq was not a CIA rogue initiative. The policy was researched at the State Department and approved at the highest levels" (*New York Times*, January 26th, 1992).

Journalist Murray Waas has done some pioneering reporting on America's relationship with Iraq throughout the 1980s. In a series of articles published in December 1990, Waas reported that in early 1982 the word in Washington from the Middle East was that Jordan's King Hussein was urging officials at the U.S. Embassy in Amman to help Saddam Hussein in the war with Iran, which had destroyed much of Iraq's oil facilities and the second-largest city and only port, Basra. The U.S. chargé d'affairs in Baghdad at the time, William Eagleton, recommended that the Administration rescind its ban on selling arms to Iraq by allowing third countries to sell weapons. Instead of lifting the arms embargo, which would have caused a furor in Congress, the Administration allowed U.S. arms to be sold to Iraq via third parties. Although technically this violated the Arms Export Control

Act, by turning a blind eye to the practice the Administration achieved its geopolitical goals in the region (*Village Voice*, December 18th, 1990).

America's allies in the region were to be used as front companies for U.S.-made arms. Waas reports that shipments were made by Jordan, Egypt, and Kuwait, with full White House approval. This was all done covertly, behind the back of Congress. One CIA official who worked with former CIA Director William Casey said that: "The Kuwaitis sent lots of money and lots of arms to Iraq, and it was all done with our knowledge. By 1982 the Jordanian military was routinely diverting American-made Huey helicopters to Iraq" (*New York Times*, January 26th, 1992). Despite the fact that U.S. export law had forbidden these third-party transfers of American-made weapons, neuther Vice President Bush nor anyone else in the Administration made any effort to stop them.

According to classified State Department cables, in late summer 1986 Saudi Arabia shipped an undisclosed number of American-made Mk-84 2000-pound bombs to Iraq. Sources in the Administration told Waas (*Los Angeles Times*, May 7th, 1992) that these Saudi transfers were done with the full approval of the U.S. government. Secretary of State James Baker called the transfers "inadvertent" and claimed that they had been brought to the attention of Congress. When President Bush was asked whether the previous Administration had authorized these transfers from Saudi Arabia to Syria in April 1982, he gave his trademark response: "No. The answer to your question is no."

Yet Waas quotes intelligence sources as saying that Secretary of Defense Caspar Weinberger was fully informed of these arms transfers. Part of the deal was that the Iraqis would supply the Americans with Soviet-made weapons such as HIND helicopter and T-72 tanks.

One 1982 deal consisted of the U.S. receiving a T-72 tank in return for four American-made 155 self-propelled howitzers. It eventually fell through for the fear the Iraqis had of the Soviets cutting off their arms pipeline if it was discovered. Another attempt a year later was made, but that fell through too when the Americans hiked the price of the weapons at the last moment. A third attempt involved Carl Perry, an executive for Hughes Helicopter, who tried to acquire a Soviet HIND helicopter. Perry contacted Colonel John Stanford, an aide to Caspar Weinberger, who put him in contact with the man who ran the covert Pentagon program to acquire Soviet weapons, Lt. Colonel Norman Blaylock. One of the partners in the deal was Sarkis Soghanalian, one of the world's biggest arms dealer and a major supplier of U.S.-made arms to Iraq.

Perry was told, however, that the Pentagon did not want to do business with the Lebanese-born Soghanalian. In fact, Perry was fired from Hughes when the company discovered that he and Soghanalian were being investigated by the Federal government in connection with violating the Arms Export Control Act by smuggling 103 combat-ready helicopters and other weapons to Iraq via Kuwait using Italian false end-user certificates.

Soghanalian claims to be a former CIA informant, which would explain his ownership of Pan Aviation Airways in Miami, a CIA proprietary company which was created after the break-up of the CIA-owned airline Air America in the early 1970s. He says the deals he put together to sell arms to Iraq were all approved by the State Department, the White House, and the National Security Council.

In 1982 Soghanalian arranged a shipment of 60 Hughes aircraft helicopters, for $25 million. Despite the effort by members of the Senate to stop the supply of helicopters to the Iraqi Army, in January 1983 Hughes received permission from the Administration to sell 30 500D and 30 300C bubble-top helicopters to Iraq, valued at $25 million, ostensibly to be used in Iraq's "Ministry of Communications and Transportation (*Flight,* January 1st, 1987). The middleman, once again, was Sarkis Soghanalian.

Waas estimated that over the last decade Soghanalian himself brokered a billion dollars' worth of arms to Iraq. Quoting a former U.S. customs agent: "If you wanted to do business in Iraq, Soghanalian was the man to see."

Waas also discovered that the Reagan Administration, through many Republican Party officials, was actually working behind the scenes to encourage and facilitate some of Soghanalian's deals to arm Saddam Hussein.

One of them, a $1.4 billion sale of French-made howitzers, was encouraged by the White House through diplomatic back channels. The French were wary of selling the weapons to Iraq for fear of angering Iran, which at that time was holding French hostages. Waas quotes U.S. intelligence files on the French howitzers sale, which shows that American intelligence agencies knew about and actively encouraged the shipment.

Another sale involved the former Attorney General under Richard Nixon, John Mitchell, who was sent to prison for 19 months on charges of obstructing justice in his role in Watergate. Mitchell, who had established a consulting firm called Global Research International in 1980, took on former Nixon military aide Colonel Jack Brennan as his president. Brennan and Mitchell helped Soghanalian get a civilian helicopter sale through Congress. A few years later Soghanalian called on Global to get Washington's approval for the sale of military helicopters, explaining that the State Department's Office of Munition Controls would be told that they were being shipped to Kuwait.

Brennan refused to consider the deal because it involved false end-user certificates. In December 1987 Soghanalian, Carl Perry, and another Hughes official, William Ellis, were indicted for that sale, but it took three years for the trio to be tried because U.S. intelligence agencies refused to make classified documents available to the courts.

Yet in 1985 Mitchell did help Hughes and Soghanalian sell Iraq 26 McDonnell-Douglas helicopters for $27.4 million; but Soghanalian refused to pay Mitchell's commission. After Mitchell died in December 1988, his heirs sued each other over the will, which left Mitchell with a mere $157,000 in assets and $141,000 in debts. Waas discovered that what the heirs were really after was a $3.5 million commission on a contract Mitchell had helped Soghanalian get to sell military uniforms to the Iraqi Army.

That deal involved Brennan, Mitchell, Soghanalian, and former Vice President Spiro Agnew, who were to have divided up a net profit of more than $180 million. Agnew represented a textile company in Tennessee, but in May 1984 when it couldn't fulfill the huge order, he called on his old boss, former President Richard Nixon, to write a letter to Romanian strongman Nicolae Ceausescu to subcontract some of the work to a Romanian company.

Soghanalian also supplied technical assistance to Saddam Hussein, again with the full support of the American Administration. Waas obtained notes by Major Charles Michael Chinn, who turned state witness and testified against Soghanalian. Chinn says he was hired by Soghanalian to train Iraqi pilots to fly a F-4 Phantom jet which the Iraqis had recently obtained from an Iranian pilot who had defected. Chinn claims he was present when Soghanalian discussed his trip to Iraq to train the pilots with the State Department's leading expert in counterterrorism, Robert Oakley, later U.S. Ambassador to Pakistan.

Complications began to arise for the Administration by the end of 1984, when Iraq was holding negotiations to purchase 45 Bell helicopters which were to have multi-mission capabilities. Senator Alan Dixon, a Democrat from Illinois, voiced his opposition to the Commerce Department for an export license, yet the sale went through.

By January 1985, the acquisition of U.S. arms by Iraq

increased dramatically. American M-60 tanks, heavy artillery, concussion bombs, and bridging materials were among the equipment used by Iraq to push Iranian troops out of the Hawr-al-Hammar swamp north of Basra. One report said that "if relations continue to improve, and if Hussein leads his country to a pro-Western tilt, the Americans may consider selling him F-15 and F-16 aircraft" (*Foreign Report*, October 1st, 1985).

U.S.-Iraqi military cooperation certainly improved. The Kuwaiti newspaper *Al Wattan* said on January 28th, 1985, that "discussions by Iraq on acquiring 45 American fighter planes began in November 1984, in addition to sophisticated radar units and special anti-aircraft missiles." The report told that military attachés had recently been exchanged between the U.S. and Iraq and that the head of the Iran-Iraq desk at the U.S. Defense Department toured the front speaking with high-ranking Iraqi officers.

In August 1985, Hughes announced the sale of 24 Model 530F commercial utility helicopters to Iraq's Ministry of Communications and Transportation. On August 26th, 1985, Hatsav, the Iraqi press agency, reported that 150 Iraqi pilots were being trained in United States Air Force bases in the Turkish city of Dierbakher near the Iraqi border, and that NATO was supervising the training. On November 17th, 1986, Hatsav reported similar training exercises at Diar in Turkey. In August, *Newsweek* claimed that there were civil technicians from the U.S. Air Force in Iraq training Iraqi pilots.

In November 1985 the U.S. government approved the sale of 45 Bell 214ST helicopters. Although considered civilian equipment, the helicopters had already been adapted for military use. The White House had assured Congress that they would not by used by the Iraqi Army.

Yet *Washington Post* correspondent Patrick Tyler spotted those very same American-made Bell civil transport helicopters while on a tour with other Western reporters visiting Kurdish areas in northern Iraq (*Washington Post*, October 6th,

The Arming of Iraq

1988). Tyler claimed he saw between six and ten of these Bell helicopters alongside Soviet-made M18 transport helicopters. Even so, the State Department insisted that the Iraqi military's evident use of the helicopters did not constitute a violation of its assurances to Congress, claiming there was no evidence they were used in actual combat.

TRANSFER OF TECHNOLOGY

More than $1.5 billion worth of dual-use products having both civilian and military uses, including helicopters, computers, and electronic equipment, were sold to Iraq between 1985 and 1990. From January 1985 to August 1990 more than 770 license applications for exports of U.S products to Iraq were approved. These sales were made behind the backs of Congress and with the full knowledge and even active support of the Reagan and Bush Administrations.

Some government officials didn't go along with the policy of arming Iraq and tried to stop it. Stephen Bryen, who from 1981 to 1988 served in the Pentagon, monitoring high-technology exports which were considered to have national security implications, says he personally tried many times to stop the export of "dual-use items," only to be circumvented by officials in the Commerce Department.

"The State Department refused to declare Iraq a 'country of concern,' which would mean imposing tighter export controls on items that would have military application" (*Boca Raton News*, May 12th, 1991).

When the Administration wasn't pushing for the sale of U.S. arms to Iraq, it was encouraging the transfer of technologies which could be used in the manufacture of sophisticated weapons, such as computer and machine-tool technology, process control, and test and evaluation equipment to repair jet engines and rocket casings. Although many of these products and technologies were available in Europe, the financing wasn't. With its massive debt problem, the United

States was one of the few countries in the world willing to extend further credit to the Iraqis.

Bryen gathered evidence that many of the products and technologies were used to help Iraq build its Saad 16 missile complex. On one occasion he discovered the proposed sale to Iraq of an analog computer system, the same type that was used in the U.S. Army's White Sands Missile Testing Program. Despite the Commerce Department's insistence that the computer had no military use, Bryen's office got hold of the advertising literature for the computer, which "bragged about its military application" (*U.S. News and World Report*, June 5th, 1991).

Former Under Secretary of Commerce Dennis E. Kloske was another Administration official who rebelled against the White House policy of arming Iraq. He told the House Foreign Affairs Subcommittee on International Economic Policy and Trade that the State Department in particular disregarded his recommendation to limit the flow of American technology to Iraq because the Administration wanted to encourage better relations with Baghdad.

One of Kloske's proposals to restrict the sale of technology to Iraq was blocked by Robert Kimmit, Under Secretary of State, and National Security Council aide Robert Haas. Kimmit would later testify before Congress: "I don't recall that position being laid out"—a standard Bush-Reagan Administration response (*Washington Post*, May 23rd, 1991).

Despite the fact that the U.S. was a signatory to the Missile Technology Control Regime (MTCR), an international monitoring system aimed at countries with the potential for developing nuclear missiles, licenses for the transfer of U.S. missile technology for the Saad 16 project were approved.

On June 8th, 1990, Kloske sent a proposal to Deputy CIA Director Robert Gates, outlining the expanded application of the MTCR to exports destined for Iraq. Gates turned down the plan (*Commonweal*, June 14th, 1991). The Commerce

Department also proposed tougher White House restrictions of U.S. exports with potential military applications to Jordan. Jordan was suspected of serving as a way station for military goods to Iraq. Gates rejected this initiative as well.

A National Security Council official said Gates did not make these decisions to reject the Commerce proposal without consulting his superiors (*Village Voice*, March 19th, 1991).

After Kloske appeared before Congress, the *Washington Post* reported on April 10th, 1991, that Commerce Secretary Robert Mosbacher was told by White House Chief of Staff John Sununu that Dennis E. Kloske should be dismissed. Both the White House and the Commerce Department denied that Kloske's resignation was requested and said he had been planning to leave.

DID ROBERT GATES HELP SADDAM GAIN CHEMICAL WEAPONS?

In early July 1991 the ABC News program *Nightline* teamed up with Alan Friedman, a *Financial Times* correspondent in New York, and broadcast a story claiming that Chilean arms dealer Carlos Carduén maintained a special relationship with the CIA. One former CIA operative contended that he had personal knowledge of at least one meeting in Florida between CIA Deputy Director Robert Gates and Carduén. Other sources confirmed that meeting to the investigators, and still other meetings in Europe.

The joint investigation followed this with a story of how the CIA knew about the transfer of cluster-bomb technology from a Pennsylvania company that shipped these weapons to Iraq. Then came a report by a company in Boca Raton, Florida, that Libya had been helped to build its Rafta chemical weapons facility. It was able to do it with the full cooperation of CIA-contracted shippers, who transferred the deadly cyanide to Libya and Iraq.

The White House denied there were any arms sales to Iraq,

and that Mr. Gates ever met with Carduén.

That's if one takes Gates at his word. During his nomination hearings to become Director of the CIA in 1987, Gates faced some tough questions by the Senate on his role in Iran-Contra. As a result, he withdrew his nomination. When William Webster resigned as CIA Director in May 1991, Gates was again nominated. Although he told the senators that despite his being number-three man on the totem pole at the CIA, he had no personal knowledge of the Iran-Contra Affair.

During the Tower Commission, Gates testified that after being informed by CIA analyst Charles Allen, on October 1st, 1986, of the illegal diversion of profits from Iranian arms sales to the Contras, he was "startled by what he told me. I told him I didn't want to hear anymore about it." What kind of intelligence agent was Gates anyway? He is being told of probably the most dramatic piece of intelligence information of the decade and is trying to tell the American public that he put his hands over his ears and made loud funny noises to himself to drown out what Allen was telling him!

When Gates had lunch with William Casey and Oliver North a week later, he told the Tower Commission that he didn't even bring up the subject. He obviously wasn't too bothered by the fact that there were illegal activities going on at the CIA. (I guess he decided that it would be better not to squeal on whoever was making the secret deals. Obviously, the last thing Gates would have wanted to be known as inside CIA circles was a snitch.)

It is understandable that as a member of Bush's Secret Team and Bush's man on the Senate Intelligence Committee, Senator David Boren, didn't grill Gates on his knowledge of U.S.-backed efforts to illegally ship arms to Iraq. There was, however, one particularly interesting line of questioning in Gates's confirmation hearings, centered on whether Gates as deputy director of the agency was aware that *intelligence* had been shared with Iraq.

In response to Senator Bill Bradley's (D-New Jersey) question, Gates said yes, and added that the law governing intelligence sharing with foreign countries "is fairly vague as it pertains to liaison relationships." While questioning Gates, Bradley implied that during these exchanges more than just intelligence was shared. Gates answered that the "materials that were provided fell within the context of that liaison relationship." Bradley pressed further, but committee Chairman David Boren (D-Oklahoma) intervened and warned Bradley against disclosing classified information. (Once again, Boren saved Bush's ass.)

Why would the CIA help Saddam Hussein acquire chemical weapons?

Former CIA agent Victor Marchetti reveals there is an attitude in the CIA that it's either conventional or nuclear weapons—nothing in between. Therefore, chemical weapons were considered gauche, not very practical. There was also a built-in bias against the efficacy of chemical weapons. They are difficult to control. They were known to backfire if the winds change. There was also the notion that chemical weapons weren't really that much of a danger, and since the U.S. and the Soviets were moving away from them, any nations still interested in them were amateurs.

Hence, if the CIA did help Saddam Hussein gain chemical weapons capabilities, they might not have thought this was a serious threat to anyone.

Although the Senate never got to the bottom of Gates's ties to the effort to arm Iraq, Don Ward, a reporter from South Florida's *Boca Raton News* did.

A key source for Ward was Richard Babayan, in mid-1992 awaiting trial in West Palm Beach jail on securities fraud charges. Babayan, who is originally from Iran, told Ward that under Gates's command he transported arms to Iraq. A key source for reports by ABC News's *Nightline* and PBS' *Frontline* investigations into the subject, Babayan testified in a closed-door House subcommittee hearing about arms sales to Iraq. He swore in an affidavit that in March 1991 he attended a series of meetings arranged by Gates to ship arms to Iraq through the Chilean arms dealer Carlos Carduén.

When the Iran-Iraq War broke out in 1980 Carlos, then a small Santiago arms manufacturer, had contacts with Iraqi Army officers interested in obtaining cluster-bomb technology, a device that scatters tiny bomblets over a wide area. The bombs were especially well suited to Iraq's unskilled air force.

Carduén defended his arms sales to Hussein by reminding his critics that he began selling Iraq weapons "when Iraq was considered a friend of the West fighting the Ayatollah Khomeini" (*Time*, December, 10th, 1990).

Babayan's family, owners of a prominent Iranian shipping company, was the sole shipper of arms to the Shah until his ouster in 1979. He claims he was an asset for Iranian intelligence, and was hired by the CIA in 1979 as part of an attempt to topple the Khomeini regime and free the 52 American hostages (*Boca Raton News*, July 7th, 1991). Babayan claims to have worked for the CIA throughout the 1980s and in 1981 was sent to Zaire to infiltrate the government in order to persuade President Mobutu Sese Seko to turn away from the Soviet Union.

In 1983 he moved to Geneva and worked as a CIA troubleshooter. One of his missions involved working in an undercover sting operation to probe former Miami Mayor Maurice Ferre. In 1984 he was based out of the offices of the Diwan Corporation, which he describes as a CIA-backed company in Geneva. It was in these offices in June 1984 where he claims he first met Gates. who introduced him to M. K. Moss, a CIA operative who also goes by the name of Mustapha El-Kastaui. The intention was to create an arms pipeline to Iraq.

Babayan was put in charge of opening bank accounts and

chartering ships to transfer the weapons. He says the arms came from NATO stockpiles in Belgium and West Germany, and from South Africa, and Latin America. Babayan contends he chartered ships from Greece and Liberia and transferred the arms from the ports of Antwerp and Rotterdam to the Iraqi port of Basra and the Jordanian port of Aqaba. From there they were transshipped overland to Iraq. Payment was made in the form of Iraqi oil sales profits diverted to Swiss bank accounts (*Boca Raton News*, July 2nd 1991; *In These Times*, October 9th, 1991).

Babayan says he worked with former U.S. Air Force general and Iran-Contra player Richard Secord in the operation. Secord calls Babayan's charges "horse manure," saying, "I've never heard of Richard Babayan."

Babayan also served as Don Ward's chief source for a series of articles on Iraqi national Ihsan Barbouti, who financed a Boca Raton cherry-flavoring plant whose cyanide-based byproduct could be used to produce poison gas (*Boca Raton News*, July 2nd, 1991). Babayan related to Ward that Barbouti told him the chemical raw materials were shipped by truck to ports near Houston and then on to Santiago, Chile. At the facilities of Carlos Carduén, they were assembled into shell casings and then flown to Baghdad.

"Despite all the bans and restrictions on him," says Babayan, "Saddam was able to obtain the best military equipment, and 95% of it was U.S. equipment. You've got to ask yourself how he circumvented all these arms export barriers. And the answer is, the CIA had to have helped. I know because I was involved in it" (*In These Times*, October 9th, 1991).

DID THE UNITED STATES HELP SADDAM HUSSEIN GAIN NUCLEAR CAPABILITIES?

An even more frightening question is: To what extent did the Bush Administration condone, and even assist, Saddam Hussein's goal of building a nuclear bomb? According to UN experts, the Iraqi leader was no more than 24 months away from acquiring nuclear weapons capability at the outset of the Persian Gulf War.

In the five years before the war, the Commerce Department licensed more than $1.5 billion worth of sensitive American exports to Iraq, many of which were used in Saddam's nuclear weapons project at Al-Atheer.

Gary Milhollin, who directs the University of Wisconsin's Project on Nuclear Arms Control—an organization that tracks nuclear exports and the spread of nuclear weapons—says that in August 1989 the Pentagon and the Department of Energy invited three Iraqi scientists to a "detonation conference" in Portland, Oregon, which assembled experts from around the world. The Iraqi scientists received information on how to produce shock waves in any configuration, on HMX, the high explosive of choice for nuclear detonation, and on flyer plates, the devices that produce the type of shock waves required to ignite A-bombs. The conference was financed by U.S. taxpayers (*New York Times*, March 8th, 1992).

It's not as if the Administration was kept in the dark as to Saddam's true intentions. Warnings that the Iraqi leader was building a nuclear bomb were silenced almost immediately after Bush took office.

In April 1992, the House Committee on Energy and Commerce headed by Congressmen John Dingell (D-Michigan) heard testimony from A. Bryan Siebert, Jr., who was the Energy Department's leading authority on the spread of nuclear weapons and who headed the department's Office of Classification and Technology Policy section. After receiving information that Iraq was purchasing parts used in nuclear industries, fuel-making equipment, and weapon triggers, Siebert urged that export controls be strengthened.

On April 15th, 1989, Siebert, his deputy Roger Heusser, and two aides wrote a memo to Energy Secretary James Watkins describing the evidence they had indicating Iraq was building an atomic bomb. They recommended that Secretary of State James Baker review the issue in the National Security Council. They wrote: "The pattern of purchases suggested the Iraqis had detailed knowledge of design for building gas centrifuges, which are key to enriching uranium for a bomb's explosive core." Siebert also detailed how Baghdad was attempting to purchase palm-size capacitors from CSI Technologies, a San Marcos, California, company, that are needed to trigger a nuclear bomb.

That memo was also given to Siebert's boss, the Deputy Assistant Secretary for Security Affairs, F. Charles Gilbert, who then sent it to Robert Walsh, the Deputy Assistant Secretary for Intelligence. Walsh told Congressman Dingell's committee that at the time he felt the warning was "overstated" and that his department was "uncomfortable with a secretarial level initiative" (*Washington Post*, April 20th, 1992). He believed that a nuclear weapons program in Iraq "had not been identified" and that while recently purchased items may have nuclear uses they also had "peaceful applications." Walsh claimed that Iraq's level of uranium enrichment technology was believed to be, "at best, in an early state of development" (*New York Times*, April 23rd, 1992).

Other Department of Energy officials testified that another reason why Siebert's initiative was stymied was that the intelligence community "was divided at the time on the importance of the warning data." Siebert told congressional investigators that after he informed his immediate boss, Troy Wade, the Assistant Secretary for Defense Programs, his initiative ceased because of an intelligence veto. Wade, who has since left government service, told the *New York Times*: "I honestly don't remember any specific initiative tied to Iraq."

The Department of Energy denied that it had tried to silence Siebert's warnings.

Dingell called the Department of Energy's failure to heed the warning "a major government failure." Yet that expla-

nation may be somewhat simplistic. In March 1992, when
Israel was thought to have transferred Patriot missile technology to China, an investigation was opened and subsequently closed within 30 days (finding no evidence to back
up the claim). If the Energy Department had received these
crucial warnings about Iraq's nuclear ambitions, why were
they not immediately investigated in the same manner? Lacka-
daisical attitudes among government officials is just too
simplistic of an answer.

Sam Gejdenson, a Connecticut Democrat who headed a
House Foreign Affairs subcommittee investigation of the
exports of sensitive U.S. technology to Iraq, claimed that these
sales were not made because the Commerce Department's
export control system "broke down" but rather because U.S.
foreign policy was to assist the regime of Saddam Hussein
(*New York Times*, January 26th, 1992). The same intentions
may have been behind the Bush Administration's policy in
arming Saddam Hussein with nuclear weapons.

Determining why the White House would want Hussein's
arsenal to include such weaponry would be the key to understanding the secret aims behind the Middle East foreign
policies of the Bush White House. While on the surface
nothing can explain the Administration's help in ensuring that
Saddam acquired nuclear capabilities, this may be only because
the larger covert agenda behind the policy remains hidden.

LOAN GUARANTEES

Helping Iraq fight Iran and build its war machine required
billions of dollars, money which the Administration couldn't
simply go to Congress and ask for. Instead, the covert operation rested on three pillars: the granting of loan guarantees
from the Export-Import Bank, loans from the Atlanta branch
of the Banca Nazionale del Lavoro, and the transfer of military
and other technologies.

Had the American people learned of these efforts, there

would have been a massive outcry in Congress. However, since they were carried out in secret, that wasn't a problem. To keep the policy secret, the President signed National Security Directive Number 26, which is believed to have ordered "pursuit of improved economic and political ties with Iraq."

The Commodity Credit Corporation (CCC) operated two export credit programs in the early days of the Reagan Administration to increase U.S. exports of grain to Third World nations. Credit was given by private banks, but guaranteed by the U.S. government. Since the program began, more than $32 billion worth of sales has been underwritten.

Due to the Iran-Iraq War, by 1983 there were severe food shortages in Iraq. The renewal of diplomatic ties with the U.S. enabled Iraq to acquire $364 million in U.S. loan guarantees for the purchase of food supplies. From 1983 until the Gulf War, more than $5 billion of Iraqi food purchases were guaranteed by the U.S. government through the program. The American taxpayer got stuck with $2 billion of loans that Iraq left unpaid.

The CCC program solved the State Department's problem of how to increase foreign aid without having to face opposition in Congres (Special Report commissioned by the Simon Wiesenthal Center from *Middle East Defense News*). Although only in existence for less than a decade, the loan-guarantees program has been transformed from a dull export-enhancement strategy into a foreign policy tool of the Administration. Credit risks took a backseat to the Administration's geopolitical policies.

For instance, at various times in the mid-1980s the Export-Import Bank was hesitant to loan Iraq more money because of Saddam's tremendous war debts, which by August 1988 had grown to more than $90 billion (one and a half times its Gross National Product). It did, however, due to tremendous political pressure put on it from senior Reagan and Bush

Administration officials.

Yet in April 1991 John Macomber, then president of the Export-Import Bank, told a congressional investigation that these two administrations had exerted no pressure on the bank to grant guarantees for $267 million in American exports to Iraq from 1987 to 1991. He said: "The test is creditworthiness. As far as we were concerned they had brought themselves up to date" (*New York Times*, April 18th, 1991).

It's not clear where Macomber got the idea that Iraq was creditworthy. At the time it still owed the Export-Import Bank $50.8 billion and another $30 billion in short-term credit to Europe and Japan.

Even after the extent of Iraqi debt became known, the Bush Administration approved an additional $500 million in new credit. In February 1992, a special report by the *Los Angeles Times* revealed that Bush personally signed the secret order to grant a billion dollars in loan guarantees to Iraq nine months before Saddam's forces marched into Kuwait. In 1989 Bush approved a presidential order granting Iraq guarantees against the opposition of the Department of Agriculture, which warned that the new assistance would enable Saddam to acquire military weapons. The *Times* claims Secretary of State James Baker personally intervened in the affair and ordered Agricultural Secretary Clayton Yeutter to grant the loans.

"It seems to me that here's a case where creditworthiness went out the window and the Administration's public policy prevailed," said Bruce F. Vento, a Democrat from Minnesota, one of the congressmen who investigated why Iraq had received such large amounts of loan guarantees from the U.S. government. "On the face of it, this is not what the Export-Import bank should have been doing" (*New York Times*, April 18th, 1991).

During these congressional hearings a report was made public which had been written by a vice president for country risk analysis at the bank in the summer of 1988. It concluded:

"With oil revenues unpredictable and insufficient to cover Iraq's financing needs, Baghdad wants to secure strategic financial partners who place their military, political and economic interest in Iraq above their requirements for repayment. Within this context, Iraq repays in full only those who provide credits in excess of payments falling due."

The report suggested that, at least by the summer of 1988, the bank realized Iraq was not going to have a difficult time repaying its debts. Nor is it clear what the report was meant to accomplish. Under those conditions, what bank, government, or otherwise would lend Iraq money? What financial institution other than the Central Bank of Iraq would put Iraq's economic, political, and military interests ahead of its ability to repay the loans? What bank would lend Iraq money knowing that it will only see repayment if it provides "credits in excess of payments falling due"?

The money wasn't used to buy only grain. Says Congressman Charles Rose (R-North Carolina): "This sleepy little agricultural program did more than just feed the Iraqi people and the Iraqi military. It also provided cash to various accounts in West Germany and other European countries as well as trucks spare parts, batteries, and spare tires (*Washington Post*, March 15th, 1991).

Some U.S. companies were told to include certain "freebies" in their shipments, if they wanted to receive the Iraqi contracts (*Washington Monthly*, April 1991). Investigative journalist Mark Feldstein, a correspondent with CNN's Special Assignment team in Washington, says the Iraqis started to demand free items, such as trucks and trailers, as conditions for winning contracts. He obtained a cable which was sent by Iraq to several U.S. wood export companies saying: "Our future business with your company will depend mainly on the range of your cooperation."

"The Iraqis have clearly extorted money from exporters," said Representative Charlie Rose, a member of the House

Operations Subcommittee. "It appears every single American company dealing with them was asked for extra sales service. What we don't know is how many companies came across" (*Boca Raton News*, May 12th, 1991).

A negative reply would cause the American firm to be blacklisted. Some companies admitted to Feldstein that they had supplied Iraq with military hardware to complete the deal, and that such methods became "standard practice in the industry" and the "price of doing business with Iraq." The kickbacks sometimes amounted to 10 percent of the value of the contract (*Washington Monthly*, April 1991).

Using these methods, Iraq acquired special trucks required to transport the SCUD and cranes to load it before launching.

Feldstein claims that as early as 1987 the United States Department of Agriculture began receiving, and ignoring, warnings that American companies were being asked to ship military goods along with the agricultural products. The attempt by the Administration to pressure the USDA and CCC to grant loan guarantees to Iraq may have been an attempt to covertly funnel U.S. aid to Iraq.

Says Rose: "This was done to avoid offending Congress. They didn't want to directly ship military systems to Iraq which would have excited Israel. Nor could they ask Congress to grant foreign aid or military sales credit. So they told USDA to be as generous as it could with agricultural credits" (*Washington Monthly*, April 1991). The policy to support Iraq with loan guarantees ran right up to the highest levels of the White House. For instance, in October 1989 Secretary of State James Baker called then-Secretary of Agriculture Clayton Yeutter and urged him to approve $1 billion in agricultural loan guarantees to Iraq, explaining that "the CCC program is important to improve and expand out relationship with Iraq, as ordered by the President in NSD-26" (*Los Angeles Times*, March 22nd, 1992). (Although the existence of the NSD is widely known, President Bush still refuses to provide a copy of it to congressional investigators and instead invokes his "executive privilege.") ✓

Even when Congress levied limited sanctions against Iraq after the gassing of Kurdish villages in northern Iraq, which would have prohibited further bank financing without a presidential waiver, the White House wrote one and President Bush signed it on January 17th, 1990, explaining that a ✗ prohibition on loan guarantees for Iraq "would not be in the national interest of the United States" (*Los Angeles Times*, March 22nd, 1992).

Why was it so vital for the national interest of the United States for Iraq to receive these loans? If the Bush Administration knew that there were widespread corruption and extortionist attempts involving these loans, why did it insist on approving another billion dollars' worth of them? In fact, for nearly two years before Saddam invaded Kuwait, the Bush Administration seems to have been aware of Iraq's diverting some of the food purchased under the loan guarantees program and exchanging it for money and arms.

In October 1989 a team of investigators from the Department of Agriculture confronted Iraqi officials with these charges. The Agriculture officials were amazed to discovered that instead of ending the aid program, the Bush Administration sought to expand it.

Documents made available to the *New York Times* (April 27th, 1992) indicate that a number of Soviet-bloc countries, Jordan, and Turkey aided Iraq in the diversions, and that nuclear technology may also have been bartered to Iraq in return for the food. The Department of Agriculture's Inspector General said at a meeting on October 13th, 1989, in the department with officials of the Commodity Credit Corporation that diverted funds were used to procure nuclear-related equipment, particularly a "nuclear fuel compounder" and a "nose cone burr."

BANCA NAZIONALE DEL LAVORO

More than a year before Saddam invaded Kuwait, on April 4th, 1989, a team of Federal and State investigators invaded the Atlanta offices of the Italian state-owned Banca Nazionale del Lavoro (BNL) and demanded to see allegedly secret files which contained information of the bank's "off-the-book" loans to Iraq recorded in "gray book" accounts.

Initially, the head office of the bank in Rome had claimed that BNL's North American headquarters in New York, which had a $500,000 lending limit, had not authorized the loans. To head off any inquiry, BNL Chairman Nerio Nesi and its president, Giocome Pedde, resigned. In testimony before the Italian Senate in December 1989, Italian Treasury Minister Guido Carli revealed that the credit requests for Iraq were "routinely" channeled to Atlanta by BNL branches in Italy and by the credits and finance departments of the BNL headquarters in Rome. He estimated that of the $2.867 billion in outlays BNL Atlanta had made, $1.017 billion went directly to the Central Bank of Iraq, $781 million to the Rafidain Bank of Baghdad, and the rest to cover letters of credit to other banks and customers (Special Report commissioned by the Simon Wiesenthal Center from *Middle East Defense News*).

Paul R. Von Wedel, former vice president, and Leigh Ann New, administrative assistant to BNL's branch manager in Atlanta, pleaded guilty to conspiracy to defraud the bank through loans BNL made to the Central Bank of Iraq (*Los Angeles Times*, March 8th, 1991). On February 28th, 1991, the Justice Department issued a 347-page indictment against ten other employees of the bank. One of them, branch manager Christopher P. Drogoul, was charged with illegally arranging more than $4 billion in unauthorized loans and credit extensions to Iraq to finance missile and chemical-weapons projects.

Says Italian Senator Francesco Forte, a member of a parliamentary commission that investigated BNL's affairs: "It was widely known in Italy that the way to finance operations with Iraq was through Atlanta" (*Time*, June 11th, 1990).

Drogoul reportedly told his lawyers: "This bank wasn't in the business of making money. It was in the business of disbursing money" (*Insight*, March 11th, 1991). In his defense he said the bank was an agent of Italian government policy. Sources close to him claimed: "BNL is not a bank. It is a source of Italian government financing" (Wiesenthal Report).

This wasn't the first time BNL, which is 93 percent owned by the Italian government, would be involved in a Middle East arms scandal. When Italian Judge Felice Casson investigated the illegal trade of Italian arms to Iran, he discovered that Abedi Tari of Islamic Republic of Iran Shipping Lines did business with two Italian affiliates of France's Luchaire firm, Sea and Consar. Luchaire was involved in French arms scandals. Payments went through branches of BNL in Singapore, Bangkok, and Hong Kong. Luchaire's man in Italy is Mario Apiano, director of the Sea Company in Turin and of Defex in Lisbon, Portugal. Defex played a major role in Oliver North's arms network to Iran and Nicaragua in the Iran-Contra Affair (*Euromoney*, October 1990).

BNL money was the lifeline of Iraqi efforts to become self-sufficient in the production of various armaments. Yet more than half a billion dollars' worth of credits that BNL Atlanta approved carry no names, so it was impossible to determine what they financed. However, an Italian intelligence report from September 1989 from SISMI, the Italian intelligence service, to Prime Minister Giulio Andreotti linked loans coming from this BNL branch to Iraq's Condor 2 missile program—a $1 billion project involving West Germany, Austria, and Brazil to develop an intermediate-range nuclear-capable missile. "It should be underlined that various domestic and foreign companies involved in the Condor 2 missile project have been helped thanks to the financial operations conducted by the BNL-Atlanta branch" (*Financial Times*,

May 3rd, 1991).

Assuming that the White House wasn't behind the effort to finance Iraq's military buildup, did it know about, yet do nothing about, a bank on U.S. soil that was loaning money to Saddam Hussein to help him purchase military equipment? Congressman Henry Gonzalez, a Democrat from Texas and chairman of the Committee on Banking, Finance and Urban Affairs in the House of Representatives, which investigated BNL, believed it did. He obtained a confidential memo showing that a top-ranking Administration official from a cabinet-level department "had knowledge that BNL money was being used to purchase military goods.

"This Administration official was concerned that the revelation of BNL financing of military articles would be bad for his particular program because it would cause considerable adverse congressional reaction and press coverage," Gonzalez revealed. "He stated in [a] memo: 'In the worse case scenario, investigators would find a direct link to financing Iraqi military expenditures, particularly the Condor missile'" (*Village Voice*, March 12th, 1991).

As with most other Reagan-Bush Administration secret agendas and scandals, it was the Department of Justice which led the effort to block any investigation. While BNL Atlanta issued more than 2500 letters of credit to Iraqi firms, only a handful of them have been disclosed. According to a report commissioned by the Simon Wiesenthal Center, a list has been compiled, but it is being kept secret by BNL, the Italian government, and by the U.S. Attorney General. None of these sources would release it to Gonzalez's committee or the Italian Senate, which conducted its own investigation into the affair, which the Italian press dubbed "Iraqgate."

The loans to Iraq were not reported to the U.S. Federal Reserve or to the bank's headquarters in Rome. When Gonzalez asked Federal Reserve Chairman Alan Greenspan for information relating to a Bank of Italy audit of BNL, he was refused.

Nor did the State Department or the Treasury Department turn over any records they had pertaining to the loans (*The Nation*, May 13th, 1991).

Former Attorney General Dick Thornburgh was equally uncooperative. On September 26th, 1990, he wrote to Gonzalez saying that he was disappointed in Gonzalez's decision to ignore the strong objections of the Department of Justice in the BNL matter. He told him: "This is a sensitive case with national security concerns"; he also stated that the congressional investigation Gonzalez was heading would "significantly diminish the Department's ability to successfully prosecute this matter."

Gonzalez wrote back on September 28th, 1990, saying that he failed to see how "interviewing employees from the Federal Reserve Board, the Federal Reserve Bank of Atlanta, the Department of Banking and Finance of the State of Georgia, and current and former employees of BNL would significantly diminish the Justice Department's ability to successfully prosecute this matter."

On October 5th, 1990, Gonzalez received a letter from FBI Director William Sessions explaining to him how worried he was "over the possibility of grand jury information being inadvertently disclosed in congressional proceedings and how the Committee's actions may prevent further cooperation by witnesses."

It's unfortunate that the heads of two of the leading judicial and law enforcement branches of the U.S. government have so little respect or confidence in Congress' ability to investigate a financial scandal. Also, if the Administration had no role in helping Saddam Hussein acquire loans from BNL, what are the "national security concerns" Thornburgh was so worried about disclosing?

Could it be that a tiny branch bank of an Italian bank could give out more than $5 billion in loans to Iraq without any official in Washington discovering it?

"Even more sobering is the suggestion that someone in the Administration did know and chose not to share this information with the Congress or the press," says Gonzalez (*Boca Raton News*, May 12th, 1991).

Gonzalez finds it difficult to believe that the U.S. intelligence community or its allies abroad did not know about the application of technology being transferred to Iraq. Or that BNL escaped the attention of the intelligence community. "These organizations monitor overseas telexes and phone conversations," he declared to Congress in February 1991. Did they fail to discover the over 3,000 telexes between BNL and Iraqi government agencies, many providing information detailing loans to companies that were building the Taji complex and other military-related projects with Iraq?"

The Democrats on the subcommittee concluded that the reason the Administration was supporting Iraq was due to an "inconsistent and unpredictable foreign policy" (*Washington Post*, June 24th, 1991). They missed the point. Far from being a policy failure, the goal of the policy was to arm Iraq—and it was a resounding success.

CHAPTER 7

Is There Any Justice at the Justice Department?

On the surface the Institute for Law and Social Research (INSLAW) Case looks like any other obscure lawsuit by a small company forced into bankruptcy because of severe cash-flow problems. But on second glance, it has the makings of a full-fledged conspiracy through a massive web of miscarriages of justice perpetrated by none other than the U.S. Department of Justice. Yet another one of the Reagan Administration's secret agendas.

I began investigating the INSLAW story in May of 1991 after I had met with a self-proclaimed former Israeli intelligence official, Ari Ben-Menashe. Ben-Menashe didn't tell me much about the INSLAW Case other than how he had given a deposition to INSLAW's lawyers. He did urge me to check it out. The next time I was in Washington, I met Bill Hamilton of INSLAW.

Bill Hamilton is not the usual stuff conspiracy scandals are made of. He isn't a gun-runner, a former intelligence official, or a spy. He is a hard-working average American from St. Louis, Missouri, who was the victim of a White House secret agenda. Only when the INSLAW story is fully understood can one even begin to digest the extent of corruption which plagued Edwin Meese's Justice Department. If more people understood the INSLAW Case, the other secret agendas and covert operations of the Reagan era would be a lot easier to believe.

The origins of this story stretch back to the late 1970s when Hamilton established the Institute for Law and Social Research as a non-profit corporation. INSLAW conducted work for state and local governments with the support of the Law Enforcement Assistance Administration (LEAA), a division of the Justice Department. With the help of LEAA grants, Hamilton developed a case management software called the Prosecutor's Management Information System (PROMIS). PROMIS was tried and tested in district attorneys' offices in large metropolitan areas throughout the U.S. and on a pilot basis in two large U.S. attorneys' offices.

When Congress decided in 1980 to axe the LEAA, Hamilton founded a for-profit corporation, INSLAW Inc. By then his software was hailed as having made an important contribution to the administration of justice, performing pioneering work on problems having to do with attrition of the criminal case load, repeat crimes by individuals, the plight of victims, and the training of police officers. Between January 1981 and March 1982 the newly formed company developed an enhanced version of PROMIS which became proprietary to INSLAW Inc.

In April 1982 Hamilton thought he had fulfilled the entrepreneur's dream by signing a three-year $10 million contract with the Justice Department to install his PROMIS software system in U.S. attorneys' offices throughout the country. The software, which was designed to track information on cases, defendants, witnesses, and evidence, would also have a special application for sorting and cross-checking data gathered by international intelligence services.

Hamilton's jubilation didn't last long. In July 1983 the government began withholding payments and by February 1985 owed him $2 million. With serious cash-flow problems and unable to pay its creditors, INSLAW, Inc., filed for reorganization under Chapter 11 of the bankruptcy laws. During this time Hamilton met with Deputy Attorney General D. Lowell Jensen to try and straighten out the payment problem. Jensen, a former San Francisco district court judge, served

with former Attorney General Edwin Meese in the District
Attorney's office in Alameda County in the mid-1970s. There,
Jensen had developed a competing program to PROMIS called
DALITE but failed to convince other district attorneys' offices
to adopt it.

When Hamilton personally encountered Jensen's opposition to PROMIS, he became convinced that he was a victim
of a personal vendetta and decided to sue the Department of
Justice for stealing his software.

But the Justice Department would have other plans for
PROMIS.

Hamilton would later learn that as far back as May 4th
or 5th, 1981, at a White House meeting, Meese intended to
launch a massive contract at the Justice Department to
implement the PROMIS software in all of the investigative
agencies and the U.S. Attorney's Office. Meese also decided
that Jensen, then head of the Criminal Division, would spear-
head the planned procurement. The only problem was that
the Justice Department didn't want to include Hamilton in
these plans. Donald Santarelli, a former presidential appointee
in the Nixon Justice Department, was told by Meese that
INSLAW, Inc., should not expect to receive the contract
(Hearing Before the Subcommittee on Economic and Commercial Law, December 5th, 1990, page 28).

It seems that almost as soon as Hamilton received the
contract, a plan was prepared to sabotage it. The Justice
Department forced the ouster of the incumbent PROMIS
project manager Patricia Goodrich and replaced her with C.
Madison Brewer, whom the Department recruited for that
purpose. Brewer had previously been dismissed by INSLAW
because Hamilton felt he lacked the experience or training
in computer software or project management that would be
a prerequisite for such a position. The Department also forced
the incumbent PROMIS contracting officer Betty Thomas out
of her job and replaced her with Peter Videnieks from the

Treasury Department's Customs Services. Elizabeth Rudd, a senior procurement official at the Justice Department, threatened during the summer of 1981 to bring charges of "nonfeasanse" against Thomas unless she resigned (Hearing, page 28).

In April 1983, three months before his contract with the Justice Department started to come apart, Hamilton received a call from Dominic Laiti, the chairman of Hadron, Inc., one of the companies controlled by Earl Brian, a close friend of Edwin Meese and Ronald Reagan. Hamilton says that Laiti told him Hadron intended to become the dominant supplier of computer software and services to law enforcement agencies and that he wanted to buy INSLAW, Inc.

Enter Earl W. Brian, a former neurosurgeon turned venture capitalist, and health secretary in Reagan's gubernatorial cabinet in California, where he served alongside Meese. In 1981 and 1982 he served in the White House as the chairman of a task force on Health Care Cost Reduction, which reported directly to Meese. In 1982, Brian also sat together with Meese on a cabinet-level White House Committee for "pro-competition."

Brian's name would later surface during Meese's confirmation hearings in 1984. It was revealed that the future Attorney General's wife had borrowed $15,000 from Edwin Thomas, a Meese advisor, to buy stock in two companies controlled by Brian, Biotech Capital Corporation, and American Cytogenetics.

Hadron had recently purchased a company which developed software for use in police and law enforcement and which was already a Justice Department contractor. PROMIS would make a perfect fit into the company's diverse product line. He told Hamilton: "We have very good political contacts in the current administration—we can get this kind of business."

When Hamilton rebuffed the offer, Laiti allegedly told him: "We have ways of making you sell."

Laiti denies ever talking to Hamilton, calling the story "ludicrous."

In mid-1983 Jensen approved a plan for Peter Videnieks, Brian's longtime investment banker, to use the sham contract disputes as justification for terminating the Justice Department's previous agreements with INSLAW. Brian and Laiti were so confident that this would drive INSLAW into bankruptcy that in September 1983 they met in New York City at the Wall Street investment bank of Allen and Company, Brian's longtime investment bank. According to Marilyn Titus, a former secretary at Hadron, Brian and Laiti went to New York "seeking $7 million in equity capital for its criminal justice expansion plans" (Hearing, page 29).

The sabotage and planned destruction of INSLAW was temporarily stalled in 1984 by an investigation led by Senator Max Baucus, a member of the Senate Judiciary Committee. Baucus was asked by the General Accounting Office to investigate allegations by a Department of Justice employee about a plan he discovered whereby "Meese and Jensen would award a massive sweetheart contract to unidentified friends for the installation of PROMIS." This was also during the investigation into Meese's family equity interests in two companies controlled by Earl Brian. By September 1984 both of the investigations had ended (Hearing, page 35).

Then, on February 7th, 1985, INSLAW filed for Chapter 11 bankruptcy protection. Later that month Meese was confirmed as Attorney General.

After INSLAW filed for protection, the Justice Department implemented another covert plan, this time to force INSLAW's liquidation. Systems and Computer Technology Inc. (SCT) of Malvern, Pennsylvania, approached (without INSLAW's knowledge) a group of INSLAW's creditors and offered $3.6 million for the company's total debts, if the consortium of creditors would force INSLAW to sell out to SCT. The creditors filed a motion in the Bankruptcy Court to strip

INSLAW of its court protection so the sale could go through, but INSLAW's lawyers stopped it and persuaded the creditors to reject SCT's offer.

"We later discovered in our own investigation that employees of SCT had met with Justice Department officials, including James Stewart, then a presidential appointee, to discuss the planned hostile takeover of INSLAW," Bill Hamilton told a congressional committee looking into the INSLAW case. "Justice officials told SCT that INSLAW's contract disputes would be resolved and I would be removed as President."

A former SCT employee, Robert Radford, gave a sworn affidavit to INSLAW which claimed that SCT had given him and other employees a script to use in disparaging INSLAW's products to its customers in state and local governments throughout the country. Hamilton later discovered that prior to the hostile takeover bid by SCT, its President, Michael Emmi had flown to the Berkshire Mountains to discuss it with Herbert A. Allen, Jr., of Allen and Company, Earl Brian's investment bankers. After that meeting Allen purchased $5 million worth of SCT stock.

Hamilton would later receive a call from Anthony Pasciuto, Deputy Director of the Executive Office for U.S. Trustees at the Department of Justice, who told him of an attempt by his boss, Thomas Stanton, to apply pressure on Pasciuto to convert INSLAW's reorganization (Chapter 11) into a liquidation (Chapter 7). This would have forced INSLAW to close up shop, putting the rights to acquire PROMIS up for grabs at an auction of the company's assets. U.S. Trustee Cornelius Blackshear gave a deposition to INSLAW's lawyers backing up Pasciuto's story. Yet after meeting with Justice officials a few days later Blackshear recanted his story, claiming he confused INSLAW with another case. When Pasciuto heard Blackshear recant, he did too.

U.S. Court of Appeals Judge George Bason believed

Blackshear's and Pasciuto's original claims and in February 1988 ruled that the Justice Department had conspired to steal 44 copies of INSLAW's proprietary software program through "trickery, deceit, and fraud." He ordered the government to pay nearly $6.8 million in lost fees and legal costs.

After he refused to rule in favor of a Justice Department motion to liquidate INSLAW, Judge Bason discovered only one month later that he would not be reappointed by the U.S. Court of Appeals. Only four of 136 federal bankruptcy judges seeking reappointment before him had ever been turned down.

In April 1988, Ronald LeGrand, Chief Investigator of the Senate Judiciary Committee, telephoned Hamilton and told him that he was calling at the request of an unnamed senior official in the Department of Justice whom he had known for 15 years and regarded as completely trustworthy. According to the official, the INSLAW Case was "a lot dirtier for the Department of Justice than Watergate had been, both in its breadth and depth, and that we [Hamilton] would be sickened if we ever learned even half of it." He also said that "the misconduct found by the court was only a small part of a much larger procurement fraud involving Meese, Jensen, and Brian." The official also said that senior career officials in the Criminal Division knew all about this malfeasance but would not disclose what they knew, even in response to a subpoena and under oath (Report, page 19).

After Justice appealed Bason's original decision, U.S. District Court Judge William B. Bryant upheld the ruling in November 1989 by affirming that the Department of Justice had acted "willfully and fraudulently to obtain property that it was not entitled to under the contract" and that "INSLAW performed its contract in a hostile environment that extended from the higher echelons of the Justice Department." The Justice Department once again pursued a further appeal.

If there was a conspiracy, The Senate's Permanent Subcommittee on Investigations never got close to revealing it.

Chaired by Sam Nunn, the committee investigated the INSLAW Case but received no cooperation from the Justice Department. In September 1989, after 17 months on the job, it released an 80-page report stating that while INSLAW had definitely been a victim of some type of personal bias, it found "no proof of the existence of a broad conspiracy against INSLAW within the Department of Justice."

The subcommittee did report, however, that its inquiry had been "hampered by the department's lack of cooperation." When the House Judiciary Committee, headed by Texas Democrat Jack Brooks, opened its own investigation in December 1990 and requested documents, they too were hindered as the Justice Department refused to allow the interrogation of its employees. Under subpoena, then-Attorney General Richard Thornburgh did produce some files, but then the Justice Department claimed that a volume containing key documents was missing and that some of the documents were too "sensitive" and "privileged" to show to Congress.

Not accepting this decision as the end of the affair, in December 1989 INSLAW filed a Writ of Mandamus seeking a higher court's order to compel Thornburgh to carry out a full investigation of the malfeasance against INSLAW which had already been found by the Bankruptcy Court and upheld by the District Court. The District Court dismissed INSLAW's petition in September 1990 because it lacked legal standing to compel a criminal investigation.

INSLAW's lawyer, former U.S. Attorney General Elliott Richardson, gave the department's Office of Public Integrity a list of more than 30 people who have supported accusations including some in the Justice Department, yet just one of them was contacted. "We believe these attempts to acquire control of PROMIS were linked by a conspiracy among friends of former Attorney General Edwin Meese to take advantage of their relationship with him for the purposes of obtaining a lucrative contract for the automation of all the department's litigating divisions," said attorney Elliott Richardson. "A comprehensive investigation would only expose criminal activity on the part of Department of Justice employees and make the department liable for large sums of money" (*Washington Post*, December 6th, 1990).

INSLAW's battle against the Justice Department took yet another queer twist when on Tuesday, May 7th, 1991, a three-member Federal appeals court issued a 15-page opinion which cast off five years of consecutive court victories and $6 million in legal costs by Hamilton by ruling that INSLAW should never had brought its case to a U.S. bankruptcy court in the first place. Ruling on a technicality, it overturned the original $6.8 million in fees and legal costs awarded by Judge Bason in 1988.

The assistant attorney general for the Justice Department's civil division told reporters after the ruling that the entire fiasco was "fundamentally a matter of commercial and contractual disagreement."

Hamilton and his lawyer, Richardson, vowed to fight to the end, claiming that the issue was now twofold: the integrity of the criminal justice system as well as compensation to individuals who have been victimized by government wrongdoing. "Putting the issue of wasting the taxpayers' money aside," said Hamilton, "two federal courts have agreed that there is a horrendous problem of misjustice at the Justice Department. This decision effectively erased those misdeeds."

Richardson and Hamilton are now trying to obtain subpoena power to confiscate copies of the PROMIS software widely believed to be in use in the United States.

In September 1990, they presented the court with documentation showing that a recently retired senior Department of Justice official informed Hamilton that in the summer of 1988 orders were issued by the Office of the Attorney General of the U.S. to implement INSLAW's PROMIS software in Department of Justice offices. This was in addition to the 42 largest U.S. Attorneys Offices already then known to be using pirated copies of the software.

Retrieving copies which have already been sold illegally to other countries' intelligence services will prove to be even more difficult. On November 5th, 1990, INSLAW received a call from Mark Valois of the Department of Communications of the Federal Government of Canada. Valois claimed PROMIS is currently in use in agencies and departments of the Canadian government, documenting more than 900 locations supported by the software, including the Royal Canadian Mounted Police and the Canadian Security and Intelligence Service. INSLAW has not sold its program to any agency or department of the Federal Government of Canada and has never had any authorized distributors in Canada. Hamilton says that in addition the CIA and National Security Agency, as well as the secret services of Great Britain, France, South Korea, Iraq, and Israel, are using unauthorized copies of PROMIS.

Hamilton, for the life of him, couldn't figure out how these foreign intelligence agencies received his proprietary software. Then, one day in May 1990 he got a call from Michael Riconosciuto, a computer software technician, who told him that the INSLAW mess was the financial reward given by the Reagan Administration to Earl Brian for his work in arranging the "October Surprise" in 1980. "October Surprise" is the alleged secret deal between members of the Reagan election campaign team and the Iranian government to delay the release of the 52 American hostages until after the presidential elections in return for a steady supply of U.S. arms for Iran to continue its war with Iraq.

Earl Brian served as Secretary of Health when Ronald Reagan was governor of California. After leaving public office in 1975, he had tried to sell the Shah a new health care system, maintaining close contacts with Iranian officials. Those connections survived the revolution, as did his ties to the U.S. intelligence network. Brian's role in "October Surprise" was to use his contacts to arrange a set of meetings in Madrid between William Casey and Mehdi Karrubi, the head of the Martyrs' Foundation and current speaker of the Iranian Parliament. Riconosciuto claims that in September 1980 he and Brian flew on the private 737 jet of Saudi Defense Attaché Prince Bandar bin Sultan, from the U.S. to Teheran, where they met with a member of the Khomeini government to arrange payment of $40 million to Iranian officials.

In an affidavit given to the U.S. Bankruptcy Court in D.C., Riconosciuto stated that in the early 1980s he served as the director of research for a joint venture between the Wackenhut Corporation of Coral Gables, Florida, and the Cabazon Band of Indians of Indio, California, located on the Cabazon Reservation near Palm Springs. The Cabazon tribe was employed as a CIA "cutout," a front, in intelligence parlance. The operation sought to develop and manufacture materials that are used in fuel-air explosives (a weapon which emits gas in mid-air, then ignites it) and biological and chemical weapons. These are the exact type of weapons the ABC News program *Nightline* alleged in its July 1991 report that the CIA transferred to Iraq.

When Hamilton checked on Riconosciuto's background he discovered that in the 1980s Riconosciuto had been trying to develop a type of bomb that would generate the force of an atomic blast with conventional explosives, and that, as president of a small R&D company, he had invented a unique miniaturized power-supply technology (*The Nation*, October 28th, 1991).

The weapons were being developed to suit the needs of number of foreign governments and forces in the Middle East and Central America, including the Nicaraguan Contras, Iraq, as well as South Africa. According to Riconosciuto, the operation maintained close liaison with certain elements of the U.S. government, including representatives of intelligence, military, and law enforcement agencies.

Riconosciuto contends that among the frequent visitors to the site was Peter Videnieks and Earl Brian. From 1983 t o 1984 Riconosciuto's job, on behalf of Brian, was to modify the PROMIS software to support the implementation of PROMIS in law enforcement and intelligence agencies worldwide. He claims that the copy he was working on came to him through Wackenhut, which had acquired it from Videnieks.

Some of these modifications he made were specifically designed to facilitate the implementation of PROMIS for the Royal Canadian Mounted Police and the Canadian Security and Intelligence Services. Earl Brian, he says, would check with him from time to time to make certain that the work would be completed in time to satisfy these agencies' schedules.

Riconosciuto says Videnieks called him in February 1991 to persuade him not to cooperate with an independent investigation of the government's piracy of PROMIS being conducted by the Committee on the Judiciary of the U.S. House of Representatives. Videnieks told him that he would reward him for a decision not to cooperate by forecasting an immediate and favorable resolution of a protracted child custody dispute in Orange County, California, being prosecuted against his wife's former husband. He also told him that "credible witnesses" would come forward to contradict any damaging claims that he made in testimony before the House Judiciary Committee.

In mid-March 1991 Riconosciuto asserts he was set up by the police in Tacoma, Washington, when he was arrested; but he had no charges brought against him. Tape recordings of telephone conversations with Videnieks were confiscated, he says, and never returned.

Brian's sale of PROMIS to international intelligence agencies is also purported by Ari Ben-Menashe, who says that between 1977 and 1987 he was employed as an intelligence officer in the External Relations Department of the Israel Defense Forces (IDF). According to Ben-Menashe, as an intelligence officer his work brought him into contact with Rafael Eitan, the Prime Minister's Anti-Terrorism Advisor, who would later be named as the Israeli intelligence agent behind the masterminding of the Pollard Affair. In a meeting that allegedly took place in December 1982 in Eitan's office, Ben-Menashe says Eitan told him that he had received a copy of the PROMIS program from Earl Brian and former National Security Advisor Robert McFarlane, for use in the IDF's Signals Intelligence Unit for intelligence purposes. Ben-Menashe claims Israel paid $5.5 million for the PROMIS system.

Eitan took Ben-Menashe aside and encouraged him to tell his superiors that Eitan was behind the acquisition of the program so that the Anti-Terrorism Advisor would be duly credited.

At another meeting at Ben-Menashe's department headquarters in Tel Aviv in 1987, Earl Brian was said to have made a "sales" presentation of the PROMIS software, stating that all U.S. intelligence agencies, including the Defense Intelligence Agency, the Central Intelligence Agency, the National Security Agency, and the U.S. Department of Justice were using PROMIS. Brian said that he, as a private U.S. businessman, had acquired the property rights to the PROMIS computer software.

Not only did these sales earn money for Brian and Co., but by selling the systems to foreign governments it encouraged these intelligence services to computerize their data, which meant their computer systems could be broken into, electronically. Hamilton calls it "a trap door" program that would allow U.S. intelligence agencies to penetrate another government's intelligence secrets and data.

Other governments could also use it for these purposes. For instance, Ben-Menashe says that Eitan worked it out with

Brian and McFarlane so that Jordanian intelligence would also be provided with a copy of PROMIS. Since Israeli intelligence had the original data codes, it could "break into" the Jordanian intelligence computer system and steal any relevant information.

Ben-Menashe contends that from November 1987 to November 1989 he was employed by the Prime Minister's Office as a Special Consultant for Intelligence Affairs. In that capacity, he maintained close contacts with Carduén Industries in Santiago, Chile, the largest suppliers of chemical weapons to Iraq. In January 1989 the owner of the firm, Carlos Carduén, boasted to Ben-Menashe that he had brokered a deal between Brian and a representative of the Iraqi Military Intelligence to sell PROMIS to the Iraqis. At an October 1987 meeting in Baghdad, Abu Mohammad of Entezamat, the security organ of the Iraqi government, told arms merchant Richard Baboyne that Iraq recently bought PROMIS after a sales presentation made by Brian and Richard Secord (Secord played a major role in arms sales to Iran and the Nicaraguan Contras from 1982 to 1986).

During a visit to Baghdad in early 1988 Mohammad told Baboyne the government of Libya had also acquired PROMIS. An official of the Korean Central Intelligence Agency revealed to Baboyne that had also bought PROMIS from Brian. In a meeting in December 1988 in Santiago, Chile, with Carlos Carduén, Baboyne was informed that Earl Brian and Robert Gates, then Deputy Director and now Director of the CIA, had just completed a meeting with Carduén on the subject of additional sales of PROMIS. (In July 1991, ABC News's *Nightline* reported that in his official capacity as deputy director of the CIA Gates was in charge of arms sales to Iraq through Carduén Industries.)

Brian has signed a sworn affidavit stating "he has never met Riconosciuto or heard of the Wackenhut-Cabazon venture, nor did he ever have any conversation with Peter

Videnieks." He claims further that "he does not know why Mr. Eitan may or may not have told Ben-Menashe during a meeting at which he [Brian] was not present" and "does not know nor has ever met Rafael Eitan," nor does he "maintain any connection to officials of the Government of Iraq."

Videnieks claims he has never met Brian or Riconosciuto, nor heard of the Wackenhut-Cabazon joint venture, nor, he says, did he ever attempt to discourage Riconosciuto from testifying.

"The various informants are not what a lawyer might consider ideal witnesses, but the picture that emerges from the individual statements is remarkably detailed and consistent, all the more so because these people are not close associates of one another," attorney Richardson wrote in an editorial in the *New York Times* (October 21st, 1991). "It seems unlikely that so complex a story could have been made up, memorized all at once, and closely coordinated."

What Richardson is saying is that for this not to have been a Justice Department conspiracy, it had to have been a conspiracy of people who got together to make it look like a Justice Department conspiracy.

Robert Parry, a former *Newsweek* journalist who produced a documentary on PBS' *Frontline* on the "October Surprise" theory, put it another way: "To think that they were conspiring together, you'd have to postulate a mastermind who not only fed these people the story years ago but slated them around the world in the hope that someone would stumble on them and ask them these questions" (*Newsday*, May 5th, 1991).

In other words, the question that needs to be posed to anyone who immediately dismisses conspiracy theories as baseless is: Why are people going around telling false tales, the same false tales no less? To besmirch the Administration? A grand Democratic Party conspiracy?

Bill Hamilton doesn't quite know what to make of all this.

All he wanted to do was fulfill the American dream of owning his own company. Instead, he got thrust into the twilight zone of a Reagan Administration secret agenda.

In October 1990 he was told by Charley Hayes, a former U.S. intelligence official, that he should "check with the Mossad because they [the Israelis] no longer have any use for Earl Brian because he did something that pissed them off."

"I was almost stunned when I heard that," said Hamilton. "How exactly does one "contact the Mossad? How do you find them? Do you phone the Israeli Embassy? I thought: Which friends of mine might know a Mossad agent?"

Hayes told them that the Mossad was angry at Brian (whom the Mossad called by his nickname, "Cash") because Brian had shortchanged the Israelis after collecting a cash payment for weapons Israel had sold Iran. The Mossad wanted to "teach Brian a lesson"; but Brian got some friends of his in the CIA to request that the Mossad do them a favor, and leave him be if he returned the money.

Hayes had some other news for Hamilton. On Saturday, April 27th, 1991, a group of former covert intelligence officials broke into the Justice Department and literally trucked away filing cabinets full of documents relating to INSLAW's case, as well as the BCCI scandal. When Hamilton asked some senior Justice officials he knew if they had heard of any records on INSLAW missing recently, they confirmed that whole file cabinets were removed. Hamilton speculates that the Justice Department arranged the heist because they expected to be subpoenaed by Congress and that it was indicative of the tremendous influence Meese still has in the government.

After Thornburgh resigned as attorney general to run for the Senate in Pennsylvania, newly designated Attorney General William P. Barr has assured Elliott Richardson that he will address his concerns. In November 1991, retired Federal Judge Nicholas J. Bua was appointed as special counsel to investigate the INSLAW Case. However, he will not have the powers of a special prosecutor nor have any independent subpoena power or be able to grant immunity.

Richardson believes the only way to get to the bottom of the Justice Department's conduct is to appoint a special counsel that does not report to the department. Otherwise, he claims, witnesses will not have the confidence to come forward.

One of the many unanswered questions of the INSLAW Case is: Why didn't Brian and Meese just set up a team of computer researchers and develop a computer program to do exactly what PROMIS could do? Probably because that would have taken too much time. PROMIS was already there. Also, there weren't too many companies out there at the time developing this particular type of software.

The most likely reason they didn't compete with INSLAW is because that would have been the honorable, decent thing to do. Meese and Brian weren't either.

THE DEATH OF DANNY CASOLARO

The INSLAW story gets even more weird. On Saturday, August 10th, 1991, the body of 44-year-old freelance writer Danny Casolaro was found naked in his hotel room bathtub in Martinsburg, West Virginia, with each wrist slashed a dozen or so times.

With no signs of struggle or forced entry into his room, the local police called it a suicide and quickly embalmed the body, even before informing Casolaro's family of the death. The hotel brought in an industrial cleaning company to clean the room, thus thwarting any further forensic investigation. After reviewing the autopsy reports, the FBI said the case was closed and that they were not interested in any further investigation.

For the past year or so, Casolaro had been absorbed in a story he termed "The Octopus," a range of scandals carried out by a group of rogue intelligence operatives who were behind everything from the Bay of Pigs to Watergate, Iran-Contra, INSLAW, BCCI, and the bankruptcy of the S&Ls. What Daniel Sheehan of the Christic Institute referred to as the "Secret Team," Casolaro called "The Octopus"—a team of covert operators who carried out clandestine operations.

Casolaro's brother, Anthony, a physician in Arlington, Virginia, says Danny was a "happy, outgoing, talkative, person who kibbitzed with everyone he met." The notion of Casolaro slashing his own wrists was difficult for him to accept; he claimed that Danny would never even go to get a physical because "he wouldn't let his finger be pricked for a blood sample" (*Baltimore Sun*, August 29th, 1991).

Others who knew Danny in the months before his death saw him as "ecstatic" and "euphoric." When he spoke with his mother on Friday evening to tell her he was on his way to see the family, she said he sounded "upbeat." One law enforcement official who spoke with him a few days before his death said that he appeared "too anxious and too eager" to have committed suicide (*The Nation*, October 28th, 1991).

For a professional writer, the so-called suicide note found beside the body sounded unusually simple. "To those whom I love the most, please forgive me for the worst possible thing I could have done. Most of all I'm sorry to my son. I know deep down inside God will let me in" (*Village Voice*, October 15th, 1991).

Not very elaborate for someone who had written a children's book and published several works of fiction. Some say if Danny's death wasn't a suicide, it would be logical that he wrote the note with the threat of a gun or death hanging over him.

Village Voice International Editor Dan Bishoff says the day after Casolaro's body was discovered he got an anonymous call which informed him of Casolaro's death and told Bishoff "his death should be scrutinized" (*The Nation*, October 28th, 1991).

Danny told many of his friends in the last few weeks before his death that his life was threatened by people who demanded he drop his investigation. He told his brother that he had been getting phone calls in the middle of the night telling him, "You gonna die." A neighbor who answered his phone remembers the voice saying, "You're dead," and after the body was found, "You're dead, you son of a bitch" (*Vanity Fair*, December 1991). The last time he saw his brother he told him if there was an accident and he died, not to believe it.

Although everyone who knew him during his last few months said that he was always carrying stacks of envelopes and files with him, the police say none of these were found in Danny's room or in his automobile. William Richard Turner claims he saw Casolaro at 4:00 P.M. on Friday evening with the folders because he gave him documents related to the INSLAW Case which he stuffed inside. They were not found by the police.

Turner, an aerospace engineer for Honeywell, detected fraud on the part of Hughes Aircraft, which had recently taken over Honeywell. He says he gave Casolaro names of Department of Defense investigators who ignored his report, and told Casolaro he had knowledge of how PROMIS was stolen from INSLAW. Turner and Casolaro met in Martinsburg, where Turner said he would turn over documents proving "a vast government conspiracy."

"Casolaro had discovered a common denominator to the theft of INSLAW's software and other recent scandals," says Hamilton, who worked very closely with Casolaro right up to his death in helping him to uncover the dirty dealing behind the theft of INSLAW's software. "A group of individuals trained in covert intelligence operations and aligned with the U.S. political leadership who were allegedly profiting from each of these scandals. These veterans of U.S. covert intelligence operations had also allegedly been selling pirated copies of INSLAW's software to foreign intelligence and law enforcement agencies and laundering the funds through BCCI. Casolaro believed some of the profits from these illegal sales made their way into a slush fund used for political payoffs and covert intelligence operations not authorized by Congress" (*St. Louis Post Dispatch*, September 19th, 1991).

When David Corn, a journalist for *The Nation*, interviewed Michael Riconosciuto in jail in Washington State, he discovered that Riconosciuto was giving Casolaro leads, one of them which led to Robert Nichols. Nichols was a former business partner of Riconosciuto when the two had tried to develop a number of different types of weapons, including a submachine pistol and an "enhanced gaseous fuel device," and powerful explosives that could produce an electromagnetic pulse to destroy an enemy's communications and electronics network.

The partnership broke up in 1984. The only hint there is of what Casolaro and Nichols talked about came from one person who regularly spoke with Casolaro, and who told him that Nichols described to him a building in the Georgetown district of Washington, D.C., where "unusual activities were occurring and that he [Casolaro] was eager to stake it out." There is no indication that he ever did (*The Nation*, October 28th, 1991).

Casolaro was warned by Nichols that his prying was dangerous. One ex-FBI agent who served as a source for Casolaro says Danny began getting into areas that were "dangerous, very dangerous" (*Vanity Fair*, December, 1991).

Riconosciuto kept steering Casolaro into Nichols' direction, telling him that he was behind many evil deeds and conspiracies, and that he was the lynchpin of the entire "Octopus" theory. Casolaro later discovered that Nichols had ties to organized crime and was involved in international money laundering. Nichols claimed to have helped with the CIA assassination attempts on Castro and Sálvador Allende.

Corn thought it almost "too coincidental" that while conducting his research, Casolaro met someone, by chance, at a restaurant who had worked for a company involved in the INSLAW Case. The person also just happened to be a friend of Peter Videnieks and asked Casolaro if he wanted him to set up a meeting. On another occasion, Casolaro and a friend met a woman at a party who insisted that she leave with them. They went back to Casolaro's house, where she talked knowingly about certain aspects of Casolaro's investigation. She told them that she was close to a former CIA official who Casolaro thought was connected to his grand conspiracy of the "Octopus."

Riconosciuto told Corn that another journalist, Anson Ng, was recently killed in Guatemala after investigating an episode involving Riconosciuto and the Cabazon Reservation.

According to a series of articles in mid-September 1991, written by Jonathan Littman in the *San Francisco Chronicle*, John Nichols took control over their (the Cazabon tribe's) affairs as "administrator." Following this, more than $250 million worth of projects poured into the reservation, which is just north of the Salton Sea, near Indio, California, and was classified by the U.S. government as a quasi-independent nation enjoying partially sovereign status.

According to Littman, those who visited the reservation included: "a maze of politicians, military officers, organized crime figures, intelligence agents, and foreign officials ranging from Saudi oil sheikhs to Nicaraguan Contras."

Like the rest of the INSLAW story, Danny Casolaro's death remains shrouded in mystery. Whatever he stumbled upon and was investigating, it hit a nerve somewhere in the U.S. government. Although he had neither served in the army nor covered military affairs, his family watched as a man whom nobody recognized wearing a tan raincoat, and another, beribboned black soldier in full army dress uniform, walked up the to the coffin, lay a medal on the lid, saluted, and walked away (*Village Voice*, October 15th, 1991).

Had Danny Casolaro written more and interviewed less,

he might be alive today to tell his story.

Casolaro wasn't the only investigative journalist who died in pursuit of Bush-Reagan covert operations. On March 31st, 1990, the body of British journalist Jonathan Moyle was found hanging from a closet in his hotel room in Santiago, Chile. Moyle, editor of the London-based *Helicopter World* trade journal, was in Chile attending an international air show. While there, he began looking into weapons sales to Iraq by Carlos Carduén. Carduén is alleged to have acted as an agent for Brian to sell the PROMIS software to Iraq. Moyle wasn't interested in intelligence software, but rather claims that Carduén had sold secondhand American-made civilian helicopters to Iraq, which were then refitted as attack helicopters (*Washington Post*, Jack Anderson column, August 28th, 1991).

Perhaps somewhere in the journalism hall of fame, if there is such an institution, there should be a wing dedicated to the memory and works of investigative journalists who sacrificed their lives so the rest of us would discover the truth.

CHAPTER 8

The Cover-Up of
the Gander Crash

The plane crash at Gander, Newfoundland, is another one of those conspiracy theories that is difficult to explain away by simply discrediting the witnesses. Witnesses to the crash were all average working people, not former spooks or arms dealers. What possible ulterior motive would the U.S. government have had for disputing the official version of events?

On December 12th, 1985, at Gander, on Canada's eastern coast, a U.S. military plane crashed killing 248 men, three women, and eight crew members, in what was the worst aviation disaster in U.S. military history, the worst ever in Canadian history, and the tenth worst in the world. Although more people died on that plane than on the Pan Am 103 that blew up over Lockerbie, Scotland, most people can barely remember the Gander incident.

The reason why few people are aware of this event—which may be directly related to Irangate—is that the U.S. government managed to cover up the entire incident and keep it safely hidden away from the American public.

Shortly after 6:00 A.M. an Arrow Air McDonald Douglas DC-8, carrying members of the U.S. Army's 101st Airborne Division, took off for Fort Campbell, Kentucky. Its passengers had completed six months of peacekeeping duties with the Multinational Force or were "observers" in the Sinai Peninsula. In the predawn darkness the plane rose to an altitude of only about 1000 feet and was in the air for a mere 15 seconds when it crashed into a ravine half a mile from the runway.

Only a twisted 20-foot section of the plane's fuselage remained intact.

Under the provisions of the International Civil Aviation Organization Treaty, to which the United States is a signatory, the Canadian government was primarily responsible for the investigation and reporting of the crash. Under that treaty, the role of the U.S. was to have been only as advisor to the Canadian investigation. The National Transportation Safety Board (NTSB) served as the lead U.S. agency in carrying out that role.

The Canadian investigation took almost four years to complete. It examined and analyzed the wreckage, flight recorders, and autopsy reports. The initial report, by the Canadian Aviation Safety Board (CASB) was issued on October 28th, 1988. It was a highly controversial report, with the board split five to four in its conclusion as to how the jet crashed. The majority ruled in favor of the explanation that the cause of the crash was icing on the wings. The dissenting four members believed that an in-flight fire from an explosion brought the plane down.

Due to the controversy the report caused in Canada, two additional reports were issued before the investigation was officially closed. Both of these found substantial fault with the original investigation and its conclusions.

During the four years following the Gander disaster, the NTSB chose to sit back and watch as the Canadian efforts became embroiled in controversy and dissension which drew into question the effectiveness of the investigation. Despite this controversy, the NTSB routinely rubber-stamped the Canadian findings, whereas subsequent reviews of the report found serious flaws in the investigation; i.e., data was gathered to prove a preconditioned concept of why the accident occurred, not to investigate and evaluate all the possibilities.

Justice Willard Z. Estey, a former Justice of the Supreme Court of Canada, completed a three-and-a-half-month review of the CASB report in July 1989 and concluded that the cause of the accident may never be discovered and that any further inquiry would be futile. He found there was not enough evidence to support either theory, an in-flight fire or icing on the wings. Nor did Estey find any impropriety in the gathering and analysis of evidence by the CASB investigation staff (*Aviation Week and Space Technology*, July 31st, 1989).

Donald Boudria, a member of the Liberal Party in Canada, at that time the opposition in Canada's parliament, said that his party was not surprised at the finding claiming that Justice Estey's mandate did not allow him to review the record of investigation carried out by the Royal Canadian Mounted Police (RCMP) in cooperation with the FBI.

The families of those who died at Gander closely followed the drawn-out proceedings in Canada. In response to the reports issued by the CASB, in January 1989 Dr. J. D. Phillips, a clinical pathologist at the Edward E. White Hospital in St. Petersburg, Florida, who had lost his only son, Sergeant James Douglas Phillips, in the crash and his wife, Zona, organized and founded "Families for the Truth About Gander." The families felt that neither report dealt with or addressed the key issues, which according to them, were terrorism, sabotage, and illegal munitions aboard the airplane.

In August of that year, Republican Congressman C. W. Young, from a district in Florida where five families of servicemen killed in the crash lived, asked Secretary of State James Baker to reopen the Gander crash investigation. Baker declined, saying that the U.S. government had no reason to doubt the outcome of the original Canadian investigation (*Aviation Week and Space Technology*, July 31st, 1989).

Another congressmen, Robin Tallon, a Democrat from South Carolina, wrote Secretary of Defense Richard Cheney and Attorney General Richard Thornburgh seeking answers to questions families were asking about the crash. They had requested that the government release the portion of the FBI report on the incident that had been censored to date (*Aviation Week and Space Technology*, July 31st, 1989).

"The real story is in those files," says Gene Wheaton, a former army criminal investigator working with the "Families for the Truth About Gander" and who along with reporter Terri Taylor for KDKA-TV in Pittsburgh has been trying to force the government to release them (*Details*, December 1990).

The Congress did eventually hold hearings on the crash in December 1990. Tallon testified: "The Subcommittee on Crime has accomplished what I believe is the most thorough research into the Gander mystery thus far. Still our combined information remains sketchy and spotty at best. Simply put, it begs much more questions under the auspices of an official forum whose sole mandate is to investigate the crash. I have been shocked and dismayed at the response I got from the various U.S. agencies. Are they lying, incompetent, lazy, or just insensitive? Many times, I don't receive the same answer. Agencies have different answers to the same questions, and sometimes the answers seem like they are intentionally misleading. At this point we need to hold all U.S. agencies which were or should have been involved in the investigation accountable."

CAUSE OF THE CRASH

One of the four dissenting voices in the CASB investigation was Les Filotas, a pilot who also holds a doctorate in aeronautical engineering and a former research director with Transport Canada. He disputed the core of the official report by the CASB that the plane crashed due to icing on the wings. In late 1991 he published a study in what has become the the definitive work yet on the Gander crash, entitled *Improbable Cause* (1991).

Harold F. Marthinsen, Director of Accident Investigations of the U.S. Air Line Pilots Association, says that the subject of icing dominated informal questioning of witnesses during the public hearings (*Aviation Week and Space Technology*, February 13th, 1989).

Clarence Bowering, the official weather observer for 32 years at Gander Airport, told Filotas that there wasn't any significant amount of precipitation during the 75 minutes the plane was on the ground (*Improbable Cause*, page 178). At the CASB inquiry he testified that at 5:00 A.M., four minutes before the DC-8 landed, he recorded "light" snow grains and "very light freezing drizzle." Bowering described "very light freezing drizzle" as scattered drops, flakes, grains, pellets, or stones occurring at a rate which would not wet or cover a surface, regardless of the duration. When he took his next reading at 6:00 A.M., less than half an hour after the DC-8 had landed, even the "very light freezing drizzle" had ceased. At 6:15 A.M. he noted that all of the freezing drizzle had ended, and that from 3:30 A.M. until 9:30 A.M. a total precipitation of two millimeters had accumulated. He claims that, at worst, "a minuscule, unmeasurable amount of freezing precipitation could have been deposited on a small percentage of the DC-8's wing surfaces" (page 181).

Filotas avers that there could have been ice on the wings when it had landed from flying through thick clouds if the crew had not activated the de-ice system. Such a theory, however, was not presented at the public inquiry.

Despite the fact that four members of the ground staff at Gander employed by the Allied Aviation Company claimed there was no ice on the aircraft wings, the preliminary report completed by the CASB on December 12th, 1987, concluded that the accumulation of ice on the wings and fuselage was the cause of the added weight and created enough drag to prevent proper takeoff.

Yet when ground workers Paul Garrett and Ray Folley were refueling the aircraft neither of them saw ice on the wings. When asked if he would notice any frost or ice on the wings, ground worker John Stuckless, said: "Yes, sure. You couldn't help but notice it. There was nothing falling that morning. His co-worker Patrick Fewer added: "Generally, if there is anything there we bring it to the attention of the crew, but there was nothing there." The remaining member of the ground crew, Craig Granter, also testified that he hadn't noticed ice on the airplane.

EYEWITNESSES

Another crucial part of the investigation concerns *when* the plane exploded. If there was icing on the wing, the plane would have exploded only after it had crashed. However, five eyewitnesses insisted they saw a blinding flash just seconds before the plane crashed.

Despite the fact that these statements were made earlier in the day of December 12th, 1985, an RCMP officer at the scene declared there was no possibility of any form of wrongdoing. Yet the official report offers no answers as to why the DC-8 experienced such a sudden loss of speed. At 95 seconds after takeoff it was traveling at 140 knots, and two seconds later, only 30 knots. The crash did not impact with the trees until 105 seconds after takeoff. Why the abrupt deceleration?

One eyewitness, Cecil Mackie, was driving his truck when the aircraft flew right over him at less than 100 feet in altitude. He later told reporters: "There was a flame on the bottom [of the plane]. It seemed like there was no engine noise. There was just a rumbling noise. I saw an orange glow coming from the underside of the plane as it passed over" (*Improbable Cause*, page 4).

Mackie was sure he had seen the flames, not just the airplane's lights.

Another truck driver, Gerald MacWhirter, noticed the aircraft crossing low over the Trans-Canada Highway a quarter-mile ahead of him. "I couldn't see the right-hand side of the airplane, but I could tell it was very bright on that side of the plane, like something was on fire," he recalled. "I couldn't see the flame, but that side was brighter than it should be. ... The plane went off to the left and I lost sight of it because of the trees. ... Later I heard a bang and saw a big puff of smoke rise up like a mushroom cloud."

A nearby resident, Ann Hurley, said: "We were driving to work when we saw this big explosion ... and it dived down very quickly."

Truck driver Leonard Loughren watched as the aircraft flew directly overhead. "There was a bright glow coming from it ... kind of underneath the plane that lit up the inside of my cab. Then all of a sudden I looked around and there was this big explosion. It lit the sky up like daylight."

Gander Airport Manager John Pittman also said he had seen a fire on board the plane before it crashed.

Judith Parsons, a car rental agent at Tilden, said she saw a flash and what appeared be be a "large orange oval object" moving through the sky. The object then "blew up, it just went in a million pieces. It was definitely not on the ground." Seconds later she saw the fireball. When air traffic controller Glen Blandford cleared the DC-8 takeoff, out of the corner of his eye he saw it level off before disappearing from view. "At that point," he says, "I saw a glow which proceeded along the lakeshore, and then a mushrooming fireball. The incoming pilot saw it too. "Tower, it looked like we have some sort of explosion off to the west," he reported.

Irving Pinkel, a private insurance investigator and consulting engineer who investigated the fire which killed three astronauts on *Apollo 1*, was hired by Arrow Air's Associated Aviation Underwriters. He visited the site six months after the Gander crash and discovered a fuselage panel from the plane's right side bearing an elliptical hole about a foot long. This hole had a "pronounced outward pucker," which Pinkel believed was punched out by a strong force, such as an onboard explosion (*Details*, December 1990).

Although the CASB preliminary report excluded it, one of the master fire warning lights located on the main instrument panel was turned on (which is usually activated by the pilot), pointing to a pre-impact fire.

Peter Boag, the CASB's chief investigator, however, refuted all of these findings, saying that the RCMP forensics people found no evidence of explosive residue and that "it was concluded that the damage occurred during break-up of the aircraft and subsequent post-impact fire."

THE AUTOPSIES

Only two days after the crash, the CASB ruled out terrorism as a possible cause. The bodies of the victims were flown to the Armed Forces Institute of Pathology (AFIP) at Dover Air Force Base in Delaware. Two months later the autopsy reports were finished. The findings revealed lethal doses of hydrogen cyanide (a product of combustion of most types of plastics) in the blood of several of the those killed, indicating a pre-crash fire on board the aircraft (Hearings Before the Subcommittee on Crime, December 4th, 1990, page 35).

The AFIP initially asserted that there was no pre-impact fire and thus the hydrogen cyanide was absorbed after death from decapitation and mutilation. Yet according to most medical experts, hydrogen cyanide can only be absorbed in the blood through inhalation, meaning that the victims whose blood contained the lethal dose had to have breathed in the hydrogen cyanide before dying.

Many of the families were concerned over how long their loved ones lived, how much they suffered in the fire, etc. Some of them asked Dr. Phillips to help them get peace of mind by evaluating the length of injuries based on the AFIP autopsy records. However, those records only listed injuries and gave no detailed description as to size and location of injuries, causes of death, or length of survival (Hearings, pages 11-12).

Many of the victims who survived the inhalation of hydrogen cyanide had increased or lethal levels of carbon monoxide in their bloodstream. Carbon monoxide is a lethal gas caused by fire and must be inhaled by a living person. It is further evidence that indicates exposure to fire before death, not absorbed after death. Many of the victims would have had to live up to five minutes after the crash to explain these levels.

"Families have attempted to get autopsy reports on their dead to alleviate their worst fears and nightmares in which their loved ones sat helplessly in utter agony in an inferno for up to five minutes," Dr. Phillips testified. "They have either been denied the autopsy report, or, having received it, find only a list of injuries with no actual cause of death. As a practicing pathologist of 25 years, I am convinced the autopsies of the victims are incomplete and demonstrate critical deficiencies. I do not feel that this flawed data can be used to preclude a pre-crash fire or explosion."

ACCIDENT OR TERRORIST ATTACK?

Could a bomb have been placed on the jet by Islamic terrorists? Were munitions brought on board by the soldiers? Were arms being flown to the Contras?

The time frame and context of the Gander crash is extremely important. In June 1985 a TWA jet was hijacked in Beirut. In October there was the *Achille Lauro* hijacking, followed by the Rome and Vienna airport massacres.

Only three weeks prior to the crash the Iranians had received a shipment of 18 HAWK missiles which were inferior to what they were expecting. "You have cheated us," the Iranian prime minister secretly warned President Reagan, "and you must act quickly to remedy this situation." A debate then took place in the National Security Council with North warning his bosses not to renege because it would invite a wave of Islamic terrorism against American targets. On December 9th,

North again warned that to "do nothing" would be "very dangerous. ... U.S. reversal now in mid-stream could ignite Iranian fire—hostages would be our minimum losses" (*Details*, December 1990). Yet the decision was made to drop the initiative to trade arms for hostages.

Two days later, the Arrow Air jet crashed. The connection of Arrow Air to other covert operations by the Reagan White House was never thoroughly investigated by either the CASB or Congress.

During Gene Wheaton's other investigation into some of the planes that were involved in Iran-Contra, he had come across Arrow Air, based at Miami International Airport. It was owned by 61-year-old George Batchelor.

"Arrow Air was one of the airlines that resulted from the breakup of Air America, the CIA proprietary airline that helped ship drugs out of Southeast Asia during the Vietnam war," Wheaton reveals. "It was one of the airlines Oliver North was using to ship arms to the Contras and other rebel forces the Reagan administration was supporting." In September 1985 one of Batchelor's planes was used to deliver TOW anti-tank missiles to Iran in a deal arranged by Oliver North in the National Security Council. The operator of the Gander aircraft was identified in the Iran-Contra investigations as "Sur International," a front company created in Miami a few months earlier. Two of the three owners of the company were former Southern Air Transport pilot Herman Duran and Jacobo "Jake" Bolivar, chief of flight operations of Arrow Air. The Gander DC-8 was leased by Arrow Air from another Batchelor-owned company, International Air Leases (*Improbable Cause*, page 202).

ISLAMIC JIHAD

Only hours after the crash, Islamic Jihad, the Shiite Moslem extremist terrorist organization, called Reuters in Beirut claiming responsibility for the tragedy. The caller asserted that the group had planted a bomb on the aircraft to prove "our ability to strike at the Americans anywhere" and that the bomb was set to blow up as the plane landed in the U.S. but exploded prematurely over Canada because the flight had been delayed. This claim was repeated in a call to the American consul-general in Oran, Algeria.

Whoever made these calls had to know that the flight had been delayed during a refueling stop in Cologne, West Germany.

A few hours after the crash, Rick Gibbons, representative of the Canadian Press News Agency in London, took a call from a man with a thick Middle Eastern accent identifying himself as an official in an embassy he wouldn't name, claiming that intelligence traffic from American and British sources indicated that an American jetliner had been sabotaged in Gander, Newfoundland.

Dismissals came instantly, beginning with the Pentagon's chief spokesman, Robert Sims: "We have no indications of explosions prior to the crash or of hostile action." While the plane was still on the ground burning, White House spokesperson Larry Speakes would declare that the accident had "definitely not resulted from a terrorist act."

How was it learned so quickly that these calls were a hoax before even one square inch of the wreckage had been examined to determine the cause of the crash? Considering the anti-terrorism and anti-Khomeini rhetoric of the Reagan years, one would think that the White House would be shouting "terrorist attack" from every rooftop, if nothing else than for propaganda purposes.

"Had they not covered up Gander immediately, Iran-Contra would have been exposed a year before it had," says Wheaton.

There has been a lot of speculation over the 41 duffle bags belonging to the members of the 101st Airborne that were removed from the plane in Cairo to make room for six mysterious boxes. Captain De Porter, the customs supervisor to the Multinational Force and Observers (MFO), claimed that it was highly unusual on such a rotation to separate the soldiers from their bags.

Ramp workers involved in loading the DC-8 were never interviewed by the CASB.

On December 11th, 1985, the day before the crash, the soldiers were flown from Ras Nasrani, Egypt, in the Sinai Desert where they were stationed to Cairo in two Egyptian Air 737s. All personal belongings including duffle bags, luggage, and military equipment were trucked into Cairo International Airport. Upon arrival at the airport no customs, immigration, baggage check, or security screening of passengers was made.

Captain Arthur Schoppaul of Arrow Air claims there was no security provided for the luggage, which remained on the ramp for five hours. Nor was there any inspection prior to loading it onto the DC-8 or any security check of the passengers or their carry-on baggage prior to boarding. "At no time was a baggage inspection carried out, neither in barracks nor at the airport," Captain Schoppaul testified.

He also said a blackout occurred while the plane was being loaded and a fight broke out among the baggage handlers, which he believes, could have had an impact on the security of the plane. Julius Graber, Arrow Air's European manager, who traveled in the jumpseat on the return trip between Cairo and Cologne, claims "there was a period of time when there was no light because the ground power unit had been pulled." He observed the "considerable number of wooden boxes among the baggage." Colonel Marvin Jeffcoat, the battalion commander, was "rather upset" and "requested that all bags be loaded—period."

"The troop commander was very concerned about those boxes," Graber recalled. "He requested that if nothing more could be loaded, that we swap bags—we would remove bags already loaded from the bellies in order to accommodate the wooden boxes. The troop commander said [these boxes] contained important military material."

Major Ronald William Carpenter, the U.S. Army liaison officer in Cairo, described the boxes as "footlockers in cardboard boxes" two feet by three feet across, and five feet in length. He said he didn't know exactly what was in the footlockers but suggested "medical records or tool kits or whatever." Captain Schoppaul said he saw four wooden boxes, each weighing nearly 160 pounds, loaded into the cabin bin. These were sealed, he says, and loaded on orders of Colonel Marvin Jeffcoat of the MFO.

When CBC journalist Carole Jerome interviewed Major Carpenter he was petrified as his superior officer stood over him watching his every word. "I've never seen anyone more nervous than that young officer," she observed. "When we were packing up to leave he turned to me and said, 'Look I'm just trying to survive.' "

Nothing more could be learned about the contents of these boxes. The cargo of the six boxes remains a mystery. Said Captain De Porter: "We do not do a detailed indication of the equipment on the manifest."

Congressman Robin Tallon did obtain transcribed copies of the FBI memos of its interviews with Captain Schoppaul and First Officer Hans Bertelesen, and learned that significant points were never followed up. Among them, Schoppaul said he believed the plane crashed possibly because of "structural failure of the aircraft on takeoff" or "explosion of a bomb," that the "B cargo compartment was left open during the night," and that "empty food carts were removed from it and replaced with full ones which were not searched," and "that the Egyptian soldier," assigned to guard the plane, "disappeared from his post several times, sometimes for as long as an hour." Hans Bertelsen told the FBI he noticed "20 or more persons milling about the aircraft with no apparent function in servicing it."

In November 1989 the National Security Subcommittee of the U.S. Congress requested that the Comptroller-General of the nation direct the General Accounting Office to "determine to the extent possible the identification of the cargo loaded aboard the Arrow Air flight prior to its departure from Cairo."

Despite numerous requests by Members of Congress under the Freedom of Information Act to the army, no itemized description of the cargo was ever released (*Improbable Cause*, page 148).

WEAPONS ON BOARD?
AN ARMS SHIPMENT?

If there was an on-board fire, could it have been caused by a terrorist attack? Or could it have been caused by an explosion of munitions on board, either carried by the soldiers or stored in the cargo areas?

While the Department of Defense did provide Tallon with a copy of what it described as the cargo's manifest, Captain De Porter testified that this was a very general accounting of the plane's contents and not the actual manifest. A blue copy of the true manifest of the plane's contents was provided to the MFO and was in the safekeeping of Major Jacques Lenclud of the MFO in Europe. The CASB did not use the genuine manifest in its investigation.

The official military report claimed that the only weapons on board were two side arms carried by the battalion commander. Yet on May 7th, 1988, the *Ottawa Citizen* reported that the RCMP did recover "large shell cases and grenade launchers in addition to M-16 rifles and automatic pistols." A report by Arrow Air official Julius Graber admitted that the cabin was often loaded with weapons on that series of missions. On December 4th, 1985, an MFO battalion was transferred out of the Sinai to Cairo en route to the U.S. Based on a report signed by Major Carpenter, these soldiers brought back sniper rifles and at least a dozen green metal ammunition boxes.

Could the DC-8 have been carrying arms en route to rebel groups such as the Nicaraguan Contras? Wheaton says it isn't inconceivable that the six crates that replaced the 41 duffle bags contained anti-tank rockets and other weapons which would have been stockpiled in U.S. weapons depots in the Sinai and were being shipped to the Contras. An alternative theory, which Wheaton believes to be equally plausible, is that the aircraft was blown up as an act of revenge for the November 1985 HAWK missile deal in which the Iranians felt the Americans were trying to cheat them by sending them an older version of the weapon. Another possible explanation is that the missiles aboard the plane caused an accidental explosion.

Wheaton believes that Arif Durrani, who is currently sitting in a Connecticut prison for illegal arms sales to Iran, holds the key to understanding the role Arrow Air played for the Administration. In his pre-trial affidavit in February 1987, Durrani describes being taken inside an Arrow Air plane in Portugal and shown its stack full of NATO missiles destined for Iran. Says Wheaton: "If true, this would at least prove that Arrow Air was hauling arms for North's network and hence it would be the reason the Administration would be interested in burying the case as quickly as possible."

HOSTAGE RESCUE MISSION

It is also possible that the contents of these boxes were related to a rescue attempt to release Americans held hostage in Lebanon.

The U.S. Army's official version states that everyone on board was a member of the 3rd Battalion, 502d Infantry, 101st Airborne Division and that only eleven were from Armed Forces Command Units. However, an early passenger manifest lists more than 50 as being outside of the 3/502. Wheaton claims that he has information indicating there were more than 20 Special Forces commandos traveling undercover, since Fort Campbell, Kentucky, was the home base of a covert aviation unit known as Task Force 160, specially trained for sensitive missions. He says that 20 of the dead were Task Force 160 helicopter pilots identified on the passenger list as "warrant officers" (*Details*, December 1990).

One persistent allegation has been that a former member of the U.S. Army claimed he was detailed from his Ranger Unit at Fort Benning, Georgia, to the 101st Airborne in the Sinai in order to participate in a covert mission. Tallon called on the U.S. Army to clarify this claim. He received no response.

Another allegation never investigated was that there was an unknown quantity of money aboard the plane which was found immediately after the crash and turned over to the U.S. Army. A firefighter at the scene claimed he found a large satchel of money weighing about 75 pounds. It was allegedly ransom money to be paid to secure the release of the hostages.

COVER-UP

"This was an extremely technical story," says journalist Carole Jerome. "The investigators had to be versed in aviation to be able to ask and answer questions. The most interesting aspect about the dissenting report by the CASB is that those dissenting were are all ones that had the most expertise and experience in determining causes of plane crashes."

If there was a cover-up, it began hours after the crash. Donald Boudria of Canada's Liberal Party immediately sensed a whitewash and charged that the board's investigators deliberately withheld crucial facts from the CASB.

A CASB spokesman said on December 13th, 1985, of the flight-data recorder tapes which had been listened to for the first time at a laboratory in Ottawa: "Both tapes are readable despite severe damage that will take several days to repair."

The *Ottawa Citizen* would quote chief investigator Peter Boag five weeks later as saying that "the failure of the cockpit voice recorder will mean the loss of critical information that could have helped explain the disaster."

A dissenting CASB member and former fighter pilot and brigadier general in the Canadian armed forces, Roger L. Lacroix, testified that the U.S. Army asked Canadian authorities to bulldoze the wreckage site 48 hours after the crash (*Aviation Week and Space Technology*, February 13, 1989).

A memo dated Febrary 24th, 1986, written by Michael Mendez, the director of maintenance for Arrow Air, to the airline owner's wife stated that U.S. Army Major General John Crosby wanted to bulldoze the site immediately (*Aviation Week and Space Technology*, February 27th, 1989). Mendez claims he was informed of this by George Seidlein, a National Transportation Safety Board (NTSB) accident investigator, who was in charge of the U.S. delegation to Gander. Seidlein denies ever hearing of Crosby's order to bulldoze the site or that Crosby ever attempted to impede any part of the investigation (*Aviation Week and Space Technology*, March 13, 1989). In the spring of 1989 the Canadian and U.S. representatives agreed to have the site bulldozed.

"Despite the fact that this was the worst aviation disaster in American military history, there was no attempt to put the plane back together," says author/pilot Les Filotas. "The CASB's assistance in the inquiry into the crash involving Air India on June 23rd, 1985, included a search for pieces under 6000 feet of ocean. By contrast, the pattern of wreckage from the Arrow Air crash was never analyzed. All traces of havoc from the 160 tons of aircraft and contents were eradicated well before the investigators submitted their first draft report. The remaining trees were cleared away, as bulldozers covered the scars in the ground with tons of topsoil. Six months after the crash, visitors to the site saw only a sloping meadow with a small stone memorial."

What worried Congressman Tallon most was why the U.S. Army maintained such a commanding profile at the crash site. Was it worried that other investigative bodies might discover that something illegal was being carried on the plane or find evidence suggesting sabotage? "The Army was in need of helicopter-borne, multi-spectrum prototype minefield sensors for its activities at the crash site," he points out. "Why was such specialized equipment needed? What was it looking for? Why was the U.S. Army in charge of obtaining this minefield sensor rather than the Canadians or the NTSB?"

One source close to the investigation told "Families for the Truth About Gander" that within the first 24 hours of the crash, over 500 telephone communications were made between American officials at Gander and the U.S. State Department, Justice Department, and Pentagon. All of these may well have been in the process of standard procedure. Yet when the CASB requested to see the records of these conversations they were told by U.S. officials that none were available because no transcripts were kept.

The involvement of the FBI in the Gander investigation is a major controversy that Tallon says needs to be clarified.

The FBI report on Gander contained 280 pages; however, 239 of them were deleted before given over to the U.S. Justice Department. Included in these missing documents are the transcripts of memos of the interviews conducted by the FBI for the RCMP of the 30 to 40 Arrow Air employees, including approximately 14 pilots. Tallon tried unsuccessfully to get a clean copy of the FBI report of the crash.

In an interview with Terry Taylor of Pittsburgh's KDKA TV in the spring of 1990, FBI Associate Deputy Director Oliver "Buck" Revell said the FBI had "no indication that it was a terrorist incident" and repeated that the agency had not conducted any investigations. "We helped only with the identification of the deceased through our identification division and our disaster team."

The search for signs of high explosives called for outside expertise, so the RCMP's Gander unit was assisted by "some explosives people who were at the site." Yet the RCMP won't identify who these "explosives people" were.

While insisting that it did not assist the Canadians with an investigation of "sabotage, terrorism, or explosive devices," the Federal Aviation Administration (FAA) claimed that the "FBI and the RCMP investigated the criminal aspects of the accident, including the possibility that an explosive device caused the crash." While the CASB admits that "at the request of the RCMP, they [the FBI] conducted a number of interviews of United States residents in order to assist the RCMP in their ongoing investigation into possible criminal activities," CASB states that it is "not aware of the exact details of the relationship between these two agencies [the FBI and the RCMP]" (Hearings, December 4th, 1990).

"One issue is clear," says Congressman Tallon. "The FBI certainly did initially assist the RCMP. Then, suddenly, all record of FBI involvement and concern disappeared."

One U.S. investigation did discover something which worried certain elements in the U.S. government. A former Pentagon investigator's inquiry had become "so public" that in August 1989 the outgoing Chairman of the Joint Chiefs of Staff, Admiral William J. Crowe, Jr., asked the army's top attorney to find out what the investigator knew. Well-placed sources told investigative columnist Jack Anderson that the "army may have been used by covert operatives who were neck-deep in the secret arms sales to Iran" (*Washington Post*, November 9th, 1989).

Those operatives allegedly told the army almost immediately after the crash that a GI had accidentally detonated a hand grenade on the plane. That report could have been enough to scare the army brass into steering any investigation away from the embarrassing prospect of the explosion caused by negligence. Anderson's sources claim that the grenade story was a hoax to persuade the army to cooperate in a cover-up of anything that would point to an explosion (*Washington Post*, November 9th, 1989).

As a result of an investigative story on October 13th, 1989, on the ABC News show *20/20*, the Gander controversy was finally brought to mainstream America. After the broadcast, Tallon was able to convince 103 Members of Congress to co-sign a letter to President Bush urging him to "explore all crash theories" (*St. Petersburg Times*, October 24th, 1989). President Bush did not even bother responding.

CONCLUSION

At the congressional hearings in Washington, December 1990, no one presented a smoking gun proving that there was an explosion on board. However, what did emerge was that evidence suggesting there was had been systemically repressed.

In his statement to the Congressional Hearings, Dr. J. D. Phillips summed up the feelings of all the families (and anyone else who has taken a serious look at the incident) when he said: "We should have been able to trust that our government had done everything it could to find the true cause of our loved ones' sudden, unexpected, untimely and tragic deaths. Begging and pleading to obtain our government's information and assistance should not have been necessary. We cannot comprehend the reason for our government's apparent lack of concern for 256 Americans who may have been murdered."

According to Tallon, the bottom line was: "Why was the possibility of sabotage not investigated by our government? Why was the U.S. government so willing to accept the CASB's version of events if there was so much evidence to the contrary?"

These questions are at the center of the Gander mystery.

CHAPTER 9

The Middle East: President Bush's New Playground

President Bush's Middle East policy can't be fully understood without a look back at how he viewed Israel during the two Reagan administrations.

In the early 1980s the combination of being pro-Israel and anti-communist was a very powerful one. You could get to the same position by considering Israel an important strategic asset or by being anti-Soviet.

However, the "Israel is a strategic asset of America" argument may have been nothing more than an election gimmick and a cover for the Administration's true intentions in the Middle East. William Quandt, a senior fellow at the Brookings Institute and a former aide to Carter advisor Zbigniew Brzezinski, says that Reagan was the first American politician to refer to Israel as a strategic ally of the U.S. that could be counted on to fight communist intrusion into the Middle East. "Until then one would have had a hard time finding senior U.S. officials using that type of language," Quandt claims. "No one in Carter's administration thought like that."

There's no doubt that Reagan himself was pro-Israel, some say instinctively pro-Israel. Former Ambassador to Saudi Arabia Robert Neuman attributes these sentiments to Reagan's idealistic vision of Israel and to the many Jewish friends he had in Hollywood.

Yet it's doubtful whether it was Reagan who was orchestrating American foreign policy in the Middle East. Neuman says Reagan had little penchant for the subject. "When you briefed Reagan on Middle East politics, like I did during the 1980 campaign and during his Presidency, you would watch as his eyes would glaze over. There was no point in going into too many details."

What mattered was not what the actual policies of the Administration were, but what the American public thought they were. As a majority of the American public has always been predisposed to Israel over the Arabs, from the 1980 presidential campaign through the two Reagan administrations it was politically astute for the Reagan White House to be identified and perceived as being pro-Israel. However, while Israeli leaders and pro-Israel lobbyists in the United States relished the thought that they now had a President who viewed them as America's number-one ally in the region, they were being hoodwinked. In fact, far from being considered a "strategic asset," in the minds of those who carried any serious weight with the President Israel was a "strategic liability."

Just below the surface, another sphere of the Reagan Administration's attitudes towards Israel existed, a world of secret agendas and foreign policies carried out behind the back of Congress.

The Reagan Administration's presiding policy towards Israel was based on the "level battlefield doctrine" (LBD), designed to weaken Israel. The White House was then (and still is today) more interested in a steady flow of Middle East oil and multi-billion-dollar sales of U.S. arms to the region than Israel's security. The Saudis can fulfill both of these needs. Israel, none.

The LBD became and some say still is today the cornerstone of U.S. policy towards Israel. The doctrine is based on a Saudi Arabian notion that the problem in the Middle East is not with the Arabs, but in Israel's reckless use of its military superiority. The Administration must ensure that the Arabs are put on a parity with Israel militarily so that Israel will be pressured into concessions which will lead to a comprehensive Middle East peace.

The doctrine expressed itself in the view that if Iran won its war with Iraq, it might "consume" Saudi Arabia and Kuwait and thus jeopardize American access to Middle East oil. This explains why the White House began supporting Iraq sometime between 1982 and 1983. The Saudis also had another reason for urging America to support Iraq. The LBD said that a strong Iraqi regime would be an effective balance against Israel so Israel wouldn't "feel so strong" and thus would be more flexible in the peace process.

Conservative ideologue Irving Kristol says that while Reagan was pro-Israel from the very beginning, Bush and Baker were not . "There was no reason to expect that they would be," he says. "They had always dealt with Arabs, not Jews" (interview with author, November 21st, 1991).

When he became President not much was known about George Bush's attitudes towards the Middle East. It may have been influenced by the views of fellow Bonesmen and former President Harry Truman's foreign policy advisors George Marshall, Dean Acheson, and Robert Lovett. All three were reportedly against U.S. support for the establishment of the State of Israel, believing it would pose a threat to U.S. hegemony over access to Mideast oil. Journalists Walter Isaacson and Evan Thomas Simon in their 1986 book cite Lovett as having said, "Israel was one ally too many" (*The Wiseman: Six Friends and the World They Made*).

Far from being pro-Israel, the Reagan years were rife with anti-Israel actions with the then-Vice President Bush leading the anti-Israel caucus in the White House. Despite Israel's being lauded as America's "strategic ally" in the region, there were few instances in which the Administration backed Israel politically against the Arabs. While it is former Secretary of Defense Caspar Weinberger who was always thought of as being the most anti-Israel of all of Reagan's cabinet, that perception may have camouflaged Bush's hostility to the Middle Eastern nation.

Weinberger himself claims that he is not anti-Israel. "While I was Secretary of Defense cooperation between the military of Israel and the U.S. was never closer," he says. "Former Prime Minister Shimon Peres and Defense Minister Moshe Arens told me ties between the two countries were never stronger. During the Reagan Administration we tried to strengthen the Israeli alliance, and without any question we did. While there were occasions when I had difficulties with Israeli policies, overall the relationship was very positive."

Whenever the Administration came crashing down hard on Israel, Bush seemed to be leading the pack.

For instance, when Israeli jets bombed Iraq's nuclear reactor in 1981, columnist William Safire wrote that "Bush led the initiative to punish Israel by withholding shipments of previously promised F-16 aircraft" (*Jerusalem Post*, November 11th, 1988).

Former Secretary of State Alexander Haig says that in the discussion in the Cabinet that followed the bombing raid, Bush demanded that the U.S. cut off all aid to Israel, economic and military, because of what Bush described as an "outrageous" breach of international law (Israel Army Radio, December 28th, 1991).

Haig also claims that Bush convinced Reagan to support a UN resolution condemning Israel for its invasion of Lebanon in 1982. During the June 1985 hijacking of a TWA plane by Shiite fundamentalists, Bush said:"All people held against international law should be released"—an obvious reference to Lebanese prisoners then being held by Israel. During the initial investigation into the Iran-Contra scandal, Bush told the Tower Commission that U.S. foreign policy was "in the grip of the Israelis" (*Jerusalem Post*, November 11th, 1988).

Secretary of State James Baker's views about Israel weren't much different from Bush's. Morris Amitay, a former executive director of American Israel Public Affairs Committee (AIPAC), remembers that during the height of the AWACS debate, Baker told him that the pro-Israel opposition to the sale was "simply hurting U.S. relations with moderate Arabs." Says Amitay: "I did not get a very good feeling about his viewing Israel as an important strategic asset during that conversation" (*Jerusalem Post*, November 11th, 1988).

Bush may have disliked Israel so much because Israeli supporters in Congress got in the way of the White House's secret agendas (something the Bush Administration is determined not to let happen). I'm sure after he was elected Baker and he sat down and plotted their revenge.

Most important, Israel interfered with the desire to sell arms to the Arabs, particularly the Saudis, who pay for their weapons in cash. For instance, in February 1986 the Administration had to postpone indefinitely a proposed $1.9 billion arms sale to Jordan of anti-aircraft missiles and advanced jet fighters—after AIPAC and pro-Israel supporters in Congress led a massive resistance to the sale. As a result of opposition the White House delayed a $1 billion arms package for Saudi Arabia.

When he became President, Bush was not going to let AIPAC repeat those victories. His administration was going to sell arms to whomever it pleased. Rather than allow Israel and AIPAC to get in the way of White House policy, Bush merely took American Middle East foreign policy underground. Like so much of Bush's policies, it became a covert operation.

PRESIDENT BUSH'S SECRET AGENDA FOR THE MIDDLE EAST

The "window of opportunity" that President Bush proclaimed is now taking place in the Middle East after the Persian Gulf War is indeed a great opportunity: an opportunity for Bush to carry out foreign policy in secret, behind the backs of the

American people.

Bush's sudden interest in peacemaking is interesting. As Vice President, the words Camp David Peace Accords never rolled off his lips. In his entire political career he had never been involved in any peace efforts, anywhere. Yet even before the Gulf War was over, he and Secretary of State Baker were calling for a comprehensive peace conference. Why the sudden interest in a peace conference?

Perhaps because it was the perfect diversion, a deflection so that the American public wouldn't suspect or detect the real hidden agenda behind Bush and Baker's policies. In fact, the plan for Madrid was a lot more grandiose than just having Arabs and Jews sit down together.

The first deal was with with Syria. Syria was vulnerable, having just lost its major backer, the Soviet Union. Baker must have told Assad: 'We have a mountain of intelligence on your support for terrorism, including the Pan Am 103 bombing. You have a choice. Either you play ball with us, or we'll release it, isolate you, and destroy you economically. We'll lay off calling you a terrorist nation and stop blaming you for the Lockerbie crash, and we'll let you have Lebanon." At the same time, Israel was probably told when Syria completed its takeover of Lebanon: "Don't interfere and in return they will leave you alone in South Lebanon."

This type of deal with Syria is understandable. The Administration wants to bring Syria under its domain now that the Soviets are no longer a player in the region.

Further evidence of a secret deal between the U.S. and Syria resulted in the death of two or three agents who had infiltrated a Palestinian terrorist organization in Syria. The agents reportedly worked either for Israel's Mossad or for another Western intelligence service. They were unmasked because of detailed information Secretary of State James Baker handed Syrian President Hafez Al-Assad and Foreign Minister Farouk Al-Sharaa during a meeting in Damascus on

September 14th, 1990, when the Administration was trying to bring Syria into the coalition against Iraq (*New York Times*, February 8th, 1991).

Intelligence officials informed the *New York Times* that they were told in February 1991 the killings stemmed from American efforts in the summer of 1990 to uncover a plot by Syria-based terrorists to assassinate the United States Ambassador to Jordan, Roger G. Harrison.

After Baker's meeting with the Syrians, there was a fierce argument between U.S. Intelligence and State Department officials over giving Assad a detailed briefing about U.S. information on Syrian involvement in terrorism. The intelligence agencies in the U.S. were worried that if the State Department confronted Assad with evidence of his country's support for terrorism, it would reveal the intelligence-gathering methods of the United States as well as compromise agents currently working undercover.

The State Department eventually won, and intelligence officials believe that Syria gave the Palestinian terrorist organization the information obtained from the briefing with Baker that enabled it to identify the undercover agents. In November or December 1990 the U.S. learned that the agents had been killed.

Several Bush Administration officials tried to deflect attention away from the affair by insisting that the undercover agents were working for the Jordanian State Intelligence Service and had infiltrated a Syrian-based Palestinian terrorist group to provide Jordan with information on terrorist activities. The officials said that Jordan shared this information with the CIA (*New York Times*, March 12th, 1991).

This is a possible explanation, if it weren't for the fact that Jordan hasn't been the target of a bomb attack by a Palestinian terrorist group in more than twenty years.

Senator David Boren (D-Oklahoma), who heads the Senate's Intelligence Oversight Committee, said that he would hold an investigation into the affair. Small wonder he didn't. He is a fellow Bonesman and one of the President's key men in Congress, who has time after time impeded investigations into Reagan and Bush White House wrongdoings.

The next part of the secret U.S.-Syria deal came in Geneva in July 1991, when Bush met Syrian President Hafez Al-Assad. Syrian Foreign Minister Farouk Al-Sharaa claims Bush made a promise to Damascus that Israel will have to return the Golan Heights. The White House responded with a statement that denied cutting a secret deal with Syria, insisting that Sharaa simply misunderstood Bush. When a reporter asked Al-Sharaa if Bush mentioned an Israeli withdrawal on all fronts, he responded, "Yes, yes, and the American administration's rejection of the annexation of one centimeter of the Golan Heights" (*New York Post*, July 26th, 1991). When *New York Times* columnist William Safire probed Administration officials as to what were the contends of a letter sent by Assad to Bush after the Geneva meetings, he discovered that "Assad had spelled out his understanding of assurances given to him over the past six weeks from the United States" (*New York Times*, July 18th, 1991).

President Bush was criticized for "cosying up to Syria" and for "repeating the same mistake the U.S. made by tilting towards Hussein in the Iran-Iraq War." What these critics don't realize is that Bush is no newcomer to foreign affairs. He's wasn't naive about the true nature of either Saddam's or Assad's regime. Architects of secret agendas rarely have much moral indignation for the ruthless nature of dictatorial rulers. For Bush, the ends justify the means.

IRAN-CONTRA II: ANOTHER ARMS-FOR-HOSTAGES DEAL

The next phase of Bush and Baker's covert policy was enacted just before the Middle East peace conference in Madrid in October 1991. It was no mere coincidence that the 17 Western hostages were released just before the start of the Madrid conference. The hostages were an embarrassment to Syria. The American public would not be sympathetic to the Arabs as long as there were American hostages being held in Lebanon. The question is: What did the U.S. give Syria, and Iran, in return?

Could it have been another arms-for-hostages deal? Iran-Contra number two?

The events which took place during the early part of March 1992 may be instrumental in revealing this scandal. They began when Israeli intelligence services first detected the *Dae Hung Ho*, a North Korean missile cargo ship loaded with SCUD-C ballistic missiles in the Persian Gulf. With it was another North Korean ship.

At the time, the Bush Administration was giving the American people the impression that they were leading the battle against the spread of ballistic missiles and the technology to make them to countries that did not possess them. On March 7th, 1992, National Security Advisor Brent Scowcroft said: "We are concerned about any type of missile proliferation. It is dangerous and destabilizing. We are always considering options." When asked what the Administration was doing to do to deal with the matter, Scowcroft replied: "We are doing what we can." Asked whether the incident over the Korean ships would come to a head soon, Scowcroft replied: "I don't know if it will ever come to a head."

When asked about media reports pointing to the Administration's concern over the matter, Pentagon spokesperson Pete Williams responded: "My concern is that all of these sources have cranked this thing up to a higher priority than it actually was for the Administration."

Western diplomats said the progress of the ships was being watched closely and the U.S. Navy knew exactly where they were (*International Herald Tribune*, March 10th 1992). Yet suddenly the aircraft carrier *America* and its entire battle group lost sight of the ships. General Joseph Hoar, who succeeded General Norman Schwarzkopf as commander of U.S. Central Command, told the House Armed Services Committee: "We were unable to locate that ship, clear and simple."

Before, the Administration was hesitant to intercept and board the ships. Now it was claiming it had lost track of them.

Hoar quickly changed the focus of the matter by suggesting that it was still unclear what cargo the ship was carrying: "The inability to find the cargo ship had dealt a blow to U.S. intelligence, depriving analysts of the oportunity to obtain details of the freighter's cargo. What we have lost by our failure to pick up that ship is, we would have been able to alert our intelligence colleagues to determine more specifically what was there" (*Washington Post*, March 12th, 1992).

Williams fed the press more nonsense when he claimed: "I can't tell you precisely why we didn't see it all the time. Perhaps it hugged the coast line and wasn't picked out of the heavy coastal traffic in that area."

One Navy official said that initially the ship wasn't a very high priority. "We were told to look for the ship, no more" (*Time*, March 23rd, 1992). Yet the vessels best suited for this task, the aircraft carrier *America* battle group, were carrying out exercises hundreds of miles away.

Is it possible that the most sophisticated and expensive collection of armed forces in the world simply lost sight of two transport ships? That everyone except the U.S. Navy knew what the cargo ship was carrying?

In fact, Israel was reminding the world that the U.S. wasn't doing anything about the North Korean ships. She let the cat out of the bag. The Administration was carrying out a secret policy to supply Iran and Syria SCUD missiles but Israeli intelligence got in the way. Embarrassed and mad as hell, the Administration decided to teach Israel a lesson.

In a classic case of media manipulation, the *Washington Times* published a story quoting Administration officials which claimed that Israel gave a Patriot missile to China. Reports in other publications followed purporting that Israel had systematically transferred or sold American weaponry or technology to Third World countries without the required permission.

Whether these reports are true or false is irrelevant to understanding the covert agenda taking place. If the reports are false then it is nothing but a smear campaign against Israel. Even then, Israel loses because nobody believes Israel would admit to it even if she had done it.

Assume for argument's sake that they are true. If the Administration wanted to go public with this information, for whatever reasons, why didn't it simply call a press conference and make an official statement. If the White House is mad as hell at Israel, why can't it come out and say so? Why have "undisclosed sources" release the story?

If the Administration had truly discovered that Israel was transferring American-made weapons to Third World countries, wouldn't the logical response have been to take a senior Israeli official aside and tell him in the sternest manner, "What you did is reprehensible and you will pay a heavy price"— and leave it at that? What does the Administration have to gain by having the affair splashed over the headlines?

All fingers point to a preconceived, orchestrated attempt either to smear Israel, or punish Israel, depending on whether Israel was guilty or not. It could not have been merely a coincidence that this information was released only days after the Administration told the American public that the U.S. Navy "lost" a ship it was tracking. If so, then was the Administration planning on leaking this information anyway? Was it also a coincidence that those reports hit the press on the eve of Israeli Defense Minister Moshe Arens' visit to the United States?

By having the media focus on the question of whether Israel transferred American weapons to other countries it deflected public attention away from the Administration's failure not to intercept the North Korean ships. It took about one day for the American public to completely forget about the ships. The technique is a perfect way to clear damaging or embarrassing incidents out of the press: Wipe out one news item by replacing it with an even bigger story. Disinformation and illusion are the name of the game.

If Israel was guilty, why would the Administration have acted the way it did? Would the White House necessarily have wanted the world to know that Israel had double-crossed them and was not to be trusted? How could the Administration not cut all aid and sales of weapons to Israel after such a breach of trust by an ally?

One possible scenario is that Israel knew of the North Korean ships and the arms deals with Syria and Iran and told Bush and Baker, "If the loan guarantees aren't approved we'll let the cat out of the bag." At that point, Bush might have said, "Just try, and see what will happen."

Why would the Administration want Syria and Iran to have improved SCUD missiles? Because America is still trading arms for hostages. Either before or after the Gulf War, it made deals with both Syria and Iran.

One sign of a deal was the $278 million the Iranians received from America. The Administration claimed that this was a coincidence and that the money that was turned over to the Iranians was "the outcome of arbitrations dating from 1981." (Iran was seeking an out-of-court settlement of its claim for $12 billion that it says the late Shah paid for arms that were never delivered.) What a remarkable coincidence! An event from ten years ago happens at the same time the hostages are being released. While the American people were being fed this, Teheran Radio said part of the agreement included a non-retaliation pledge from the U.S. (*Newsweek*, December 16th, 1991).

Was it also by chance that it was Syria and Iran which

organized the hostage release and it was these same two countries which took delivery of the SCUDs?

Just as in the first Iran-Contra, the Americans wanted their hostages back and were willing to trade arms to get them released. In fact, it may have been a new way for the Administration to secretly arm countries: providing weapons by not reacting.

SETTLING SCORES WITH HEZBALLAH

There was another aspect to the hostage release that was yet another Bush-Baker secret agenda. It was revealed to me by my good friend Barry Chamish, author of the controversial book *The Fall of Israel*.

America was mad as hell at Hezballah for the killing of more than 300 Americans by bombing the American Embassy and the U.S. marines' barracks in the early 1980s, and for the kidnapping and torturing to death of Beirut CIA chief William Buckley. For years, America and the CIA were helpless to fight back because innocent hostages were held by Hezballah.

Yet the U.S. Army could hardly just walk into Lebanon and destroy Hezballah bases. The only way to get at Hezballah was through Israel.

In late February 1992, three Israeli soldiers were killed by Palestinian terrorists who had infiltrated a basic training camp. The next day an Israeli helicopter crew killed Sheik Abbas Musawi, the leader of the fundamentalist Hezballah Party in Lebanon. Then, in retaliation the Shiites shelled northern Israel with about a hundred Katyusha rockets over a three-day span. Following this, the Israel Defense Forces entered Lebanon to crush their bases.

On the surface, none of this makes any sense. Sunni Arabs kill Israeli soldiers, so Israel retaliates by assassinating the leader of Shiites in Lebanon, who are declared enemies of the Palestinians?

Could America have asked (i.e., demanded) Israel to wait for a serious incident and use it as a pretext to avenge Hezballah? The average Westerner cannot sort out the subtleties of Arab groups and Israel will be assumed to have reacted to an Arab atrocity in its usual manner. In fact, there was almost no White House reaction to the killing of the Hezballah leader.

Meanwhile, the very same week, Israeli police arrested two of the four new members of the Palestinian delegation to the Washington peace talks. Barely a word was heard from Washington of the arrest of half the new delegates to Baker's peace conference scheduled for a week later.

Why would Israel go along with doing America's dirty work by retaliating against the Shiites? One reason could have been for leniency at the peace table. In return for helping, America could have promised Israel that there would be no talk of returning territories or the creation of a Palestinian state, only limited autonomy. Surprisingly, the Americans have not pressured Israel to return the Golan or any parts of the West Bank. Even more surprisingly was that in the February round of peace talks it was the Palestinians who were scolded by the Administration for "grandstanding" to the media.

BUSH AND SHAMIR

The overt relationship between America and Israel can't be fully understood without considering the covert ties between their two heads of state. Both George Bush and then Israeli Prime Minister Yitzhak Shamir are products of the covert world, Bush as head of the CIA and Shamir as station chief for the Mossad in France.

Both leaders probably have rooms full of incriminating information on the other's involvement in covert (and illegal) operations. Yet neither wants to be the first to reveal anything for fear of retaliation. In fact, intelligence sources in Israel say that since April 1990, Prime Minister Shamir's Office has been gathering files and documentation on Bush's involvment in Iran-Contra.

One question which no one has sufficiently answered is: Why did Israel not retaliate against Iraqi SCUD attacks in the Persian Gulf War? What did the Administration promise (or warn) Israel if they struck back?

There could have been a deal struck that if Israel didn't retaliate it was led to believe it would get the $10 billion in U.S. loan guarantees. Then, the Administration might have reneged. Or, that deal could have been made before the Madrid conference as an inducement for Israel to release its Shiite prisoners so the Western hostages could be freed.

BUSH'S SECRET DEAL AT KENNEBUNKPORT

The granting of the loan guarantees will no doubt win Bush a few points in the Jewish community. But he was given a further hand by Rabin, who may have handed a file over to Bush's people about Hillary Clinton's involvement with the New World Fund and its contributions to the PLO. What a remarkable coincidence that these revelations should be made public just when Rabin was visiting the U.S.! Despite his statements that "Israel will in no way interfere with the American election," the new Israeli Prime Minister might have just done that by helping Bush secure the Jewish vote.

While the focus of the loan guarantees should have been on the economics of the problem—for instance, whether these monies would produce the desired result of homes and jobs for the Russian Jewish immigrants—economic principles were never discussed. For everyone involved, the issue was never about humanitarian aid for the immigrants, but rather about how to exploit them for political gain.

Former Prime Minister Yitzhak Shamir used them as a way to apply pressure on President Bush to show the Israeli people how tough he could be. The Labor Party, headed by

Yitzhak Rabin, used them in the Israeli election to convince the Russian immigrants that the Likud's failure to get the guarantees was the reason there were no jobs for them. Bush exploited them to ensure a Labor victory, and now is using them in an election gambit to secure the Jewish vote in November.

When newly elected Rabin came to the U.S. on his first official visit in early August 1992 for his head-to-head at Kennebunkport with Bush, observers of American-Israeli relations were claiming that the President's granting of loan guarantees had recharged the bilateral relations between the two countries. Yet the real change had occurred in the covert, not the overt, world.

When Bush entered the White House in 1989, he no longer needed Israel to carry out his dirty work of training and arming anti-Communist rebel groups throughout the Third World. The Cold War was winding down and Israel under the leadership of Yitzhak Shamir began to call in its markers with the White House. Over the next few years, American-Israeli relations hit an all-time low.

Those dossiers and records of Bush's involvement in Iran-Contra are now safely in the hands of Rabin's office.

What do Bush and Rabin have on each other?

In the summer of 1986, then-Vice President Bush met with Amiram Nir, Israel's advisor on terrorism to former Prime Minister Shimon Peres, at the King David Hotel in Jerusalem. Nir outlined for Bush efforts taken throughout the past year (1985-1986) "to gain the release of the hostages." He told Bush: "We are dealing with the most radical elements." That was the meeting that Bush claimed "he couldn't remember much about the briefing, nor did he fully understand what Nir was saying at the time," adding, "I didn't know what he was referring to when he was talking about radicals, nor did I ask."

Shortly before the Vice President's trip, Rabin appointed

Jonathan Pollard's recruiter, Aviem Sella, to head the Tel Nof Air Force base. In protest, Bush refused to tour any Israeli military installations, even a new air base that the Americans had helped build. Bush was mad hopping mad at Rabin since Pollard was spying on Americans during Rabin's tenure as Defense Minister. Despite Rabin and Peres' denials, Pollard was not a "rogue operation," but was passing his information directly to the Defense Ministry.

One of the reasons why Rabin escaped unscathed from the Pollard scandal was his vast knowledge of Bush's role in Iran-Contra, specifically what Nir told Bush in this meeting. Bush kept quite about Rabin's role in the Pollard affair while Rabin remained silent about Bush's knowledge of U.S. arms sales to Iran.

Did Bush give Rabin an assurance at Kennebunkport that Pollard wouldn't be released in order to keep Rabin's role in the scandal secret? Shortly after the recent Israeli elections, Yitzhak Shamir wrote a letter to President Bush formally asking him to try to seek Pollard's release. the timing of the request wasn't by coincidence—it had to do with something that Shamir had neglected to get around to while he was still Prime Minister. It was his way of striking at Bush's and Rabin's Achilles heels. Although the letter was widely reported in Israel, it never became an issue in America. Had it, it might have put Bush into a position where he might have been pressured to act.

In fact, Shamir used the same technique in the early stages of the battle over the loan guarantees. Shamir's closest advisors in the U.S. had told him not to postpone the request, arguing that the White House and American public opinion were not behind Israel, and he pressed ahead on the issue. Coming just two months before the Madrid Conference, Bush was forced to deny the request so as to save face with the Arabs.

Indeed, a new era in "strategic Israeli-American cooperation" may have already begun. Just days after Rabin's victory, one of Bush's most trusted aides and former Assistant Secretary of Defense Richard Armitage proposed joint Israeli-American aid projects for the Moslem republics of Uzbekistan, Kazakhastan, Kirgizistan, Turkemenistan, and Tadzhikistan. More than four million dollars has been allocated for the first stage of the "program."

Bush's intentions and America's secret involvement in the conflict in Yugoslavia are unknown. Has Rabin agreed to do America's dirty work again?

With Rabin serving both as Prime Minister and Defense Minister, highly secret information on joint U.S.-Israeli covert initiatives will only have to pass by *his* desk alone. Shamir was in a position to defend Israel's interests and refused to be manipulated by Bush. Rabin (and Foreign Minister Shimon Peres as well) is but a pawn in the American President's hands.

I challenge any Middle East analyst to come up with answers to these three questions: Why was it so important for the U.S. to befriend and arm Saddam Hussein and why did he refuse to oust him? Why did the White House rehabilitate Syria's President Hafez Al-Assad by shifting blame for the Lockerbie bombings to Qaddafi? Why was it only in 1989 that the American-Israeli relationship began to crumble?

Answers to these questions are the key to understanding Bush's Middle East politics.

CHAPTER 10

Did the Bush Administration Cover Up the Government's Involvement in the Bombing of Pan Am 103?

If the entire story behind the bombing of Pan Am 103 over Lockerbie, Scotland, in December 1988 is ever fully exposed, most people just simply won't believe it. Not only were various agencies of the U.S. government at least partially responsible for the terrorist attack, the Bush Administration tried to cover up its involvement. And, as Vice President, Bush is reported to have made as many as four secret trips to Damascus offering arms to Syria in return for the hostages.

If the true story behind Pan Am 103 ever finally does come out, Yuval Aviv can take much of the credit.

I met a lot of strange characters during the research for this book, but Yuval Aviv was by far the most intriguing. I met Aviv for the first time in October 1991. After a three-hour meeting, I walked out of his Madison Avenue office with my head spinning. Aviv had a certain charm about him that makes him very likable, even if you don't quite trust his information or understand his motives. He claims to be a former Mossad official who immigrated to the U.S. in 1978. Shortly after, he opened his own investigating firm, called Interfor.

Aviv told me a lot of stories, some of which I have already checked out and found to be false. Some were verified by other sources. As with most sources that investigative journalists come across, some of Aviv's information was good, some wasn't. Where Aviv does come through with flying colors, though, is his version of what happened to Pan Am 103, the plane that blew up over Lockerbie, Scotland, on December 21st, 1988.

Aviv's firm was hired by Pan Am's insurer in the spring of 1989 to investigate the crash. Of all the journalists and intelligence sources I met who knew Aviv, all of them agreed that his report on Pan Am 103 is the closest thing yet to the truth. The only problem is that what he has to say about the incident isn't what the Bush Administration wants to hear. In September 1989, Interfor's report was made public. In it, Aviv claimed that a CIA team headquartered in Western Germany is largely responsible for the bombing.

That's not what the U.S. Administration claims. For the first two years after the crash all the evidence pointed to Syria and Iran as the culprits. It was believed that Iran bankrolled the operation in retaliation for the July 3rd, 1988, shooting down of an Iranian plane killing 290 people in the Persian Gulf by the U.S.S. *Vincennes*. Previously, U.S. investigators had traced a wire transfer of several million dollars from Teheran to a bank account in Vienna controlled by the Popular Front for the Liberation of Palestine General Command under the leadership of Ahmad Jabril (*U.S. News and World Report*, November 25th, 1991).

The outbreak of the Gulf War changed all that. When Saddam's troops rolled into Kuwait, the Administration needed to bring Syria into the coalition effort. The following summer Bush sat down with Assad in Geneva and ushered in a new era in Syrian-American relations. As a result, focus had to be deflected away from Syrian-sponsored Ahmad Jabril's terrorist group.

Lo and behold, in November 1991 U.S. prosecutors announced their three-year investigation produced no evidence that either Iran or Syria were involved. Instead, they believed two Libyan intelligence officials and the Tripoli government were responsible for the bombing (*New York Times*, November

15th, 1991). President Bush would publicly remark: "The Syrians took a bum rap on this" (*Time*, April 27th, 1992).

The U.S. government based its case on a tiny piece of plastic embedded in a shirt that had come from the suitcase that held the bomb. Miraculously, it survived two harsh Scottish winters. A British forensic expert matched the fragment of the bombtimer used to destroy a French DC-10 jet that exploded over Africa nine months after the Lockerbie tragedy and found them to be identical. Based on this evidence, indictments were issued for Libyan intelligence officials. (It seems the Justice Department would have looked a little silly asking Muammar Qaddafi to turn himself in to the American authorities.)

American and British investigators speculate that Iran and Libya were plotting simultaneously to blow up an American jet, but the Libyans succeeded first. Qaddafi, it was claimed, wanted revenge for the 1986 bombing of Tripoli and Benghazi by U.S. warplanes. (Why did he wait more than two and half years to get it?) They say the bomb was first loaded as unaccompanied baggage on an Air Malta flight which departed Luqa Airport in Malta and connected with the Pan Am flight in Frankfurt. Why a terrorist would take such an indirect route and risk detection was left unexplained.

The official U.S. government's version of events is quite different than Aviv's. The former Israeli intelligence official explains that his investigation revealed that the origin of the terrorist attack was actually a rogue CIA group protecting a Syrian drug operation which transported drugs from the Middle East to the U.S. via Frankfurt. Aviv says the CIA did nothing to break up the drug operation because the traffickers were also helping them send weapons to Iran to facilitate the hostage release and to the Nicaraguan Contras.

Part of Aviv's assertions were backed up by NBC News a year later, when it reported on October 30th, 1990, that the Drug Enforcement Administration (DEA) was investigating a Middle East-based heroin operation to determine whether it was used by the terrorists to place a bomb on Pan Am 103. NBC said Pan Am flights out of Frankfurt had been used by the DEA to fly informants and heroin into Detroit as part of its sting operation. It claimed the terrorists might have discovered what the DEA was doing and switched one of their bags with one containing the bomb.

The DEA denied any connection to the undercover operation (*Barron's*, December 17th, 1990).

Aviv explains that the method of drug smuggling was quite simple. One person would check a piece of luggage onto the plane and an accomplice working in the baggage department would switch it with an identical piece containing the narcotics. He says that fatal night, a Syrian terrorist organization knew how the drug operation worked and slipped a bomb inside a suitcase on the plane.

Aviv asserts that Monzer Al-Kassar, a Syrian drug and arms smuggler, set the drug-smuggling operation up through Frankfurt in 1987. The CIA, the DEA, and the West German secret police (the BKA) observed its activities, but didn't interfere so as to acquire information. Al-Kassar is well connected. The head of Syrian intelligence, Ali Issa Duba, is his brother-in-law, and his wife is related to Syrian President Hafez Al-Assad.

This was the same Monzer Al-Kassar who helped Oliver North supply Polish-made weapons to the Nicaraguan Contras in 1985 and 1986. Along with his three brothers, Al-Kassar had built a multi-million-dollar empire on military deals in Eastern and Western Europe. Administration officials who discussed these deals said Al-Kassar had clear business links with the Abu Nidal terrorist organization (*Los Angeles Times*, July 17, 1987).

The officials said that Al-Kassar maintained offices in Warsaw and was a major broker of the Polish-owned weapons company Cenzin. The first arms purchase by North from Al-Kassar, totaling $1 million, was sent by boat to an unidentified Caribbean port in the fall of 1985 and was later distributed to the Contra fighters. In April of that year a second shipment of

Polish arms was sold to the CIA as part of this transaction (*Los Angeles Times*, July 17th, 1987). In another part of the deal, more than $42 million was laundered through BCCI bank accounts in the Cayman Islands. Al-Kassar earned more than $1 million (*Private Eye*, October 25th, 1991).

Aviv wrote in his report that a special hostage rescue team was on the doomed aircraft led by army Major Charles McKee, who had discovered that a rogue CIA team in Frankfurt, called COREA, was protecting the drug route. According to a special report in *Time*, COREA used front companies for its overseas operations: Sevens Mantra Corp, AMA Industries, Wilderwood Video and Condor Television Ltd. The report revealed that Condor did its banking through the First American Bank, a subsidiary of the Bank of Credit and Commerce International.

After explaining what he had learned to CIA headquarters in the U.S. and receiving no response, McKee decided to take his men home without the required permission. He planned to bring back to the U.S. proof of the rogue intelligence team's connection to Al-Kassar. If the government tried to cover it up, he would release the information. Al-Kassar discovered this and reported McKee's attempt to make their own "travel arrangements" back to the U.S. through the rogue CIA team in Frankfurt (*Covert Action*, No. 34, Summer 1990).

Although neglected in the American press, there were at least four, and possibly as many as eight, CIA and other U.S. intelligence agency operatives from Beirut aboard Pan Am 103 (*Covert Action*, No. 34, Summer 1990). Could they have been the target? In his book *Lockerbie: The Tragedy of Flight 103*, David Johnson disclosed that the CIA investigators removed a suitcase from the crash site that belonged to McKee. It was returned a few days later, and "found" empty.

The PBS investigative program *Frontline* reported in January 1990 that the bomb was put on the plane at London's Heathrow Airport, where a baggage handler switched suitcases belonging to CIA officer Matthew Gannon. According to the

Frontline investigation, the only piece of luggage not accounted for from the flight belonged to Gannon.

Frontline claims the intelligence officials were a "strong secondary target." A May 1989 report in the Arabic newspaper *Al-Dustur* revealed that McKee's team's movements were being monitored by David Lovejoy, "an American agent" who Aviv claims was passing information to the Iranian Embassy in Beirut, which told the Iranian chargé d'affaires of the team's travel plans (*Time*, April 27th, 1992).

Aviv believes that the CIA team in Frankfurt allowed Al-Kassar to continue to smuggle drugs into the U.S. in return for help in arranging the release of the American hostages. The drug operation, he says, went as far back as spring 1987.

In the fall of 1988, the Syrian-based Popular Front for the Liberation of Palestine leader, Ahmad Jabril, discovered the operation. So as not to interfere with Al-Kassar's activities, Jabril originally targeted an American Airlines plane, but the Mossad discovered this and tipped off the airline. When the plan changed and the target became a Pan Am airliner, once again a Mossad agent tipped off German secret police 24 hours before the flight. When a BKA surveillance agent keeping watch over the suitcase supposedly filled with drugs noticed that this time the luggage was a different color and size, he passed this information on to the CIA team, who relayed this to their superiors. These reportedly said, "Don't worry about it. Don't stop it—let it go" (*Barron's*, December 17th, 1990).

Aviv says the BKA did just that.

A lengthy article on Aviv's report in the financial weekly *Barron's* quotes one Mideast intelligence specialist in the government as suggesting: "Do I think the CIA was involved? Of course they were involved. And they screwed up. Was the operation planned by the top? Probably not. I doubt they sanctioned heroin importation—that came about at the more zealous lower levels. But they knew what was going on and didn't care." The expert went on to say that his agency has "things that support Aviv's allegation, but we can't prove it. We have no smoking gun. And until the other agencies of the government open their doors, we will have no smoking gun."

These government agencies didn't open their doors. In September 1989 Pan Am subpoenaed the FBI, CIA, FAA, DEA, National Security Council, National Security Agency, Defense Intelligence Agency, and the State Department requesting documents relating to the case. According to Pan Am's attorney Gregory Buhler, "the government quashed the subpoenas on grounds of national security" (*Barron's*, December 17th, 1990).

Further signs of a cover-up were revealed by investigative columnist Jack Anderson, who claimed that President Bush and British Prime Minister Margaret Thatcher held a transatlantic phone conversation after Bush's inauguration in which they agreed that the investigation into the case should be "limited" in order to avoid harming the two nations' intelligence communities. Thatcher has acknowledged that the conversation took place, but denied she and Bush conspired to interfere with the investigation (*Covert Action*, No. 34, Summer 1990).

In its investigative report, *Time* revealed that a former agent for the Defense Intelligence Agency (DIA), Lester Knox Coleman III, has signed an affidavit which described the CIA-sanctioned operation. In 1987 Coleman was transferred to the Drug Enforcement Agency (DEA) and was assigned to Cyprus, where he witnessed the growing trade in heroin originating in Lebanon. Coleman's DEA front in Nicosia was the Eurame Trading Co. Ltd., located near the U.S. Embassy. His job was to keep track of Al-Kassar's movement and report to the DEA attaché in Cyprus, Michael Hurley. Coleman says he was paid in checks drawn on the BCCI branch in Luxembourg (April 27th, 1992).

A number of investigative journalists believe that Aviv stumbled onto just one piece of a larger puzzle. In August 1991, Larry Cohler, a writer for the *Washington Jewish Week*, reported on a set of secret negotiations which took place between Syria and the United States government over the release of the hostages and which led to a number of covert trips by Bush to Damascus.

Over an all-you-can-eat Indian lunch one afternoon, Cohler told me an incredible story that complements Aviv's conclusions.

According to a confidential Pentagon memo that Cohler gained access to, for reasons still unknown, officials in the Reagan Administration failed to pursue a series of Syrian offers to free the American hostages held in Lebanon. The Syrian overtures began in 1985 and continued through mid-1989.

A number of former government officials involved in the secret Syrian negotiations say they were never told why the Syrian offers were not acted upon, while others say the Syrian offers were not genuine. Still others claim there was too little preliminary action by the U.S. government to determine for certain whether the initiatives were genuine or not (*San Francisco Chronicle*, July 21st, 1991).

The center of the controversy was a memo dated March 17, 1987, which described a meeting attended by Lawrence Ropka, Jr., a principal deputy of Assistant Secretary of Defense for National Security Affairs Richard Armitage. Written by Ropka's military assistant, Lt. Andrew Gambara, it claimed that American businessmen and a former executive secretary to Richard Nixon, Robert D. Ladd, told Pentagon officials in December 1985 that he had a contact with a Lebanese businessman who introduced him to Fasih Makhail Ashi, a judge in Syria's Inspector General's Office. The judge claimed he had information regarding the fate of the seven American hostages held in Lebanon. Ashi said that the Syrians were "prepared to assist in the release of the hostages if Reagan called Assad and requested his support" (*San Francisco Chronicle*, July 21, 1991).

Syria's aims were simple enough. It wanted closer ties with

the U.S. The memo said that once Reagan called, "Syria would facilitate the release and transfer of the hostages without any *quid pro quo* from the U.S." It said further that Ladd had already brought this to the attention of Oliver North at the NSC and that someone would follow it up. A former official in Armitage's office said the memo was sent to a special government agency, the Vice President's Task Force on Terrorism, a group of high-ranking officials from the White House, State Department, NSC, CIA, and other intelligence agencies headed by George Bush.

Two of Armitage's aides acknowledged that the Syrian initiative was discussed during a number of interviews with Ladd and his attorney. Ladd said that after hearing the Syrian offer he arranged for Ashi to come to the U.S. to be questioned over a period of days by the Task Force. Ashi asserts he spoke in the name of General Ghaza Kenan, head of Syrian military intelligence, and even passed on details about the fate of the kidnapped CIA chief in Beirut, William Buckley.

Ashi returned to Syria but received no reply. In February 1987 he contacted Ladd, and again said Syria would help the Americans release the hostages. Ladd tried unsuccessfully to persuade government officials to meet in Paris with Ashi. A longtime senior aide to Armitage claimed Ashi could not prove the offer was genuine. "It was my sense there was nothing there," he said (*San Francisco Examiner*, July 21st, 1991). "I was told there wasn't enough information from Ashi to run it upstairs."

However, a former official in Armitage's office said that he thought Ashi's overtures should at least be checked out, as the American government could have sent someone from the Paris Embassy to meet him. Ladd said that only because of his persistence U.S. intelligence officials eventually agreed to meet with Achi. Then, in the early part of the summer of 1989 the CIA, without any explanation, canceled the meeting.

Despite the cancellation, Ashi called Ladd back, saying that the hostages would be released if Ladd would come to Damascus for them. In August Ladd was prepared to fly to Damascus when Ashi called back to take back the offer, saying that a tug-of-war over releasing the hostages had developed between Kenan and other factions of the Syrian Army.

The congressional investigators did look into why the Administration didn't follow up on these initiatives and why, when Syria offered to help release the hostages, they were put on hold. They questioned a number of individuals, including a former Pentagon official, Peter Probst, who took part in some of the meetings. He told Cohler that it was one of several he and other officials had with Ladd on the Syrian overture. He said nothing further on the matter.

Could the Administration have been pursuing another path to free the hostages? Cohler learned from different sources that Bush made as many as four secret trips to Damascus in early 1986, allegedly offering arms to Syria in return for the hostages. Congressional investigators were told by their sources that in the spring of 1988, in the middle of the presidential campaign, Bush made one final trip to Syria telling the Syrians that the time was right to make a deal. Then, the Syrians stalled.

At that point the Syrians might have grasped the leverage they actually had over Bush and wanted to up the ante (*In These Times*, August 7th, 1991). It's also possible that Bush might have been attempting an "October Surprise" of his own by having the hostages delivered to a Republican White House just in *Time* for the presidential election in November 1988.

Aviv says that when these overtures failed, Bush and the CIA turned to Al-Kassar as a middleman. (A covert deal made with drug smugglers is less likely to be exposed than one with a government or head of state.) Al-Kassar had some experience in these types of operations and at least one victory under his belt: he was used by the French government in March 1988 to free its hostages held in captivity in Lebanon.

George Bush may have wanted the same deal.

CHAPTER 11

What Was President Bush's Secret Agenda in the Gulf War?

Was Desert Storm another George Bush secret agenda? A mixture of public disinformation, media deflection, and a few mirrors? Did George Bush desperately want a war in the Persian Gulf? Did he arrange it?

The mystery of the Gulf War lies in the President's actions: Why did he order General Schwarzkopf to cease the ground attack after only 100 hours and not destroy Saddam Hussein when he had the chance? How could it be that the man the American people were told was as evil as Hitler was allowed to remain in power? Why instead of being dead or deposed, does he still pose a threat to his neighbors?

Why did the Administration literally have to be "forced" to help the Kurds? Bush had no sooner finished bombing Iraq back to the Stone Age when the Administration announced that it couldn't help the Kurds because that would be interfering with the internal affairs of a sovereign state (Iraq). Somehow the American people bought that line that Bush was seriously upset over being forced to interfere in Iraq's affairs. This was at the same time he was urging Iraqis to overthrow Saddam.

Why didn't America get rid of Saddam Hussein? Because the last thing the Saudis wanted was an Iraq run by Shiites. Saddam Hussein is better than an Iraq with no clear leader. America also wanted to keep Iraq territorially intact to offset the ambitions of other would-be regional powers, such as Iran and Syria.

Hussein also plays a useful role for the President. He's a

perceived enemy. Like Qaddafi and Khomeini before him, Hussein serves as a focal point. Bush realizes that the American public will buy simple messages, such as "They're evil, we're good. They support international terrorism. We fight international terrorism. Therefore they're evil, we're good."

If none of this makes any sense it is because the Gulf War was a covert operation and, like most covert operations, if you don't know the reasoning behind the secret agenda, from the outside everything looks absurd.

Now, with all the talk of SCUD missiles that didn't get destroyed and an existing Iraqi nuclear threat, Bush is portraying Hussein as an enemy all over again. As the election nears, the rhetoric will will intensify so that the American people have a simple message to remember: "Bush is tough on dictators. He kicked Saddam's butt." No doubt Bush's election message will remind Americans how the Gulf War was a great victory. It wasn't, but the truth doesn't matter. What's important is the image given to the media and hence to the American public.

WAS THERE AN AMERICAN PLOT TO SUCKER HUSSEIN INTO INVADING KUWAIT?

It remains a mystery as to why in late July the Kuwaitis weren't trembling with fear as 500 Iraqi tanks and 100,000 troops poised on their border. Instead of trying to appease him, they mustered up the courage to stand up to Saddam, even snubbing their noses at him. Yet literally minutes after the first cannon shot was fired, the Kuwaiti royal family were on planes bound for their short life in exile.

Could President Bush have tricked Hussein into believing that the U.S. would sit back and do nothing if he invaded Kuwait?

In the best tradition of his mentor, General Henry Stimson, Bush believed that it was time for America to go to war to boost national pride and to rid the country of the Vietnam complex for good. The scandal over the collapse of the nation's savings and loans was in the headlines. Neil Bush was in trouble. For President Bush, there was no better time for a war.

Nor is it too difficult to believe that Saddam would think that with all the support and aid he had received from the U.S., the last thing he expected the Americans to do would be to wage war on him. All Bush had to do was lead Hussein to believe that the U.S. wouldn't interfere if he invaded Kuwait.

What about a secret deal between the United States and Saudi Arabia? We may never know, because Bush refused to explain what he was referring to when he informed Congress on August 9th, 1990, that he received "requests" from King Fahd and Kuwait. Months later, when asked, the Administration would still not reveal either to the House or the Senate the nature of these "requests" or the U.S. response to them. This refusal violated the Case-Zablocki Act of 1972, which obliges the Secretary of State to submit to Congress within 60 days the substance of all international accords, written or oral (*Time*, November 19th, 1990).

Secret cooperation between the Kuwaitis and the CIA certainly existed before August 1990. A document released to Reuters news agency after the Iraqi invasion of Kuwait revealed that Brigadier General Fahd Ahmad-al-Fahd, the chief of the Emir's security forces, visited the CIA, November 12-18, 1989, and met with CIA chief William Webster. Part of the agreement was to train 128 of the Emir's personal body-guards, as well as securing American help in computerizing the Kuwaiti State Security Department. The CIA admitted that Webster met Al-Fahd, but called the document a forgery (*Village Voice*, March 5th, 1991).

Another secret agreement may have led directly to Hussein's invasion. A summit was held in Jidda, Saudi Arabia, on July 31st, 1990, between Hussein, Saudi King Fahd, and the Emir of Kuwait. Kuwait pledged $10 billion to Iraq to help pay its war debts.

In May 1990 at a Gulf Cooperation Council meeting, Saddam had demanded $30 billion. The Kuwaitis eventually reneged on the $10 billion offer and told Saddam they would only contribute $500,000. Thus it's possible that Hussein might have moved his troops up to the Kuwaiti border as a means to pressure Kuwait into coughing up more money (*Village Voice*, March 5th, 1991).

Jordan's King Hussein intervened in the negotiations and tried to convince the Kuwaiti royal family to be more conciliatory towards Iraq, urging Kuwait not to underestimate the Iraqis. However, Sheikh Sabeh told him, "We are not going to respond to Iraq. . . . If they don't like it, let them occupy our territory . . . we are going to bring in the Americans" (*Village Voice*, March 5th, 1991).

A few days later King Hussein claims the Emir told his senior military officers that if the Iraqis invaded, they must hold them off for 24 hours. He is reportedly to have told them that "American and foreign forces would land in Kuwait and expel them."

In a note to Saudi King Fahd, the Emir of Kuwait said: "We are stronger than they [the Iraqis] think."

WHAT DID APRIL GLASPIE TELL SADDAM HUSSEIN?

Did U.S. Ambassador to Iraq April Glaspie deliberately mislead Saddam Hussein as part of a premeditated effort to encourage him to attack Kuwait, thus giving Bush a pretext for moving troops into the region? If so, did she then take the rap for Bush?

In September 1990, Saddam Hussein released a transcript to the Western press of his July 25th conversation with Glaspie. It indicates that Glaspie told him that the U.S. had "no opinion" about Iraq's dispute with Kuwait or other such "Arab-Arab" issues. The tone of the text was conciliatory, leaving Hussein with the impression that the U.S. wouldn't interfere if he invaded Kuwait.

The State Department never commented on the Iraqi transcripts. It was only in March 1991, when Glaspie testified before Congress, that she responded to the text, calling it "a total fabrication" and "disinformation." She says it omitted her "tough talk" and distorted her words.

Why did it take more than seven months for the Administration to let her respond? The State Department claimed the Administration didn't want to "damage its sensitive negotiations with Hussein" (Obviously, Bush comparing Hussein to Hitler a few hundred times *during that time* didn't jeopardize these negotiations.)

When the House and Senate asked to see the cables Glaspie sent to the State Department after the July 25th meeting, Secretary of State Baker initially refused. He claimed that, if made public, they would have violated the confidentiality of diplomatic cables, making foreign leaders reluctant to speak with U.S. ambassadors.

During her testimony in front of Congress in March 1991, Glaspie says she repeatedly warned Hussein not to use violence in his border dispute with Kuwait. She claims the Iraqi leader ignored these warnings because he was too "stupid" to understand how the U.S. would act (*New York Times*, March 21st, 1991).

In July 1991, when the cables were finally declassified, a group of Senators concluded that there were major discrepancies in Glaspie's testimony. Chairman of the Senate Foreign Relations Committee Senator Claibourne Pell (D-Rhode Island) said Glaspie's version of the events were "inconsistent" with the cables. Senator Alan Cranston (D-California) charged that Glaspie "deliberately misled the Congress about her role in the Persian Gulf tragedy" (*New York Times*, July 12th, 1991).

When asked by Senator Joseph Biden what she told Saddam about U.S. intentions, she replied: "I told him orally that the U.S. would protect Kuwait, which it considered its vital interest in the region" (*Washington Post*, July 12th, 1991). Says Pell: "In no place does she report clearly delivering the kind of warning she described in her testimony to the committee" (*New York Times*, July 12th, 1991).

When the cables from Glaspie to the State Department were released they clearly showed that Glaspie was lying, possibly to protect either Baker or Bush. So, why, then did the Bush Administration declassify the cables? Playwright and novelist Steve Tesich offers one possible reason:

"The fact that the Bush Administration felt safe in declassifying those cables shows it was no longer afraid of the truth because it knows that the truth will have little impact on us. The Administration's message to us was this: We've given you a glorious victory and we've given you back your self-esteem. Now here's the truth. Which do you prefer?" (*The Nation*, January 6th, 1992).

AMERICA DIDN'T GO TO WAR TO SAVE KUWAIT

An equally important question as to why Bush wanted to take the U.S. to war in the Persian Gulf is how he prepared the American public to accept this decision.

One method was to convince the American people that the Kuwaitis were the victims of horrendous atrocities perpetrated by invading Iraqi soldiers. By creating sympathy for the Kuwaiti people, Bush was able to thrust his war aims through Congress.

The Washington-based Hill and Knowlton (H&K) public relations firm played a major role in this effort. H&K was paid $5.6 million to improve Kuwait's image in the U.S. after the Iraqi invasion in August 1990.

H&K claimed that they were working for an exile-based group, Citizens for a Free Kuwait, and not specifically for a foreign government. However, when ABC's John Martin checked documents filed with various government agencies registering "Citizens for a Free Kuwait," they revealed that nearly all of the $12 million to fund the group had come directly from the government of Kuwait.

"I resent that on an issue that should be decided by information from experts so much is being spent to influence me and the American public," said Congressman James A. Hayes, a Democrat from Louisiana who supported President Bush's decision to send U.S. troops to the Gulf. "This serious cause is being advertised like T-shirts or basketball shoes. That's immoral" (*Washington Post*, December 19th, 1990).

A major problem H&K faced was the image of Kuwait in America, particularly its lack of democracy and poor record on human rights. To change this image, H&K paid more than a million dollars to the polling company of Wirthlin Group, which organized "focus groups" to determine what would "move" or "upset" the American people. They discovered that atrocity stories would be the best stimulus.

On November 27th, 1990, a few days before the UN Security Council voted whether to employ military force if Iraq did not remove its armed forces from Kuwait by January 15th, H&K went to work. They plastered the walls of the Council chamber with vivid photos allegedly of Kuwaitis who had been killed, tortured, and mutilated by Iraqi soldiers. This was done without any prior permission from the Security Council members. The display was sponsored by "Citizens for a Free Kuwait."

How did H&K "hijack" the UN Security Council for the benefit of one of its clients?

Investigative journalist Arthur Rowse looked into the affair and discovered that it was probably due to the high-level connections the firm maintained with the White House. Its president and chief executive officer was Craig Fuller, who previously served as Bush's chief of staff during the two Reagan Administrations. Robert Gray, founder of Gray and

Co. which merged with H&K in 1986, was a longtime Republican Party insider who served as Ronald Reagan's inaugural committee co-chairman in 1981, and was a close friend of President Bush and White House Counsel C. Boyden Gray.

Rowse reports that during an address to the Public Relations Society of America meeting in New York City, H&K's Managing Director Donald Deaton boasted: "Once President Bush had ordered U.S. troops to Saudi Arabia last August [1990] the information needed to form value judgments about this action was generally unavailable—as well as any effective mechanism by which Kuwaiti citizens could tell their story to the American people" (*The Progressive*, May 1991).

In Deaton's own words, a private public relations firm's efforts helped persuade the United States to go to war.

Five weeks before the UN Security Council display, on October 10th, 1990, the U.S. House of Representatives was treated to a similar session by H&K. The firm's chief lobbyist, Gary Hymel, told Rowse that he had lined up the witnesses and helped prepare their testimony, including a twelve-minute videotape which detailed alleged atrocities committed by the Iraqis. On January 8th, 1991, another "performance" was staged for the House Foreign Affairs Committee.

Another "coup" for H&K was the charge that Iraqi soldiers had allowed 312 infants to die after being removed from their incubators at three hospitals. It wasn't until after the war was fought that these accusations were found not to be true. Chris Hedges of the *New York Times* interviewed Kuwaiti hospital authorities, who said the charges were false. On March 15th, 1991, John Martin of ABC News spoke with Kuwaiti health officials, who also verified that the incubator story was not correct.

However, that one incident may have influenced the Congress enough for it to support President Bush's request to go to war. ABC's Martin reported in January 1991 that in the Senate, seven senators mentioned the incubator atrocity in the debate over whether to go to war. In the House, a leading proponent for the war, Representative Henry Hyde of Illinois, declared: "Now is the time to check the aggression of this ruthless dictator, whose troops have bayoneted pregnant women and have ripped babies from their incubators in Kuwait."

Arthur Rowse discovered that H&K spent nearly $650,000 to produce video news releases, which were broadcasted by many television stations. Medialink, a distributor of these types of electronic press releases, claims that two of H&K's videos made their "top ten list" in total number of viewers who saw them. One of the pieces on the destruction in Kuwait was seen by more than 60 million Americans. Another, which surveyed the violations of human rights in Kuwait by the Iraqis, was watched by more than 35 million viewers.

Rowse also found that while H&K may not have had anything to do with the publication of the 154-page book *The Rape of Kuwait*, by Knightsbridge Publishing Company, the small publishing house in New York City ran a first printing of 1.2 million copies and pursued a heavy advertising campaign in the media. Knightsbridge denies that either H&K or the Kuwaiti government subsidized the book; however, it is very unusual for a small publisher to print more than a few hundred thousand copies of a paperback and have enough money left over to run a promotional campaign in major media outlets. The Kuwaiti Embassy in Washington told Rowse that it had purchased 200,000 copies and the Citizens for a Free Kuwait obtained enough copies of the book to include it in the thousands of information packages prepared and distributed to the public by H&K.

It's anyone's guess as to how different events in the Persian Gulf would have turned out had H&K not been involved in the effort to convince the American public that it was necessary for them to go to war to save the Kuwaiti people.

Says Congressman James Hayes: "It's illegal for me to accept campaign money from a foreign government. It should also be illegal for a foreign government to pay a third party to bankroll a political campaign in the United States" (*The Progressive*, May 1991).

THE $200 BILLION REASON AMERICA NEEDED A WAR IN THE MIDDLE EAST

Operation Desert Storm wasn't about Kuwait. It was about Saudi Arabia. Bush wanted that war. He needed a war in the Middle East to determine whether the $200 billion investment in CENTCOM, a combination of communication and air defense systems, infrastructure, and weaponry, would work.

Former National Security Advisor Frank Carlucci claims: "We created in the Pentagon CENTCOM, a separate command for the Middle East to serve America's military purposes in the region."

In addition to containing 60 percent of the world's known oil reserves, the Persian Gulf is in the soft underbelly of the Soviet Union. It completes a circle of U.S. influence in the Middle East: Egypt, Turkey, and Pakistan.

CENTCOM was vital to American interests in the region. It was also an integral part of the covert U.S.-Saudi relationship, itself one of the best-kept secrets of the Reagan and Bush Administrations.

Scott Armstrong, a former reporter for the *Washington Post*, an investigator for the Senate Watergate Committee, and coauthor with Bob Woodward of *The Brethren*, has followed this covert relationship since the AWACS debate in the early days of Reagan's first administration. The most sophisticated part of the CENTCOM system is its Command, Control, Communications, and Intelligence capabilities. It is much more than the ability of computers to network information. It's able to create an accurate picture of all data available. Although it is probably the most advanced system of its type in the world, it's worthless without its U.S. technicians and servicemen operators.

Armstrong says that, along with CENTCOM, the series of bases the Americans have built in Saudi Arabia were crucial to Desert Storm. Had they not been there, it might have taken a year or two to defeat Iraq. Had the CENTCOM network not been in place, he doubts the Administration would have pushed for the war.

"Bush wanted to breathe life into the bases. Without them we wouldn't have known what targets were hit, or what the enemy was up to. More SCUDS would have hit Saudi Arabia and Israel. The system is the reason why the Iraqi air force didn't get off the ground. Radar, missiles and planes would have operated with less than one-quarter their efficiency and accuracy. Decisions could be taken in hours which would have taken weeks or even months in other battlefields. Would we still have won? Yes, but not without losing 30,000 or 40,000 lives" (*Mother Jones*, November/December 1991).

Some Reagan Administration officials, like former Defense Secretary Caspar Weinberger, contend that the reason for the AWACS sale was strictly "to give greater defense capacity to Saudi Arabia" (interview with author, November 7th, 1991). Others, like Geoffrey Kemp, who was a member of the National Security Council, concede: "The Saudi Arabian bases were a part of the overall game plan."

Armstrong points out that there is no written treaty between Saudi Arabia and the United States. Congress knows only that the U.S. has a strategic relationship with the Saudis, but it doesn't know the details of it.

"Although no defense pact exists," says Armstrong, "the U.S. does, however, have an 'unwritten' but explicit obligation to defend the Saudi royal family. Both sides realize that if the two countries exchanged a piece of paper with a signature on it, it would be considered a treaty and would have to be presented to Congress, which might not ratify it.

AWACS," he points out, "passed by only two votes in a Congress controlled by the Republicans. Would Congress accept America's commitments to NATO if they were simply the result of a series of discreet decisions? This is exactly the relationship the U.S. has to the Saudis."

It was the AWACS debate, which Armstrong covered for the *Washington Post*, that first started his investigation into America's secret relationship with the Saudis. He says that the figures that were being given to Congress about the scope of the sale were slanted. While the Administration claimed the value of the military equipment being sold to Saudi Arabia was $550 million, it was at least ten times that much.

Also, more than 90 percent of the value of the deal was left unaccounted for. The AWACS deal provided a cover for the construction of the bases, since only about $50 million of the entire $5.5 billion package was for the AWACS planes. Armstrong says he was told by Richard Secord, then Deputy Assistant Secretary of Defense for the Middle East, that 90 percent of the arms package was for "spares, training, and ground equipment."

"Nobody asked how could it be that the planes only made up 10 percent of the value of the contracts," says Armstrong.

With the American public focused on the AWACS planes, the rest of the deal snuck through. To keep the debate out of the public eye, the Saudis agreed to an American plan for a simple oral understanding between the then head of the Saudi air force, Colonel Fahd Abdullah, and chief of the U.S. military group in Saudi Arabia, Major General Charles L. Donnelly, Jr. (*Mother Jones*, November/December 1991).

Armstrong maintains that the key issue in this "secret agenda" was to minimize congressional review by breaking down military purchases into smaller packages that were below the dollar limits requiring congressional approval. One method used was that instead of purchasing military aircraft, the Saudis acquired commercial jets and upgraded them to military specification with avionics obtained from other countries.

Little press or congressional attention was paid to these deals because the Administration used private corporate think tanks, such as Boeing Corp., BDM Corp., and Mitre Corp., to advise the Saudis on how to construct the overall system. Mitre told the Saudis how to integrate their radar, missile systems, fighters, and command-communication posts into one network, similar to the NORAD system in the U.S. or NATO's NADGE. The country was divided into five regions with each having its own system and operating center, linked together into a central headquarters by satellite. Armstrong says that each was capable of commanding an air war from Egypt to Pakistan, or from the southern Soviet Union to the Indian Ocean.

When he checked on the Saudi side, Armstrong found that the AWACS sale was part of a deal that involved sending the U.S. Rapid Deployment Force to the region in the event of war. The Saudis agreed that they would pre-position essential material for the Rapid Deployment Force to use. Through all this, Armstrong discovered that the series of superbases and weapons systems for use by the U.S. in event of a war were all "off the books."

Little was heard about the secret bases after the AWACS sales were approved. A few years later Pentagon sources told Armstrong that information on the matter had been compartmentalized and that members of the cabinet, and the NSC, and even the President didn't really know all the details. Oliver North would later tell him it was part of a "loose arrangement" between the U.S. and Saudi Arabia.

The major question now is: What type of access will the U.S. have to these networks of bases and weapons systems in the future? The Saudis want to minimize the U.S. presence on their soil while at the same time they realize there has to a significant-enough presence of the U.S. military to serve as a viable deterrent.

"The U.S. wants to preposition equipment there but the Saudis say no, we will man the bases," says Armstrong. "The U.S. says we can't rely on non-U.S. servicemen to operate the equipment. I believe Secretary of Defense Dick Chaney promised the Saudis that the secret relationship could continue in secret, and that no admission of a permanent U.S. base would be made nor would there be any public treaty."

According to the Constitution, the President can sign a defense treaty with a foreign government only with the consent of the Senate. Carrying out foreign policy in secret, behind the backs of Congress and the American people, may be unconstitutional, but that didn't stop the the Reagan and Bush Administrations.

Secret agendas weren't meant to be discussed in the Halls of Congress.

HOW THE WHITE HOUSE COVERED UP ITS SUPPORT FOR SADDAM HUSSEIN

It isn't only the mountain of evidence which ties the Bush and Reagan Administrations to the arming or Iraq that is so alarming, but also the extent to which the Bush White House went to try to cover up these policies after they were discovered following the Persian Gulf War.

Take the case of Robert Bickel. Bickel claims that he uncovered evidence that the Bush Administration colluded with Iraqi officials to help Saddam Hussein to obtain advanced weapons systems, some of which were instrumental in providing Iraq with nuclear weapons capabilities.

Bickel was a former U.S. Customs informant. A series of documents provided by Bickel, sent to Iran-Contra Independent Counsel Lawrence Walsh in November 1990, expose "the activities not only of the Iraqi government and its agents but also the activities of the U.S. government, its senior officials, and its agencies in assisting and supporting the Iraqi acquisition. This includes support of these activities by senior officials in the administration and agencies of our government including Department of Agriculture, Department of State, Department of Commerce, Central Intelligence Agency, Federal Bureau of Investigation, Foreign Counter Intelligence and U.S. Customs Service in quashing legitimate investigations of these illegal activities and in maintaining the covert nature of these activities by operating to discredit individual citizens who have come forward to report suspected violations" (Unclassified, December 1990; *Newspaper for the Association of National Security Alumni*, page 2).

Bickel was hired as a consultant to Southern Brokers International (SBI) of Houston, Texas, in 1989 to acquire technical equipment for a client who, he was told, was a purchasing agent for the Iraqi defense ministry. The equipment involved was all subject to U.S. arms exports controls and Bickel reported this to U.S. Customs, which then initiated an investigation.

Bickel told C. A. (Tony) Hardin, the head of SBI, of his report to Customs. Hardin told him that he was acting as a CIA asset. After a few meetings between Hardin and Customs, the investigation was canceled and the Iraqi agent was able to purchase all the equipment requested.

More than a year later Bickel was working with Kenneth Brumfield, a regional coordinating officer for U.S. Customs, on a report on the use of U.S. oil and gas technology for covert or military use by foreign governments as part of an effort by Customs to stifle the export of these types of technology to hostile states. Bickel claimed that a certain type of gamma-ray neutron exploration device which had already been sent to Iraq could be used as a nuclear-bomb detonator. While the device is used to measure geological formations in oil wells, it also has an application, when modified, to shoot a neutron beam into plutonium, which would trigger a chain reaction and hence a nuclear explosion. When UN inspectors searched

Iraq's nuclear facilities in September 1991, they found documents which indicated Iraq was going to use a neutron pulse to trigger its nuclear bombs. The Halliburton Company in Texas, which was the chief supplier of these items to the Iraqi defense ministry, had exported them without a valid license (*The Forward*, March 20th, 1992).

Bickel also told Brumfield about the aborted 1989 investigation. Just before Brumfield was going to give his report before a gathering of regional Customs directors in Washington, he was told to return to Houston, and was indicted for making nine false statements in an unrelated grand jury investigation. Brumfield claims he was set up because of his technology investigation, and remains suspended from his official duties.

It's believed Bickel had secretly copied and distributed to certain people confidential internal Customs Service documents relating to the investigation of Iraqi arms acquisitions, and how and why the investigations were stopped. Currently, the House's Government Operations Subcommittee on Mismanagement and Misconduct is investigating the Bickel case. Texas Democrat Henry Gonzalez, who is chairman of the House Banking Committee, claims the cover-up is being run directly out of the National Security Council and the White House.

Attempts to uncover how the Atlanta branch of the Italian bank Banca Nazionale del Lavoro (BNL) gave Iraq more than $4 billion in loans were also hampered by the Bush White House. The Administration seemed to be more concerned with damage control than with rooting out corruption at the bank. After the FBI had raided BNL's offices on August 4th, 1989, the CIA's Director of Intelligence wrote in a memo on November 6th that "the loss of BNL financing, and, more important, any reducing in U.S. agricultural credit guarantees because of negative publicity about the scandal, probably would damage U.S.-Iraqi commercial ties" (*New York Times*,

March 20th, 1992).

Robert L. Barr, Jr., the former United States Attorney in Atlanta, was prepared to return an indictment against certain Iraqi officials in October 1989, but after being passed on to the Justice Department in Washington, it was never returned.

Government investigators in the case have repeatedly claimed that the Administration has hampered their work and that the State Department has restricted them from traveling abroad to interview witnesses and suspects who figured prominently in the BNL case. They also charge that they were discouraged from filing criminal charges against the Central Bank of Iraq and that the Justice Department requested in 1989 and 1990 that the Federal Reserve Bank in New York and Washington, D.C., delay regulatory action against BNL (*New York Times*, May 3rd, 1992, March 20th, 1992).

When Congress raised questions about whether Secretary of State James Baker personally telephoned Clayton Yeutter, then Secretary of Agriculture, to intervene and ensure that Iraq received a billion dollars in agricultural loan guarantees, the Administration tried to limit the information it provided to Congress.

After a meeting on April 8th, 1991, Special Assistant to President Bush C. Nicholas Rostow wrote a memo to department officials saying that "alternatives to providing documents should be explored." Rostow told the various agencies being subpoenaed to give verbal briefings to Congress and not to deliver crucial documents, as well as explained how withholding information could be justified on national security and foreign relations grounds (*Los Angeles Times*, March 8th, 1992).

"The Agricultural Department clearly misled me and my subcommittee," Charlie Rose, chairman of the House Agricultural Committee subcommittee recently said. "Clearly, there was pressure at the highest levels of the Bush Administration to see that Iraq got continuing and large amounts of loan guarantees, although the Administration knew there were abuses and kickbacks" (*Los Angeles Times*, March 8th, 1992).

Said Senate Agriculture Committee Chairman Patrick J. Leahy: "I am very concerned that in an effort to cover up its secret dealings to aid Saddam Hussein, the Administration refused to tell the American people the truth. At a time when Saddam Hussein was expanding his military operations, the Administration ignored its own experts and used taxpayer money to secretly help Iraq" (*Los Angeles Times*, March 8th, 1992).

Another attempted cover-up was the Commerce Department's issuing of licenses for goods to be shipped to Iraq. Congressional investigators claim that there were numerous instances where the phrase "military use" was removed from the license for products and technologies sent to Iraq.

Despite the power of subpoena, with more than 100 of them already issued by congressional investigators, important records were still being kept from Congress.

Texan Henry Gonzalez summed up the attempted cover-up best by saying: "It used to be that cover-ups were sort of ad hoc events—a mad scramble to provide damage control. The Rostow Gang advances the notion that cover-up mechanisms have become an integral cog in the machinery of the Bush Administration" (*Washington Post*, March 17th, 1992).

President Bush has yet to face any serious questions over what he might know of the pressure exerted by people in his Administration to grant Iraq loan guarantees, or what U.S. government agencies know about the BNL scandal, or of the transfer of military technology to Iraq. But is it possible that the Administration and the President were not involved in or aware of the buildup of Iraqi conventional and unconventional weapons capabilities? This is the same question as whether George Bush could not possibly have known about the secret effort to fund the Contras.

He knew everything. How could it have been any other way?

HOW TO DETECT A SECRET AGENDA? LOOK FOR AN UNCLEAR POLICY

After supporting Saddam for nearly eight years, why did the Bush Administration so eagerly want to go to war against him? Only two years earlier, Under Secretary of State Robert Kimmitt stated his belief at a 1989 meeting at the National Security Council that Iraq was "influential in the peace process" and "a key to maintaining stability in the region?" (*Wall Street Journal*, December 7th, 1990).

Most experts agree that President Bush's policy towards Saddam Hussein since the end of the Gulf War has been anything but logical. Laurie Mylroie, author of the recent book *Saddam Hussein and the Crisis in the Gulf*, and a professor at the Center for Middle East Studies at Harvard University, in a 1991 study entitled "The Future of Iraq" for the Washington Institute for Near East Policy claimed that the Administration's language towards Hussein's regime was puzzling with phrases such as: "No one would weep if Saddam were overthrown," and that "the Iraqi people should take matters into their own hands and force Saddam Hussein to step aside." These statements make no sense. For six solid months Bush told the world Saddam Hussein was an evil dictator who had to be stopped. Yet when that moment was imminent, despite the fact that the President had a decisive military option at his disposal, the best he could offer the Iraqi people was a few pats of encouragement on the back.

"How could the Iraqi people, largely unarmed and living under a regime of systemized terror, decide their own future?" asks Mylroie. "And when, against the odds, they attempted to do so, as the Kurds and the Shi'a—75 percent of the Iraqi population—rose in revolt immediately after the cessation of hostilities, the United States offered them little support, despite its overwhelming military superiority in the region."

No sooner had it completed the most concentrated and intense aerial bombing in military history when the White House announced "the U.S. would not interfere in Iraq's internal affairs."

Who would have been offended had America sided with the rebels? The Iraqi people, who the Bush Administration claimed were the victims of Saddam's ruthless terror? Was Bush concerned about a UN censure and accusations of his "blatant violation of Iraqi sovereignty"?

On March 1st, 1991, an aide to the National Security Council declared: "Our policy is to get rid of Saddam Hussein, not his regime" (Staff Report to the Committee on Foreign Relations, May 1st, 1991).

Why was the Administration so concerned about the longevity of the Ba'ath regime? Did they think the rebellion was coming from his own party, rather than from the Kurds and the Shi'a?

Mylroie points out that there was no reason for Bush to fear a "breakup" of Iraq: The Kurds had repeatedly reaffirmed their commitment to a program of autonomy within a democratic Iraq, and the Shi'a had no separatist agenda. She also contends that many Sunni Arab elements would have thrown their support to the rebels if they thought they were going to be the new rulers of Iraq. She questions the assumption that fixating exclusively on a coup was reasonable since it wasn't clear the elite had the will and the means to do so. She points out that when one Administration official claimed "the uprisings almost made it inevitable that there would not be a coup" (*Washington Post*, April 20th, 1991), it was in effect to blame the victim.

On March 26th, a senior official of the White House explained a decision the Administration had made to let Hussein put down rebellions in his country without American intervention: "Bush believes Saddam will quash the rebellions and, after the dust settles, the Ba'ath military establishment and other elites will blame him for not only the death and destruction from the war, but the death and destruction from putting down the rebellion. They will emerge and install a new leadership and will make the case it is time for new leaders and a new beginning" (*Washington Post*, March 29th, 1991).

And they'll live happily ever after too. In other words, you wait and see, something good will come out of all this. Bush certainly went a long way to ensure not offending Saddam. Was the Administration prepared to sacrifice tens of thousands of Iraqi lives based on the "hope" that one day everything will turn out all right?

Instead of putting the U.S. and coalition forces at the disposal of the rebels, Bush was telling us that, in the long run, the rebels will be better off without American armed forces' help because they will emerge stronger after defeating Hussein. Does Bush mean the Iraqi people will be prouder of their achievements if they, and they alone, dispose of Saddam? That the Iraqi people will make Hussein feel so ashamed for the damage he has caused them, he will resign and flee in shame?

What led Bush to believe that all of a sudden, after more than a decade of Saddam's dictatorial rule the Iraqi people were going to wake up and and discover the evils of dictatorship and the virtues of pluralism? If so, how come they didn't do it after the ruinous war with Iran which Saddam dragged them into?

Mylroie says that a major drawback of White House policy was that there could be no real debate over a deliberately vague policy. This misses the point. It is exactly the goal of the White House—to give the public ambiguous signals as to its true intentions, which serves to quash any debate. (How can a policy be debated if it isn't even understood?)

The decision not to destroy Saddam was yet another Bush

secret agenda. The last thing the White House wanted was a stable Iraq or an Iraq run by forces which the Administration would have no control over.

CONCLUSION

Bush's media manipulators had America believe they went to war in the Persian Gulf to stand up to a bully or to defend Saudi Arabia or to free Kuwait. President Bush was presented as someone who went on a moral crusade to demonstrate to the world that America is the vanguard of freedom and was prepared to go to war to safeguard the democratic ideals it cherishes. That was media disinformation. One of the secret agendas behind the Persian War war was the need for Bush to have U.S. troops stationed in Saudi Arabia to man the $200 billion string of military bases there called CENTCOM. These bases are vital to the strategic control of the world. They were too valuable to be left in the hands of the Saudis.

That's one reason. There are likely others, but they remain hidden from the public's eye because no investigative journalist has yet uncovered them.

Yet President Bush's actions in the Persian Gulf war can't be fully understood unless the reason why the Bush and Reagan Administrations went out of their way to support Saddam Hussein in the first place is understood.

The most common reason given by Administration officials (after the fact) was that the Saudis, America's long-standing vested interest in the region, was petrified of the Iranians winning the Gulf War and thus consuming the Persian Gulf with Islamic fundamentalism. Yet this assertion was never confronted.

Says Iran-Contra player Richard Secord: "The pro-Iraqi tilt came fairly early on in the Reagan Administration. I was against it. I don't know of any responsible opinions, militarily speaking, who believed an Iranian victory would cause a Muslim fundamentalist tide to sweep over the rest of the Arab world in a domino-like fashion" (author interview, November 7th, 1991).

Besides, financial support for Iraq from the U.S. via loan guarantees and loans from BNL increased after the Iran-Iraq War ended. The White House went way beyond just keeping Saddam strong to fight Iran to a standoff. They created a military monster.

Nor does the arguments that the U.S. government supported Saddam to strengthen bilateral trade between the two nations make much sense, After the Iran-Iraq War, Iraq was heavily in debt. The Administration had to lend Saddam the money to buy American food and weapons.

Another favorite of the Bush apologists is that "if the U.S. had better relations with Iraq it would reform Saddam's record on human rights." President Bush even said on one occasion that the U.S. tried to help Iraq in order to "bring Iraq into 'the family of nations.'"

These arguments should be highly suspect. Morality rarely defines relations between foreign leaders, national interests do. (If this statement came from Jimmy Carter it would be easier to accept. For some reason George Bush is just not easily associated with a high level of morality.)

If the White House's consideration for supporting Saddam was to reform his evil ways, why didn't every other ruthless dictator in the world receive loan guarantees to purchase food and advanced military technologies? There is absolutely no indication that either the Bush or Reagan Administration cared one iota about Saddam's human rights record. In fact, it was Congress who had to urge the White House to enact sanctions against Iraq after the gassing of the Kurds in 1988. Nor should the claim that the Administration "failed to understand the true nature or intent of Saddam" or that the "intelligence community failed to inform the White House of the Iraqi buildup" be readily accepted. Statements such as these completely understate the wealth of information available to modern statesmen. President Bush knew the exact nature of Hussein's regime as well as he did of the rule of Hafez Al-Assad of Syria. It makes no sense that every newspaper columnist, rabbi, political analyst, and think-tanker can understand that guys like Hussein and Assad are nasty people, but the President of the United States, with all the intelligence and high-quality information available to him and his staff, remains in the dark, is naive, and gets taken in by the dictator. Doesn't the Oval Office subscribe to *Time*, *Newsweek*, *The New Republic*, *Commentary*, and *The American Spectator*?

Arguments such as the White House policy went "astray" and "took on a life of its own" are equally ridiculous. The direction of foreign policies can change in a matter of days. Sanctions can be imposed almost immediately. If the Administration discovered that Saddam had gassed the Kurds or was building a nuclear bomb, and didn't like it, it could have stopped its support for Saddam on the spot.

A more logical reason why the Reagan and Bush Administrations went to such lengths to arm and support Iraq may have been the hostility Bush and other members of both Administrations had towards Israel.

In July 1991, I met William Northrup, an Israeli intelligence asset and part-time arms dealer who shared an interest with me in Iran-Contra and the secret agendas of the Bush and Reagan Administrations. He attributed the policy of supporting Iraq to the "equal playing field doctrine" that the Administration used in balancing its Middle East policy.

This doctrine, which was never publicly acknowledged by the White House, is based on the notion that the problem in the Middle East is not with the Arabs, but in Israel's reckless use of its military superiority. Therefore, the Administration must ensure that the Arabs are put on a parity with Israel militarily so that Israel will be pressured into concessions. This, it was believed, would satisfy the Arabs.

This explains why as soon as Bush became President in 1989, support for Iraq intensified. Bush must have wanted to teach Israel a lesson for all the times that the pro-Israel lobby in the U.S. killed arms deals with the Arabs. When Bush got into the Oval Office, he could finally get even.

Although this reason doesn't account for why Bush went to war against Saddam, that may be due to a completely separate secret agenda, which remains hidden from Congress and the American people. With George Bush at the helm, there's no reason to believe that there is only one covert agenda in place at any given time.

Chapter 12

What Is a Covert Operation?

"A covert operation is, in its nature, a lie."
Oliver North in his testimony
before the Iran-Contra
congressional investigations

The major problem investigative journalists have in determining the secret agenda behind covert operations is the secrecy which surrounds these activities.

Gary Sick discovered this during his investigation into the "October Surprise" scandal.

"For those conducting a covert action, there are three layers of protection against disclosure," he says. "First, there is the culture of secrecy surrounding such operations. People are sworn to silence, and they take their oaths with the utmost seriousness. Second, there is compartmentalization. Ideally, in a covert action almost no one should have the whole picture. Especially those at a lower level should have as little information as possible about any activities except those required to fulfill their mission. The third layer of protection is culpability. If the covert operation involves criminal actions, the source will be reluctant to subject himself to possible prosecution. That inhibition is greatly strengthened if those he is accusing happen to be in positions of great political power" (*October Surprise: America's Hostages in Iran and the Election of Ronald Reagan*).

These layers of protection pose a major obstacle to journalists seeking to expose a covert operation. Sick points out that the "need to know" is the rule, and if it is rigorously observed, even a disgruntled operative will only be able to reveal one tiny dimension of the operation. Thus, even exposing one aspect of the adventure, doesn't reveal the wider secret agenda.

"If the operative is also a suspect character, which is typically the case, then deniability is even easier to maintain, since he can easily be discredited by the 'respectable' people who planned the operation."

For these reasons, most covert operations never get discovered. The covert operations that are exposed are usually the unsuccessful ones that screw up.

ROBERT SENCI

Whatever Robert Senci was involved in before he was arrested is a good example of a covert operation that wasn't successful, became public, but still didn't expose the wider secret agenda it was supporting.

During the summer of 1991, I became good friends with William Northrup. He was arrested along with Israeli General Avraham Baram in Bermuda in April 1986 and was illegally deported to the United States on trumped-up charges of "conspiracy" to defraud the U.S. government. He gave me Bobby Senci's number and told me to call him. "Bobby's part of the Brown Helmut Society," said Northrup, using the term to refer to those in the Iran-Contra Affair who went to jail for merely carrying out the orders of their superiors. "The ones that got dumped on," Northrup liked to say.

On March 22nd, 1988, Robert Mario Senci was found guilty by a Washington, D.C., court of six counts of mail fraud, four counts of first-degree theft, and eleven counts of interstate transportation of stolen securities. His lawyer told the jury he was authorized to spend the $2.5 million he was accused of stealing by a high-ranking Kuwaiti Airlines official who was also a member of the Kuwaiti royal family.

Senci was involved in a covert operation that to this day has yet to be exposed. By going to jail rather than opening his mouth, Senci was simply abiding by the rules set down for covert operators. "If you get caught, you go down and keep your trap shout," Northrup would tell me.

From 1977 until his arrest in 1986, Senci was the local sales manager in Washington for Kuwaiti Airlines, a perfect cover for his covert activities. According to testimony given during the trial, he took payments sent by the airline to the cultural division of the Kuwaiti Embassy in Washington and deposited them in several bank accounts. Kuwaiti Airlines officials testified that Senci was not authorized to maintain the account.

Senci claimed most of the money was spent on a mission by the CIA to forge ties with moderates in Iran who would ultimately be spying for the agency. The plan, Senci said, was approved by the Kuwaiti government because of its own vulnerability to Iranian Islamic fundamentalism.

The CIA admitted that it had a "relationship" with Senci from late 1983 until the time of his arrest. Robert Carter, as former aide to CIA director William Casey, wrote a letter to the judge on Senci's behalf, saying, "I know that Mr. Senci was often involved in highly technical and extremely important meetings around the world. These meetings on many occasions were held to further the interests of the United States government."

Although he faced a ten-year prison sentence, Senci was given only six months. Before being arrested, Senci told the court: "I solemnly swear before the court, and to almighty God, that I am a patriot and that what I did was for my country and fellow man."

What did Senci do? In an exclusive interview in the *Village Voice* (July 23rd, 1991), Senci says he worked closely with CIA Director William Casey in "Republicans Abroad," an organization created to further Republican Party goals abroad. A front for covert activity would be a better description for it, as it was used, for example, for a CIA operation to recruit Iranian spies and to gain information on Americans being held hostage in Lebanon. It enabled Senci to get close to potential spies in the Iranian community in Europe.

Senci says he worked with Carter and was also a consultant for the powerful Washington lobbying firm of Robert Gray Ltd., known for its close ties to the Administration and U.S. intelligence bodies. (In November 1983, Robert Owen, an aide to then-Senator Dan Quayle and Oliver North's co-operator of the Contra supply operation, began working for Gray and Co. to improve the image of the Contras in Congress.) Says Senci: "Gray was also the chief lobbyist for the Kuwaiti government to encourage the U.S. to go to war in the Persian Gulf in November and December 1990."

In what might have become a second Iran-Contra, in late 1985, Habib Moallem, an Iranian contact of Sensi's, proposed that Iran would trade oil and the American hostages in return for U.S. help in reconstructing its oil refineries, which had been bombed by the Iraqis. He says the proposal was the brainchild of William Wilson, the U.S. Ambassador to the Vatican, who arranged for Senci and Moallem to meet Vice President Bush, Casey, and a number of people from Robert Gray's lobbying firm. The meeting got leaked to the press and never took place, but plans were drawn up by Casey, Senci, and Carter to initiate the deal.

WILLIAM HERRMANN

On May 17th, 1985, William Herrmann returned to his London hotel room and was arrested with a suitcase full of counterfeit American money. Herrmann had been arranging a sale of 10,000 TOW missiles from the U.S. and Israel through Iranian arms dealer Cyrus Hashemi.

"In early March 1985, I got the orders from Oliver North to issue pro-forma invoices for 10,000 TOW missiles from Cyrus Hashemi via Bank Melli," Herrmann claims.

The deal was to have been done through Hashemi, Manuchar Gorbanifar, and Herrmann, with full American knowledge. The TOW missiles would be shipped out of Israel. The problem was, the Israelis wanted to get paid in advance and the Iranians wanted the goods before payment was made. Israel wanted to sell an additional 300 M-48 tanks to Iran, but that deal didn't go through due to the conflict over the TOW sale.

Back in the early 1960s Herrmann had started a freight-forwarding company in New York and from time to time did contract work for the CIA. By the early 1970s he had established himself in Frankfurt and was a full-time arms dealer. He had made some excellent contacts in the intelligence and law enforcement community and was asked to participate in an operation to break up a European counterfeiting ring printing U.S. currency.

Herrmann worked with the FBI to infiltrate the "Action Directe" terrorist organization in Belgium. This operation began in February 1985 just before the Iranian arms deal was set into motion.

"Ten days before my arrest I inspected the distribution points for Action Directe's counterfeiting ring," Herrmann told me at our first meeting we had at the Barbizon Hotel in Manhattan. "I posed as a buyer and told them I was going to get rid of the counterfeit cash for them."

He says the legal attaché at the American Embassy was to have made all the necessary arrangements and provide cover for him, but didn't. (Herrmann says legal attachés at American embassies all over the world are FBI agents.) Instead, Herrmann was left out to dry, and would later discover that the order for this came directly from North, who, he claims, believed Herrmann was complicating the deal by pressuring the Iranians to release the money.

"The American and the Israelis wanted payment in advance and I was advising the Iranians not to do that," says

Herrmann. "After Michael Ledeen had brought Amiram Nir in to handle the Israeli side of the sale, North thought there were too many people involved in the deal and decided to get rid of some. I guess I was expendable."

If what Herrmann is saying is true, it sheds entirely new light on the official story of the Iran-Contra Affair. Michael Ledeen, a consultant to the National Security Council, says he traveled to Israel in the spring of 1985 to seek Israel's help in getting the U.S. hostages freed. Israel's counterterrorism chief, Amiram Nir, doesn't officially enter the Iran-Contra story until December 1985, when then-Prime Minister Shimon Peres appointed him to take charge of future arms sales to Iran. No mention is made in Israel's official version of events or the Iran-Contra investigations of a sale of TOW missiles as early as the spring of 1985.

In December 1985 before his trial, a friend of Herrmann's attended a Christmas party at the American Embassy and met the legal attaché and the liaison officer between M15 and the Royal Air Force. The friend pumped everyone he met to find out if he knew anything about the case. The legal attaché was very drunk and told him, "We have instructions from Washington to throw the book at him. We're going to nail that son of a bitch."

In March 1986 after a three-week trial in London, Herrmann was found guilty of counterfeiting and remained in an English jail from March 1986 until February 1987 before being transferred to a prison in Pennsylvania. He remained there until his release in December 1988.

One of the reasons the Reagan Administration may wanted to have Herrmann "out of the picture" was because in 1980 he met with an Iranian official, Hamid Naqashan, to procure arms for the Revolutionary Guards. A few deals followed and the two became friends. Herrmann says that on the day the hostages were released he had dinner in Teheran with Naqashan, who told him he had attended meetings in Paris in late October where an arrangement was made not to release the hostages until Reagan was sworn in as President (*October Surprise*, pages 153-54).

I met with Herrmann a number of times during my final trip to New York. He is indeed bitter over having paid a price for North's follies, and is determined to find out the whole story behind the White House's secret agenda that he was sacrificed for.

PIA VESTA

The *Pia Vesta* Affair is a classic covert operation bearing the signature of the Reagan-Bush White House. It is an example of just how far the Administration went to get its hands on black money it could use for other covert operations.

The scandal was first reported by David Corn (*In These Times*, June 22-July 5th, 1987), a regular contributor to *The Nation* and one of America's leading investigative journalists.

The *Pia Vesta* Affair was essentially about arms smuggling. Sometime in June 1986 the *Pia Vesta*, a Danish freighter loaded with Soviet-bloc weaponry, was unable to dock in Peru and instead went to Panama. There, Manuel Noriega seized the ship and its contents. Nothing more is known about the fate of the weapons.

Corn discovered the affair from information released in the Iran-Contra investigations. He came across a memo from Barbara Studley, a Miami radio personality and part-time arms dealer who had helped General John Singlaub in the Contra supply effort. The memo was sent to Oliver North and stated that Studley had met with arms dealer David Duncan in August 1986 in Washington and that he had information that could "damage President Reagan, Bush, the Republican Party and the National Security Council." Studley told North: "Disclosure of covert 'Black Money' could have untold ramifications."

Studley informed North that Duncan was threatening to

go public with a story about a covert operation to supply Soviet-made, anti-aircraft weapons to UNITA rebel groups in Angola via South Africa. Duncan claimed a French arms dealer, Georges Starckmann, had arranged the deal by purchasing the arms from the Soviet Union with end-user certificates indicating they were destined for Peru. Yet Duncan, who was enlisted to carry out the Peru end of the deal, says this was a cover and the Peruvian Navy was going to receive a completely different supply of arms at much-reduced prices.

Corn says that Duncan knew Starckmann stung the South Africans by cashing the $27 million letter of credit they gave him. It was to have included the items listed on the letter of credit, but didn't.

The ship carrying these weapons, called the *Pia Vesta*, was bound for Peru. The South Africans were told their weapons would be on a second ship leaving East Germany once the first ship arrived in Peru, so as to assure the Soviets the deal was legitimate. In mid-journey, it was to be diverted to South Africa.

The only problem was that there was never a second ship.

Duncan contends that he believed all along that it was a legitimate deal, albeit covert, essentially an operation to arm the UNITA fighters. It wasn't until October 1986 that Duncan says he found out from a South African intelligence agent that the money for the deal had actually come from Saudi Arabia, which provided it as a favor to the United States.

In the Iran-Contra hearings it was revealed that as part of the AWACS deal, Saudi Arabia promised to fund rebel fighters supported by the U.S. in Afghanistan and Nicaragua.

The entire operation may have simply been a way for Casey and North to get their hands on nearly $30 million from the Saudi Arabians for use by the CIA in covert operations.

SOLOMON SCHWARTZ AND THE NORBISTOR AFFAIR

The difference between a secret agenda and a covert operation is that a secret agenda is an overall policy while a covert operation is just one part of a secret agenda. Many covert operations make up a secret agenda.

Says former CIA agent Victor Marchetti: "Covert operations are very attractive to agents who can't deal with the bureaucracy between departments inside the government or the constant leaks that happen when too many sectors of a government are aware of a particular policy. People like North are attracted to them because they admire the ability of the covert operators to get things done, with no questions asked, by anyone. And besides, if you screw up, who cares, nobody knows what you're doing in the first place."

Covert operations sometimes do screw up. When they do, and details of them hit the press, they sound crazy because what doesn't get reported is the secret agenda behind the covert operation: in other words, the policy the covert operation was serving.

Such was the case of Solomon Schwartz. Schwartz was caught in a sting operation by U.S. customs agents on February 21st, 1984, at Kennedy Airport. The seized cargo was more than 500 Ruger rifles, 100,000 rounds of ammunition, electronic torture equipment, and a specially armed chocolate-colored Cadillac bound for Poland (*Newsweek*, April 23rd, 1984).

Schwartz had falsely filled out end-user certificates declaring the weapons were destined for the Mexican government. Customs officials said it was the first time they had encountered anyone trying to smuggle weapons into the communist bloc.

Schwartz claims the operation was sanctioned by Oliver North and the Defense Intelligence Agency (DIA). The DIA says it "listened, but that's all," to a plot by Schwartz to obtain two Soviet-built T-72 tanks from Poland so the U.S. could analyze the alloys used in the armor (*Newsweek*, April 23rd,

1984). The DIA did acknowledge that it "expressed interest in the tanks," but it denies authorizing Schwartz's actions (*Los Angeles Times*, January 24th, 1987). Schwartz told Federal investigators he had been given $15 million by the DIA as part of a plan to buy two Soviet T-72 tanks from corrupt Polish generals. Schwartz had already managed to smuggle the operations manual out of Poland (*Village Voice*, August, 21st, 1990).

The DIA wasn't the only U.S. defense or intelligence agency hoping to acquire a T-72 tank. Ahmed Heidari, an Iranian arms dealer, told Gary Sick that after William Casey became director of the CIA in 1981, the U.S. made a major effort to acquire a T-72 by approaches to both Iran and Iraq. Certain officials in the Pentagon believed that the T-72 had "a virtually impenetrable armor, which was supposed to be layered with different composites and laminates, more powerful than anything ever seen" (*Village Voice*, December 18th, 1990).

A year later the U.S. Attorney General's Office slapped Schwartz with an indictment for conspiring to sell 1300 night-vision devices to Argentina during the Falklands War and to ship F-4 Jet aircraft parts to Iran and Iraq. Schwartz told the court that due to his special relationship with Israel he was asked to go there to help North arrange for a shipment of 1000 TOW missiles and Cobra military helicopters to Iran. "I was told that the National Security Council was directly involved in this operation, and that the FBI was overseeing the project to ensure there was no problem," Schwartz said.

In Israel, Schwartz met General Yossi Peled, who provided him with end-user certificates from Pakistan. A few weeks later, Schwartz claims, he flew to the Dominican Republic and met with Contra leader Adolfo Calero, who was in the market for light military weapons. Schwartz set up a supply route to him subsidized with profits from arms sales to Iran. Schwartz contends the network he set up was taken over by

Richard Secord.

Although Federal District Court Judge Thomas C. Platt, Jr., wrote that Schwartz "had a relationship with certain agencies of the U.S. government," he denied his motion that he was authorized by the U.S. government to carry out his action (*New York Times*, December 27th, 1986).

In 1989 Schwartz was sentenced to ten years in prison and fined $70,000. His lawyers said the government offered to reduce his sentence if he carried out a sting operation against other arms dealers, but Schwartz refused, contending his activities had been authorized by the U.S. government.

Between the time he was first arrested in 1984 and late 1986 Schwartz was involved in a coup attempt to overthrow Jerry Rawlings, the President of the West African republic of Ghana.

Why would the U.S. want to overthrow Ghana?

Relations between the Reagan Administration and the left-leaning government of Jerry Rawlings were never very friendly, particularly since Rawlings had good relations with Libya's Muammar Qaddafi.

In July 1985 a relative of Rawlings became romantically involved with Sharon Scrannage, a young women who worked for the CIA. She allegedly turned over the names of and information on CIA agents who had penetrated the Ghanaian government. After the mercenaries were caught and awaiting trial in Brazil, one of them wrote from his prison cell: "Jerry Rawlings has pissed off not only the Company [the CIA] but its cousins [the Mossad] in the Middle East" (*San Jose Mercury News*, October 29th, 1986). By involving itself in the covert operation, Israel was hoping to spring one of its agents held by Ghana after he was exposed by the CIA employee.

The coup was a joint venture with Schwartz as the key contact between Argentina, the Israelis, the South Africans, and the State Department's Office of West African Affairs.

Schwartz had good contacts in Argentina. Through Kevin Kattke, a rogue agent who worked for Oliver North in the Caribbean, he was introduced to Godfrey Osei. Osei told one of the mercenaries involved in the plot: "I came to Washington with no experience and I went to the front door of the CIA. They put me on hold for a couple of years. Then, things started happening" (*San Francisco Chronicle*, December 29th, 1986).

The CIA put people in contact with him and in early 1986 everything started to come together.

No one quite knew who Osei was. He had been imprisoned on fraud charges in Ghana, and presented himself to the mercenaries as a former defense minister in Rawlings' government. He told the Argentine authorities he was an envoy of the Ghanaian Defense Ministry and was authorized to purchase $200,000 worth of weapons, munitions, and explosives from the Argentine army production conglomerate, Fabricaciones Militares (*Atlanta Constitution*, October 26th, 1986).

To procure financing for the operation, Osei offered a seaside gambling concession to the Chinese Mafia in New York, who backed the coup with $500,000. He also promised one of the mercenaries, Ted Bishop, cocoa- and coffee-marketing rights in Ghana (*San Jose Mercury News*, June 22nd, 1986).

It was Bishop who arranged the purchase of 6 tons of weapons for the job. According to mercenary Timothy Carmody, Bishop was the connection to Schwartz, who, he was told, was an agent for Israeli intelligence and who worked out of the offices of Bophusthawa International in New York (*San Francisco Chronicle*, December 29th, 1986). In November 1986 investigative journalist Jack Anderson contacted Solomon Schwartz at a company called B International in New York.

Bishop told the mercenaries that the plot was sanctioned by the White House. He would often boast to them that he had "walk-in access to the highest office in the land—the National Security Council" (*San Francisco Chronicle*, November 11th, 1986) and that he worked for a "lieutenant colonel" who worked for "an admiral" at the National Security Council (NSC).

When they were eventually caught, one of the mercenaries repeated what Bishop had told him: "I worked for the National Security Council and I report to a Marine colonel in Room 357 of the White House Executive Office Building" (*San Jose Mercury News*, December 27th, 1986).

John Early of Albuquerque, New Mexico, was the military leader of the mercenaries. He was a contributing editor of *Soldier of Fortune* magazine, operated a parachute training school in Albuquerque, and spent nearly four years in the Rhodesian Air Force. Those who knew him said he was a "shadowy figure" involved in clandestine activities in Laos in the 1960s and later in El Salvador (*San Francisco Examiner*, March 29th, 1987).

The entire group consisted of one Argentinian and eight American Vietnam veterans. Their six-week mission was to escort the six tons of weapons and rendezvous with a ship off the Ghana coast. The weapons were purchased from the Argentinian Army, which also transported and loaded them on the vessel.

An attack of the city of Accra would follow. They would then train a force of about 100 Ghanaian dissidents to overthrow Rawlings. The plan also included freeing CIA agents imprisoned by Rawlings and destroying a Libyan training center.

The plot was doomed from the start. The equipment and arms were less than adequate. The boat to transport them to Africa arrived two weeks late. Then, the Argentine captain wanted another $50,000 for the trip.

Early began to get suspicious about Bishop when he failed to show up for the final certification of the cargo by port authorities. After he had a Tampa private detective check Osei out, he discovered that Osei had no official ties whatsoever to the Ghana government. The mercenaries began to question their mission and the person in charge, Solomon Schwartz (*Atlanta Constitution,* October 26th, 1986). Six hundred miles off the Brazilian coast they decided their mission was comprised and that they might get killed in Africa.

When they turned back and ran ashore north of Rio de Janeiro the Brazilian police suspected they were going to sell the weapons they had on board to right-wing landowners in order to bloc a proposed land reform. The police seized the boat and its cargo and put the men in jail.

Early and the Argentine captain were sentenced to five years in prison and the other seven Americans four years. When Carmody told his wife he needed "iron enriched" tablets, she knew exactly what he meant and sent him four hacksaw blades in a box of powdered milk (*Atlanta Journal,* December 27th, 1986). On December 15th, 1986, he and three others escaped by climbing down the prison walls with a ladder made out of knotted sheets. With the help of bush pilots who took them on short hops, they made it through the jungle to La Paz, Bolivia. In late February 1987 the remaining mercenaries were extradited to Argentina, where they jumped bail and returned to the United States.

The CIA and Solomon Schwartz have denied involvement in the operation. The State Department said the men were operating as free agents, yet throughout the affair Schwartz's telephone records showed that he was in continuous contact with the State Department's West Africa desk (*San Francisco Examiner,* March 22nd, 1987).

In March 1987, Doug Foster, currently the editor of *Mother Jones,* wrote a lengthy piece about the Nobistor Affair for the *San Francisco Examiner.* He quoted two government officials who claim that Godfrey Osei kept in close contract with the State Department's Office of West African Affairs about his coup plans. Ed Perkins, then head of that office and, after, Ambassador to South Africa, acknowledged to Foster that he had met with Osei in late 1985 but insisted that the "routine meeting" was held at Osei's request. He denied knowing Osei very well or supporting his plans.

Another official from the NSC, who moved over to the CIA in 1987, says that sometime in late 1985 Ambassador Perkis referred Ghanaian exiles seeking U.S. help for a coup attempt to Oliver North and the National Security Council. The official claims the meeting was held in an attempt to "discourage, rather than promote" the effort to overthrow Rawlings.

It would be extremely difficult to believe that Solomon Schwartz would contract this job out to a group of private mercenaries if he wasn't acting on behalf of the U.S. government. How many individuals act on their own to stage a coup?

Considering the ties Schwartz and some of the mercenaries had to North's office, a better guess would be that the Norbistor Affair was yet another secret agenda of the Reagan-Bush White House.

COVERT OPERATORS AREN'T SO COVERT

An amazing phenomenon I have come across in investigating secret agendas is that some of the players in these covert operations were willing to talk with me. When I met Carole Jerome in Toronto in October 1991 she was investigating the "October Surprise" story. Looking over her note pad of phone numbers, she asked me if I wanted to talk with Richard Secord. "Does he talk to journalists?" I asked. She said, "Give him a try."

In September 1990 I spent two afternoons at Yaacov Nimrodi's house in Savion, a plush Tel Aviv suburb, talking to him about Iran-Contra. Now I was going to ring up "secret team" member Richard Secord, a major player in the covert world and ask him what he thought about Iran-Contra. I didn't realize it would be so easy to enter this world of spies, intelligence agents, and arms dealers. You can just phone these people up.

On November 7th, 1991, I called Richard Secord and introduced myself as an Israeli journalist writing a book about American-Israeli relations. (I figured I couldn't just come out and say I was writing a book about covert operations.) He did have a few interesting things to say, such as:

On the Iran-Contra Affair, he believed that had "Reagan come clean early on it would have become a footnote in his Presidency." He said Poindexter was in favor of Reagan's coming forward, but Meese and Nancy protected the President.

"I advocated as early as July 1986 that the Administration go public with this operation because it was leaking even then and we knew it was," Secord says. "When I learned that Gorbanifar was dealing with Kashoggi, for me that was the beginning of the end. Gorbanifar was notorious for double and triple dealing and not keeping his mouth shut."

Secord is convinced Oliver North was victimized by the Administration and put into a position "which nobody should be put into." Avers Secord: "He was clearly a scapegoat. I blame President Reagan for not standing up and taking the heat."

On procuring arms for the Contras, Secord believes that ultimately it was a private initiative and in complete accord with U.S. policy. "Foreign policy was not privitized," he concludes. "Private entities were used."

Secord doesn't like the term "diversion" to describe the use of profits from arms sales to Iran to buy arms for the Contras as it implies a change of plan. "There was no diversion, it was a private commercial operation," claims Secord. In his summation of Iran-Contra, Secord offers: "One of the things I hate about these covert operations is all the crazy cowboys it attracts. Compared to the Bay of Pigs this was nothing, a droplet in a great big sea."

CHAPTER 13

The Role of Disinformation in Covert Operations

Most people have never had to confront the concept of disinformation. Unfortunately, most people also believe what they read in the newspapers and weekly magazines such as *Time* and *Newsweek*. And some governments leak information to news organizations as a deliberate attempt to have them publish information which they know to be false but want the public to believe. In this respect, disinformation is nothing more than a lie that everyone believes.

There's probably no better example of the way disinformation was exploited by the Reagan-Bush White House than in the events following the attempted assassination of Pope John Paul 11. To students of media manipulation and disinformation, it is what occurred *after* Turkish-born Mehmet Ali Agca shot the Pope on May 13th, 1981, in St. Peters Square that is important.

The "Bulgarian Secret Service" theory didn't even emerge until November 1982, when Agca himself claimed that several Bulgarian embassy officials in Rome helped him carry out the crime. Yet there was no evidence linking Agca to his so-called accomplices, and in March 1986 they were were all acquitted due to insufficient evidence (*Time*, April 7th, 1986).

Agca was active in the neo-fascist right in Turkey, the Gray Wolves, which was affiliated with the Nationalist Action Party (NAP). Formed in the mid-1960s, one of NAP's goals was to reunite all Turkish peoples in a single nation. On

February 1st, 1979, Agca's gang, Malatya, which was based in eastern Turkey, killed a prominent newspaper editor. Although it wasn't clear that he was the culprit, Agca was sent to prison.

After Agca claimed he was aided in the Pope's near-assassination by the Bulgarians, Reagan Administration (so-called) terrorism experts such as Claire Sterling, author of *The Terror Network*, and Michael Ledeen, journalist and possibly disinformation expert, wrote a number of articles in American newspapers and periodicals. Despite any hard evidence linking the Bulgarians or the KGB to Agca, Sterling and Ledeen's conclusions of the affair became the accepted version. They argued that Agca's membership in the Gray Wolves was merely a cover for his Bulgarian and KGB links and later "left-wing actions," such as killing the Pope. In other words, Agca successfully infiltrated and maintained membership in Gray Wolves over a number of years, but information on that group's activities were not the main goal of his cover.

Both Sterling and Ledeen claimed that the plot was hatched during Agca's July 1980 visit to Bulgaria and that the KGB and/or Bulgarian secret service wanted to kill the Pope because of his declaration of support for the Polish trade union, Solidarity. Agca had threatened the Pope once before, in 1979. Solidarity wasn't created until August 1980, a month after Agca visited Bulgaria.

Sterling claims that since Agca spent three weeks in Bulgaria in the summer of 1980, which, she averred, must mean Bulgaria was deeply involved in the attack. Yet Agca spent the same or longer periods of time in twelve other countries, yet these governments were not found by Sterling to be involved in the plot. Would the Soviets really believe that by killing the Pope, Solidarity would no longer be a potent political force in Poland? In fact, if anything, the death of their "beloved Pope" would only strengthen the Poles' resolve. Also, if the KGB was going to arrange to kill the Pope, would they choose as their assassin someone who had been previously convicted of murder?

Edward S. Herman, a professor at the University of Pennsylvania and author of *The Real Terror Network: Terrorism in Fact and Propaganda*, is an expert in disinformation. He immediately saw that the Reagan Administration was trying to "disinform" the American public.

Herman points out that not a single witness (outside of Agca himself) has ever been produced to support any of Agca's claims of contacts with Bulgarians. Additionally, all of his *supposed* meetings and travels with them were frequent and in conspicuous places. In contrast, with one exception, every proven transaction by Agca, from his escape from a Turkish prison in 1979 to the day he shot the Pope, including all transfers of money or guns, was with or through a member of the Gray Wolves (*Covert Action*, Spring 1985).

When Agca first implicated the Bulgarians, he said he visited the homes of these officials and even accompanied them on shopping expeditions in Rome.

"To believe Agca means accepting that he socialized with his Bulgarian co-conspirators and that he visited them in their homes and met them in some of Rome's best-known restaurants and pubs," says Herman. "When he needed to speak with them, he simply picked up the phone and called their embassy."

William Hood, a veteran CIA agent, notes that in this devious plot to assassinate one of the world's most influential religious leaders, "there was absolutely no secrecy or compartmentalization."

A major question is: Why did it take Agca more than eighteen months to "remember" his Bulgarian connection? Was he being coached? Herman suggests that, considering his right-wing background, Agca would have no ideological conflict blaming the communists. It would certainly keep the investigations away from the Gray Wolves.

Although supposedly in solitary confinement, Major Petrocelli of SISMI, the Italian Secret Service, met Agca in Ascoli-Piceno prison on December 29th, 1981, as did Lt. Colonel Giuseppe Belmonte of SISMI (*La Repubblica*, October 23rd, 1984).

Following these visits, on February 2nd, 1982, Agca told his lawyer that the "services" had promised him that if he talked, his sentence would be reduced to ten years at most. He was also told he would be released into the general prison population if he didn't cooperate (not something a killer of a Pope sitting in an Italian jail would relish). In May 1982, Agca started talking about the Bulgarian connection.

Could the U.S. government have been behind Agca's sudden recollection?

In a letter sent to the U.S. military attaché in Rome in August 1983, Agca implies that he made his confessions at the direction of U.S. personnel. The letter describes the longstanding relationship between Captain Ernest Till of the Embassy staff and Agca (*Washington Post*, January 19th, 1985). It reads: "For two years you have done everything necessary in view of our mutual friendship and interest. ... What crime have I committed? You told me to begin, and I began to speak" (*La Repubblica*, January 18th, 1985).

If the Soviets weren't involved, why would Agca want to kill the Pope? According to Michael Dobbs of the *Washington Post*, who met Agca in Turkey and in Italy, Agca had an image of himself as a top-flight international terrorist and he desired publicity. "Terrorism represented for him the way to leave his mark on the world," Dobbs says (*Washington Post*, October 14th, 1984).

The problem with that explanation is that it left no role for the disinformation experts in the White House to play in manipulating American public opinion.

The outcome proves that it doesn't matter what the truth is; only what the public perceives to be the truth. To this day most Americans believe that the Bulgarian secret service and the KGB were behind the plot. Disinformation works.

DISINFORMATION AS A DIVERSIONARY TACTIC

Disinformation has a number of aims. One of them is as an effective means of keeping the public focused in one direction while the Administration is off carrying out another secret agenda.

The first Reagan Administration took the battle cry of the "threat of terrorism" and etched it deep into the minds of the American public. The concept was simple: Terrorism was the world's leading evil and the Soviet Union was behind all acts of international terrorism.

By 1984 the White House had veered away from the slogan "the Soviets are behind all acts of terrorism." Instead, "Middle Eastern terrorism" had become America's number-one enemy. By focusing the public on the so-called threat of terrorism, the Administration was able to carry out its covert operations in Central America, Afghanistan, Africa, etc. It was the perfect diversionary measure. As long as the public believed that the Administration was being "tough on terrorists" there was no danger of other secret agendas being exposed.

While terrorism presented a major threat to some countries, such as Israel, Spain, and England, it was never more than a minor irritant to the United States. The major terrorist attacks against American targets were the bombing in April 1983 of the American Embassy in Lebanon, the attack on the U.S. marines barracks in October 1983, the hijacking of a TWA plane over Europe in June 1985, and the downing of Pan Am 103 over Scotland. These were all perpetrated by Iranian-controlled Shiite groups based in Lebanon. The full stories behind these attacks have yet to be told, but when they are, they will probably reveal that they were the result of failed

American promises to deliver arms to Iran.

In the context of Middle East politics, Libya's Colonel Muammar El-Qaddafi was a destabilizing factor, but was he ever really a serious threat to America? While most terrorist experts believed Palestinian terrorist groups trained in Lebanon and Syria were behind the December 27th, 1985, bombings at the Rome and Vienna airports, the Reagan Administration insisted it had "irrefutable" proof that Libya was behind the attacks. It never produced any evidence, but kept on referring to the Libyan guilt as "obvious."

The same technique was employed after the April 1986 bombing of the La Belle Discothèque in West Berlin, which killed a GI, a Turkish woman, and injured more than 200 others. Immediately following the attack the White House said, "Our evidence is direct, it is precise, and it is irrefutable." Once again, the Administration produced nothing.

That's not to say Qaddafi wasn't a ruthless dictator and a supporter of terrorism. Yet the "Madman Qaddafi" label the Administration's disinformation experts gave him and the grave threat to America they ascribed to him had more to do with the image the White House media manipulators created than anything Qaddafi actually did.

The Ayatollah Khomeini was treated in the same way. But if dislike of his regime were based on the actual number of people killed, it would not come close to the vicious rule of any one of a number of dictators in Africa or Central America that the Reagan and Bush Administrations supported.

When the Administration wants to plant disinformation in the media to manipulate the public's perceptions, it is usually "intelligence sources" which are quoted. Most journalists at mainstream publications may think themselves to be quite important when an intelligence official offers them some "exclusive" information for publication. What they may not realize is that there may be a covert operation behind that information to manipulate the public's perceptions.

The only information intelligence agencies would want to be published is data they *want* the public to know. There is no pressure on intelligence agencies to issue press releases. A simple "No comment" is accepted by all.

A good example of this was when *Newsweek* reported in November 1981 that U.S. intelligence officials had discovered that Qaddafi had sent a "hit squad" to the U.S. to kill President Reagan. By the end of December the *New York Times* and the *Los Angeles Times* ran stories proving the story was a hoax, and revealing the sources of the false rumors. Yet most Americans didn't remember the denials or the end result. They only remembered that Qaddafi was their enemy.

Another example of intelligence officials putting out disinformation occurred in mid-February 1992. While every terrorism expert agreed that Syria and Iran were behind the bombing of the Pan Am 103 jet over Lockerbie, Scotland in December 1988, the Administration insisted that Libya was the guilty party. U.S. intelligence sources were quoted by the *Washington Post* as stating that they had information saying that the two Libyans they believed responsible for the Pan Am 103 bombing had been executed by Qaddafi. This is a double whammy. A simple piece of information given to the press serves two purposes: It saves the Administration from having to demand the extradition of the two men, which Qaddafi would obviously never agree to. And, it reminds the American public that Qaddafi is a ruthless dictator who routinely executes his own people.

No information was given to prove the claim, or why Qaddafi would execute someone who supposedly carried out his orders. When a British lawyer claimed the next day he had seen the two alive and well just days before, nothing more was heard of their apparent execution.

Disinformation also plays a role when the Administration wants to have the public believe it is acting in a certain way. For instance, in February 1992 CIA Director Robert Gates

visited Egypt and Israel to apparently discuss "covert operations to bring down Saddam Hussein." Being an election year,
it was important for the American people to hear that "Bush
was now going to get tough with Hussein."

If the U.S. was going to initiate covert operations to topple
Hussein's regime, would these plans be announced in advance?

THE CREDIBILITY FACTOR

The Reagan and Bush Administration disinformation experts
developed a unique concept enabling them to pursue their
secret agendas. It was called "deniability factor," which meant
that if accused of any wrongdoing by anyone or asked about
it by a reporter, an Administration official could skirt the issue
by simply denying involvement or knowledge of the affair,
or call the allegations "baseless." If another country or group
of people outside the White House were thought to have
supplied arms to the Contras, or were selling arms to Iran,
then it was done "without White House knowledge."

The technique worked well. The public was told straight
out there was no secret, covert effort to resupply the Contras;
therefore, the Vice President and his staff could not have been
involved in it. Any report which inferred the opposite was
considered to be an attempt to "smear the White House."
Those who told a different story to journalists or Senate
investigators were found to be "not credible." (It seems nobody
but White House officials are given the benefit of the doubt
that they are telling the truth.) The question of why the person
would want to wrongfully accuse the official is never addressed.

The disinformation experts knew that the majority of
Americans would take their elected officials at their word (or
be unable to do anything about it if they didn't).

Another technique the Reagan-Bush Administrations used
to deflect any accusations of illegal activity was to cause

suspicion of the credibility of the accusers.

What does it actually mean for someone not to be credible? For the most part, everyone is credible, until someone calls into question his or her credibility. This is where the manipulation of the media comes into play. To discredit someone, all that has to happen is for a rumor to be spread or a negative article to appear in the press. That person will be forever discredited.

The Reagan and Bush Administrations have honed this technique. For instance, Bush responded to allegations that his Office was involved in a guns-for-drugs operation to support the Nicaraguan Contras by personally accusing Senator John Kerry of allowing "slanderous" allegations to leak from his investigative committee. Despite the fact that Kerry's chief witness was not charged with any crime, Bush destroyed his credibility in the eyes of the public by saying, "The guy who they are quoting is the guy who is trying to save his own neck."

José Blandón, a former Panamanian diplomat and General Manuel Noriega's top political aide testified before a Senate investigating committee in February 1988 on Noriega's alleged drug-trafficking activities and his involvement with U.S. intelligence agencies. The CIA and Defense Department quickly discredited him by calling him an "untrustworthy leftist."

From the question of a witness' or a source's veracity comes the credibility factor, the investigative journalist's worst nightmare.

The handicap all investigative journalists have is that the only people who will talk to them are those with axes to grind, or former arms dealers sitting in prison. The problem with "proving" their allegations is that the covert operators have no desire for the facts to be revealed. Thus the investigator does not have the luxury of choosing sources. To be a witness to the seedy world of arms dealing and covert operations requires one to have been a member of it.

Says Gary Sick, one of the main proponents of the "October Surprise" theory: "The 'respectable' people who plotted and carried out a covert operation refuse to comment or, at worst, fabricate stories to protect themselves and their reputations; because of their 'respectability' most people are inclined to believe them. The contractors who were hired to do the dirty work are not 'respectable' at all, and if they decide to tell their story, most people assume they are lying" (*October Surprise*, page 215).

Another problem is that investigative journalists are expected to prove that a certain official was involved in an illegal act or behind a covert operation. With no access to intelligence documents, this becomes a near-impossible task. When they are presented with information which could prove these officials' guilt, the likelihood of disinformation becomes a major threat. For that reason, journalists rarely possess the "smoking gun" so many of their critics demand before accepting claims of government wrongdoing.

Yet the role of the investigative journalist shouldn't be to provide evidence of illegal activities, but merely to bring attention to the possibility of these actions. It is up to the judicial branch of a government to carry it further. Unfortunately, that's not what happened in the Iran-Contra investigations.

THE CONSPIRACY AGAINST CONSPIRACY THEORIES

Can it be that all investigative journalists (myself included) are simply wrapped up in conspiracy theories and are jumping to conclusions? That men and women who filled the cabinet spots in the Reagan and Bush White Houses were good, honest, decent people who would never contemplate illegal or unconstitutional activities? That whatever evidence links these actions to the White House was due to their underlings, who hatched up these covert operations and secret agendas behind their bosses' backs?

It's logical for most people to render conspiracy theories as the products of lunatics. Rather than feel the need to investigate a certain conspiracy theory, it's easier to dismiss both the theory and the advocate. This is human nature. Thus, the burden of proof of a conspiracy is always on the advocate of the theory. That's understandable.

However, it's not intellectually honest for the critic to merely say, "You can't prove it, therefore it didn't occur." The only logical response to any conspiracy theory is: "I don't know, it could have happened. We need to do more research to determine if it is true." The best response an investigative journalist could give to someone who immediately discounts a conspiracy theory is: "Well, have you done any research on this subject? No? Then shut up and listen, because I have and here is what I've come up with."

The bottom line on conspiracy theories is that some of the allegations and theories are false. However, when one is investigating White House covert operations and secret agendas, and the actions of intelligence operatives, agencies, arms dealers, and crooked politicians, no theory should be discounted outright nor should any investigator be "shot down" for suggesting a certain hypothesis. In this world, all is possible.

WHY THE MAINSTREAM MEDIA MISSED THE STORY

Why hasn't any major publication thoroughly investigated Iran-Contra and President Bush's involvement in the scandal? How did the American people let the whitewash of the Iran-Contra investigations pass with no one being found guilty? Why didn't *Time* or *Newsweek* produce at least one cover story on Bush's role in Iran-Contra or attempt to prove, through the number of conflicting statements he had made, that he was lying? Instead of investigating the scandal, why did the mainstream press merely transmit the official line?

According to Mark Hertsgaard, author of *On Bended Knee: The Press and the Reagan Presidency*, the media's failure to get to the bottom of Irangate was due to an article of faith among most American journalists that they are not supposed to insert their own judgments into their reporting.

"This may sound true in theory," says Hertsgaard, "but in practice it means that a reporter cannot say that the sky is blue unless a government official—or, in this case [John Poindexter's trial] a judge or jury—says the sky is blue. The danger, then, is that the reporter becomes a mouthpiece for the government rather than writing the truth as he or she sees it. I don't think that's what the Founding Fathers had in mind when they talked about a free press" (*The Nation*, July 2nd, 1990).

The American media has stopped seeing itself as serving and delivering the public's "right to know"? Instead of searching for the truth, the major publications are saying to the American public: "Don't worry, everything is okay in Washington, it's these far-out leftist publications and their writers that keep coming up with these conspiracy theories."

The lethargy of the mainstream press may simply be a reflection of the society it is reporting on. Americans have become politically lazy. Few of them care one way or the other if George Bush has come clean about his role in Iran-Contra. According to the prevailing attitude, all politicians are crooks. If so, why should the American public care if George Bush is a liar?

CHAPTER 14

Intrigue in the Ozark Mountains

While the American public was riveted on presidential candidate and Arkansas Governor Bill Clinton's extra-marital affairs, they missed the real scandal which if it became widely known would have doomed Clinton's election chances. If the American voters have any doubts about Bill Clinton's credibility, they should look no farther than a tiny airport in Mena, Arkansas.

Airplanes play an important role in covert operations. According to former CIA agent Victor Marchetti, the roots of the CIA's ties to clandestine airlines stretches back to the Civil Air Transport, which was established in China in 1946, even before the CIA was created. CAT was an offshoot of General Claire Chennault's Flying Tigers and during its early days flew missions of every type supporting Chiang Kai-shek's unsuccessful effort to retain control of the Chinese mainland. It eventually reorganized as a CIA proprietary holding company called Pacific Corporation. Air America, Air Asia, and Intermountain Aviation soon followed.

After the Vietnam war, Air America was too big to operate domestically so the CIA broke it up into a string of interrelated covert airlines which they sold to outside operatives: Global Airlines, Global, Capital, Continental Air Services, South Air Transport, and Southern Cross, all fell under the Air America umbrella. The CIA wanted to keep these assets intact for its privitized operations. Each of them had their own separate ground staff, pilots and mechanics.

"Through a series of front companies, commonly known as "cutouts" and by laundering, or disguising, the ownership of the airplanes, these aircrafts could be used for clandestine purposes," says Gene Wheaton, a former criminal investigator for the U.S. military and a leading expert on the use of airplanes for covert actions. "If journalists or state investigators came close to exposing them, the companies would simply be shut down and the planes would be leased to another firm. I found companies which consisted of nothing more than a piece of paper in a file cabinet."

During his investigations into covert airlines, Wheaton discovered that William Blakemore, one of Bush's closest friends, allowed his ranch in Brewster County near Marathon, Texas, to be used for commando and assassination training, and to move weapons to and from the U.S.

Wheaton was told that Charles Beckwith of the Delta Force, who was in charge of the failed Desert One mission to rescue the U.S. hostages held in Iran in 1980, was heading up the training on the ranch. Beckwith admitted to Wheaton that there were covert operations going on, but that he wasn't heading up the training. In early 1989 Austin newspapers began exposing the scandal.

Wheaton's investigation into airplanes used for covert operations by Ollie North's network led him to the Intermountain Regional Airport at Mena, Arkansas, 130 miles west of Little Rock in Polk County. It was being used by Oliver North's team of operatives who were running guns to Nicaragua and drugs from Central America.

Why Mena? One reason may be that Mena is in Arkansas' 3rd Congressional District, represented by Republican John Paul Hammerschmidt, a longtime friend of President Bush. He was one of two (out of six) Arkansas congressional representatives who supported federal aid to the Contras.

The story behind the illicit activity at Mena first hit the

mainstream press in October 1989 when investigative journalist Jack Anderson wrote a column describing an airport in the tiny town of 5,000 in the Ozark Mountains that was used by Barry Seal, a notorious drug smuggler from 1982-1986. Although Seal was killed in 1986 by the Medellín cartel, local police still think the airport is being used by drug smugglers. Sources familiar with the ongoing activities to ship private aid to the Contras told Anderson: "They pushed Ollie North aside and kept going."

The drug-smuggling operation prospered until 1984, when Seal was convicted on drug charges in Miami and was given a ten-year sentence. Yet in return for immunity, Seal was offered a deal by Oliver North's network and by the Drug Enforcement Agency to work undercover to discredit the Sandinista government. Seal agreed to fly his C-130 transport plane to Managua to pick up 750 kilos of cocaine from a high-ranking Nicaraguan official. The entire transaction would be recorded with hidden cameras.

Anderson discovered that since Seal's death a new cast of characters have settled in at the Mena airport. One businessman called himself "an international aircraft delivery company," another "delivers aircraft parts all over the world." State police told him they couldn't figure out why these international aviation service companies picked a remote base like Mena in the Ozarks to run their operations out of. Wheaton told Anderson that one of the strange occurrences at Mena was at a private airstrip 15 miles from the town. Until a year ago the strip was used for commando training to teach pilots how to land without using their lights.

When Bill Alexander, a Democratic Congressman from Arkansas, asked the General Accounting Office (GAO) in Congress to investigate government involvement in the activities at Mena, he was told the National Security Counsel instructed other White House agencies not to cooperate with the investigation.

On June 10th, 1991, a C-130 cargo plane crashed shortly after takeoff from the Luanda International Airport in Angola.

On board was the 34-year-old son of Charles and Clara Hendricks, Chuck, an airplane cargo loadmaster and mechanic. Chuck died along with ten other people on the plane, three of them Americans, including the nephew of a Republican Congressman from Pennsylvania, Curt Weldon. The flight-data recorder and its blackboxes were never found.

Hendricks told his parents he was flying famine relief missions for the Angolan and U.S. government. After the crash, the Hendrickses discovered the plane was actually heading for a diamond mine in Angola carrying alcohol, cigarettes, and other provisions (*Washington Post*, December 30th, 1991). They also discovered that the owner of the plane was alleged to have maintained closed ties with the CIA, and at one point in time had shipped weapons to Iran in the Iran-Contra Affair.

The Hendrickses sent letters to the National Transportation Safety Board and the office of both President Bush and Vice President Quayle, requesting an explanation. They were told that since the crash occurred in a country which the U.S. maintains no diplomatic relations with, the U.S. government was unable to investigate it. However, when they contacted the plane's manufacturer, Lockheed Corporation, they were informed by a crash investigator at the company that "his superiors told him he could not look into the incident."

Along with other families of the American victims on the plane the Hendrickses hired a private investigator to do a paper trail to determine who the plane was registered to. That led to CZX Productions, a Delaware firm which leased it to Carib Air Transport Corporation of the West Indies while Unitramn International of Frankfurt, Germany, hired the crew.

The families discovered that one of the partners in CZX was Dietrich Reinhardt, who was also the head of Unitramn. One of the airlines he owned, St. Lucia Airways, transported shipments of Hawk aircraft missiles to Iran in 1985. During the Iran-Contra hearings, St. Lucia Airways was described as a "CIA proprietary" airline. The British press revealed that the downed

C-130 had an expired tail number that was once assigned to St. Lucia Airways. It was also discovered that St. Lucia had been used by Oliver North's network to transport arms to Angolan rebels.

Contacted in Florida by investigative journalist Jack Anderson and Dale Van Atta, Reinhardt denied any involvement of any type with CIA covert activities, but did say that the purpose of the flights to Iran and Angola was "classified."

In April 1992 the TV investigative program *A Current Affair* broadcast a story on the Angolan crash. Geraldo Rivera's *Now It Can Be Told* looked at the larger story on the mysterious activities at the Intermountain Regional Airport at Mena. Mena was also the base which serviced the C-123 plane carrying Eugene Hasenfus, shot down in Nicaragua in October 1986—which exposed the secret effort to supply weapons to the Contras.

In the late 1980s the state police in Arkansas investigated certain aspects of the case and gave their information to the U.S. Attorney's Office in Fort Smith. It was believed to be sufficient enough to obtain indictments, but a federal grand jury never took any action in the case. This illicited allegations that the Bush-Reagan Administration was orchestrating a cover-up.

A student group at the University of Arkansas called the Arkansas Committee headed by Mark Swaney and Tom Brown, which called on Governor Clinton to open a full investigation into the foul play going on at Mena. Swaney claimed that Clinton was protecting Bush, adding, "They don't want this to be investigated" (*Arkansas Democrat Gazette*, April 7th, 1992). A Clinton campaign spokesperson, Max Parker, replied, "The state has reached the limit of what it can do," claiming that "the case is under federal, not state jurisdiction."

State Investigator Russell Welch believes the scandal reaches "from Mena, Arkansas, to the White House." At one point in Welch's investigation he was told by federal agents that the case was being handled "differently" from others (*Mena,*

Star, April 14th, 1992).

Deputy State Prosecuting Attorney Charles Black says that when he asked Clinton in 1988 to provide financial assistance so the state could conduct its own grand jury investigation, Clinton never replied (*Time*, April 20th, 1992).

Arkansas Congressman Bill Alexander is a staunch opponent of Mena and wants the airport shut down, saying it has been responsible for drugs entering his state. He and Arkansas State Attorney General Winston Bryant have sent boxes of evidence to Iran-Contra independent council Lawrence Walsh for further investigation.

When Alexander met with Clinton the Governor told him he had allocated $25,000 in state funds to investigate the matter and told State Police Chief Tommy Goodwin to tell Polk County authorities that the funds were available. However, Joe Hardegree, then Polk County prosecuting attorney, claims he never received the offer, verbally or otherwise.

Deborah Robinson, a reporter in Arkansas who has closely followed the scandal, says that the Arkansas Committee filed a Freedom of Information request which demanded access to "letters, memoranda of meetings, telephone records and financial records" relating to the governor's offer of financial assistance for a Mena prosecution. The group was told by Clinton's legal counsel, Field Wasson, Jr., that "this office has been unable to find any such records" (*In These Times*, February 12th, 1992).

In late 1991, Alexander did receive a $25,000 federal grant from the Justice Department's State Law Enforcement Assistance Fund to investigate Mena. Yet the money has been held up behind a wall of bureaucratic excuses in Little Rock (*The Nation*, March 23rd, 1992).

It was first revealed that the airport at Mena, Arkansas, was involved in covert operations in the mid-1980s when a convicted drug smuggler turned Drug Enforcement Agency informant, Barry Seal, was gunned down in Baton Rouge, Louisiana, by a Colombian drug traffickers hit team. It was during this time that Bill Duncan, then an investigator with the Internal Revenue Service, began looking into the activities of Rich Mountain Aviation at Mena, which he believed was part of Seal's operation.

In the spring of 1989 Duncan was called into the office of a lawyer for the IRS, who told him if he continued to pursue his investigation it would lead to "an extremely high level official in the administration." Duncan says he was told to perjure himself at an upcoming hearing in the House Judiciary Subcommittee on Crime by testifying that there had been no tampering with the Mena investigation by any government official. He was also told never to mention a report he had received from an employee of Freddie Hampton that former U.S. Attorney General Edwin Meese received a $350,000 bribe from Seal. Duncan refused, and quit the IRS (*In These Times*, February 12th, 1992; Unclassified, February-March 1992).

He then joined the Arkansas Attorney General's Office as an investigator and told a House subcommittee in the summer of 1991 that he collected evidence which pointed to "a bizarre mixture of drug smuggling, money laundering and covert operations." He claimed the activities implicated "contract operatives of the U.S. intelligence services."

Duncan's reports were confirmed by Terry Capehart, an auxiliary Polk County sheriff's deputy at the time of Seal's arrival on the scene and who also ran a small machine shop at the airport. Capehart began to notice mysterious late-night activity going on at Mena, such as cargo doors being added to Seal's planes, alteration of serial numbers on the tails of planes, and extra fuel tanks being added. This was all being done without Federal Aviation Administration approval.

Capehart discovered that Freddy Hampton, the owner of Rich Mountain Aviation, would receive large bundles of money from Seal. Hampton's secretary, Lucia Gonzalez, told state police: "Hampton's financial status was improving greatly when there

was no apparent difference in the amount of work being done."
Another secretary, Kathy Gann, says it was her job to buy cashier's
checks at Union Bank in Mena of less than $10,000 with the money
Seal gave Hampton (*In These Times*, February 12th, 1992).

Deputy State Prosecuting Attorney Charles Black charges
a federal cover-up, adding that Duncan had put together a very
well documented and well supported case that certain individuals be indicted for money laundering and perjury. He says that
while it was standard practice that case investigators be called
upon to testify at a grand jury, U.S. Attorney Mike Fitzhugh and
Asa Hutchinson didn't call either Duncan or Welch to the stand.
Out of 20 witnesses investigators gave to Fitzhugh, only three
were subpoenaed to testify. When Hampton's secretary Kathy
Gann took the stand, she wasn't even asked about her knowledge of money laundering at local banks.

Reporter Deborah Robinson discovered that two acquain-
tances of U.S. Assistant Attorney Steve Snyder had said that
Snyder confided to them that his office had been ordered to drop
the case by the Miami Drug Enforcement Agency. Others
charged that then-Attorney General Edwin Meese interfered
with the federal grand jury in order that the case would not be
fully investigated.

Governor Clinton's ties to Mena and Contra resupply effort
were revealed through a defamation of character lawsuit filed
against him by Larry Nichols. Nichols worked for the Contra
cause in Honduras and later lobbied for Contra aid in Washington. It was also through this case that Clinton's extra-marital
relationship with Genny Flowers was revealed.

In 1988, Clinton appointed Nichols marketing director of
the Arkansas Development Finance Authority (ADFA), an office
Nichols used to meet with to Contra leader Adolfo Calero, his
brother Mario, and Iran-Contra figure retired Major-General
John Singlaub (Unclassified, February-March 1992). When the
press began questioning Clinton about Nichols' appointment
(he wasn't at all qualified) and the use of a state office for pro-

Contra purposes, he fired Nichols, claiming that he made un-authorized calls to Central America. Nichols refused to take the heat and turned around and sued Clinton for defamation of character (*The Nation*, February 10th, 1992).

The Arkansas Committee acquired under the Freedom of Information Act Nichols' phone records when he was em-ployed at ADFA. They showed no calls to Central America.

Clinton's ties to the covert operations at Mena were ex-posed through the court case of Terry Reed. Reed, who worked for the CIA's Air America operation in Thailand during the Vietnam War, was in the machine tool business. He says in early 1981 he received a call from his CIA contacts from his days at Air America; they told him they could kick a lot of business his way if Reed would help the Agency monitor "trade-secret leaks to communist countries" (*Covert Action*, Summer 1991).

In March 1983 his contacts told him of a new covert oper-ation called "Private Donation," which enabled citizens to do-nate items to the Contras and would later have them replaced. If the individuals wanted to consider the items donated lost or stolen, insurance companies would reimburse the owners. Two weeks later Reed discovered that his Piper turbo-prop plane had been stolen from the Joplin, Missouri, field where he left it when he returned from a Florida air show and developed engine trouble. Reed filed a claim with his insurance company and received a check for $33,000.

In 1985 Reed received a phone call from William Cooper, an old Air America friend who had been involved in flying arms to the Contras. Cooper died in the October 5th, 1986, plane crash over Nicaragua that exposed then-Vice President Bush's ties to the Contra supply effort. Cooper told Reed that his airplane had been stolen by Oliver North, but would be returned soon. Hav-ing already filed a claim for theft, Reed was worried and thus was told to rent a hangar to store it.

In mid-1986, his CIA contacts told him that there was a lot of money to be made in his business in Mexico, and the CIA would stir more contracts his way if he would be involved in supporting the Contra effort. He was asked to establish a front company called Machinery International which would be under the direction of Felix Rodriguez, Bush's personal link to the Contra operation.

Reed moved his family to Guadalajara, Mexico, and became increasingly aware of the illegal activities the CIA, such as their using the same arms export network to run drugs, particularly cocaine, back into the U.S. Just as was trying to disengage himself from the operation, Arkansas State Police were mysteriously told where they could find Reed's plane, which he had declared stolen more than four years earlier.

Reed discovered that information on him had been given to the FBI and the U.S. Customs Service and he was being considered by these two agencies as "armed and dangerous." After his wife's parents were harassed by federal agents, Reed surrendered to police in Kansas City. He and his wife were charged in June 1988 with four counts of federal postal fraud based on receiving an insurance payment under a false claim. In a court motion in February 1989 Reed countered the charges and described how his plane had been "stolen" by North's Contra network via "Project Donation" and said that when he told them he wanted out, they had the plane "reappear." Reed claimed he was simply a disposal asset, used and manipulated by U.S. intelligence agencies. Once it became apparent he knew too much, he was considered too dangerous to simply let walk out the door.

Charges against Reed's wife were eventually dropped. The defense's witness list included many CIA agents, so the court enacted the Classified Information Procedure act on it and prevented his lawyer from calling them to the stand. The government refused Reed's request to turn over North's diaries, notes and records, which Reed said he needed to prove his innocence. On November 9th, 1990, the prosecution announced there was insufficient evidence to prosecute.

Evidence the defense wanted to use in their clients' behalf wound up in Clinton's mansion long after it was to be in the federal court's possession. Reed is now suing the Arkansas state police officials, who, he claims, set him up on the mail fraud charges. One of them is Buddy Young, head of security for Governor Bill Clinton.

According to Young, on October 8th, 1987, Tommy Baker, a former Arkansas state police officer and a close friend of Young, says he just happened to be passing by Reed's hanger when a "powerful gust of wind blew the door open and exposed Reed's plane." Young said that after he was contacted by Baker, he gave the aircraft's registration number to the National Crime Information Center to determine if the plane was stolen. Baker was told it wasn't, and then tried to determine if the markings had been changed. They had, and on October 21st he turned the case over to the FBI.

Yet on October 5th, before the so-called gust of wind opened the hanger door, Young had called in an incorrect registration number even before Baker said he first saw the plane.

On July 5th, 1991, Reed charged that the two presented false evidence for the purpose of furthering a false prosecution (*The Nation*, February 24th, 1992). It was established that Young made calls from Bill Clinton's mansion, and later admitted that he and Baker had tampered with the plane, and obtained warrants on the basis of misrepresentation. A federal judge in the case, Frank Theis, said that Baker and Young "acted with reckless disregard for the truth."

The whole story behind Bill Clinton's ties to Mena may yet be revealed. Criminology professor Allan Block of Penn State University, one of the nation's leading academic scholars of the international drug traffic, has a book on Mena in the works.

Says Congressman Alexander: "I have never seen a whitewash job like what has been executed in this case. There has been a conspiracy of the greatest magnitude that has not been prosecuted" (*In These Times*, February 12th, 1992).

CHAPTER 15

Follow the Money Trail: Who Looted the S&Ls?

While the Reagan-Bush Administration repeatedly told the American people that the deregulation of the nation's savings and loans was going to benefit consumers because less regulation on the industry would provide a more efficient allocation of capital, nothing could have been further from the truth. In the end it will cost the American public (a conservative estimate) more than $500 billion to bail out the failed thrifts.

Yet only a fraction of the money lost in S&L failures has been documented. The media attention on cases where bank officials spent lavishly on cars, lavish condos, and boats accounts for only a small portion of the total money lost. Where did the rest go? An even more probing question is: To what extent was the looting of the S&Ls preconceived, an instrument to move enormous amounts of government funds out of the public (government) sector offshore to be used for covert operations in certain intelligence agencies? And, did the Bush-Reagan Administrations attempt to cover up the entire affair?

In July 1987 the White House chose Danny Wall to replace Edwin Gray as Chairman of the Federal Home Loan Bank Board. Gray lost his job when he started to speak out against the corruption that was going on and the true extent of the S&L fraud. Wall served as a top aide to Republican Senator Jake Garn of Utah from 1981, when Garn was chairman of the Senate Banking Committee and had become a favorite of S&L owners. When Wall was appointed in 1987, Senator Leach would remark: "The industry got to choose outright its regulator."

It was Wall who drafted the infamous deregulation bill which came to be known as the Garn-St. Germain Act. This shifted the savings and loan depositors' money, which was now to be insured for $100,000 instead of $40,000, from conventional to risky investments.

One of the S&L scandals which the Bush administration is believed to have played a direct role in helping to cover up was the Silverado Banking, Savings and Loan Association in Denver, Colorado, where the President's son Neil was a director.

Kermit Mowbray, a former president of the Topeka branch of the Federal Home Loan Bank (FHLB), one of the regional regulators charged with monitoring Silverado, testified under oath in June 1990 in Washington. He claimed he received orders from Washington to delay the closure of Silverado for 45 days in 1988, to avoid having it influence Bush's election chances (*Vanity Fair*, October 1990). Mowbray said he couldn't remember who told him to do that, or who made the call. Only that the order came in late October 1988.

At the same time a request was made by the Colorado state S&L regulatory body to seize the thrift immediately. James Moroney, a former supervisory analyst at the FHLB, asserted that Silverado was insolvent as far back as 1986.

CIA TIES TO THE S&L CRISIS

Did the CIA use certain S&Ls to launder money for covert operations or move money offshore?

In a series of articles in the *Houston Post* which concluded an eight-month investigation, journalist Pete Brewton discovered that 22 S&Ls and two banks that had to be bailed out by the government had links to the CIA, 16 in Texas alone.

Between 1983 and 1985, the First National Bank of Maryland was used by a CIA proprietary to make payments for covert operations, including the purchase of at least $23 million worth of weapons. Called Associated Traders, the CIA-linked proprietary company used accounts at First National to buy guns for covert operations in Nicaragua, Angola, Chad, and Afghanistan (*Covert Action*, No. 35, 1990).

These links were exposed when a former executive of the bank, Robert Maxwell, went public with the knowledge that Associated Traders was a CIA front company. Maxwell claims he was asked to commit crimes, such as hide the company's activities, which should have been identified on all letters of credit. Maxwell resigned from the bank when he was unable to receive, in writing, from his superiors that the actions he was being asked out to carry out were legal.

Maxwell then filed a $20 million lawsuit in the Maryland Federal District Court against the bank, claiming he was physically threatened and was then forced to leave his job. In response, the bank's attorney filed a brief which stated that "a relationship between First National and the CIA and Associated Traders was classified information which can neither be confirmed nor denied" (*Washington Business Journal*, February 5th, 1990).

Another S&L which maintained ties to the CIA was the Palmer National Bank in Washington, D.C., founded in 1983 by a $2.8 loan from Texan Herman K. Beebe to Harvey D. McLean, Jr. Brewton linked Beebe to at least a dozen failed S&Ls in the Southwest U.S. Beebe had served nearly a year in federal prison for bank fraud. *Inside Job*, by Stephen Pizzo, Mary Fricker, and Paul Muolo, 1989, the first book to document the S&L scandal, calls Beebe's banks "potentially the most powerful and corrupt banking network ever seen in the U.S." Beebe controlled, directly or indirectly, over 55 banks and 29 S&Ls in six Southern states, Colorado, and California.

McLean's partner in the business venture was Stefan Halper, George Bush's foreign policy director during the presidential primaries in 1980. Halper was in charge of the operations center in Arlington, Virginia, which maintained a constant watch on developments in the Carter campaign effort to free the U.S. hostages held in Teheran. Most of the staffers were former CIA agents. Halper has been tied to the "Debategate" scandal which revealed that Carter's notebooks of his 1980 presidential debates with Reagan were stolen and wound up in the hands of the Republican campaign. A congressional investigation initiated in 1983 and chaired by Don Albosta discovered that Halper "ran a highly secretive operation which involved a number of retired CIA officials"; and it is widely believed that Halper was put in charge of the operation to thwart Carter's efforts to free the hostages before the presidential elections, also known as the "October Surprise" conspiracy.

Palmer National served as the bank for Oliver North's National Endowment for the Preservation of Liberty (NEPL), headed by Carl "Spitz" R. Channell, which was used by North to send money and weapons to the Nicaraguan Contras. One contribution of $30,000 to the NEPL came from Silverado Banking, Savings and Loan Association's third-largest borrower, E. Trine Starnes, Jr. (*The Guardian*, October 31st, 1990).

When his real estate empire collapsed in the late 1980s, Starnes failed to repay more than $7.5 million in loans to Silverado. In a civil lawsuit against the Board of Director of Silverado, the Federal Deposit Insurance Corporation found that "the loans were made despite the fact that Silverado had no previous experience with Starnes, and that Starnes had a previous history of financial instability." It also stated that Silverado was "willing to make large sums available to Starnes even for speculative and poorly underwritten projects. "

Starnes was invited to the White House in January 1986 by Channell to hear a briefing from President Reagan on getting Congress to resume aid to the Contras. Starnes's "donation" went to fund the NEPL's Central American Freedom

Program, a propaganda campaign by the Reagan Administration. The program provided film tapes to local TV stations which alleged Sandinista atrocities.

Another bank for which Pete Brewton uncovered ties to the CIA was the Indian Springs State Bank in Kansas City, Kansas. Brewton was particularly interested in the connection between Indian Springs and Global International Air, an air charter company owned by a former Iranian, Farhad Azima. Brewton discovered that Azima was the fourth-largest stockholder in Indian Springs and that the bank had made numerous unsecured loans to Global Air. Global filed for bankruptcy in 1983 and Indian Springs followed it in 1984.

Global International Air was used by Oliver North's network on a number of occasions to ship arms, including a 1986 shipment of 23 tons of TOW missiles to Iran by Race Aviation, another company owned by Azima. When federal officials, including Former Assistant U.S. Attorney Lloyd Monroe, began to investigate Indian Springs' collapse, they were told to "back off from a key figure in the collapse because he had ties to the CIA." One source told Brewton the FBI did not investigate because it was told by the CIA that Azima was "off limits" (*Houston Post*, February 8th, 1990).

Azima's ties to the CIA stretch back to the late 1970s, when he acted as a transporter for EATSCO, Egyptian American Transport and Services Corp, which was owned by ex-CIA agents, including Thomas Clines, Theodore Shackley, and Richard Secord. Says criminal investigator Gene Wheaton: "Global was the aviation arm of EATSCO. It was owned through cutouts—third parties." Brewton quoted a private investigator in Houston who concurred with Wheaton, saying: "Wilson, Clines, and Secord incorporated Global."

Azima maintained some unusually close ties to the Republican Party. The Federal Election Commission revealed that from 1983 to 1988, he gave more than $54,000 to the Republican campaign, and, from 1984 to 1986, $27,000 to the

President's Dinner Committee. In 1986 he was even allowed to reschedule his testimony in a federal court case so he could attend a Washington function for key Republican donors. One pilot, Franck Van Geyso, who worked for Global for four years, told Brewton, "Any time we had a little problem with the feds, Azima would jump on a plane to Washington and straighten it out."

Brewton discovered a mysterious payment from Global International to Anthony Russo in 1981 of $25,000. Russo, a convicted conspirator to promote bribery and prostitution, was an employee of Indian Springs and a member of the advisory board of Global International. He was paid the money to escort Liberian dictator Samuel Doe on a "goodwill trip" of the U.S. which was paid for by Uncle Sam.

Van Geyso says that when Global's planes were in Miami, Southern Air Transport, a former CIA proprietary that was later sold to ex-CIA lawyer James Bastian, did the maintenance work. Van Geyso and other former pilots say they flew guns to Latin America and returned to the U.S. with drugs.

Another CIA-linked player to the failed S&L scandal was Robert L. Corson, who in March 1986 purchased the Kleberg County Savings and Loan in Kingsville, Texas, for $6 million and changed its name to Vision Banc Savings. To receive permission from state regulators to buy the bank, Corson presented a 1985 letter of recommendation from Judge Jon Lindsay to the Texas Savings and Loan commissioner. Lindsay headed President Bush's 1988 president campaign in Harris County, Texas. Judge Lindsay would later say that he hardly knew Corson, leading some investigators to believe that he did it as a favor to Bush. It was later revealed that Lindsay received a $10,000 campaign contribution and trip to Las Vegas from Corson (*Houston Post*, February 11th, 1990).

Journalist Brewton discovered that Corson was identified in federal law enforcement records as a "known money launderer." One former CIA operative told Brewton that

Corson "frequently acted as a mule for the agency," meaning that he carried large sums of cash from country to country.

When Corson purchased the bank it boasted assets of $70 million. Four months later it was bankrupt. In another unsavory deal, a $20 million loan to finance a Florida land purchase was arranged by Miami lawyer Lawrence Freeman, a convicted money launderer for drug runners (*Houston Post,* February 4th, 1990). Another participant in the Florida deal was Hill Financial Savings in Red Hill, Pennsylvania, which put in $80 million. Hill Financial was one of the 22 failed thrifts that the *Houston Post* linked to ties to the CIA. Hill Financial cost the U.S. taxpayers $1.9 billion.

The Sunshine State Bank in Miami was yet another failed bank which had ties to the CIA and the White House. Sunshine's owner, Ray Corona, was convicted in 1987 of racketeering, conspiracy, and mail fraud. Corona bought Sunshine in 1978 with $1.1 million in drug monies supplied by José Antonio "Tony" Fernandez, who was later indicted on charges of smuggling 1.5 million pounds of marijuana into the United States. His co-conspirator was Eulalio Francisco Castro, whose marijuana-smuggling charges were dropped because he began training Nicaraguan Contras on a farm near Naples, Florida (*Houston Post,* February 18th, 1990).

Lloyd Monroe, a former prosecutor with the Justice Department, says that although he is convinced the CIA either masterminded or condoned a certain amount of S&L fraud, proving it would be extremely difficult. He claims the reason Congress and federal regulatory agencies haven't been more aggressive in rooting out the corruption is because important government officials are aware of the CIA's involvement. "CIA and high government officials who might have had ties to people involved in S&L fraud can maintain the face of 'plausible deniability' that they didn't order or condone anything improper," says Monroe. "The CIA knows that these people are going to use their financial institutions for CIA purposes and are going to come to the CIA when they get into trouble" (*Houston Post*, February 4th, 1990).

Although the authors of *Inside Job*, Pizzo, Fricker, and Muolo, suspected CIA involvement in many failed S&Ls, they did not directly investigate the subject for their book. They did, however, conclude that: "Time and time again during our research we ran into people at failed thrifts who claimed to have connections with the CIA. We ran into individuals who we discovered were dealing secretly with the Contras, moving large sums of money here, there, and off to nowhere for what they claimed were covert purposes. Experts have wondered how so many billions of dollars could just vanish from the thrift industry without a trace. If some of that money were channeled into the Contra pipeline or used to serve other legal or illegal covert purposes, that could certainly be one answer. We didn't have time to investigate, but we want to be on the record as saying that we finally came to believe something involving the CIA and Contras was going on at the thrifts during the 1980s. After all, deregulation created enough chaos to accommodate just about anyone's purpose. And taking out loans from federally insured institutions, giving the money to the Contras, and letting federal insurance pick up the losses does have the flavor of what Ollie North might think was a "neat idea."

Not too surprising, the House Intelligence Committee, which did investigate links between the CIA and S&L failures, found no evidence to support the claims. It ended a nine-month preliminary inquiry into allegations that the CIA had fraudulently used the S&L funds with the conclusion that those charges were "based primarily on second-hand information" (*Wall Street Journal*, December 24th, 1990).

Due to the lack of will by certain members of Congress to challenge the White House and the intelligence agencies, the American people know nothing of what really went on at the S&Ls in the 1980s. If it weren't for the diligent efforts of investigative journalists like Pete Brewton, the failure of the S&Ls would have gone down in financial history as being solely about a failed free-market initiative. Yet how many more S&Ls were tied to the White House, the CIA and/or organized crime that Brewton *wasn't* able to expose?

The bottom line is whether the White House, Vice President Bush on down, knew what was happening, allowed it to continue, or actively covered it up. Or, even orchestrated what occurred and planned the whole scheme from the start.

If the hundreds of millions, some say billions, of dollars are ever finally located (probably in offshore banks), the American people might get a glimpse of who really was behind the biggest financial scandal in their nation's banking history.

THE BCCI AFFAIR WASN'T JUST A BANKING SCANDAL

To understand the roots of the BCCI scandal means to first stop calling it an "Arab bank." Albert Mokhiber, President of the American-Arab Anti-Discrimination Committee, points out: "The 'Arabs,' who number more than 200 million, have about as much to do with the Bank of Credit and Commerce International or any other financial institutions as 'Americans' have to do with crack-cocaine" (*New York Times*, Letters to the Editor, August 29th, 1991).

BCCI was neither an Arab- nor a Pakistani-owned bank. Its real owners, and objectives have yet to be exposed.

Like the S&L scandal, the Bush Administration has done everything in its power to prevent the truth from surfacing. To say that the White House "covered up" the scandal is an understatement.

A Senate subcommittee was established and headed by Senator John Kerry to investigate the BCCI affair. From the start, the committee encountered resistance from the Administration, specifically from the Justice Department, which ordered key witnesses not to cooperate and refused to hand over key important documents.

There were also charges that the Justice Department understaffed FBI and U.S. Attorney teams assigned to the BCCI case. Says New York District Attorney Robert Morgenthau, who initiated criminal action against BCCI officials: "We had no cooperation from the Justice Department since we first asked for records in March 1990," Morgenthau said. "In fact, they are impeding our investigation, and Justice Department representatives are asking witnesses not to cooperate with us" (*Time*, July 29th, 1991).

Legal efforts to prosecute BCCI stem from an October 1988 grand jury indictment in Tampa, Florida, of the bank and nine of its employees for money laundering. The case was made possible by the valiant work of Robert Mazur, then a U.S. Customs agent who led the undercover sting operation which produced the Tampa indictments. He left the Customs Service in 1988, saying that he was disgusted over the government's failure to pursue leads concerning secret BCCI ownership of US banks and alleged payoffs to U.S. politicians. The Justice Department even tried to prohibit John Kerry's committee from taking testimony from Mazur.

Despite overwhelming evidence, in 1990 the Justice Department offered the bank a plea bargain which avoided a trial. BCCI paid a fine of a mere $15 million.

Critics of the Justice Department's treatment of BCCI say that the $15 million fine the bank received in the Tampa case was a joke, and let the top ranks of BCCI off the hook. Said Kerry: "They plea-bargained in reverse. They let off the upper people and shut off the rest of the investigation. I know as a mater of fact that evidence that should have been followed up wasn't, witnesses that should have been talked to weren't, events that should have been exhaustively analyzed weren't" (*Newsweek*, August 5th, 1991).

The plea bargain, however, may have been the only way to keep BCCI from standing trial, and perhaps revealing what the White House was trying to keep hidden. Senate investigator Jack Blum says that he didn't believe there was ever an effort to plea-bargain the individual defendants because they never spent much time in jail but instead were housed in a condominium under guard by local police. This, he believed, was to keep them out of the prison culture, where they would have quickly come to understand that the only real "out" for someone in their position would be a plea bargain.

Yet even after the bank was, in fact, let off the hook, the Justice Department wanted to ensure that they continue operating. In a letter to Gerald Lewis, Florida State Controller of the Department of Banking, from the chief of the Justice Department's narcotic and dangerous drug section, Charles S. Saphos, a request was made that Lewis not shut BCCI down. It stated: "We are . . . requesting that BCCI be permitted to operate in your jurisdiction" (*Newsweek*, August 5th, 1991).

Another congressional investigation, led by Congressman Charles Schumer of the House Judiciary Subcommittee on Crime and Criminal Justice, believed that someone in the Justice Department told the prosecutor to "slow down, to lay off BCCI." Said Schumer: "I don't know if this is true, but when we interviewed law enforcement people in this case, Justice has insisted someone from the White House sit in" (*Time*, November 11th, 1991).

Schumer's own report, which was based on a review of Federal documents, asserts that as far back as 1983 various Federal law enforcement agencies and officials knew or received reports that BCCI was involved in money-laundering activities. The Internal Revenue Service itself received at least 13 allegations, and the Drug Enforcement Administration was involved in at least 125 cases "having something to do with BCCI (*New York Times*, September 6th, 1991). "All the rogues knew about this bank," said Schumer. "How come none of the regulators did?" (*New York*, August 5th, 1991).

One reason may be that the CIA didn't want them to find out.

The CIA first produced a report on BCCI in 1986, but only referred to what it called "unorthodox and unconventional practices." Former Customs Commissioner William Von Raab said the report he received from the CIA was as "bland as porridge" (*Washington Post*, August 11th, 1991).

A later CIA report, a 30-page document issued in May 1989, contained mini-profiles of BCCI managers and a long list of its branches and shareholders. Even by 1989, the only thing the CIA would admit that it knew about the bank was that it was "a source of undetermined reliability" and that BCCI established a Washington, D.C., presence in late 1987 with the purchase of First American Bankshares. It goes on to describe BCCI as a bank that "has a reputation for doing business with anyone, and using whatever means are available to preserve anonymity when the depositor request it." No mention is made of BCCI's ties to Palestinian terrorist Abu Nidal, money-laundering operations in cooperation with Manuel Noriega, or arms sales to Iran and Iraq.

Richard Kerr, who was acting CIA chief before Robert Gates was chosen to run the agency in September 1991, said the CIA did nothing more than maintain a few "ordinary bank accounts" at BCCI and that they were "lawful and proper." He claimed that the agency made an "honest mistake" by not sending the Federal Reserve Board a 1985 report (which casts doubt on the veracity on the 1986 report) which showed that BCCI secretly owned First American Bankshares. Federal agencies only discovered this fact in 1990.

During the Senate investigation on the BCCI affair in August 1991, Senator Kerry reported that when his staff asked for a copy of a 1988 CIA memorandum on BCCI's corporate criminality, they were told it didn't exist. Later, the CIA said it did exist, but was "extremely sensitive" in nature and handed it over. One sentence, however—stating that BCCI already owned American banks and that the CIA knew that in 1982—was deleted.

A frustrated Kerry told his fellow senators: "The entire question about secrecy in government is once again raised by this issue. Too often too many of use have seen instances where information that people want to keep away from the accountability process is merely classified. There is no rightful reason for it to be classified, there is no matter of national security of urgency contained therein, but it is classified, and thereby we have a secret government kept away from the people."

What was the Administration trying to hide or cover up?

Covert arms sales may be one thing. One mysterious event in the BCCI investigation occurred during August 1991 but received little media coverage in the United States. Anson Ng, a British journalist who worked for *The Financial Times*, was found shot to death in his Guatemala City apartment. Guatemalan authorities claimed the murder was the work of common criminals, but independent journalists familiar with the case say Ng, who was found with a bullet wound in his head, was struck in the neck, was not robbed, nor were his personal items stolen.

BCCI was at the center of a complex affair concerning allegations of illegal shipments of American-made arms to Guatemala's military. Did Ng get too close to the truth? According to people who talked by phone with Ng in the days before his death, he told them he was working on a "big story" related to arms trafficking allegedly carried out by BCCI in collusion with top leaders of the Guatemalan military.

Another covert operation the Bush Justice Department may not have wanted to reveal is the use of the bank as a conduit to funnel $2 billion in U.S. aid to mujahideen rebels fighting the Soviets in Afghanistan. Although hidden from public view, it is widely believed that a large chunk of that covert funding was stolen by corrupt Pakistani officials using

BCCI accounts.

It may be more than just a coincidence that BCCI has Pakistani roots. Blum told Kerry's committee: "People repeatedly told me that this bank was a product of the Afghan War and people who were very close to the mujahideen have said that many of the Pakistani military officials who were deeply involved in assisting and supporting the Afghan rebel movement were stealing our foreign assistance money and using this bank both to hide the money they stole, to market American weapons that were to be delivered that they stole, and to market and manage the funds that came from the selling of heroin that was apparently engineered by one of the mujahideen group. This is an issue that has largely been unexplored in public."

Adds a U.S. intelligence agent: "If BCCI is such an embarrassment to the U.S. that forthright investigations are not being pursued, it has a lot to do with the blind eye the U.S. turned to the heroin trafficking in Pakistan" (*Time*, July 29th, 1991).

Potentially, probably the most explosive of ties between BCCI and the Administration may be concealed in records which recorded the bank's U.S. transactions, including bribes paid to congressmen and senators. Those records were most likely destroyed, possibly by U.S. government officials.

Kerry's committee received one letter from a federal law enforcement official who complained to him that "tons of documents were not reviewed . . ." and that "the CIA put a halt to certain investigative leads" in the Tampa case. "We had drug traffickers, money launderers, foreign government involvement, Noriega, and allegations of payoffs by BCCI to U.S. government political figures. I will not elaborate on who these U.S. government figures were alleged to be, but I can advise you that you don't have all of the documents. Some were destroyed or misplaced" (*Time*, November 11th, 1991).

Federal Reserve officials say the only evidence of BCCI's ownership of First American Bankshares, CenTrust, and other U.S. banks was hidden in a secret cache of BCCI documents seized when English regulators seized the bank's records in early summer of 1991.

Former Customs Commissioner William Von Rabb said that his department desperately wanted the large amount of BCCI documents which were seized by the British authorities and were subject to a number of lawsuits in Great Britain because of efforts by BCCI to prevent the documents from being given to U.S. investigators. Eventually, the documents were turned over to the United States through the Customs Services. Yet Von Rabb was prohibited by the Treasury Department from receiving any of the files. They were sealed up by his own customs agent, and sent directly to the Treasury Department. The agents from Customs were told that Von Rabb was not to have access to any information on the BCCI case.

BCCI bank records from Panama City relating to Noriega's dealings with the bank were also put off-limits to U.S. investigators. They mysteriously disappeared in transit to Washington while under the protection of the Drug Enforcement Administration. The DEA claimed it had "no idea what happened to the documents" (*Time*, July 29th, 1991).

Probably the most controversial set of "missing documents" is an alleged list, bribery list to be more accurate, kept by BCCI officials. It contained, supposedly, the names of 105 members of both Houses of Congress.

Senator Kerry had enough suspicions about the reported list to have asked William Taylor, staff director of banking supervision and regulation at the Federal Reserve, about them. "Have you or any of your investigative staff seen an alleged list of U.S. officials reportedly prepared by officials at BCCI that indicates payoffs or bribes in any form?" Kerry asked. Taylor replied: "We have been hearing about this list for the past four weeks. We have not been able to find such a list."

Kerry also asked Robert Mazur, the undercover customs agent who was chiefly responsible for exposing the crimes at the Tampa branch of BCCI, if he believed that Capcom, the Chicago-based commodities firm that was used by BCCI to launder billions of dollars, was used as a delivery system to pay off political and government officials. Mazur said he had no information on this matter.

Reports of the list have come from other corners. Sources told *Time* magazine in its July 29th, 1991, edition that one BCCI Washington representative distributed millions of dollars in payoffs to U.S. officials during the past decade. "In America, it was easy; money almost always worked, and we sought out politicians known to be corruptible," another source boasted.

Lloyd's of London claimed it offered evidence it held of bribery and kickbacks made to U.S. attorneys in Miami. Lloyd's claims the Justice Department completely ignored the offer (*Time*, July 29th, 1991).

During the Senate hearings Senator Jesse Helms asked: "Why the lack of action on BCCI by this administration, so good at managing the crises they themselves create? During the past years there were no lack of danger signs concerning this full-service banking service for terrorists, for drug mobsters, for nuclear proliferators, for assorted rogues and professional confidence men. Who were they afraid of offending, and why? Or, why were they so incompetent in their pursuit of greed's global reach." It wasn't incompetence. Nor was the BCCI affair simply a financial scandal about the clandestine take-over of a few American banks or a bank that was used by drug dealers, arms merchants, and money launderers without anyone in Washington finding out.

The reason why the White House failed to act when it knew in 1988 that BCCI was secretly in control of other banks was not that it would have been embarrassing to the White

House since those ties ran through Democrats like Clifford Irving, David Paul, and Bert Lance. It was only when documents revealing money laundering and secret financial transactions between Bush and Saddam Hussein and Manuel Noreiga, and bribes paid to congressmen and senators, were threatened to be exposed, that the Administration decided it was time to take action and move in to cover up the scandal.

Interestingly, very few members of Congress have demanded action on BCCI. One politician who certainly wouldn't like to see the truth about BCCI unfold is Senator Orrin Hatch from Utah. In an effort to shift blame for the BCCI scandal onto the Democrats, Hatch issued an extensive report detailing to David Paul the Miami S&L CenTrust meetings and phone conversations with Senator John Kerry and other Democratic senators.

Those contacts may lead to another aspect of the scandal, however, that is not where the source of foul play at BCCI lies. Blum told Kerry's investigation: "There was an army of people in Washington on all sides trying to say this bank was a wonderful bank, that the people involved in it were honest, good, and true people, and that anybody who said they were the criminals that I was making them out to be had to be crazy."

That "army" was being led from the office of Robert Altman, BCCI's lawyer, with the help of Hatch.

Nothing was quite as shocking as Hatch's February 22nd, 1990, speech on the Senate floor. He was the first and sole supporter of the Justice Department and Attorney General Richard Thornburg's deal with BCCI which settled for BCCI's paying a simple $15 million fine. Hatch painted BCCI as the crime of a few "bad apples," that BCCI could offer important cooperation and assistance in the global drug war, and commended the bank's management for responding to the laundering charges as "a responsible corporate citizen." He also asserted there was no "systematic money laundering uncovered in the BCCI case, despite the bank's pleading guilty to 31 felony counts.

If that weren't incredible enough, Hatch warned that if the U.S. government singled out BCCI, it would give "the wrong message to our friends in the Middle East" and not serve "the national interest."

A short while after giving that speech, Hatch contacted BCCI on behalf of Monzer Hourani, a Houston real estate development which Hatch had financial ties to. Thus, even after BCCI was facing major drug-laundering charges in the U.S. courts and while it was being hounded by U.S. government investigators, Hatch was calling up the bank's CEO, Swaleh Naqvi, and asking him to approve a loan to his good friend Monzer.

Hourani told NBC News on November 26th, 1991, that Hatch told him in 1989 that he knew people at BCCI and that he might be able to put in a good word with them for him.

Hourani was tied to Mohammad Hammoud, who was acting as a front man for BCCI Holdings Luxembourg. Hatch claimed earlier that he wasn't aware of the ties between BCCI and Hammoud until 1990, and that he learned of them only after reading about them in a Washington business magazine. He said their conversations were about the Middle East, Lebanon's leadership, and the hostage crises.

Yet when in the mid-1980s Hourani found himself in debt to a few S&Ls, Hatch wrote a letter to the Federal Savings and Loan Insurance Corporation on July 31st, 1986, explaining how Monzer had been a victim of one of the failed thrifts, Mainland Savings in Houston. When the letter was discovered, Hatch claimed he was unaware of it "until the past few days" and that a staffer must have used "an automatic pen" to put his signature on it (*Wall Street Journal*, December 3rd, 1991) (not your standard letter for the automatic-pen people).

The *Houston Post* reported that in 1987 Texas state banking regulators suspected Hourani of criminal actions and sent a "criminal referral" to the FBI. At the time, Hammoud was a money-mover for Hezballah, holding the Lebanese Shiite organization responsible for the U.S. hostages in Lebanon. Hammoud, says Hourani, had friends among Lebanon's Christian factions, and Hourani had similar contacts in Syria. Hammoud and he worked with Iran-Contra middleman Adnan Khashoggi and Hatch on a number of "private" schemes to free U.S. hostages held by terrorists in Lebanon (*New Republic,* January 27th, 1992). Hatch hosted Khashoggi on trips to Washington and convinced him to make substantial investments in Hatch's home state of Utah.

Hammoud died in May 1990 while he was visiting his doctor in Switzerland. His insurance company refused to pay his life insurance policy because they claim his corpse was found to be four inches shorter than the height recorded at his last medical examination earlier that year (*Wall Street Journal,* November 21st, 1991).

If the American people are ever to discover U.S. government links to BCCI, Hatch's office would be a good place to start. His response to this monstrous financial scandal is nothing short of astounding. His ties to Hourani, and other BCCI dealmakers, and his "private" efforts to get the U.S. hostages then held in Lebanon released, should be the focus of a thorough congressional investigation.

Jackson Stephens and George Bush, Jr.'s, ties to BCCI should also be investigated.

Little Rock, Arkansas, financier Jackson Stephens and the good fortune that fell on Harken Energy is a prime example of how it pays to be a good friend of President Bush.

The Stephens group investment firm, Stephens Inc., is reportedly to be worth nearly $1 billion. Stephens helped BCCI executives in the late 1970s to find key American investment opportunities, such as First American Bankshares. He was a major contributor to President Bush and part of Team 100, a Republican group where membership required a

$100,000 donation to Bush's election campaign. Stephens' wife, Mary Anne, was the 1988 co-chairman of the Bush for President drive. In September 1977, Jimmy Carter's former Office of Management and Budget director Bert Lance recommended that BCCI officials meet his good friend Jackson Stephens to discuss acquisition of National Bank of Georgia. Stephens met with Agha Hasan Abedi, founder and head of BCCI. Stephens was a defendant in the suit against BCCI in its attempt to take over First American Bankshares.

Stephens was the major mover behind the deal that enabled a company run by President Bush's son George Jr. to win a lucrative contract to drill for oil in Bahrain. The only problem was that Harken Energy had never sunk a well and was millions in debt.

Stephens had a friend, Michael Ameen, a Houston oil consultant who had "close" contacts with Kamal Adham, a major shareholder in BCCI and the former chief of the Saudi Arabian intelligence service, and Abdullah Taha Bakhsh, a Saudi investor who controls nearly 17 percent of Harken's stock. While he was working on the deal, Ameen was also serving as a paid consultant to the U.S. State Department, and briefed incoming U.S. ambassador to Bahrain, Charles Hoestler. Hoestler, also a member of the Bush Team 100, was a financial advisor to Mohammad Hammoud, who was "tied" to Senator Orrin Hatch through Hezballah moneyman Monzer Hourani.

Stephens convinced the Union Bank of Switzerland to invest $25 million in Harken. At the time, Union Bank was involved in a joint venture with BCCI in another Swiss bank. (What was so attractive about Harken, then, that the Union Bank pumped that type of money into it and rescued it from its debt woes?)

No one in the oil industry has been able to figure out exactly how Harken Energy won the contract, or for that matter how it manages to stay in business. Although it continues to lose money, Bush Jr. and other directors of the company receive six-figure salaries and generous stock options. Says Phil Kendrick, Harken's founder, who remains a minority shareholder: "There's been so much promotion, manipulation, and inside deal making. It's been a fast numbers game" (*Time*, October 28th, 1991).

Harken Energy was formed in the late 1970s. In 1984 it was taken over by Alan Quasha, whose father was "tied" to the Nugan Hand Bank scandal in Australia in 1980 where it was revealed that a secret team of covert operators were laundering billions in profits from the drug trade out of Laos. Before long, Harken passed the $100 million mark. In 1991 the company lost $40 million and watched its shareholder equity drop more than $3 million, $70 million since 1988.

George Bush, Jr.'s, own dealings with Harken are in question. He sold nearly $850,000 worth of Harken's stock just a week before the company showed very poor quarterly earnings and lost more than 60 percent of its value over a half-year period. The Securities and Exchange Commission sought an explanation from Bush after only learning about the sale more than eight months after the fact. Bush said he filed it on time, but it "got lost."

A few years later, Bush Jr. came to the rescue, and a group of investors received more than $2 million worth of Harken stock in exchange for his 180-well Texas oil operation, Spectrum 7 Energy Corp., which was awash in red ink. (Young George seems to have a knack of making money where none exists.)

Among Bush Jr.'s first investor group was James R. Bath, a Houston aircraft broker, who invested $50,000 with Bush when he created his Arbusto Energy Co. (which earned, of course, no profit) before it merged with Spectrum. With Saudi financier Ghaith Pharaon, BCCI cutout major BCCI shareholder Khaled bin Mahfouz, and former U.S. Treasury Secretary John Connally—all of them investors—Bath was a director of Houston's Main Bank. This small community bank held only $58 million in deposit, yet had been buying $10 million a month in $100 bills for some unknown purpose (*Time*, October 28th, 1991).

Bath, a Bush friend, controlled a fleet of companies tied to his aircraft business. Bill White, Bath's former partner, and another good friend of the President from Bush's Texas Air National Guard days, is currently embroiled in a number of lawsuits. White claims Bath was a front man for CIA business operations, and that he used his connections with the Bush family to cloak the development of a lucrative array of offshore companies designed to move money and airplanes between Texas and the Middle East. The same firm that incorporated Bath's companies in the Cayman Islands, did the same for a money-collecting front company created by Oliver North. Private records obtained by reporters at *Time* showed that Bath was a "representative" for several wealthy Saudi families. Bath referred to himself as "a small, obscure businessman."

As soon as Bush Jr. came aboard, he brought along Abdullah Taha Bakhsh, whose was said to be "a reclusive Saudi." Then the Bahrain deal came along. Bahrain hadn't made a new oil find since 1932, but a seismic survey suggested a large geological formation under the sea (*Wall Street Journal*, December 6th, 1991).

In 1989 the Bahrain government suddenly and mysteriously broke off talks with Amoco, which it had held for the past two years, to discuss the project with Michael Ameen. Harken claims Bahrain was looking for a small American company because a larger company might not "have had the commitment" to stick with the project. (I'm sure Amoco would really have ignored the project.) The deal was signed, even though Harken admitted it couldn't finance the drilling on its own. It signed an agreement with Bass Enterprises Production of Fort Worth, which was controlled by the Bass family. The Basses have contributed more than $200,000 to the Republican

Party in recent years (*Wall Street Journal*, December 6th, 1991). (What a surprise. More friends of Bush from Texas.)

Talt Othman, a director of Harken who manages investments for Sheik Abdullah Taha Bakhsh, is also an active member of the Arab-American Council on the Middle East and a close friend of former White House Chief of Staff John Sununu. Within six months of the signing of the agreement with Bahrain, Othman was added by the White House to a select list of 15 Arab-Americans who meet periodically with President Bush and National Security Advisor Brent Scowcroft to discuss American Middle East policy.

Everyone from the President on down says there's nothing fishy about the arrangement and that Harken won the Bahrain contract on its own merit. A more likely answer is that the entire affair was yet another of President Bush's covert operations designed either to launder money, fund covert operations, or illicitly enrich Bush's immediate family. Take your pick.

EVIL STUFF IN CHICAGO

The part of the story of BCCI that has never been told was given to me by investigative journalist Sherman Skolnick.

I'm convinced that fate means a lot when one is investigating covert operations. When I met Skolnick in April 1992 it was just at that point in time where I needed someone to fill in the missing pieces. It was only after I heard what Skolnick had been investigating that I could really understand what the scandal was all about.

In 1963 Skolnick established an organization called "Citizen's Committee to Clean Up the Courts," a public interest group which investigated and exposed public corruption, especially in the courts. Self-educated in law, Skolnick claims that his Freedom of Information suit in 1959 led to the disclosure of several pages of a suppressed report of a President's Crime Commission, called the Blakey Report, showing links in Chicago between the Federal judiciary and organized crime, and how the mob murdered a Chicago Federal Appeals judge. Between 1969 and 1973 he investigated bribery charges against the 7th Court Circuit Federal Appeals Judge, Otto Kerner, Jr.

Skolnick got national exposure as a result of his research into the suspicious plane crash in December 1972 in which 12 Watergate figures died, including Mrs. E. Howard Hunt, who was carrying a suitcase with $2 million inside. The Hunts were allegedly blackmailing Nixon about his role in the murder of JFK. In the case, Skolnick sued the National Transportation Safety Board (NTSB), charging them with a cover-up of the scandal. As a result, the NTSB reopened its hearings and Skolnick presented them with 1300 pages of documents from NTSB's own files demonstrating foul play.

In 1987 Skolnick investigated the mysterious death of Chicago's first black mayor, Harold Washington. The medical staff confirmed his charges that Washington was poisoned.

Skolnick contends that Saddam Hussein and George Bush maintained a financial relationship and that this is what the Bush Administration is trying to hide.

"For ten years," says Skolnick, "Hussein has received kickbacks from the other Middle East oil nations which went through BCCI. This deal was arranged by President Bush, and went through companies such as Pennzoil, which was created by William Liedtke, Jr., and Liedtke's brother, who along with Bush created Zappata Petroleum Co. in the early 1960s. Bush profited financially from the deal."

Skolnick points to a case currently in the Federal District Court in Chicago: "People of the States of Illinois ex rel William Harris versus the Board of Governors of the Federal Reserve System, Number 90C 6863." On May 10th, 1991, the case came before a three-judge appeals panel. One of the judge's law clerks leaked information that one of the judges was pressing to release the records. Skolnick says that the

Justice Department then started circulating stories that one of the panel members, Judge Richard Posner, was being investigated for eight instances of bribery in other cases.

"Posner was pressuring the other judges to release the records. The Justice Department wanted this information about the bribery cases known so they could blackmail the three-judge panel not to release the documents relating to Bush and Saddam," Skolnick believes.

After attending the hearings on the case, he stopped one of the lawyers, who was from the state solicitor general's office, which represents the state banking commissioner, who is in charge of the Italian Banca Nazionale del Lavoro's Chicago branch records. Skolnick said to the lawyer: "Sources tell me that the records being fought over in this court involve huge private deals between Bush and Saddam Hussein. Not government-to-government deals, but huge private deals." She replied: "You are absolutely correct." Skolnick asked: "Why is the bank commissioner so afraid that these records might be revealed?" She said: "It might cause a run on the bank. It might cause widespread lack of confidence in banks in general. It would tend to cause a great disruption."

Skolnick then asked the general counsel for the bank commissioner the same questions. He responded: "Mr. Skolnick, I want you to also know that the Justice Department is resisting the release of other non-bank records involving Bush and Saddam."

In other words, under-the-table records.

Skolnick says that the reason Senator Kerry or anyone else, for that matter, is aware of a list of congressmen and senators who were bribed by BCCI is that at least four major media organizations, and the Federal Reserve, received photocopies of it which came straight from the files in London of the Bank of England, which seized all of BCCI's London documents in early summer 1991. One establishment, apparently blocked from publishing it by his editor, revealed the list to Skolnick.

Skolnick says that large sums of cash were physically brought into Chicago by two channels: the Chicago branch of the Banca Nazionale del Lavoro (BNL), the same bank whose Atlanta branch granted more than $5 billion worth of loans to Saddam Hussein. On Columbus Day weekend in 1988, BCCI's facilities in the U.S., including its Chicago branch, were seized on order from the Administration to quash documentation on this illegal activity.

Chicago was a city awash in illegal money laundering. There was talk then in Chicago of the futures exchanges being used by "organized crime to launder money" (*The London Economist*, January 28th, 1989). One congressional staffer remarked: "A lot of people think evil stuff is going on there in Chicago" (*Wall Street Journal*, November 5th, 1987).

Money was believed to have been laundered by having it fed into the bank accounts of four commodity brokers headquartered in Chicago. On September 5th, 1986, U.S. Attorney Anton Valukas announced an 11-count Federal grand jury indictment against a team of money launderers, led by Boston Witt, former attorney general of New Mexico. Also indicted was Shahid Riky from the Chicago branch of the Bank of Credit and Commerce.

Another indication of the money laundering going through Chicago resulted in a series of undercover operations by the FBI, called "Sour Mash," within the Chicago Mercantile Exchange in January 1989. The two-year investigation, also headed by Valukas, sought to root out a wide range of illegal trading practices, and eventually indicted 46 commodities traders. However, Valukas was probably hoping to expose evidence of more systematic corruption at the level of senior executives of the exchange's clearing firms.

In November, two former members of the Chicago Board of Trade (CBOT) were given jail terms of five and six years. In sentencing the two, Judge Marvin Aspen called CBOT, America's largest futures exchange, the "tip of the iceberg," a "cesspit," and "ripe for corruption and abuse" (*The London Economist*, November 12th, 1989).

A major player in the scheme was Capcom Futures Inc., which was fined $500,000 in October 1989 and was forced to withdraw its membership in the Chicago Mercantile Exchange. Its London-based affiliate, Capcom Financial Ltd., was also expelled by the Futures, Brokers and Dealers, a regulatory body which oversees British commodity markets, and fined $700,000.

Capcom worked closely with BCCI, and played a major role in papering over losses at BCCI in mid-1980s for as much as $1.3 billion. Senate investigator Jack Blum revealed that at one point Capcom's "gross transaction rate" totaled almost $90 billion in an eight-month span (*Wall Street Journal*, November 22, 1991). It is believed that Capcom was created as a front so BCCI could launder drug money through the Chicago commodity exchanges.

Capcom Financial Services had been founded in 1984 by Bob Magness, of Tele-Communications, one of America's largest cable TV firms. You guessed it. Magness is "close" to Bush. He joined four Middle Eastern businessmen ostensibly in an offshore operation to speculate in financial and commodities markets. One of them was Kamal Adham, former chief of the Saudi Arabian intelligence service. The other was Syed Ziauddin Akbar, the former head of BCCI's treasury operation.

Magness and Senior Vice President Larry Romrell sat on the board of Capcom from 1985 to 1990. Romrell's spokesman said he was introduced to "some of the Arabian principals" of Capcom through "friends of friends of friends." The mouthpiece added: "The proceedings were conducted mostly in Arabic and Urdu, and Mr. Romrell frankly didn't understand most of what went on." (That sounds like a George Bush answer if I've ever heard one.)

Robert Mazur, the former Customs Service undercover

agent, testified to the Senate that "we came to learn that it was Mr. Akbar's plan to launder drug proceeds through the transactions of Capcom." Mazur had presented himself as a middleman for drug lords and was told by two officials at BCCI's Florida branch that Capcom could launder the money. Mazur was introduced to Akbar in London.

Mazur explained that Akbar told him how Capcom uses so-called mirror-image trading to create accounts that would use different shell corporations. If orders to both buy and sell a commodity are made at the same time, and no loss or gain is insured, it still incurs fees which can be reported were earned on those transactions. The fees could then be allocated to a third party (*Wall Street Journal*, November 22nd, 1991). The Chicago Mercantile Exchange charged that Capcom was involved in another scheme where money was shifted around among different accounts of Capcom shareholders. Investments were taken out of one account and put in another with no record of the transfers.

"Because these transactions would be scrambled among many billions of dollars' worth of transactions, it would take forever for anyone to ever find them," Mazur concluded.

Akbar and Capcom are defendants in two civil lawsuits in the United States and Britain by the government of Panama to recover millions of dollars that were allegedly stolen by Noriega. More than $20 million of Noriega's money had been traced from BCCI's branch in Panama through banks in six countries to a trading account at Capcom (*Washington Post*, September 29th, 1991). It is believed that Noriega's account was part of the millions of dollars of unexplained payments found by British regulatory agencies which audited Capcom's accounts.

A mysterious third individual tied to Capcom is Robert Powell, who the *Washington Post* discovered worked in aircraft operations and maintenance firms which had ties with the U.S. government stretching back to the Vietnam War

(*Washington Post*, September 29th, 1991). Powell admitted he had had business connection with Kamal Adham since 1968, when Adham was head of Saudi Intelligence, and that he had long done business with BCCI. When asked why he accepted an offer to invest in Capcom, Powell replied: "Because it was in my interest to place BCCI." The offer came not from Adham, but from the then head of BCCI's branch in Oman, Pakistani banker Syed Ziauddin Akbar.

The White House's connection to the growing scandal in Chicago was likely through U.S. Secretary of Agriculture Clayton Yeutter, who was a former Chicago Mercantile Exchange president. Yeutter agreed to be character witness for Brian Monieson, who was himself a former chairman of the Mercantile Exchange. Monieson faced charges that two of his commodity brokers in his company, GNP Commodities, defrauded customers. The Commodity Futures Trading Commission, a regulatory agency, banned Monieson from trading for life.

Skolnick says that BCCI merely took advantage of the already existing close relationship with the commodity exchanges in Chicago and members of both Houses of Congress. He says that, one by one, various congressmen and senators flew into Chicago to deliver their "speeches" and collect their honoria from either the Chicago Board of Trade, the Chicago Board Options Exchanges, or the Chicago Mercantile Exchange.

He also reveals that Bush had a joint business venture with Panama's former dictator Manuel Noriega through the Continental Bank of Chicago. He believes the reason the BCCI officials in Tampa were offered such a sweetheart deal by the Justice Department is because they warned that if they were going to prison, they would release documents showing Bush's private business ventures through their bank with Noriega and Hussein.

Skolnick also discloses that BCCI was actually formed

with seed money from the Bank of America and that its largest shareholders aren't Arab Sheiks or Pakistani frontmen, but the Rothschild banking family from their bases in Chicago, Paris, London, and Switzerland.

He says: "Until just recently Henry Kissinger and David Rockefeller sat on the consulting board of BNL. These are the two men who should be dragged before a committee of Congress and asked about what they know about BCCI, BNL, and secret deals between Bush and Saddam. No doubt, this is where the roots of scandal are."

After meeting Skolnick I realized something: the laundering of dirty money and drug trafficking can't exist if the White House didn't want it to. He led me to the conclusion that a large portion of the money laundering that was (is) going on in America, both by BCCI and others, was tied to the White House and President Bush.

Could it really be that the highest levels of the U.S. government are involved in plots to import drugs and launder money, I asked myself? Yes. Bush is behind BCCI. Behind Noriega. America, wake up! For about the thousandth time, Bush has pulled the wool over your eyes. He's hoodwinking you with a few mirrors to deflect your perception of reality. He is BCCI.

CHAPTER 16

Who Really Rules America, and Why?

When Arkansas' governor Bill Clinton was running for governor in October 1990, his campaign was in deep financial trouble. He called on Jackson Stephens, a member of the Bush 100 club in Little Rock, and the prime mover behind Harken Energy's bid to win a lucrative oil-drilling contract in Bahrain. Stephens helped Clinton raise nearly $100,000, and receive a $2 million line of credit from the Worthen National Bank. This was done, it is believed, through one of Stephens' associates, Curt Bradbury, a former employee of his who is now chief executive officer of Worthen National Bank. Jackson Stephens is chairman of the bank.

Jackson Stephens is a perfect example showing how Bush and Co. play both sides of the fence. Stevens was the lifeline of Clinton's campaign. Like Jimmy Carter, Clinton was a Southern Democrat created by the Council on Foreign Relations and Trilateral Commission. That could be why so many voters are saying, "There's no difference between the two parties."

"There really isn't," says covert operations investigator Gene Wheaton. "Bush's people are behind them both. Someone like Bill Clinton is a perfect Democratic candidate for Bush to run against. If the race becomes too close, Clinton's ties to the Mena scandal can be leaked. If for some reason Bush loses, his team of covert operators will still have their man in the White House."

Next to the Freemasons, the Council on Foreign Relations (CFR) and the Trilateral Commission (TC) are probably the most misunderstood organizations operating on American soil. Yet all three organizations are part of a global conspiracy to dominate the world, a goal not too distant from George Bush's alumni at their secret society, Skull and Bones. In fact, the term President Bush is credited with coining, a "New World Order" comes right out of the Freemason handbook.

A recently published book explains the connection between Freemasonry, the Council on Foreign Relations and the Trilateral Commission. It's called *En Route to Global Occupation: A High-Ranking Government Liaison Exposes the Secret Agenda for World Unification*. It was written by Indianan Gary Kah and published in 1992 by Huntington House in Lafayette, Louisiana.

Kah's book came at an opportune time in my research. I was trying to discover some logical explanation of how Bush's covert operations and secret agendas all fit together. What were the real reasons for their existence? This book put a lot into perspective. Not only are Kah's conclusions enlightening, but his sources and data are very well documented, some by people who wrote about the questionable intentions of Masons two and three centuries ago. In fact, Kah discovered that as an organization, the Masons possess an archives of two-and-half million documents and a library of sixty thousand books.

"The mere existence of such a collection suggests that Freemasonry was more than a large group of citizens organized for community service," he says.

Most dictionaries describes the Freemasonry movement as simply "a secret international fraternity." Yet the New World Order global-domination groups like the Council on Foreign Relations and the Trilateral Commission trace their history back to The Illuminati, a secret order founded in Ingolstadt, Bavaria, on May 1st, 1776, by Adam Weishaupt, a professor of canon law at the University of Ingolstadt and a well-known Freemason. The organization was an order within an order. It was a higher form of Freemasonry: Illuminized Freemasonry. The Illuminati, as it was known, was created to carry out the plans of the Freemasons to create a "one world movement" by gaining power in the policy-making circles in European governments to influence the decisions of European leaders.

On July 16th, 1772, at the Masonic Congress at Wilhelmsbad, representatives of all the Freemasons and Illuminati met—numbering more than three million members. The Congress enabled the Illuminists to solidify their control over the various secret lodges in Europe so they would become the leaders of the "one world movement." Weishaupt was also successful in convincing many Christian leaders to join the order by telling them that The Illuminati was a Christian organization and that its purpose was to unify the world for the sake of Christ.

The Bavarian government quickly understood what the Freemasons were up to but failed to seize their secret documents and destroy the movement. The Illuminati did nothing under its own name, but established other organizations to carry out its agenda. If something went wrong and the initiative was exposed, it could claim it had nothing to do with it. This is similar to what the Bush and Reagan Administration did to hide its secret agendas: it protected itself by having these actions carried out via a secret team of covert operators.

With Masonic lodges established throughout Europe, the movement maintained influence in all political and social movements. Kah reveals that it was even largely responsible for the French Revolution, through the Jacobin Society and Napoleon Bonaparte, who was a Mason. Volaire, Robespierre, Danton, and Marat were all prominent Freemasons.

In the late eighteenth century The Illuminati moved its headquarters from Bavaria to Frankfurt and hooked up with the Rothschild banking family. The Freemasons needed money to finance their efforts to build a New World Order. At that time the Rothschilds were a relatively small banking concern in Frankfurt, but by cooperating with the secret societies they were able to expand their banking operations through their extensive international business and political contacts with Freemasonry.

At the forefront of the drive to bring the Freemasonry movement to the U.S. in the late 1700s was Alexander Hamilton. The Secessionist Movement established in Charleston, South Carolina, was also the American headquarters of Scottish Rite Freemasonry. The influence of Illuminized Freemasonry on the movement was considered to be partly responsible for inciting the Americans to Civil War. The Theosophical Society, Christian Science and Unitarianism, the Jehovah's Witnesses, and the Mormon Church were all founded by Freemasons.

Kah reveals that the Federal Reserve System was a creation of the Freemasons, one which gave the European Illuminists a permanent role in America's finances. Most people don't realize that the Federal Reserve System is not a government body. It was established in 1913 as a privately held corporation owned by stockholders. In a passage in the Federal Reserve Act, it is stated that the identities of the Fed's Class A stockholders would not be revealed.

The term "New World Order" has been used by Freemasonry since the days of Weishaupt to describe the coming world government. On the back of a one-dollar bill are the words "Novus Ordo Seclorum," which is Latin for "The New Order of the Ages" or "New World Order." Kah discovered that one of Freemasonry's secret symbols was the pyramid with the all-seeing eye of Osiris or Baal above it, just as it is on the one-dollar bill. The New World Order is symbolized by the capstone being separated from the rest of the pyramid. When the New World Order comes into being, and a "one world government" will have been created, the capstone will rejoin the rest of the pyramid, symbolizing the completion of the task.

According to R. E. McMaster, publisher of a financial newsletter called *The Reaper*, the top eight stockholders of the Federal Reserve System are the Rothschild Banks of London and Berlin, Lazard Brothers Banks of Paris, Israel Moses Seif Banks of Italy, Warburg Bank of Hamburg and Amsterdam, Lehman Brothers Bank of New York, Kuhn, Loeb Bank of New York, Chase Manhattan Bank of New York, and Goldman, Sachs Bank of New York.

There has been some opposition to Freemasons and their New World Order agenda. The father of Charles Lindbergh fought the creation of the Federal Reserve Bank as a Congressman and later conducted an investigation into the cartel, warning: "This Act establishes the most gigantic trust on earth. When the President [Wilson] signs this bill the invisible government of the Monetary Power will be legalized. ... The worst legislative crime of the ages is perpetrated by this banking and currency bill."

Congressman Louis T. McFadden, who chaired the House Banking Committee during the 1920s, also tried unsuccessfully to expose the the plot. In the 1950s, Congressman Carroll Reece of Tennessee headed the Reece Committee to investigate major tax-exempt foundations linked to the same people who controlled the Federal Reserve: the Rockefeller, Ford, Carnegie, and Guggenheim foundations. These foundations served as tax shelters for the wealth created by the international banking cartel.

The Reece Committee discovered that a great deal of the research in the social sciences, public education and international affairs that these foundations supported promoted ideas that advocated socialism and globalism. For instance, the United Nations Association, the Institute of Pacific Relations, and the Council on Foreign Relations were all created and continue to be influenced by these foundations. René Wormser of the Reece Committee stated that the influence of the major foundations had "reached far into government, into the policymaking circles of Congress and into the State Department."

In the 1960s and early 1970s Congressman Wright Patman of Texas chaired the House Banking Committee and tried to expose the "one world" plot by calling for an audit of the Federal Reserve.

In the 1970s and 1980s Congressman Larry P. McDonald was a ferocious critic of the power and influence the Rockefeller family had as well as of their secret intentions. In 1976 he wrote in the introduction to Gary Allen's *The Rockefeller File*: "The drive of the Rockefellers and their allies is to create a one-world government combining super-capitalism and Communism under the same tent, all under their control. ... Do I mean conspiracy? Yes I do. I am convinced there is such a plot, international in scope, generations old in planning, and incredibly evil in intent."

The Rockefeller File revealed that the Rockefellers had nearly two hundred trusts and foundations, and that the number of foundations indirectly controlled by the family was in the thousands. Allen discovered that because banks owned by Rockefeller, such as Chase Manhattan, are trustees for other U.S. foundations, they have the right to invest and to vote the stock of these institutions through the banks' trust departments.

The Rockefellers' influence in public education was also investigated by Allen, who wrote: "The foundations [Carnegie and Rockefeller] stimulated two-thirds of the total endowment funding of all institutions of higher learning in America during the first third of this century. During this period the Carnegie-Rockefeller complex supplied twenty percent of the total income of colleges and universities and became in fact, if not in name, a sort of U.S. Ministry of Education."

Both of these foundations supported John Dewey's socialist philosophy. Dewey became the "father of progressive education" and probably more than any other thinker influenced the future direction and perspective of American educators. Allen points out that since America's public school system was decentralized, the foundations had concentrated on influencing schools of education, particularly Columbia, the spawning ground for Deweyism, and on financing the writing of textbooks which were subsequently adopted nationwide.

The Reece Committee investigated the control of the foundations over teacher training schools, and concluded: "Research and experimental stations were established at selected universities, notably Columbia, Stanford, and Chicago. Here some of the worst mischief in recent education was born. In these Rockefeller-and-Carnegie-established vineyards worked many of the principal characters in the story of the suborning of American education. Here foundations nurtured some of the most ardent academic advocates of upsetting the American system and supplanting it with a Socialist state."

Kah points out that traditionalist teachers, who had strongly resisted Deweyism, found themselves swamped by education propagandists backed with millions of Rockefeller-Carnegie dollars. He also discovered that the National Education Association (NEA), the country's chief education lobby, was also being financed by the Rockefeller and Carnegie foundations. By 1934 the NEA had adopted John Dewey's philosophy of humanism, socialism and globalism, and incorporated it into the classroom.

The Rockefeller Foundation also supported the publishing of textbooks that promoted Marxist propaganda while the NEA promoted them.

Money to establish the Council on Foreign Relations (CFR) came from the Rockefeller and Carnegie foundations, which also created the CFR's sister organization, the Institute of Pacific Relations. The CFR has about 2500 members, the majority of whom live in New York, Washington or Boston.

It has has 38 branch affiliates throughout the U.S..

One vocal critic of the CFR was Rear Admiral Chester Ward, a former CFR member for sixteen years, who claimed: "The most powerful clique in these elitist groups have one objective in common—they want to bring about the surrender of the sovereignty and the national independence of the United States."

One of the early investigators of the CFR's intentions was FBI agent Dan Smoot, who wrote: "The ultimate aim of the CFR is to create a one-world socialist system and make the U.S. an official part of it."

Former Congressman John Rarick asserted: "The CFR is 'the establishment.' Not only does it have influence and power in key decision-making positions at the highest levels of government to apply pressure from above, but it also finances and uses individuals and groups to bring pressure from below, to justify the high-level decisions for converting the U.S. from a sovereign Constitutional Republic into a servile member state of a one-world dictatorship."

The CFR doesn't hide its real intentions. On February 17th, 1950, CFR member James Warburg told the Senate Foreign Relations Committee: "We shall have world government whether or not you like it—by conquest or consent." A CFR position paper published in 1959 stated that its purpose was to advocate the "building of a new international order ... including states labeling themselves as Socialist." In the April 1974 issue of the CFR's journal, *Foreign Affairs*, Richard Gardner writes: "The New World Order will have to be built from the bottom up rather than from the top down ... but in the end run around national sovereignty, eroding it piece by piece, will accomplish much more than the old-fashioned frontal assault."

One of the reasons Kah discovered that most Americans know nothing about the true intentions of the CFR is because, like Freemasons, the CFR requires that the minutes from all important meetings remain top secret. Nothing said in council meetings is allowed to be discussed with non-CFR members. The CFR works much the same way the founder of the Illuminati, Adam Weishaupt did: surrounding leaders in high places with members of the council, targeting key advisory positions in the executive branch of the U.S. government, and applying this tactic to education, the media, the military, and banking.

The ultimate goal of the CFR, says Kah, is to influence all aspects of society in such a way that one day Americans would wake up to discover themselves in the midst of a one-world system, whether they like it or not. Its hope was to get Americans to the point where entertaining a world government would seem as natural and American as baseball and apple pie.

Kah points out that the CFR was successful in gaining control of the Democratic Party in the 1920s and 1930s, the Republican party in the 1940s, with the help of Franklin D. Roosevelt and the State Department.

"The organization became virtually an agency of the government when World War II broke out," René Wormser stated in the Reece Committee.

The tremendous influence the CFR had in the State Department was responsible for getting the U.S. to create and join the UN. The idea for a United Nations of governments, a limited form of one-world government, was made to President Roosevelt by Secretary of State Cordell Hull, who on December 22nd, 1941, suggested that the President establish a Presidential Advisory Committee on Post War Foreign Policy. The land which housed the United Nations buildings was donated by John D. Rockefeller, Jr. Ten of the committee members were from the CFR. In the 1945 founding conference of the UN, nearly fifty CFR members were in the U.S. delegation.

Kah believes that the CFR used its influence in public education and the media to cast a favorable image for the

UN among the American public. "The immediate purpose of the UN was to warm the Americans up to the idea of global government. It was all part of the conditioning."

The CFR was also the catalyst behind the creation of the Bilderbergs, the Club of Rome, and the Trilateral Commission.

The Bilderbergs were named after the Bilderberg Hotel in Oosterbeek, Holland, where the group first met in 1954. Consisting of nearly 100 policy makers from NATO, its leadership was interlocked with the CFR. It was funded by the Rockefeller and Ford foundations, with its purpose to "regionalize Europe." Former U.S. ambassador to West Germany George McGhee has revealed that the Treaty of Rome, and hence the European Common Market, were nurtured at the Bilderberg meetings. Why was the so-called unification of Europe in 1992 so important? Before anyone had time to look around, the deed was done.

The ultimate goal of the Bilderbergs is similar to that of the CFR. The group's first chairman, Price Bernhard of the Netherlands, whose family is the major shareholder in Royal Dutch Shell Oil, wrote: "It is difficult to reeducate the people who have been brought up on nationalism to the idea of relinquishing part of their sovereignty to a supernational body. ... This is the tragedy."

Kah discovered that the American Bilderberg membership includes: Henry Kissinger, Cyrus Vance, Robert McNamara, Donald Rumsfeld, George Ball, Gerald Ford, Henry Grunwald, Sheppard Stone (of the Aspen Institute for Humanistic Studies, a sister organization of the CFR), David and Nelson Rockefeller, and Zbigniew Brzezinski. Virtually every American member of the Bilderbergs is a current or former member of the CRF. European participants include prime ministers, foreign ministers, and financial leaders such as Helmut Schmidt, Rumor of Italy, Baron Edmond de Rothschild, and Valéry Giscard d'Estaing.

The Club of Rome, established in 1968, claims to have

"solutions" for world peace and prosperity, nearly all of which include the concept of world government. About 25 members of the CFR belong to the American faction of the Club of Rome.

The Trilateral Commission (TC) was established by David Rockefeller in 1973 to promote world government by encouraging economic interdependence among the superpowers. Zbigniew Brzezinski drafted the commission's charter and became its first director. Its membership is comprised of leaders from North America, Japan and Western Europe. Writer Gary Kah found that most, if not all, of the important Frenchmen who are members of the commission also belong to the Grand Orient Lodge of Freemasonry.

The activities of the commission echoed and complimented the "one world view" efforts of its sister organizations, the Bilderbergs and the Club of Rome. Some say it is also a mirror image of the CFR as all eight American representatives to the founding meeting of the commission were also members of the CFR.

Kah did some simple arithmetic and discovered that while the Reagan Administration appointed no less than 75 members of either the CFR or the TC, when Bush entered the White House an astounding 350 members of these two organizations received positions in the executive branch. Bush, Brent Scowcroft, Richard Cheney, Lawrence Eagleburger, Nicholas Brady, Alan Greenspan, Dick Thornburgh, Colin Powell, and Carla Hills are all either past or present members of either the TC or the CFR.

Since the Eisenhower Administration, CFR/TC members who have also served as national security advisors to the President include: Henry Kissinger, Brent Scowcroft, Walt Rostow, Zbigniew Brzezinski, Robert McFarlane, Frank Carlucci, and Colin Powell.

Presidents who were members of CFR/TC are John F. Kennedy, Richard Nixon, Gerald Ford, Jimmy Carter, and George Bush. Franklin D. Roosevelt was a member of the

Masonic Lodge as was Harry Truman, Lyndon Johnson, Gerald Ford, and Ronald Reagan. Presidential losers are also well represented in the CFR/TC. They include Adlai Stevenson, Barry Goldwater, George McGovern, and Michael Dukakis. Their membership serves to stack the ticket so that no matter who wins, the New World Order people have to come out on top.

Kah is quick to point out that many of those who join either of these organizations may not be aware of the ultimate purpose for which they were established. Nevertheless, they do become influenced by these organizations' philosophies.

What role does President Bush play in all this? His Skull and Bones group, which he was a member of during his days at Yale University, has Masonic overtones whose rituals are similar to The Illuminati. The Skull and Bones are also the secret symbols of Freemasonry.

There are three versions of the roots of the Order of Skull and Bones. One is that it was an outgrowth of an earlier British or Scottish Freemasonry group established at All Souls College at Oxford University in the late 17th century. Another is that it grew out of the German "nationalistic" secret societies of the early 19th century. Still another is that it has roots only in America, and that its founders adopted some of the rituals of European Freemasonry.

Those who deny the hypothesis that "Freemasonry is intent on taking over the world" is the ultimate conspiracy ought to research the subject as Kah has done. Before I began researching the subject of the Bush and Reagan Administrations' covert operations and secret agendas I too would have called anyone promoting these ideas as "conspiracy nuts."

But if one believes, as I now do, that George Bush has an imperialistic agenda for America's future which includes global domination via a New World Order, why should the Freemasons' plans to do the very same thing—which were devised centuries ago—be so hard to believe?

Conclusion

I set out to examine what a covert operation and a covert operator are. President Bush is an example of both. He is a grave threat to the future of a free and democratic American society. He is the reason why democracy and life in general took a sharp nose-dive in the past three decades. He and his secret team of covert operators is the reason why Americans stopped caring.

But what do the American people really know about him? President Bush has become so powerful that he has never been questioned over any of his political actions. His closest scuffle with a congressional investigation was during the Iran-Contra proceedings, yet he wasn't even required to testify. Why not? How did the second-highest political leader in the country get away without being called upon to give his version of the events?

Because George Bush has corrupted the American system to such an extent that he can get away with any crime. What does the mainstream press know about his scandals? He told them he didn't know anything about trading arms for hostages. What does that mean, then—that he was in the dark? Political discourse was going on at the highest level of the U.S. government but the Vice President didn't even feel the need to become involved with the negotiations? Why not? In fact, the public's knowledge of Iran-Contra is nothing more than the tip of the iceberg, a window onto a covert world that had been in high gear since George Bush entered the White House.

For most people, this covert world might as well exist in

another dimension. To understand what's going on requires a great deal of background knowledge and research. I spent the past two years getting just that.

In the early months of 1992 my good friend, author Barry Chamish, and I read through every one of the news clippings I had gathered from my research, and interpreted their meaning. We saw covert operations in paragraphs from *Time* and *Newsweek* that everyone else ignored. When we started to scrutinize the events of the 1980s as they related to Bush's policies, we realized that what we thought we had seen the first time around was nothing more than a pile of disinformation. On second look, events weren't occurring naturally but were being orchestrated. A secret team of covert operators were deciding what the American public believes.

I think of and consider myself very literate in international relations and American-Israeli politics. I write regularly on contemporary Middle East subjects. Yet I realize now that I knew precious little of what really moved American foreign policy in the Middle East in the 1980s or of America's covert relations with Israel.

Part of the problem is that too many Americans simply don't care whether George Bush is carrying out a secret agenda and violating the Constitution. No mainstream publication thoroughly investigated his involvement in Iran-Contra. Bush could claim he wasn't involved in anything, knew nothing, and remembered little, and nobody said a word. Congress allowed these investigations to be whitewashed.

How did he get away with this? Because Bush knows how to manipulate the American public's perceptions and to distort their understanding of events. His secret was to create simplistic images for the public to focus on. The American public was told that Saddam Hussein was the bad guy and George Bush was the good guy. If the Soviet Union, Arab dictators, and terrorist leaders were all evil, the Administration was good.

Another tactic was the creation of the "plausable deniablity" phrase/excuse. Anytime a White House covert operation was exposed, somehow by whipping this argument out the Administration was excused from being questioned.

Why did Congress allow Bush to simply deny he was involved in operations to arm rebel groups? Because it was unable to get to the bottom of the scandal. Investigations into BCCI, Iran-Contra, or what the Bush/Reagan Administrations knew about supplying Iraq with military technology have been blocked by the Department of Justice. When Congress is powerless to investigate government corruption, it means Congress is no longer the highest authority in the land. By making this so, Bush corrupted the legislative branch and polluted the entire blood system of the American Federal governmental system.

I can live with know-it-alls and other political analysts who have never researched this topic, but will bark and hoot about how they know for sure that all conspiracy theories are bunk. Well, they're not. That's why my readers should consider this work as a whole. George Bush. Skull and Bones. Drug trafficking by the CIA. The assassinations of JFK and RFK. The Council on Foreign Relations and the Trilateral Commission. There is a global conspiracy founded on the Freemasonry notion of a New World Order and global domination and President Bush plays a major part in it.

While many will disagree with this conclusion, at least some of the evidence will be in the public domain. Think of what I have written as an anthology or an almanac. It will establish a whole new field of investigation for scholars studying the subject of secret agendas, covert operations, and global domination.

After a careful reading of it, close the book and ask yourself whether you can honestly say that everything is still okay in Washington, D.C., and that the Bush-Reagan Administrations served the American people in a straightforward and honest manner? Could it be that what I have uncovered was going on but nobody in the White House knew about it? Or they knew, but did nothing to stop it?

Is it possible that even though the Reagan Administration lobbied Congress for aid to support the Contras, the White House didn't direct the secret supply effort to the Contras? That private individuals were operating and financing this secret operation to arm the Nicaraguan rebels, but the White House was not aware of it, or if it was, did nothing to stop it even when they knew it was constitutionally illegal?

Is it possible that the second-highest elected official in the U.S. government would be kept in the dark about the policies being carried out in the governing institutions he presided over? Can a lone Lt. Colonel in the National Security Council decide to trade arms for hostages without the Vice President being aware of it? Does Bush contend he disagreed with the operation but North and Casey went ahead with it anyway, behind his back?

Consider the recent banking scandals of BCCI, the S&Ls, and BNL-Atlanta. Could the various agencies of the U.S. government have had no idea as to what BCCI was doing? How could the looting of the S&Ls continue for nearly a decade without anyone in the White House finding out or doing anything to stop it? Did it really come as a surprise/ shock to members of the Bush Administration that secret loans from BNL's Atlanta branch were made to Saddam Hussein?

If the Administration wasn't aware of these covert activities, with all of the investigative resources available to them why couldn't they expose the perpetrators? Assuming that the White House didn't know, who then was orchestrating these covert operations?

These White House scandals are bad enough. The attempt to cover them up is worse, and they could *not* have occurred without the President's knowledge. Do the actions taken by the Justice Department in these scandals reflect those of an administration intent on rooting out the corruption in the system?

Some people have tried to explain away these scandals by suggesting that they were the result of "negligence" in various agencies of the U.S. government. According to this theory, Iraq acquired billions of dollars in loan guarantees and advanced U.S. military technology because a few bureaucrats at the Commerce Department forgot to look under a stack of papers. And BCCI was able to secretly acquire control of U.S. banks because Federal regulatory agencies were asleep on the job?

While individuals can be sloppy or lazy, could the hundreds, perhaps thousands, of people who work in the various agencies of the U.S. government all have been negligent? Wasn't anyone able to catch glaring contradictions and errors in the conduct of policy, even years after these so-called mistakes were made?

I'm the first one to admit that I have no smoking guns. Yet my speculation wasn't undertaken without strong circumstantial evidence. When investigative journalists go up against people like George Bush, it's not an even playing field. We have no access to secret CIA documents to prove the existence of covert operations or secret policies. We can't manipulate the media and public perceptions. Even Congress was unable to subpoena crucial White House documents to complete its investigations.

The only weapon I have is the information contained in this book. I didn't pluck it out of the air, nor did the investigative journalists I have used as my primary sources. All I ask is that Bush's statements such as "I have answered those charges before and I'm just not going to respond to them anymore" or "I don't remember what was said at that meeting" don't fool anyone. If Bush is allowed to get away with these excuses, then the American people are suckers. National leaders can only evade questions and claim total memory loss to the uninformed.

Could it be that all of the instances and events I have revealed were nothing more than the product of conspiracy "theories" and the imaginations of investigative journalists run wild? That they have no basis in reality, are baseless allegations, and are intended merely to smear and discredit the Bush and Reagan Administrations?

If I am branded a "conspiracy theorist," then this means that all of the journalists and investigators whose research I've quoted in this book are also "conspiracy theorists." Or that they are all in on my "conspiracy." To trash my research means to discredit nationally recognized and award-winning journalists such as Martin Kilian, Robert Parry, Larry Lifschultz, Peter Trubel, Alan Friedman, Carole Jerome, Jonathan Marshall, Edward Herman, Murray Waas, David Corn, Christopher Byron, Ron Rosenblum, Douglas Franz, Pete Brewton, Jonathan Kwitny, Christopher Hitchens, Jack Anderson, Andrew Cockburn, Jack Colhoun, Scott Armstrong, Kenneth Timmerman, Leslie Cockburn, Larry Cohler, Fred Kempe, Jim Hoagland, Bill Remple, Allan Nairn, Tim Winer, Scott Malone, Jeff Gerth, and Kevin Buckley. Rather than simply ignoring the goings-on, the dedication to the truth of these and other investigative journalists have enabled the deceit of the Bush-Reagan White House to be documented. More than anything else, theirs is an example of how the fourth estate can work for the public good.

Despite spending the last two years investigating this subject, my guess is that I've only scratched the surface. I know in my gut that the true scope of the Bush-Reagan covert operations is far beyond what I've exposed.

I believe hundreds of billions of dollars were moved offshore from looting the S&Ls and via budget deficits and Star Wars myths to fund covert operations aimed at toppling communism. It wasn't simply a coincidence that South American drug lords and Central American and Caribbean localities like the Cayman and Antilles Islands, Antigua, and Panama became centers of secret international finance in the 1980s. Or that despite three conservative administrations and endless attacks on how the Democrats are soft on crime, America never witnessed as much drug flow and money laundering as it did during the Bush-Reagan years.

In 1981 America's leading covert operator, George Bush, absconded with U.S. foreign policy and carried it out behind closed doors. During the past twelve years the White House has been a cesspool of secret government, covert operations, miscarriages of justice, and financial corruption. Through a combination of illusions, deceit, disinformation, and mirrors, Bush was able to overthrow the American system.

Americans may think they are accurately perceiving reality, but since the early 1980s they have been snookered and hoodwinked by George Bush's disinformation and secret agendas. Bush is making a mockery of their perceptions. America's political fortunes have been hijacked while the majority of the American public continues to believe Bush is a fairly decent guy who has a large family, plays golf, and goes on hunting and fishing trips.

How can Bush simply say he didn't know anything about a policy that originated in the White House? Why is he allowed to whip out this "plausible deniability" argument, and then never have to face the question again? Why is he never put on trial for what he knows? Reagan may have been the Teflon President, but Bush doesn't even get asked about a scandal long enough for his possible knowledge of it to become a scandal. When did an American politician become so untouchable?

The only way to stop the Freemasonry agenda is to recognize it exists and isn't just some wild conspiracy theory. Only by public awareness and further study and knowledge of the subject can we win the battle over how we believe and what we perceive is America's involvement in international events.

As for George Bush, his crimes are the worst of all—they are the "crimes of a President."

4.	5.
body	and
building	did
radio	bed
modify	bad
ready	hand
louder	cold
under	loved
window	second

II. PHRASES

dreaded incidents	dented fenders
desired goods	drugged dentists
doubtful doodling	standard precedent
dainty dessert	addicted to candy
deserved delight	deductible dividend

decidedly dumbfounded
deserted dead-end
dutiful dieting daughter
doggedly defended freedom
determined debater

III. SENTENCES

1. Engaged in Dallas, married in Des Moines, honeymooned in Deauville, divorced in Denver.

2. A domain divided against itself definitely does not long endure.

3. Dauntless daredevils dangled dangerously and defied defeat.

4. Don't devote days and days to despair, dawdling, and delaying decisions.

5. Demoralizing, outmoded procedures denied democratic dividends and decisions.

6. Avoiding duty, details, and devotion definitely does not decrease domestic discord.

7. Old doddering daddies don't dance divinely with discothèque debutantes.

(Make up three sentences loaded with "d" words, *saying each aloud* before you write.)

8.

9.

10.

"l" as in lady

TO PRONOUNCE:

a) Thin tongue tip darts up and touches upper gum ridge. Say as quickly as possible, "la, la, la, la, la, la."

b) Note the position of the tongue for the "t" sound when finishing the words in Column 1 below. Use the same position to begin words with "l" in Columns 2 and 4.

1.		2.	3.		4.
hit	—	lit	hist	—	list
set	—	let	bode	—	load
tot	—	lot	tiffed	—	lift
hate	—	late	oft	—	loft
root	—	loot	aft	—	laughed
route	—	lout	apt	—	lapped
fast	—	last	short	—	lord

Caution:

The tongue should not feel heavy as in making a "w" but light and agile as in articulating "t." Contrast the following:

1.			2.		
wean	—	lean	wed	—	led
weep	—	leap	wet	—	let
week	—	leak	wag	—	lag
weed	—	lead	wap	—	lap

3.			4.		
wake	—	lake	wise	—	lies
wade	—	laid	wink	—	link
wait	—	late	winch	—	lynch
ware	—	lair	wisp	—	lisp

I. WORDS

1.	2.	3.	4.
locate	ball	blaze	able
like	call	blame	bubble
lake	bill	claim	capable
leave	hill	click	durable
lounge	wall	flank	edible
lunatic	will	flicker	inimitable
lily	tall	slack	lovable
lovely	tole	slick	manageable

II. PHRASES

(Sail through the "l"s fast, pronouncing half as much "l" as you think you need.)

1.	2.
alone at last	yelled for help
along a lane	tell a tall tale
laws of the land	fill lanterns with oil
looseleaf calendars	three million Italians
light loads	William won a medallion
lovable lasses	bleak and blustery
legs of lamb	plump and pleasing plums
plastic plaques	flock to the flag
flash and flicker	clever clowns
climb the cliff	licorice lollypops

III. SENTENCES

1. Be likable, lovable, and livable or you're liable to be leavable, left, and lonesome.

2. A little farm well tilled,
   A little barn well filled,
   A little wife well willed,
   Give me, give me.

—JAMES HOOK

3. If you want knowledge, you must toil for it; if good, you must toil for it, and if pleasure, you must toil for it. Toil is the law. Pleasure comes through toil and not by self-indulgence and indolence. When one gets to love his work, his life is a happy one.

—JOHN RUSKIN

4. In order to love people and to be loved by them, one must train oneself to gentleness, humility, the art of bearing with disagreeable people and things.

—LEO TOLSTOY

5. The money-getter who pleads his love of work has a lame defense, for love of work at money-getting is a lower taste than love of money.

—AMBROSE BIERCE

6. If you will think about what you ought to do for other people, your character will take care of itself. Character is a by-product, and any man who devotes himself to its cultivation in his own case will become a selfish prig.

—WOODROW WILSON

7. Applause waits on success. The fickle multitude, like the light straw that floats on the stream, glide with the current still, and follow fortune.

—BENJAMIN FRANKLIN

(Make up three sentences loaded with "l" words, *saying each aloud* before you write.)

8.
9.
10.

"ng" as in singing

TO PRONOUNCE:

The back of the tongue is raised almost to the soft palate and stays up there clinging like a suction cup, the sound comes out of the nose. Contrast this with "n" where the tip of the tongue touches the front upper gum ridge. In the mirror, observe that the back of the tongue and the palate meet on "ng."

Say "ng" followed by "ah"—do not say "gah"—over and over.

Caution:

The sound must end in a hum! Do not end it with the hard "g" or a "k" click, nor with a simple "n."

I. CONTRAST

Say "n", then "ng" several times until you can *distinguish* between them: n-ng, n-ng, n-ng.

A. Now:

front hum		back hum	front		back
sin	—	sing	taken	—	taking
sun	—	sung	lighten	—	lighting
ban	—	bang	ribbon	—	ribbing
tan	—	tang	cannon	—	canning
win	—	wing	bacon	—	baking

B. Watch for and practice the distinctions between the following words. See that the words with "ng" spelling do not have the "k" or "g" clicking sound:

1.					2.		
Click		*Click*		*Back Hum*			
bag	—	bank	—	bang	sink	—	sing
hag	—	Hank	—	hang	wink	—	wing
rag	—	rank	—	rang	rink	—	ring
tag	—	sank	—	sang	think	—	thing
sag	—	tank	—	tang	tug	—	tongue

3.			4.		
dog	—	dong	bagging	—	banging
log	—	long	rigging	—	ringing
lug	—	lung	gagging	—	ganging
brig	—	bring	rigging	—	ringing
wig	—	wing	wigging	—	winging

II. PHRASES

Practice the following. (Be sure that you do *not* carry the "g" over to the following vowel!) Southerners: pronounce the back hum sound of "~~ng~~" *not* front tongue tip sound of "n."

1.	2.
belo~~ng~~ing out	swi~~ng~~ing up
carryi~~ng~~ off	gleami~~ng~~ eyes
amo~~ng~~ us	goi~~ng~~ over
thro~~ng~~ing in	growi~~ng~~ old
fli~~ng~~ing at	bri~~ng~~ing up
wi~~ng~~ing over	believi~~ng~~ all
wro~~ng~~ art	falli~~ng~~ out
cli~~ng~~ing on	pouri~~ng~~ out
comi~~ng~~ at	Lo~~ng~~ Island
wro~~ng~~ing us	swarmi~~ng~~ over

III. EXCEPTIONS

A. Although the "g" is not pronounced in long, strong, young, it is pronounced in the comparative and the superlative.

longer	longest
stronger	strongest
younger	youngest

B. Words in which the "ng" is in the middle and where, if the following syllable were cut off, the remainder would have no meaning to the full word.

See: anger (ang?) dangle (dang?)
angry (ang?) jungle (jung?)
linger (ling?) single (sing?)
finger (fing?)
hunger (hung?) length (leng?)—pronounced "k"
strength (streng?)— " "

IV. A. 1. Adoring not boring, bugging not hugging.
    2. Blaming not flaming, roaring not soaring.
    3. Chanting not panting, booming not zooming.
    4. Kissing not hissing, deceiving not believing.
    5. Dawning not morning, hurrying not scurrying.
    6. Angling not tangling, lingering not fingering.

B. 1. Believing but grieving, craving but raving.
   2. Quivering but shivering, dating but waiting.
   3. Working but shirking, homing but roaming.
   4. Towing but rowing, winking but thinking.
   5. Raving but craving, rousing but carousing.

C. 1. Shooting and looting and rooting and tooting.
   2. Dining and wining and eating and bleating.
   3. Brightening and whitening, enlightening and
       frightening.
   4. Gunning and sunning and running and fun-
       ning.
   5. Giving and living or sinning and winning.

"r" as in red

TO PRONOUNCE:

Lift the tongue so that its sides contact the upper side teeth. Then the tongue tip should point upward.

Caution:

1. Do not purse lips as in pronouncing "w" consonant or you will get a baby sound as "wabbit" for "rabbit."

2. For foreign-speaking people: There should not be any gargling sound at the back of the tongue. It is very difficult for many Europeans to eliminate this trill. There should be no vibration of the tongue. The "r" sound in English is much higher in the mouth than in other languages. Say "no tongue tension" aloud before every "r" word.

I. WORDS

1.	2.	3.
er—rabbit	are	already
"—race	bear	around
"—ran	car	every
"—read	dear	harrow
"—ready	chair	morning
"—red	far	orange
"—ride	fur	parrot
"—right	hear	story
"—round	her	very
"—run	near	weary

4.	5.
berate	brag
carry	brim
deride	brother
glory	crew
horrid	crop
morrow	dress
perish	drink
pouring	group
terrible	grasp
tyranny	ground

II. CONTRAST

1.			2.		
weep	—	reap	wait	—	rate
week	—	reek	wail	—	rail
weed	—	read	ware	—	rare
weal	—	real	wide	—	ride
wed	—	red	wise	—	rise
wad	—	rod	wink	—	rink
watt	—	rot	wench	—	wrench
won	—	run	wake	—	rake

III. PHRASES

1.	2.
droopy group	through trials
pretty proud	cramped and crowded
print programs	cream of the crop
present problems	create a crisis
trim trees	creeping crocodiles

IV. SENTENCES

1. Reading, writing, and 'rithmetic aren't enough to turn the trick in these electronic days of computers.

2. There is nothing stronger and nobler than when man and wife are of one heart and mind in a house; a grief to their foes, and to their friends great joy, but their own hearts know it best.   —HOMER

3. Armstrong, Aldrin, and Collins, three men of courage, heroes of this world, explorers and discoverers of outer space.

4. Loving kindness is greater than laws; and the charities of life are more than all ceremonies.

5. Rioters and revolutionaries resolutely refuse to respond to recommendations.

6. Every generation tends to edit and correct the faults of its predecessors.

7. Grow to greatness by grappling with and overcoming your problems, going through not around them.

(Make up three sentences loaded with "r" words, *saying each aloud* before you write.)

8.
9.
10.

"s"

TO PRONOUNCE:

For Lispers: any or all of these hints can help you!

A. 1. Head up to ceiling—let tongue fall back in throat.

2. Make a hissing sound as though hissing a villain.

3. Aim a thin breath stream through opening of the two upper front teeth close to the gum line.

4. Tip of tongue points to upper gum ridge but doesn't touch anywhere, sides of tongue anchor lightly to upper side teeth, furrow tongue lengthwise.

5. Check in mirror to see that you do not see the tongue at any time.

6. Teeth held loosely together as though nibbling corn; upper teeth should overlap lower teeth.

B. Lean chin on back of hand. Keep tongue retreated as in looking at ceiling. Hiss!

For Sibilizers:

The idea is to fuzz up or put whiskers on the "s" so it is not as piercing. To do this nestle tongue tip against lower teeth and aim breath stream low over tongue and lower lip. Try almost to lisp. Do Column 5 below which has the "th" sounds and let them influence the Column 6 words, leaving tongue in *almost* the same position for both.

I. WORDS

1.		2.	3.		4.
toe	—	sew	ssseen	—	sheen
tot	—	sot	ssseep	—	sheep
tat	—	sat	ssseek	—	sheik
too	—	Sue	ssseat	—	sheet
told	—	sold	sssad	—	shad
tame	—	same	sssop	—	shops
tub	—	sub	sssock	—	shock
tell	—	sell	sssod	—	shod
tip	—	sip	Swiss	—	swish
tight	—	sight	class	—	clash

5. (Contrast) 6.

thin	—	sin
think	—	sink
thank	—	sank
thaw	—	saw
thong	—	song
thick	—	sick
bath	—	bass
worth	—	worse
truth	—	truce
forth	—	force

7.	8.	9.
lapse	squeak	strike
crops	squat	stream
backs	square	straw
trucks	squint	strap
shocks	small	scram
cooks	smirk	scroll
stuffs	smart	script
roofs	smoke	scratch
puffs	skim	sprig
staffs	scant	spray

10.

lend(s)	—	sends
cat(s)	—	sats
cart(s)	—	starts
gate(s)	—	sates
torte(s)	—	sorts
mate(s)	—	states
rot(s)	—	slots
route(s)	—	suits
pate(s)	—	spates
short(s)	—	snorts

II. PHRASES

Read each phrase. Say each one in front of the mirror, watching to see that the teeth are together. (Retract the tongue.)

1.
sink or swim
spic and span
soft as silk
Mississippi
serve yourself and save
sin, sex, and sensuality

2.
stop, shop, and save
supersonic sports
serendipity swings
parsley, spinach, watercress
please pass the strawberries
scrimp and save

III. SENTENCES

1. Fashion forces us to face society with scanty skirts.

2. Suspicion centered on the southern senator's statements on taxes.

3. Superior wisdom certainly dominates the Supreme Court's decisions.

4. Sara serves watercress sandwiches and iced cider laced with cinnamon.

5. Spices and salt seem to spruce up simple recipes.

6. She substitutes saccharin for sugar sometimes.

7. The happiness of life is made up of minute fractions—the little, soon-to-be-forgotten charities of a kiss or

smile, a kind look, a heartfelt compliment—countless infinitesimals of pleasurable and genial feeling.

—SAMUEL TAYLOR COLERIDGE

(Make up three sentences loaded with "s" words, *saying each aloud* before you write.)

8.

9.

10.

"t"

TO PRONOUNCE:

Tongue tip touches upper gum ridge lightly like a feather tip. Take it away quickly.

Caution:

Do not overpronounce "t" so it comes out "tsoy" instead of "toy," "tsime" instead of "time," "tsell" instead of "tell," etc. If you have trouble with "t" do the following like a machine gun or a woodpecker or a dripping (not a splashing faucet: t-t-t-t-t. Also do the same with d-d-d-d-d-d.

I. WORDS

1.	2.	3.	4.
to	it	into	rotate
toy	out	after	totem
tie	got	until	lettuce
time	not	city	better
talk	late	pretty	sweater
town	soft	sometime	letter
took	want	beautiful	actor
tall	last	sister	octave
table	about	water	affectation
today	basket	wanted	expectation

II. PHRASES

1.
twenty trumpets
twice twelve
trunk for trinkets
trials and tribulations

2.
twenty-two times
true to Tony
triumphed and tripled
tribal treasure trove

3.
twin treatments
two Saturday nights
triplets tried
travel tickets

III. SENTENCES

1. To be addicted to candy or cigarettes is to taste purgatory.

2. The cost of theater tickets is too high for us to accept third-rate entertainment.

3. To test tranquility try to rest and to do without activity.

4. Respect the child. Be not too much his parent. Trespass not on his solitude.   —RALPH WALDO EMERSON

5. Television audiences are frequently irritated by interviewers who inflict stupid questions on their subjects.

6. Life is short, the art long, opportunity fleeting, experience treacherous, judgment difficult.

—HIPPOCRATES

7. In giving a talk, take advantage of the first twenty seconds to impress listeners with anecdotes or quotations.

(Make up three sentences loaded with "t" words, *saying each aloud* before you write.)

8.

9.

10.

"th" as in them (and "th" as in thin)

TO PRONOUNCE:

Tongue tip pushes against cutting edge of upper teeth.

Caution: Do not substitute "d" or "t" for "th." Memorize: the, this, that, these, them, those, there.

I. WORDS

1.

the*	not	duh
they	"	day
that	"	dat
them	"	dem

2.

this	not	dis
these	"	deez
there	"	dare
those	"	doze

3.

though	not	dough
with	"	wit
than	"	Dan
thy	"	die

*Pronounce "the" as "thuh" except before words beginning with a vowel where it is pronounced "thee."

II. PHRASES

1.

another brother
mother and father
without bother

2.

smooth lathe
bother breathing
feathers and leathers

3.

unclothes and bathes
other weather
gather together

4.   **5.**

the bonds   with deals
the closings   with gains
the debentures   with investments
the sales   with losses
the transactions   with profits

6.

without backing
without inquiring
without interviewing
without counting
without thinking

III. SENTENCES

1. Thatched or thorny, thick or scrawny, flabby or brawny, a man's a man for all that.

2. The thirsty, thwarted, and thoughtless thump tables, thunder and threaten until their thirst is thoroughly slaked.

3. Mathematicians and even theologists, theocrats and therapists are thankful for thoughtful theorems.

4. Things have their day and their beauties in that day.
—GEORGE SANTAYANA

5. The work of progress is so immense and our means of aiding it so feeble; the life of humanity is so long, that of the individual so brief, that we often see only the ebb of the advancing ways, and are thus discouraged. It is history that teaches us to hope.   —ROBERT E. LEE

6. Wise men say, and not without reason, that whoever wishes to foresee the future must consult the past; for human events ever resemble those of preceding times. This arises from the fact that they are produced by men who have been, and ever will be, animated by the same passions, and thus they must necessarily have the same results.
—NICCOLÒ MACHIAVELLI

7. The technique that protects the voice is the same that gives you the thrust of enthusiasm.

(Make up three sentences loaded with "th" words, *saying each aloud* before you write.)

8.
9.
10.

"v"

TO PRONOUNCE:
Bite the lower lip hard.

Caution:
Foreign-language-speaking people often confuse the "v" consonant and pronounce it as a "w." Distinguish between the articulation of each. For "w" the lips are completely rounded as in whistling or in pronouncing "oo" and the lip is not bitten.

I. WORDS

1.	2.	3.	4.
vast	view	valuable	avert
van	vine	villain	avoid
vat	valve	vitamins	avow
veto	virtue	volatile	event
vent	visit	volume	eventually
vote	vocal	vulture	evict

II. CONTRAST

vase	—	ways	(oo) ways
vane	—	wane	(oo) wane
vent	—	went	(oo) went
vine	—	wine	(oo) wine
veer	—	weird	(oo) weird
vile	—	while	(oo) while

III. SENTENCES

1. Vivacity and verve are valuable for vocal variety.

2. Volcanic revolutions provoke violence and often provide victims not victories.

3. Vitamins of various vegetables vastly improve vitality.

4. Voters vowed to evaluate the virtues and vices of the visiting candidates.

5. Vim and vigor will vastly benefit your visage and verbalizing.

6. Verily, verily wish, work and wait and never wonder.

7. Avoid Venice and Virginia in very warm weather and Vladivostok in winter.

(Make up three sentences loaded with "v" *saying each aloud* before you write.)

8.
9.
10.

B. Readings for Color and Effectiveness

Following are some selections that have appealed to me enough, for their language or their message, so that I thought them useful and interesting for reading aloud. Obviously these are only a surface scratch on the numberless memorable passages of literature. I am sure you have many favorites of your own, and I hope you will add many more.

Study these passages to see how you can profit by their style and thinking. Notice the multifarious ways in which the authors add to their color, expressiveness, and power.

Read the excerpts aloud, not once but many times. On each reading, aim at some particular quality of delivery: pacing; emphasis; variety; sincerity; pauses. Bring out the full value of the words, but shun like the plague any impression of "giving a recitation."

Read sometimes as though you were talking to a small group, close at hand. At other times read as though you were addressing a crowd of hundreds. This practice will help you to strengthen your projection and to maintain audience interest some day when you are giving a talk of your own. The concepts and turns of phrase, too, will provide useful approaches to your own speech preparation. Also, some passages may serve as useful quotations in your own speeches.

Select your readings according to your needs. All of the

selections can be read aloud with great profit by anyone, no matter what the purpose.

OPENING—HUMOR

1. I appreciate very much your generous invitation to be here tonight.

You [newsmen] bear heavy responsibilities these days and an article I read some time ago reminded me of how particularly heavy the burdens of present-day events bear upon your profession.

You may remember that in 1851, the New York *Herald Tribune,* under the sponsorship of Horace Greeley, included as its London correspondent an obscure journalist by the name of Karl Marx.

We are told that the foreign correspondent Marx, stone broke and with a family ill and undernourished, constantly appealed to Greeley and managing editor Charles Dana for an increase in his munificent salary of £5 per installment, a salary which he and Engels labeled as the "lousiest petty bourgeois cheating."

But when all his financial appeals were refused, Marx looked around for other means of livelihood and fame, and eventually terminated his relationship with the *Tribune* and devoted his talents full time to the cause that would bequeath to the world the seeds of Leninism, Stalinism, revolution, and the Cold War.

If only this capitalistic New York newspaper had treated him more kindly, if only Marx had remained a foreign correspondent, history might have been different, and I hope all publishers will bear this lesson in mind the next time they receive a poverty-stricken appeal for a small increase in the expense account from an obscure newspaperman.

—JOHN F. KENNEDY

2. I recently read that the preamble to the Declaration of Independence contains 300 words. The Ten Command-

ments has 297. The Gettysburg Address comes in at 267, while the Lord's Prayer has less than 100.

However, a recent report from the Federal Government on the pricing of cabbages allegedly contains 26,911 words. I will confine my remarks to something between the Lord's Prayer and the pricing of cabbages.

—CHARLES L. GOULD

3. I won't make the same mistake this morning that I made at a speaking engagement last Saturday. I was at the Arizona State Penitentiary . . . with a round-trip ticket . . . to speak to a group of inmates. Without thinking, I began by saying, "It's good to see so many here this morning." In trying to correct my blunder, I made an even greater mistake. I said, "What I meant is, I'm pleased to speak to such a captive audience."   —KEITH L. FLAKE

4. When I say that we are both in the "security" business, there are some people who will say that I'm playing with words. That you from Wall Street and I from the Pentagon have a different view of security. Your security interest is bonds and stock; mine is bombs and shock.

Like most things today, we have our specialties.

—VINCENT F. CAPUTO

5. A well-known literary man objected to Lincoln's calling a certain Greek history "tedious." The man said to Lincoln: "Mr. President, the author of that history is one of the profoundest scholars of the age. Indeed, it may be doubted whether any man of our generation has plunged more deeply into the sacred fount of learning."

"Yes," said Lincoln, "or come up drier."

All too many people seem to plunge deeply into the sacred fount of learning, and still manage to come up quite dry. I don't understand this, for learning, scholarship, ought to be exciting, and when anyone makes it dull and dry, he has gotten off the track somewhere.

—CLIFFORD D. OWSLEY

OPENINGS—SERIOUS

1. In this symposium my part is only to sit in silence. To express one's feelings as the end draws near is too intimate a task.

But I may mention one thought that comes to me as a listener in. The riders in a race do not stop short when they reach the goal. There is a little finishing canter before coming to a standstill. There is time to hear the kind voices of friends and to say to oneself: The work is done. But just as one says that, the answer comes: "The race is over, but the work is never done while the power to work remains. The canter that brings you to a standstill need not be only coming to rest. It cannot be, while you still live. For to live is to function. That is all there is to living."

And so I end with a line from a Latin poet who uttered the message more than fifteen hundred years ago, "Death plucks my ear and says: 'Live—I am coming.'"
—OLIVER WENDELL HOLMES on his ninetieth birthday

2. Man's fascination with Tomorrow is as old as man himself.

From the dawn of his imagination, he has tried to peer behind the "curtain's magic fold" to where Bret Harte said "the glowing future lies unrolled."

He has speculated about the future for profit, for amusement, out of simple curiosity . . . and sometimes for reasons bigger than himself.

And sometimes, he has, indeed, looked into Tomorrow.
—ORVILLE FREEMAN

3. The habit of reading is one of the greatest resources of mankind; and we enjoy reading books that belong to us much more than if they are borrowed. A borrowed book is like a guest in the house; it must be treated with punctiliousness, with a certain considerate formality. You must see that it sustains no damage; it must not suffer while un-

der your roof. You cannot leave it carelessly, you cannot mark it, you cannot turn down the pages, you cannot use it familiarly. And then, some day, although this is seldom done, you really ought to return it.

But your own books belong to you; you treat them with that affectionate intimacy that annihilates formality. Books are for use, not for show; you should own no book that you are afraid to mark up, or afraid to place on the table, wide open and face down.   —WILLIAM LYON PHELPS

4. My friends: No one not in my situation can appreciate my feeling of sadness at this parting. To this place, and the kindness of these people, I owe everything. Here I have lived a quarter of a century, and have passed from a young to an old man. Here my children have been born, and one is buried. I now leave, not knowing when or whether ever I may return, with a task before me greater than that which rested upon Washington. Without the assistance of that Divine Being who ever attended him, I cannot succeed. With that assistance, I cannot fail.

—ABRAHAM LINCOLN (Farewell to Springfield)

CONCLUSIONS

1. Sure I am that this day now we are the masters of our fate, that the task which has been set before us is not above our strength, that its pangs and toils are not beyond our endurance. As long as we have faith in our cause and unconquerable will power, salvation will not be denied us.

In the words of the Psalmist: "He shall not be afraid of evil tidings, his heart is fixed, trusting in the Lord."

—WINSTON CHURCHILL before the United States Congress,
December 26, 1941

2. In the elimination of war lies our solution, for only then will nations cease to compete with one another in the production and use of dread "secret" weapons which are evaluated solely by their capacity to kill. This devilish pro-

gram takes us back not merely to the Dark Ages, but from cosmos to chaos. If we succeed in finding a suitable way to control atomic weapons, it is reasonable to hope that we may also preclude the use of other weapons adaptable to mass destruction. When a man learns to say "A" he can, if he chooses, learn the rest of the alphabet too.

—BERNARD M. BARUCH

3. Let's tell them that the victory to be won in the twentieth century, this portal to the golden age, mocks the pretensions of individual acumen and ingenuity. For it is a citadel guarded by thick walls of ignorance and mistrust which do not fall before the trumpets' blast or the politicians' imprecations or even the generals' baton. They are, my friends, walls that must be directly stormed by the hosts of courage, morality, and of vision, standing shoulder to shoulder, unafraid of ugly truth, contemptuous of lies, half-truths, circuses, and demagoguery.

—ADLAI STEVENSON, 1952 acceptance speech

4. We are a nation of many nationalities, many races, many religions—bound together by a single unity, the unity of freedom and equality. Whoever seeks to set one nationality against another, seeks to degrade all nationalities. Whoever seeks to set one race against another, seeks to enslave all races. Whoever seeks to set one religion against another, seeks to destroy all religion.

—FRANKLIN D. ROOSEVELT

5. Neither let us be slandered from our duty by false accusations against us, nor frightened from it by menaces of destruction to the government, nor of dungeons to ourselves. Let us have faith that right makes might, and in that faith let us to the end dare to do our duty as we understand it.   —ABRAHAM LINCOLN, Cooper Institute

6. Where, after all, do universal human rights begin? In small places, close to home—so close and so small that they cannot be seen on any map of the world. Yet they are the world of the individual person: the neighborhood he

lives in, the school or college he attends, the factory, farm or office where he works.

Such are the places where every man, woman and child seeks equal justice, equal opportunity, equal dignity without discrimination. Unless these rights have meaning there, they have little meaning anywhere.

—ELEANOR ROOSEVELT

7. With malice toward none; with charity for all; with firmness in the right, as God gives us to see the right, let us strive on to finish the work we are in; to bind up the nation's wounds; to care for him who shall have borne the battle, and for his widow, and his orphan—to do all which may achieve a just and lasting peace among ourselves, and with all nations.

—ABRAHAM LINCOLN, Second Inaugural Address

8. God grant that not only the love of liberty but a thorough knowledge of the rights of man may pervade all the nations of the earth, so that a philosopher may set his foot anywhere on its surface and say: "This is my country."   —BENJAMIN FRANKLIN

9. Grant us a common faith that man shall know bread and peace—that he shall know justice and righteousness, freedom and security, an equal opportunity and an equal chance to do his best, not only in our own lands, but throughout the world. And in that faith let us march toward the clean world our hands can make.

—STEPHEN VINCENT BENÉT

10. It is not the critic who counts; not the man who points out how the strong man stumbled, or where the doer of deeds could have done them better. The credit belongs to the man who is actually in the arena; whose face is marred by dust and sweat and blood; who strives valiantly; who errs and comes short again and again; who knows the great enthusiasms, the great devotions, and spends himself in a worthy cause; who at the best knows in the end the triumph of high achievement; and who at the

worst, if he fails, at least fails while daring greatly; so that his place shall never be with those cold and timid souls who know neither victory nor defeat.

—THEODORE ROOSEVELT

11. Let our object be our country, our whole country, and nothing but our country. And by the blessing of God, may that country itself become a vast and splendid monument, not of oppression and terror, but of wisdom, of peace, and of liberty, upon which the world may gaze with admiration forever. —DANIEL WEBSTER

12. A revival of integrity and character can mean a renewal of freedom. The nurturing of values that maintain society's moral tone is going on every day in the financial market place as in the classroom. These values manifest themselves more dramatically through what men and women do than through what they say, and they can never be any better than the generation that holds them in trust.

To some, this may seem an impossibly arduous burden; but others it will inspire to greatness.

—GEORGE CHAMPION

13. I believe that man will not merely endure; he will prevail. He is immortal, not because he alone among creatures has an inexhaustible voice, but because he has a soul, a spirit capable of compassion and sacrifice and endurance. The poet's, the writer's, duty is to write about these things. It is his privilege to help man endure by lifting his heart, by reminding him of the courage and honor and hope and pride and compassion and pity and sacrifice which have been the glory of his past. The poet's voice need not merely be the record of man, it can be one of the props, the pillars to help him endure and prevail.

—WILLIAM FAULKNER

MISCELLANEOUS READINGS

1.   Those who compare the age in which their lot has fallen with a golden age which exists only in imagination, may talk of degeneracy and decay; but no man who is correctly informed as to the past, will be disposed to take a morose or desponding view of the present.

—THOMAS MACAULAY

2.   Unceasingly contemplate the generation of all things through change and accustom thyself to the thought that the nature of the Universe delights above all in changing the things that exist and making new ones of the same pattern. For everything that exists is the seed of that which shall come out of it.   —MARCUS AURELIUS

3.   Appearances to the mind are of four kinds: things either are what they appear to be; or they neither are, nor appear to be; or they are, and do not appear to be; or they are not, and yet appear to be. Rightly to aim in all these cases is the wise man's task.   —EPICTETUS

4.   Men, by their constitutions, are naturally divided into two parties: 1. Those who fear and distrust the people, and wish to draw all powers from them into the hands of the higher classes. 2. Those who identify themselves with the people, have confidence in them, cherish and consider them as the most honest and safe, although not the most wise, depository of the public interests.

—THOMAS JEFFERSON

5.   Behavior seemeth to me as a garment of the mind, and to have the conditions of a garment. For it ought to be made in fashion; it ought not to be too curious, it ought to be shaped so as to set forth any good making of the mind, and hide any deformity; and above all, it ought not

to be too strait, or restrained for exercise or motion.

—Francis Bacon

6. Anybody can become angry—that is easy; but to be angry with the right person, and to the right degree, and at the right time, and for the right purpose, and in the right way—that is not within everybody's power and is not easy.   —Aristotle

7. Whenever you are angry, be assured that it is not only a present evil, but that you have increased a habit, and added fuel to a fire . . . If you would not be of an angry temper, then, do not feed the habit. Give it nothing to help its increase. Be quiet at first, and reckon the days in which you have not been angry. "I used to be angry every day; now every other day; then every third and fourth day." And if you miss it so long as thirty days, offer a sacrifice of thanksgiving to God.   —Epictetus

8. We are never so virtuous as when we are ill . . . It is then a man recollects that there are gods, and that he himself is mortal; . . . and he resolves that if he has the luck to recover, his life shall be passed in harmless happiness.   —Pliny the Younger

9. For just as I approve of a young man in whom there is a touch of age, so I approve of the old man in whom there is some of the flavor of youth. He who strives thus to mingle youthfulness and age may grow old in body, but old in spirit he will never be.   —Cicero

10. You may not carry a sword beneath a scholar's gown, or lead flaming causes from a cloister . . . a scholar who tries to combine those parts sells his birthright for a mess of pottage . . . when the final count is made it will be found that the impairment of his powers far outweighs any possible contribution to the causes he has espoused. If he is fit to serve in his calling at all, it is because he has learned not to serve in any other, for his singleness of

mind quickly evaporates in the fire of passions, however holy.   —LEARNED HAND

11.   We seek an open world—open to ideas, open to the exchange of goods and people, a world in which no people, great or small, will live in angry isolation.

We cannot expect to make everyone our friend, but we can try to make no one our enemy.

Those who would be our adversaries, we invite to a peaceful competition—not in conquering territory or extending dominion, but in enriching the life of man.

As we explore the reaches of space, let us go to the new worlds together—not as new worlds to be conquered, but as new adventures to be shared.

                —RICHARD M. NIXON, Inaugural Address, 1969

12.   Peace does not appear so distant as it did. I hope it will come soon, and come to stay; and so come as to be worth the keeping in all future time. It will then have been proved that among free men there can be no successful appeal from the ballot to the bullet, and that they who make such an appeal are sure to lose their case and pay the cost.   —ABRAHAM LINCOLN

13.   . . . Not to destroy but to construct,
        I hold the unconquerable belief
        that science and peace will triumph over ignorance
            and war
        that nations will come together
        not to destroy but to construct
        and that the future belongs to those
        who accomplish most for humanity.

                                        —LOUIS PASTEUR

14.   We have seen what the space program has already done to make America more secure, more comfortable, more prosperous, and, above all, more progressive. An invaluable stockpile of the required skills and techniques has been developed in recent years through the government-

industry partnership in defense, aerospace, and atomic
energy programs and under the incentives inherent in the
free world. I am optimistic about the future because we
have the resources needed to meet the immense challenges
of our era. The proper use of these will unlock the expanding vistas of a bright future. But all of us must share the
responsibility of insuring the right balance among enthusiasm, imagination, and reality.   —JOHN R. MOORE

15.   We know that the only alternative to private competition is government monopoly of enterprise. We know
that when government monopolizes production, distribution, and employment, it is no longer the servant of men—
it is their master. And, therefore, we know that economic
liberty and political liberty are inseparable parts of the
same ball of wax—that we must keep them both, or we
shall lose them both.   —BENJAMIN FAIRLESS

16.   Newspapers give the impression that railroads are
dead or dying. Obituaries are not in order. Actually, we're
a growth industry. We're on the way up. Don't expect us
to spread our wings and fly. But believe me, gentlemen,
the railroads are emerging as a spirited industry—the best
that's roared down the track in quite a while. This nation
has long needed us. In the years ahead, we're going to
make it want us, too.
—THOMAS GOODFELLOW, Pres. Assoc. of Amer. Railroads

MISCELLANEOUS READING FOR LIGHT TOUCH

1.   The number of things a small dog does naturally is
strangely small. Enjoying better spirits and not crushed
under material cares, he is far more theatrical than average man. His whole life, if he be a dog with any pretensions to gallantry, is spent in a vain show, and in the
hot pursuit of admiration. Take out your puppy for a walk,
and you will find the soft little ball of fur clumsy, stupid,
bewildered, but natural. Let but a few months pass, and

when you repeat the process you will find nature buried in convention. He will do nothing plainly; but the simplest procedures of our material life will all be bent into the forms of an elaborate and mysterious etiquette.

—ROBERT LOUIS STEVENSON

2. So, 37 per cent of life is luck. We have to plan to accept the mystery of luck, but we keep in mind what Charlie Brown said one day too. Charlie and Lucy were playing marbles and Lucy was a humdinger. As she knocked agate after agate of Charlie's, and steelies as well, he kept saying, "Luck, luck, luck." In the second frame it was more of the same. In the third frame Lucy is going saucily down the street with all of Charlie's marbles and he is saying, "Luck, luck, luck." But when she gets around the corner he says, "Boy, that girl can really play marbles."

—JOHN P. LEARY

3. "Papa is a preferable mode of address," observed Mrs. General. "Father is rather vulgar, my dear. The word papa, besides, gives a rather pretty form to the lips. Papa, potatoes, poultry, prunes, and prism, are all very good words for the lips; especially prunes and prism. You will find it serviceable, in the formation of a demeanor, if you sometimes say to yourself in company—on entering a room, for instance—'Papa, potatoes, poultry, prunes and prism, prunes and prism.' "   —CHARLES DICKENS

4. There are members of Parliament so enamored of the spoken word that if waylaid, en route, to the House, an important speech in their pocket, they would, at the cry, "Your type-transcript or your trousers" (if hesitantly) part with the latter. A taxi and a tailor could save *that* situation; the other loss, nothing. Again, there are those sad persons we see, with next to nothing to say, and no hope of saying it without the paper, from which they lift reluctant eyes an anxious moment, for would-be human glances.   —A. P. ROSSITER

READINGS TO HELP THE LISTENER SEE

1. On the verge of the forest we paused to inquire our way at a log house, owned by a white settler or squatter, a tall rawboned old fellow, with red hair, a lank lantern visage, and an inveterate habit of winking with one eye, as if everything he said was of knowing import. He was in a towering passion. One of his horses was missing; he was sure it had been stolen in the night by a straggling party of Osages encamped in a neighboring swamp; but he would have satisfaction! He would make an example of the villains. He had accordingly caught down his rifle from the wall, that invariable enforcer of right or wrong upon the frontiers, and, having saddled his steed, was about to sally forth on a foray into the swamp; while a brother squatter, with rifle in hand, stood ready to accompany him.

—Washington Irving

2. The general attention had been directed from himself to the person in the carriage, and he was quite alone. Rightly judging that under such circumstances it would be madness to follow, he turned down a bye street in search of the nearest coach-stand, finding that after a minute or two he was reeling like a drunken man, and aware for the first time of a stream of blood that was trickling down his face and breast.

—Charles Dickens

3. President Franklin D. Roosevelt (speaking of the Lend-Lease program prior to World War II): Suppose my neighbor's home catches fire, and I have a length of garden hose four or five hundred feet away. If he can take my garden hose and connect it up with his hydrant, I may help him put out his fire. Now, what do I do? I don't say to him before that operation, "Neighbor, my garden hose cost me $15, you have to pay me $15 for it." I don't want $15—I want my garden hose back after the fire is over.

READINGS—FOR SMOOTH, FLOWING SPEECH

1.   The proverbs of all nations, which are always the literature of reason, are the statements of an absolute truth without qualification. Proverbs, like the sacred books of each nation, are the sanctuary of the intuitions. That which the droning world, chained to appearances, will not allow the realist to say in his own words, it will suffer him to say in proverbs without contradiction. And this law of laws, which the pulpit, the senate and the college deny, is hourly preached in all markets and workshops by flights of proverbs, whose teaching is as true and as omnipresent as that of birds and flies.   —Ralph Waldo Emerson

2.   No man is an island, entire of itself;
    Every man is a piece of the continent, a part of the
        main;
    If a clod be washed away by the sea, Europe is the
        less,
    As well as if a promontory were, as well as if a
        manor of thy friend's or of thine own were;
    Any man's death diminishes me, because I am in-
        volved in mankind;
    And therefore never send to know for whom the
        bell tolls; it tolls for thee.   —John Donne

3.   Flowers have an expression of countenance as much as men or animals. Some seem to smile; some have a sad expression; some are pensive and diffident; others again are plain, honest and upright, like the broadfaced sunflower and the hollyhock.   —Henry Ward Beecher

4.   Though I speak with the tongues of men and of angels, and have not charity, I am become as sounding brass, or a tinkling cymbal. And though I have the gift of prophecy, and understand all mysteries, and all knowl-

edge; and though I have all faith, so that I could remove
mountains, and have not charity, I am nothing. And though
I bestow all my goods to feed the poor, and though I give
my body to be burned, and have not charity, it profiteth
me nothing. Charity suffereth long, and is kind; charity
envieth not; charity vaunteth not itself, is not puffed up . . .
Charity never faileth . . ."

—I Corinthians 13:1–4, 8

5. To everything there is a season, and a time to every
        purpose under the heaven:
    A time to be born, and a time to die;
    A time to plant, and a time to pluck up that which
        is planted;
    A time to kill, and a time to heal;
    A time to break down, and a time to build up;
    A time to weep, and a time to laugh;
    A time to mourn, and a time to dance;
    A time to cast away stones, and a time to gather
        stones together;
    A time to embrace, and a time to refrain from
        embracing;
    A time to get, and a time to lose;
    A time to keep, and a time to cast away;
    A time to rend, and a time to sew;
    A time to keep silence, and a time to speak;
    A time to love, and a time to hate;
    A time of war, and a time of peace.

—Ecclesiastes 3:1–8

6. I asked God for strength that I might achieve,
        I was made weak, that I might learn to
            humbly obey;
    I asked for health, that I might do greater things,
        I was given infirmity, that I might do better
            things,
    I asked for riches, that I might be happy,
        I was given poverty, that I might be wise;
    I asked for all things, that I might enjoy life,

I was given life, that I might enjoy all things;
I got nothing that I asked for
But everything I had hoped for;
Almost despite myself, my unspoken prayers were
answered.
I am among all men, most richly blessed.

—AUTHOR UNKNOWN

7.   Thinking cannot be clear till it has had expression.
We must write, or speak, or act our thoughts, or they will
remain in half torpid form. Our feelings must have expression, or they will be as clouds, which, till they descend in
rain, will never bring up fruit or flower. So it is with all
the inward feelings; expression gives them development.
Thought is the blossom; language the opening bud; action
the fruit behind it.   —HENRY WARD BEECHER

8. You cannot pluck out the mystery of the human
heart. Go placidly amid the noise and the haste and learn
what peace there may be in silence. Speak your truth
quietly and clearly; and listen to others, even the dull and
ignorant; they too have their story . . . If you compare
yourself with others you may become vain and bitter;
for always there will be greater and lesser persons than
yourself.

9.   Enjoy your achievements as well as your plans.
Keep interested in your career, however humble; it is a
real possession in the changing fortunes of time. Exercise
caution in your business affairs, for the world is full of
trickery. But let this not blind you to what virtue there
is; many persons strive for high ideals; and everywhere
life is full of heroism.

10.   Be yourself. Especially do not feign affection. Neither be cynical about love; for in the face of all avidity
and disenchantment it is as perennial as the grass. Take
kindly the counsel of the years, gracefully surrendering the
things of youth. Nurture strength of spirit to shield you in
sudden misfortune. But do not distress yourself with imaginings. Many fears are born of fatigue and loneliness. Beyond a wholesome discipline, be gentle with yourself. You

are a child of the universe no less than the trees and the stars; you have a right to be here.

—AUTHOR UNKNOWN. Found at Adlai Stevenson's bedside after his death.

11.   When the conduct of men is designed to be influenced, persuasion, kind, unassuming persuasion, should ever be adopted. It is an old and true maxim that "a drop of honey catches more flies than a gallon of gall." So with men. If you would win a man to your cause, first convince him that you are his sincere friend. Therein is a drop of honey that catches his heart, which, say what he will, is the great high-road to his reason, and which, when once gained, you will find but little trouble convincing his judgment of the justice of your cause, if indeed that cause really is a good one.   —ABRAHAM LINCOLN

12.   May the road rise to meet you,
      May the wind be always at your back,
      May the sun shine warm upon your face
      And the rains fall soft upon your fields,
      And, until we meet again,
      May God hold you in the palm of his hand.
                                        —GAELIC PRAYER

13.   Give us grace and strength to persevere. Give us courage and gaiety and the quiet mind. Spare to us our friends and soften to us our enemies. Give us the strength to encounter that which is to come, that we may be brave in peril, constant in tribulation, temperate in wrath and in all changes of fortune, and down to the gates of death, loyal and loving to one another.
                                —ROBERT LOUIS STEVENSON

C. Punchliners

Ability

The university brings out all abilities including incapability. —CHEKHOV

Skill to do comes of doing.

—RALPH WALDO EMERSON

We judge ourselves by what we feel capable of doing, while others judge us by what we have already done.

—LONGFELLOW

Absence

The same wind snuffs candles yet kindles fires; so, where absence kills a little love, it fans a great one.

—LA ROCHEFOUCAULD

Accent

I once knew a fellow who spoke a dialect with an accent.

—IRVIN COBB

Accomplishment

Be ashamed to die until you have achieved some victory for humanity. —HORACE MANN

Accidents

The way some people drive you'd think they were late for their accident. —EDDIE CANTOR

Acting

The art of acting consists in keeping people from coughing.   —SIR RALPH RICHARDSON

I don't act—I react.   —JOHN WAYNE

Action

Action may not always bring happiness; but there is no happiness without action.   —DISRAELI

You will recall what Senator Dirksen said about the rocking chair—it gives you a sense of motion without any sense of danger.   —JOHN F. KENNEDY

Actions

All our actions take their hue from the complexion of the heart, as landscapes their variety from light.

—FRANCIS BACON

Adversity

Adversity introduces a man to himself.

—ANONYMOUS

There is no education like adversity.   —DISRAELI

What on earth would a man do with himself if something did not stand in his way.   —H. G. WELLS

Advertising

Doing business without advertising is like winking at a girl in the dark; you know what you're doing, but nobody else does.   —STEWART H. BRITT

Advertising is nothing more than the arts of persuasion practiced in mass media.   —ARTHUR E. MEYERHOFF

You can tell the ideals of a nation by its advertisements.

—NORMAN DOUGLAS

Advice

Advice is like castor oil, easy enough to give but dreadful uneasy to take.   —JOSH BILLINGS

To profit from good advice requires more wisdom than to give it.   —JOHN CHURTON COLLINS

I am glad that I paid so little attention to good advice;

had I abided by it I might have been saved from some of my most valuable mistakes.   —GENE FOWLER

A bad cold wouldn't be so annoying if it weren't for the advice of our friends.   —KIN HUBBARD

If you can tell the difference between good advice and bad advice, you don't need advice.
                         —OKMULGEE (Okla.) Rotary Club Bulletin

I sometimes give myself admirable advice, but I am incapable of taking it.   —MARY WORTLEY MONTAGU

Old men are fond of giving good advice, to console themselves for being no longer in a position to give bad examples.   —LA ROCHEFOUCAULD

How is it possible to expect that mankind will take advice when they will not so much as take warning?
                                                         —JONATHAN SWIFT

Age

Middle age occurs when you are too young to take up golf and too old to rush up to the net.
                                          —FRANKLIN PIERCE ADAMS

To me, old age is always fifteen years older than I am.
                                                    —BERNARD BARUCH

Middle age is when you have a choice of two temptations and choose the one that will get you home earlier.
                                                         —DAN BENNETT

In youth we run into difficulties, in old age difficulties run into us.   —JOSH BILLINGS

Middle age is the time when you begin to exchange your emotions for symptoms.   —JACOB BRAUDE

Many people's tombstones should read: "Died at 30. Buried at 60."   —NICHOLAS MURRAY BUTLER

Old age isn't so bad when you consider the alternative.
                                                —MAURICE CHEVALIER

Everything I know I learned after I was thirty.
                                              —GEORGES CLEMENCEAU

No matter how young I think, I can't get under sixty.
                                                    —BILL COPELAND

Youth is a blunder, manhood a struggle, old age a regret.   —DISRAELI

It's not how old you are but how you are old.

—MARIE DRESSLER

Growing old is an emotion which comes over us at almost any age; I had it myself between the ages of 25 and 30.   —E. M. FORSTER

Middle age is when your age starts to show around your middle.   —BOB HOPE

You've reached middle age when all you exercise is caution.   —FRANKLIN P. JONES

Forty is the old age of youth, fifty is the youth of old age.   —VICTOR HUGO

Senescence begins and middle age ends the day your descendants outnumber your friends.   —OGDEN NASH

A man loses his illusions first, his teeth second, and his follies last.   —HELEN ROWLAND

The first forty years of life give us the text; the next thirty supply the commentary on it.   —SCHOPENHAUER

It's not like running out of gas; it's more like burning out your bearings.   —DR. ELVIS STAHR

Agnostic

Don't be an agnostic. Be *something*.

—ROBERT FROST

Alimony

Alimony is like buying oats for a dead horse.

—ARTHUR (BUGS) BAER

You never realize how short a month is until you pay alimony.   —JOHN BARRYMORE

Billing minus cooing.   —MARY C. DORSEY

A man's cash surrender value.

—TOASTER'S HANDBOOK

Ambition

Ambition raises a secret tumult in the soul; it inflames the mind, and puts it into a violent hurry of thought.

—JOSEPH ADDISON

All ambitions are lawful except those which climb upward on the miseries or credulities of mankind.

—JOSEPH CONRAD

America

We must dream of an aristocracy of achievement arising out of a democracy of opportunity.

—THOMAS JEFFERSON

Ours is the only country deliberately founded on a good idea. —JOHN GUNTHER

Intellectually I know that America is no better than any other country; emotionally I know she is better than every other country. —SINCLAIR LEWIS

The American dream does not come to those who fall asleep. —RICHARD M. NIXON

Anger

Two things a man should never be angry at; what he can help and what he cannot help. —THOMAS FULLER

When angry, count four; when very angry, swear.

—MARK TWAIN

The size of a man can be measured by the size of the thing that makes him angry. —J. KENFIELD MORLEY

Apology

Nine times out of ten, the first thing a man's companion knows of his shortcoming is from his apology.

—OLIVER WENDELL HOLMES

Architects

A doctor can bury his mistakes, but an architect can only advise his client to plant vines.

—FRANK LLOYD WRIGHT

Argument

Never argue with a woman when she's tired—or rested.

—H. C. DIEFENBACH

You raise your voice when you should reinforce your argument. —SAMUEL JOHNSON

In most instances, all an argument proves is that two people are present. —TONY PETTITO

Art

Art, like morality consists in drawing the line somewhere.   —G. K. CHESTERTON

A man who works with his hands is a laborer; a man who works with his hands and his brain is a craftsman; but a man who works with his hands and his brain and his heart is an artist.   —LOUIS NIZER

When love and skill work together expect a masterpiece.
—JOHN RUSKIN

In life beauty perishes, but not in art.
—LEONARDO DA VINCI

Automation

The real danger of our technological age is not so much that machines will begin to think like men, but that men will begin to think like machines.   —SIDNEY J. HARRIS

It's going to be a tough decision when the purchasing agent starts negotiating to buy the machine that's to replace him.   —DAVE MURRAY

Babies

Babies do not want to hear about babies; they like to be told of giants and castles.   —SAMUEL JOHNSON

Baldness

There's one thing about baldness: it's neat.
—DON HEROLD

Baldness may indicate masculinity, but it diminishes one's opportunity to find out.
—SIR CEDRIC HARDWICKE

Banking

Bank accounts are like toothpaste; easy to take out but hard to put back.   —ROBERT ACKERSTROM

Beauty

Beauty is not caused. It is.   —EMILY DICKINSON

Beauty is all very well at sight, but who can look at it when it has been in the house three days?
—GEORGE BERNARD SHAW

Beginning

A journey of a thousand leagues begins with a single step.   —CHINESE PROVERB

Behavior

Manners are the happy ways of doing things.
                                    —RALPH WALDO EMERSON
Some people take everything on a vacation but their manners.
                        —MARSHALLTOWN, IOWA, TIMES-REPUBLICAN
We have committed the Golden Rule to memory; let us now commit it to life.   —EDWIN MARKHAM
One of the very best of all earthly possessions is self-possession.   —GEORGE D. PRENTICE

Belief

Some things have to be believed to be seen.
                                    —RALPH HODGSON
Some men like to understand what they believe in. Others like to believe in what they understand.
                                    —ANONYMOUS

Bigamy

The only crime on the books where two rites make a wrong.   —BOB HOPE

Birth Control

It may boil down to a little pill whether or not the world comes to its right census.   —CURRENT COMEDY

Books

On how many people's libraries, as on bottles from the drugstore, one might write: "For external use only."
                                    —ALPHONSE DAUDET

Bore

He is not only dull himself but the cause of dullness in others.   —SAMUEL FOOTE

A bore is a man who deprives you of solitude without providing you with company.

—GIAN VINCENZO GRAVINA

The secret of being a bore is to tell everything.

—VOLTAIRE

Boredom

Some people can stay longer in an hour than others can in a week.   —WILLIAM DEAN HOWELLS

A yawn is a silent shout.   —G. K. CHESTERTON

Borrowing

A moneylender serves you in the present tense, lends you in the conditional mood, keeps you in the subjunctive, and ruins you in the future.   —JOSEPH ADDISON

Before borrowing money from a friend, decide which you need more.   —ADDISON H. HALLOCK

Brevity

All pleasantries ought to be short—and for that matter, gravities too.   —VOLTAIRE

Business

Few people do business well who do nothing else.

—LORD CHESTERFIELD

The business of America is business.

—CALVIN COOLIDGE

Competition is getting keener all the time; are you?

—ELMER LETERMAN

Good will is the one and only asset that competition cannot undersell or destroy.   —MARSHALL FIELD

I don't meet competition. I crush it.

—CHARLES REVSON

Next to knowing all about your own business, the best thing is to know all about the other fellow's.

—JOHN D. ROCKEFELLER

Business World

A company is known by the men it keeps.

—MELLON INSTITUTE NEWS

Busy

Bees are not as busy as we think they are. They just can't buzz any slower.   —KIN HUBBARD

Buying

People will buy anything that's one to a customer.
—SINCLAIR LEWIS

Camping

He who believes that where there's smoke there's fire hasn't tried cooking on a camping trip.
—CHANGING TIMES

Capability

If there's a job to be done, I always ask the busiest man in my parish to take it on and it gets done.
—HENRY WARD BEECHER

Celebrity

Someone who works hard to become well known and then wears dark glasses to avoid being recognized.
—HAPPY VARIETY

Challenge

The Difficult is that which can be done immediately; the Impossible that which takes a little longer.
—GEORGE SANTAYANA

Prosperity is a great teacher; adversity is a greater; possession pampers the mind; privation trains and strengthens it.   —WILLIAM HAZLITT

Chance

He that leaveth nothing to chance will do few things ill, but he will do very few things.
—MARQUIS OF HALIFAX

Character

You must look into people as well as at them.
—LORD CHESTERFIELD

Every man has three characters—that which he exhibits, that which he has, and that which he thinks he has.

—ALPHONSE KARR

The shortest and surest way to live with honor in the world is to be in reality what we appear to be.

—SOCRATES

Charity

Charity begins at home, and justice begins next door.

—CHARLES DICKENS

Our charity begins at home, and mostly ends where it begins.   —HORACE SMITH

Charm

If you have charm, you don't need to have anything else; and if you don't have it, it doesn't matter what else you have.   —J. M. BARRIE

Cheerfulness

Cheerfulness keeps up a kind of daylight in the mind, and fills it with a steady and perpetual serenity.

—JOSEPH ADDISON

A cheerful face is nearly as good for an invalid as healthy weather.   —BENJAMIN FRANKLIN

A cheerful look makes a dish a feast.

—A. P. HERBERT

Children

For adult education nothing beats children.

—BANKING

Diogenes struck the father when the son swore.

—ROBERT BURTON

You can tell that a child is growing up when he stops asking where he came from and starts refusing to tell where he's going.   —CHANGING TIMES

Hooky is when a small boy lets his mind wander—and then follows it.   —CIRCLE ARROW RETAILER

We have not passed that subtle line between childhood and adulthood until we have stopped saying, "It got lost," and say, "I lost it."   —SYDNEY J. HARRIS

There is little use to talk about your child to anyone; other people either have one or haven't.

—Don Herold

Children have more need of models than of critics.

—Joseph Joubert

Insanity is hereditary. You can get it from your children.

—Sam Levenson

Children aren't happy with nothing to ignore,
And that's what parents were created for.

—Ogden Nash

The surest way to make it hard for children is to make it easy for them. —Eleanor Roosevelt

Circumstance

Man is not the creature of circumstances,
Circumstances are the creatures of men. —Disraeli

Citizens

Whatever makes good Christians, makes them good citizens. —Daniel Webster

City

If you would be known, and not know, vegetate in a village; if you would know, and not be known, live in a city. —Charles Caleb Colton

City Life

City life: millions of people being lonesome together.

—Henry David Thoreau

Civilization

The end of the human race will be that it will eventually die of civilization. —Ralph Waldo Emerson

The path of civilization is paved with tin cans.

—Elbert Hubbard

It wouldn't be so bad if civilization were only at the crossroads, but this is one of those cloverleaf jobs.

—"Senator Soaper"

Civilization is a movement and not a condition, a voyage and not a harbor. —Arnold Toynbee

Classes

There may be said to be two classes of people in the
world; those who constantly divide the people of the world
into two classes, and those who do not.

—ROBERT BENCHLEY

Clothes

It is an interesting question how far men would retain
their relative rank if they were divested of their clothes.

—HENRY DAVID THOREAU

She looked as if she had been poured into her clothes
and had forgotten to say "when."   —P. G. WODEHOUSE

Cold

A cold is both positive and negative; sometimes the Eyes
have it and sometimes the Nose.

—WILLIAM LYON PHELPS

Committee

A committee is a group that keeps minutes and loses
hours.   —MILTON BERLE

Common Sense

Common sense is, of all kinds, the most uncommon. It
implies good judgment, sound discretion, and true and
practical wisdom applied to common life.

—TRYON EDWARDS

Common sense is not so common.   —VOLTAIRE

Company

Misery loves company, but company does not re-
ciprocate.   —ADDISON MIZNER

Compliment

Every day you look lovelier and lovelier and today you
look like tomorrow.   —CHARLIE MCCARTHY

I can live for two months on a good compliment.

—MARK TWAIN

Some people pay a compliment as if they expected a
receipt.   —KIN HUBBARD

Computer

To err is human; to really foul things up requires a computer. —BILL VAUGHAN

Conference

A conference is a gathering of important people who singly can do nothing, but together can decide that nothing can be done. —FRED ALLEN

A meeting of the bored. —RUSSELL NEWBOLD

Confessions

Confessions may be good for the soul but they are bad for the reputation. —THOMAS ROBERT DEWAR

Connections

Many a live wire would be a dead one except for his connections. —WILSON MIZNER

Conscience

Conscience and reputation are two things. Conscience is due to yourself, reputation to your neighbor.

—ST. AUGUSTINE

Reason often makes mistakes, but conscience never does.

—JOSH BILLINGS

Conscience is thoroughly well bred and soon leaves off talking to those who do not wish to hear it.

—SAMUEL BUTLER

Once we assuage our conscience by calling something a "necessary evil," it begins to look more and more necessary and less and less evil. —SYDNEY J. HARRIS

Conscience: the inner voice which warns us that someone may be looking. —H. L. MENCKEN

Conservatism

What is conservatism? Is it not adherence to the old and tried, against the new and untried?

—ABRAHAM LINCOLN

Conservative

I never dared to be a radical when young
For fear it would make me conservative when old.
                                        —ROBERT FROST

Consideration

Be kind and considerate to others, depending somewhat
upon who they are.   —DON HEROLD

Contentment

Enjoy your own life without comparing it with that of
another.   —CONDORCET
When we cannot find contentment in ourselves it is use-
less to seek it elsewhere.   —LA ROCHEFOUCAULD

Control

In the order named, these are the hardest to control:
Wine, Women, and Song.   —FRANKLIN PIERCE ADAMS

Conversation

The true spirit of conversation consists in building on
another man's observation, not overturning it.
                                —EDWARD BULWER-LYTTON
His conversation does not show the minute hand, but
he strikes the hour very correctly.
                                        —BENJAMIN FRANKLIN
Conversation is the slowest form of human communica-
tion.   —DON HEROLD
Conversation should be fired in short bursts; anybody
who talks steadily for more than a minute is in danger of
boring somebody.   —HARLAN MILLER
The less men think, the more they talk.
                                        —MONTESQUIEU
I often quote myself; it adds spice to my conversation.
                                —GEORGE BERNARD SHAW
Conceit causes more conversation than wit.
                                        —LA ROCHEFOUCAULD
It is better to ask some of the questions than to know
all the answers.   —JAMES THURBER

Cooking

Fish, to taste right, must swim three times—in water, in butter, and in wine.   —POLISH PROVERB

Let the salad-maker be a spendthrift for oil—a miser for vinegar—a statesman for salt—and a madman for mixing.   —SPANISH PROVERB

Courage

Fear gives sudden instincts of skill.
                                —SAMUEL TAYLOR COLERIDGE

Fortune favors the audacious.   —ERASMUS

Nature reacts only to physical disease, but also to moral weakness; when the danger increases, she gives us greater courage.   —GOETHE

I have never thought much of the courage of the lion-tamer; inside the cage he is, at least, safe from other men.
                                —GEORGE BERNARD SHAW

Courtesy

True politeness consists in being easy with one's self, and making every one about one as easy as one can.
                                —ALEXANDER POPE

We cannot always oblige, but we can always speak obligingly.   —VOLTAIRE

Courtship

The word "engagement" has two meanings: in war it's a battle, in courtship it's a surrender.
                                —GENERAL FEATURES CORPORATION

Coward

To sin by silence when they should protest makes cowards out of men.   —ABRAHAM LINCOLN

Crime

If you do big things they print your face, and if you do little things they only print your thumbs.
                                —ARTHUR (BUGS) BAER

We enact many laws that manufacture criminals, and then a few that punish them.   —JOSIAH TUCKER

Critic

A drama critic is a man who leaves no turn unstoned.
                                            —GEORGE BERNARD SHAW

Criticism

There is always something wrong with a man, as there is with a motor, when he knocks continually.
                                            —COLUMBIA RECORD

Clean your finger before you point at my spots.
                                            —BENJAMIN FRANKLIN

The actor who took the role of King Lear played the King as though he expected someone to play the ace.
                                            —EUGENE FIELD

Even the lion has to defend himself against flies.
                                            —GERMAN PROVERB

I don't like yes men. I want you to tell me what you really think—even if it costs you your job.
                                            —SAM GOLDWYN

The trouble with most of us is that we would rather be ruined by praise than saved by criticism.
                                            —NORMAN VINCENT PEALE

Critic: One who finds a little bad in the best of things.
                                            —JOSEPH P. RITZ

When you point your finger at someone else, you have three fingers pointed at yourself.   —LOUIS NIZER

The scenery in the play was beautiful, but the actors got in front of it.   —ALEXANDER WOOLLCOTT

Cures

There's something alive about a kitchen, the way it smells and sounds and feels. Maybe sick people would all live longer if they sat in kitchens.
                                            —CHRISTOPHER MORLEY

Curiosity

Curiosity is the only intelligence test which tells what one may become as well as what one is.
                                            —SATURDAY REVIEW

Why do they call it idle curiosity when it's pretty close to the one thing never idle?   —MARION STAR

Debt

The house was more covered with mortgages than with paint. —George Ade

Debt is a trap which a man sets and baits himself—and catches himself. —Josh Billings

Deception

Nothing is so easy as to deceive one's self, for what we wish, that we readily believe. —Demosthenes

Necessity is the mother of deception.

—Belle Sarnoff

Decision

When a decision has been made and the die is cast, then murder the alternatives. —Mrs. Emory S. Adams, Jr.

Making up your mind is like making a bed; it usually helps to have someone on the other side.

—Gerald Horton Bath

A woman's final decision is not necessarily the same as the one she makes later. —H. N. Ferguson

Deeds

One good deed has many claimants.

—Yiddish Proverb

Democracy

The tyranny of the multitude is a multiplied tyranny.

—Edmund Burke

Democracy is based upon the conviction that there are extraordinary possibilities in the ordinary people.

—Harry Emerson Fosdick

Republics end through luxury; monarchies through poverty. —Montesquieu

Democracy is a form of government in which it is permitted to wonder aloud what the country could do under first-class management. —"Senator Soaper"

Dentist

A dentist at work in his vocation always looks down in the mouth. —George D. Prentice

Depressions

Depressions may bring people closer to the church, but so do funerals.　—CLARENCE DARROW

Description

When something defies description, let it.
　　　　　　　　　　　　　　　　—ARNOLD H. GLASOW

Diet

She used to diet on any kind of food she could lay her hands on.　—ARTHUR (BUGS) BAER

Eat breakfast like a king, eat lunch like a prince, but eat dinner like a pauper.　—ADELLE DAVIS

The sad thing about most diets is they do so much for the will power and so little for the waistline.
　　　　　　　　　　　　　　　　—"GRAND OLE OPRY"

Another good reducing exercise consists in placing both hands against the table edge and pushing back.
　　　　　　　　　　　　　　　　—ROBERT QUILLEN

Differences

People differ. Some object to the fan dancer, and others to the fan.　—ELIZABETH W. SPALDING

Diligence

Everything yields to diligence.　—ANTIPHANES

Diplomacy

Diplomacy: lying in state.　—OLIVER HERFORD

Diplomacy is to do and say the nastiest thing in the nicest way.　—ISAAC GOLDBERG

A diplomat is a man who remembers a lady's birthday but forgets her age.　—AUTHOR UNKNOWN

Discipline

Say what you will about the Ten Commandments, you must always come back to the pleasant fact that there are only ten of them.　—H. L. MENCKEN

Discretion

There's a time to wink as well as to see.

—BENJAMIN FRANKLIN

Discussion

I'll discuss anything. I like to go perhaps-ing around on all subjects. —ROBERT FROST

Dissatisfaction

It's when you're safe at home that you wish you were having an adventure. When you're having an adventure you wish you were safe at home. —THORNTON WILDER

Divorce

Divorce is what happens when the marriage you thought was a merger turns out to be a conglomerate.

—"HOT LINES"

People wouldn't get divorced for such trivial reasons if they didn't get married for such trivial reasons.

—BRIDGEPORT STAR

Doctor

A man who tells you if you don't cut something out, he will. —FRANK ROSSITER

Dogs

If dogs could talk, perhaps we'd find it just as hard to get along with them as we do with people.

—KAREL ČAPEK

Doubt

To believe with certainty we must begin with doubting.

—STANISLAUS LESCYNSKI

I respect faith, but doubting is what gets you an education. —WILLIAM MIZNER

Drinking

Some men are like musical glasses; to produce their finest tones you must keep them wet.

—SAMUEL TAYLOR COLERIDGE

Bacchus has drowned more men than Neptune.

—GARIBALDI

Wine makes a man better pleased with himself; I do not say that it makes him more pleasing to others.

—SAMUEL JOHNSON

There is a devil in every berry of the grape.

—THE KORAN

Liquor talks mighty loud when it gets loose from the jug.   —JOEL CHANDLER HARRIS

I drink to make other people interesting.

—GEORGE JEAN NATHAN

I'm not willing to sacrifice the control of physical and mental ability that drinking and smoking take away for what they give in return.   —PIERRE TRUDEAU

I must get out of these wet clothes and into a dry martini.   —ALEXANDER WOOLLCOTT

Driving

Drive carefully! Remember: it's not only a car that can be recalled by its maker.   —CONSUMERS DIGEST

Duty

One trouble with the world is that so many people who stand up vigorously for their rights fall down miserably on their duties.   —GRIT

A sense of duty is useful in work but offensive in personal relations.   —BERTRAND RUSSELL

He who eats the fruit should at least plant the seed.

—HENRY DAVID THOREAU

Earnestness

Earnest people are often people who habitually look on the serious side of things that have no serious side.

—VAN WYCK BROOKS

Economy

So often we rob tomorrow's memories by today's economies.   —JOHN MASON BROWN

Editing

I have made this a rather long letter because I haven't had time to make it shorter.   —Pascal

The hardest thing for some people to say in 25 words or less is "Good-by."   —Tony Pettito

Education

I find that a great part of the information I have was acquired by looking up something and finding something else on the way.   —Franklin P. Adams

The primary purpose of education is not to teach you to earn your bread, but to make every mouthful sweeter.
—James Angell

I have never let my schooling interfere with my education.   —Mark Twain

There is nothing so stupid as an educated man, if you get off the thing that he was educated in.
—Will Rogers

Universities are full of knowledge; the freshman brings a little in and the seniors take none away, and knowledge accumulates.   —Abbot Lawrence Lowell

Education is what remains when we have forgotten all that we have been taught.
—George Savile, Marquis of Halifax

A man who has never gone to school may steal from a freight car; but if he has a university education, he may steal the whole railroad.   —Theodore Roosevelt

Ego

Most men are like eggs, too full of themselves to hold anything else.   —Josh Billings

The personal pronoun "I" should be the coat of arms of some individuals.   —Comte De Rivarol

When a man is wrapped up in himself he makes a pretty small package.   —John Ruskin

Eloquence

Eloquence is logic on fire.   —Lyman Beecher

Emotions

This is the greatest paradox; the emotions cannot be trusted, yet it is they that tell us the greatest truths.

—Don Herold

Encouragement

Correction does much, but encouragement does more; encouragement after censure is as the sun after a shower.

—Goethe

Entertainment

Nightclub: A place where they take the rest out of restaurant and put the din in dinner.   —Reader's Digest

Enthusiasm

Every production of genius must be the production of enthusiasm.   —Disraeli

He came to his job fired with enthusiasm and left it the same way.   —Max Rubin

Equality

Though all men are made of one metal, yet they were not cast all in the same mold.   —Thomas Fuller

Men are made by nature unequal. It is vain, therefore, to treat them as if they were equal.

—James Anthony Froude

The only real equality is in the cemetery.

—German Proverb

Evaluation

The injury we do and the one we suffer are not weighed in the same scales.   —Aesop

Executive

The mark of a true executive is usually illegible.

—Leo J. Farrell, Jr.

Exercise

Whenever I feel like exercise, I lie down until the feeling passes.   —Robert M. Hutchins

The only exercise I get is when I take the studs out of one shirt and put them in another. —RING LARDNER

Experience

Experience increases our wisdom but doesn't reduce our follies. —JOSH BILLINGS

To stumble twice against the same stone, is a proverbial disgrace. —CICERO

I believe in getting into hot water; it keeps you clean. —G. K. CHESTERTON

Experience is not what happens to a man. It is what a man does with what happens to him. —ALDOUS HUXLEY

Experience is the name everyone gives to his mistakes. —OSCAR WILDE

Eyes

The eyes of the dead are closed gently; we also have to open gently the eyes of the living. —JEAN COCTEAU

The sky is the daily bread of the eyes. —RALPH WALDO EMERSON

There's so much to say but your eyes keep interrupting me. —CHRISTOPHER MORLEY

Face

There are people who think that everything one does with a serious face is sensible. —G. C. LICHTENBERG

He had the sort of face that, once seen, is never remembered. —OSCAR WILDE

Facts

Every man has a right to his opinion, but no man has a right to be wrong in his facts. —BERNARD BARUCH

Faith

All I have seen teaches me to trust the Creator for all I have not seen. —RALPH WALDO EMERSON

I have no faith, very little hope, and as much charity as I can afford. —T. H. HUXLEY

Let us have faith that right makes might; and in that faith, let us, to the end, dare to do our duty as we understand it.   —ABRAHAM LINCOLN

I can see how it might be possible for a man to look down upon the earth and be an atheist, but I cannot conceive how he could look up into the heavens and say there is no God.   —ABRAHAM LINCOLN

Faith is the force of life.   —TOLSTOY

I can believe anything, provided it is incredible.

                                  —OSCAR WILDE

Fame

Fame is the perfume of heroic deeds.   —SOCRATES

Familiarity

Though familiarity may not breed contempt, it takes off the edge of admiration.   —WILLIAM HAZLITT

Family

The first half of our lives is ruined by our parents and the second half by our children.   —CLARENCE DARROW

Most parents don't worry about a daughter till she fails to show up for breakfast, and then it's too late.

                                  —KIN HUBBARD

All happy families are alike, but each unhappy family is unhappy in its own way.   —TOLSTOY

There is little less trouble in governing a private family than a whole kingdom.   —MONTAIGNE

Fashion

Fashion is made to become unfashionable.

                                  —GABRIELLE CHANEL

Fashion is gentility running away from vulgarity, and afraid of being overtaken.   —WILLIAM HAZLITT

She had a passion for hats, none of which returned her affection.   —STORM JAMESON

High heels were invented by a woman who had been kissed on the forehead.   —CHRISTOPHER MORLEY

I see that the fashion wears out more apparel than the man.   —SHAKESPEARE

A fashion is nothing but an induced epidemic.

—GEORGE BERNARD SHAW

Women's styles may change but the designs remain the same. —OSCAR WILDE

Fashion is a form of ugliness so intolerable that we have to alter it every six months. —OSCAR WILDE

All women's dresses are merely variations on the eternal struggle between the admitted desire to dress and the unadmitted desire to undress. —LIN YUTANG

Fault

She is intolerable, but that is her only fault.

—TALLEYRAND

Fear

If a man harbors any sort of fear, it percolates through all his thinking, damages his personality, makes him landlord to a ghost. —LLOYD C. DOUGLAS

There's nothing I'm afraid of like scared people.

—ROBERT FROST

The misfortunes hardest to bear are those which never happen. —JAMES RUSSELL LOWELL

Of all the liars in the world, sometimes the worst are your own fears. —RUDYARD KIPLING

In this world, there is always danger for those who are afraid of it. —GEORGE BERNARD SHAW

To him who is in fear everything rustles.

—SOPHOCLES

It takes up too much time, being afraid.

—PIERRE TRUDEAU

Feeling

Half our mistakes in life arise from feeling where we ought to think, and thinking where we ought to feel.

—JOHN CHURTON COLLINS

Figures

She had a lot of fat that did not fit.

—HERBERT GEORGE WELLS

Nothing is so fallacious as facts, except figures.

—GEORGE CANNING

Flattery

He soft-soaped her until she couldn't see for the suds.

—MARY ROBERTS RINEHART

The art of telling another person exactly what he thinks of himself.   —PAUL H. GILBERT

Flattery never hurts a man unless he inhales.

—HARRY EMERSON FOSDICK

Men are like stone jugs—you may lug them where you like by the ears.   —SAMUEL JOHNSON

Flirtation

Flirtation, attention without intention.

—MAX O'RELL

Folly

A good folly is worth whatever you pay for it.

—GEORGE ADE

If fifty million say a foolish thing it is still a foolish thing.   —ANATOLE FRANCE

Food

No man is lonely while eating spaghetti—it requires so much attention.   —CHRISTOPHER MORLEY

Fools

A learned fool is more foolish than an ignorant fool.

—MOLIÈRE

Forgiveness

Forgive others often, yourself never.

—PUBLILIUS SYRUS

Freedom

In free countries, every man is entitled to express his opinions—and every other man is entitled not to listen.

—G. NORMAN COLLIE

All men are born free and unequal.   —GRANT ALLEN

A man's worst difficulties begin when he is able to do as he likes.   —T. H. HUXLEY

We must be willing to pay a price for freedom, for no price that is ever asked for it is half the cost of doing without it.   —H. L. MENCKEN

Liberty means responsibility. That is why most men dread it.   —GEORGE BERNARD SHAW

Friends

A true friend is one soul in two bodies.   —ARISTOTLE

Friend: one who knows all about you and loves you just the same.   —ELBERT HUBBARD

Friendship

Love is blind; friendship tries not to notice.
—OTTO VON BISMARCK

The only way to have a friend is to be one.
—RALPH WALDO EMERSON

Friendship is the best gift you can give yourself.
—ELMER LETERMAN

Fun

Fun is like life insurance; the older you get, the more it costs.   —KIN HUBBARD

Future

I try to be as philosophical as the old lady from Vermont who said that the best thing about the future is that it only comes one day at a time.   —DEAN ACHESON

My interest is in the future because I am going to spend the rest of my life there.
—CHARLES FRANKLIN KETTERING

The trouble with our times is that the future is not what it used to be.   —PAUL VALÉRY

Giving

The world is composed of takers and givers. The takers may eat better, but the givers sleep better.
—BYRON FREDERICK in *Ohio State Grange Monthly*

Golf

A game where the ball always lies poorly and the player well.   —READER'S DIGEST

I play Civil War golf—out in 61—back in 65.

—DOROTHY SARNOFF

Golf is a good walk spoiled.   —MARK TWAIN

Gossip

Too often when you tell a secret it goes in one ear and in another.   —LESLIE E. DUNKIN

Rare is the person who can weigh the faults of others without putting his thumb on the scales.

—BYRON J. LANGENFELD

She poured a little social sewage into his ears.

—GEORGE MEREDITH

Busy souls have no time to be busybodies.

—AUSTIN O'MALLEY

Government

We sometimes wonder whether the members of Congress would have to mend their fences so often if they had not sat on them so much.   —CHRISTIAN SCIENCE MONITOR

Isn't it a shame that future generations can't be here to see all the wonderful things we're doing with their money?   —EARL WILSON

Graduation

Some men are graduated from college cum laude, some are graduated summa cum laude, and some are graduated mirabile dictu.   —WILLIAM HOWARD TAFT

Grammar

Grammar school never taught me anything about grammar.   —ISAAC GOLDBERG

Grief

The busy have no time for tears.   —LORD BYRON

The swallows of sorrow may fly overhead, but don't let them nest in your hair.   —CHINESE PROVERB

Sorrows are like thunderclouds—in the distance they look black, over our heads scarcely gray.

—JEAN PAUL RICHTER

Guest

No one can be so welcome a guest that he will not annoy his host after three days.   —PLAUTUS

Habit

Cultivate good habits—the bad ones all grow wild.

—DETROIT HOME GAZETTE

The unfortunate thing about this world is that good habits are so much easier to get out of than bad ones.

—W. SOMERSET MAUGHAM

Habits are at first cobwebs, then cables.

—SPANISH PROVERB

Hair

What's on the head is not as important as what's in it.

—MILTON RAYMOND

Happiness

Not in doing what you like but in liking what you do is the secret of happiness.   —J. M. BARRIE

There is no cosmetic for beauty like happiness.

—LADY MARGUERITE BLESSINGTON

Action may not always bring happiness, but there is no happiness without action.   —DISRAELI

Though we travel the world over to find the beautiful, we must carry it with us or we find it not.

—RALPH WALDO EMERSON

Human felicity is produced not so much by great pieces of good fortune that seldom happen, as by little advantages that occur every day.

—BENJAMIN FRANKLIN

Happiness makes up in height for what it lacks in length.

—ROBERT FROST

We act as though comfort and luxury were the chief requirements of life when all that we need to make us really happy is something to be enthusiastic about.

—CHARLES KINGSLEY

Most folks are about as happy as they make up their minds to be.   —ABRAHAM LINCOLN

Hate

Hating people is like burning down your own house to get rid of a rat.   —HARRY EMERSON FOSDICK

People hate, as they love, unreasonably.

—THACKERAY

Health

He who has health has hope, and he who has hope has everything.   —ARABIAN PROVERB

My constitution was destroyed long ago; now I'm living under the bylaws.   —CLARENCE DARROW

Help

The best place to find a helping hand is at the end of your arm.   —ELMER LETERMAN

Hesitation

He who hesitates is sometimes saved.

—JAMES THURBER

Hindsight

Ah, the insight of hindsight!   —THURSTON N. DAVIS

Hobby

Hard work that you would be ashamed to do for a living.   —GILBERT NORWOOD

Honor

Our own heart, and not other men's opinion, forms our true honor.   —SAMUEL TAYLOR COLERIDGE

Hope

Appetite, with an opinion of attaining, is called hope; the same without such opinion, despair.

—THOMAS HOBBES

Hosts

People are either born hosts or born guests.

—Max Beerbohm

Hotels

Where you give up good dollars for bad quarters.

—Billy Rose

Sign outside a small hotel: "Have your next affair here."

—Speaker's Encyclopedia

Houses

A man's dignity may be enhanced by the house he lives in, but not wholly secure by it; the owner should bring honor to the house, not the house to its owner.

—Cicero

Humanity

I love my country better than my family; but I love humanity better than my country.   —Fénelon

You must not lose faith in humanity. Humanity is an ocean; if a few drops of the ocean are dirty, the ocean does not become dirty.   —Gandhi

After all there is but one race—humanity.

—George Moore

Humor

Humor is the good-natured side of truth.

—Mark Twain

Ideas

Great ideas need landing gear as well as wings.

—Adolph A. Berle, Jr.

Ignorance

Everybody is ignorant, only on different subjects.

—Will Rogers

Illusion

Illusion is the first of all pleasures.   —Voltaire

Image

To know oneself is to foresee oneself; to foresee oneself amounts to playing a part.   —PAUL VALÉRY

Imagination

A man's life is dyed the color of his imagination.
—MARCUS AURELIUS

Imagination is more important than knowledge.
—ALBERT EINSTEIN

Anything one man can imagine, other men can make real.   —JULES VERNE

Imagination is the eye of the soul.   —JOUBERT

Impossibility

You cannot make a crab walk straight.
—ARISTOPHANES

The airplane, the atomic bomb, and the zipper have cured me of any tendency to state that a thing can't be done.   —R. L. DUFFUS

Improbable

The improbable happens just often enough to make life either disturbing or delightful.
—WILLIAM FEATHER

Improvement

It is necessary to try to surpass one's self always; this occupation ought to last as long as life.
—QUEEN CHRISTINA

Indecision

There is grief in indecision.   —CICERO

Inferiority

No one can make you feel inferior without your consent.
—ELEANOR ROOSEVELT

Infidelity

The plural of spouse is spice.
—CHRISTOPHER MORLEY

Inflation

A little inflation is like a little pregnancy—it keeps on growing.   —Leon Henderson

Influence

Goethe said there would be little left of him if he were to discard what he owed to others.
—Charlotte Cushman

It is only the people with push who have a pull.
—Thomas Robert Dewar

I am a part of all that I have met.
—Alfred Lord Tennyson

Interest

You must learn day by day, year by year, to broaden your horizon. The more things you love, the more you are interested in, the more you enjoy.
—Ethel Barrymore

Intolerance

If the bell of intolerance tolls for one, it tolls for all.
—Henry Seidel Canby

Intuition

Intuition is reason in a hurry.   —Holbrook Jackson

A woman's guess is much more accurate than a man's certainty.   —Rudyard Kipling

Invention

How come, if necessity is the mother of invention, all this unnecessary stuff gets invented?
—General Features Corporation

Italy

The Creator made Italy from designs by Michelangelo.
—Mark Twain

Joy

Real joy comes not from ease or riches or from the praise of men, but from doing something worthwhile.

—SIR WILFRED GRENFELL

Grief can take care of itself; but to get the full value of joy you must have somebody to divide it with.

—MARK TWAIN

Judgment

Next to knowing when to seize an opportunity, the most important thing in life is to forgo an advantage.

—DISRAELI

Jury

A jury consists of twelve persons chosen to decide who has the better lawyer.   —ROBERT FROST

Justice

By the just we mean that which is lawful and that which is fair and equitable.   —ARISTOTLE

Justice is too good for some people, and not good enough for the rest.   —NORMAN DOUGLAS

Justice is the constant desire and effort to render to every man his due.   —JUSTINIAN

Justice is spontaneous respect, mutually guaranteed, for human dignity, in whatever person it may be compromised and under whatever circumstances, and to whatever risk its defense may expose us.   —P. J. PROUDHON

Kindness

The kindness planned for tomorrow doesn't count today.

—NEWARK (Del.) POST

Loving kindness is greater than laws; and the charities of life are more than all ceremonies.   —THE TALMUD

Knowledge

Strange how much you've got to know before you know how little you know.   —BEST QUOTATIONS

To be conscious that you are ignorant is a great step to knowledge.   —DISRAELI

There are two great boosters which propel a man into the upper spaces of society and accomplishment—knowledge and wisdom.   —Selig Edelman

Our knowledge is the amassed thought and experience of innumerable minds.   —Ralph Waldo Emerson

He was not made for climbing the tree of knowledge.
—Sigrid Undset

Lady

A lady is a woman in whose presence a man is a gentleman.   —Peg Bracken

Land

If a man owns land, the land owns him.
—Ralph Waldo Emerson

Language

Slang is language that takes off its coat, spits on its hands, and goes to work.   —Carl Sandburg

England and America are two countries separated by the same language.   —George Bernard Shaw

Laughter

Laughing is the sensation of feeling good all over, and showing it principally in one spot.   —Josh Billings

Men show their character in nothing more clearly than by what they think laughable.   —Goethe

Law

Laws too gentle are seldom obeyed; too severe, seldom executed.   —Benjamin Franklin

A successful lawsuit is the one worn by a policeman.
—Robert Frost

Be you never so high, the law is above you.
—Thomas Fuller

Law is experience developed by reason and applied continually to further experience.
—Roscoe Pound, Time, May 5, 1958

The execution of the laws is more important than the making of them.   —Jefferson

Innocence finds not near so much protection as guilt.
—LA ROCHEFOUCAULD

Leadership

One of the tests of leadership is the ability to recognize a problem before it becomes an emergency.
—ARNOLD H. GLASOW

We don't want to be like the leader in the French Revolution who said, "There go my people. I must find out where they are going so I can lead them."
—THE KENNEDY WIT

The shepherd always tries to persuade the sheep that their interests and his own are the same.   —STENDHAL

Learning

Histories make men wise; poets, witty; mathematics, subtile; natural philosophy, deep; morals, grave; logic and rhetoric, able to contend.   —BACON

There are more men ennobled by study than by nature.
—CICERO

We can easily forgive a child who is afraid of the dark; the real tragedy of life is when men are afraid of the light.
—PLATO

Iron sharpens iron; scholar, the scholar.
—THE TALMUD

Lecturer

Lecturer: one with his hand in your pocket, his tongue in your ear, and his faith in your patience.
—AMBROSE BIERCE

Leisure

The secret of being miserable is to have leisure to bother about whether you are happy or not.
—GEORGE BERNARD SHAW

Liberal

I can remember way back when a liberal was one who was generous with his own money.   —WILL ROGERS

Life

Life is a long lesson in humility.   —J. M. Barrie

Life is like playing a violin solo in public and learning the instrument as one goes on.   —Samuel Butler

The tragedy of life is not so much what men suffer, but rather what they miss.   —Thomas Carlyle

Life is too short to be small.   —Disraeli

You've got to love people, places, ideas; you've got to live with mind, body, soul; you've got to be committed; there is no life on the side-lines.

—Bess Myerson Grant

It is but a few short years from diapers to dignity and from dignity to decomposition.   —Don Herold

Life can only be understood backwards, but it must be lived forwards.   —Søren Kierkegaard

Life is easier to take than you'd think; all that is necessary is to accept the impossible, do without the indispensable, and bear the tolerable.   —Kathleen Norris

Life is not a spectacle or a feast; it is a predicament.

—George Santayana

The process of living is the process of reacting to stress.
—Stanley J. Sarnoff, *Time*, November 29, 1963

Begin at once to live, and count each day as a separate life.   —Seneca

As is a tale, so is life: not how long it is, but how good it is, is what matters.   —Seneca

Simply the thing I am shall make me live.

—Shakespeare

Life is no brief candle to me; it is a sort of splendid torch which I have got hold of for the moment, and I want to make it burn as brightly as possible before handing it on to future generations.

—George Bernard Shaw

It is better to burn the candle at both ends, and in the middle, too, than to put it away in the closet and let the mice eat it.   —Henry Van Dyke

Listening

We have two ears and only one tongue in order that we may hear more and speak less.   —Diogenes

No man would listen to you talk if he didn't know it was his turn next.   —EDGAR WATSON HOWE

A good listener is not only popular everywhere, but after a while he knows something.   —WILSON MIZNER

Love

When a couple of young people strongly devoted to each other commence to eat onions, it is safe to pronounce them engaged.   —JAMES MONTGOMERY BAILEY

Love is the delightful interval between meeting a beautiful girl and discovering that she looks like a haddock.
—JOHN BARRYMORE

Love is said to be blind, but I know lots of fellows in love who can see twice as much in their sweethearts as I can.   —JOSH BILLINGS

The way to love anything is to realize that it might be lost.   —G. K. CHESTERTON

Love is an ocean of emotions, entirely surrounded by expenses.   —THOMAS ROBERT DEWAR

If you would be loved, love and be lovable.
—BENJAMIN FRANKLIN

As soon as you cannot keep anything from a woman, you love her.   —PAUL GERALDY

No one knows the worth of woman's love till he sues for alienation.   —OLIVER HERFORD

He gave her a look that you could have poured on a waffle.   —RING LARDNER

Come live in my heart and pay no rent.
—SAMUEL LOVER

Love has the power of making you believe what you would normally treat with the deepest suspicion.
—PIERRE MARIVAUX

Love is the triumph of imagination over intelligence.
—H. L. MENCKEN

Most of these love triangles are wreck tangles.
—JACOB BRAUDE

Love is a gross exaggeration of the difference between one person and everybody else.
—GEORGE BERNARD SHAW

To love her was a liberal education
                              —WILBUR DANIEL STEELE

Luck

I am a great believer in luck, and I find the harder I work the more I have of it.   —STEPHEN LEACOCK

He is so unlucky that he runs into accidents which started out to happen to somebody else.
                              —DON MARQUIS

The only good luck many great men ever had was being born with the ability and determination to overcome bad luck.   —CHANNING POLLOCK

Luxury

Give me the luxuries in life and I will willingly do without the necessities.   —FRANK LLOYD WRIGHT

Any bare necessity—with taxes added.
                              —DAVID CROWN

Lying

I can't tell a lie—even when I hear one.
                              —JOHN KENDRICK BANGS

No man has a good enough memory to make a successful liar.   —ABRAHAM LINCOLN

The tombstone is about the only thing that can stand upright and lie on its face at the same time.
                              —MARY WILSON LITTLE

Man

Every man is a volume, if you know how to read him.
                              —WILLIAM ELLERY CHANNING

It is easier to know mankind in general than man individually.   —LA ROCHEFOUCAULD

Man is the greatest miracle and greatest problem on earth.   —DAVID SARNOFF

Man was made at the end of the week's work when God was tired.   —MARK TWAIN

Mankind

One small step for a man, one giant leap for mankind.
—NEIL ARMSTRONG

The human race is in jeopardy whenever power, insensitivity and ignorance are joined together whatever the national banner. —NORMAN COUSINS

Man-Woman

The test of a man is how well he is able to feel about what he thinks. The test of a woman is how well she is able to think about what she feels.

—MARY MCDOWELL

Dancing is wonderful training for girls, it's the first way you learn to guess what a man is going to do before he does it. —CHRISTOPHER MORLEY

Most men hope that their lean years are behind them; women hope that theirs are ahead. —READER'S DIGEST

A woman is perturbed by what a man forgets—a man by what a woman remembers. —ARCH WARD

I like men who have a future and women who have a past. —OSCAR WILDE

To a smart girl, men are no problem—they're the answer. —ZSA ZSA GABOR

Manners

When Civil Service was a commodity obtainable in restaurants. —JACOB BRAUDE

Men make laws; women make manners.

—DE SÉGUR

Happiness is the best teacher of good manners; only the unhappy are churlish. —CHRISTOPHER MORLEY

Good breeding consists in concealing how much we think of ourselves and how little we think of the other person. —MARK TWAIN

Marriage

Some women work so hard to make good husbands that they never quite manage to make good wives.

—MARY ALKUS

If you are afraid of loneliness do not marry.

—CHEKHOV

Marriage is a feast where the grace is sometimes better than the dinner. —CHARLES CALEB COLTON

Don't think because there's a ring on your finger you don't have to try anymore.

—HAL DAVID, *Wives and Lovers*

It destroys one's nerves to be amiable every day to the same human being. —DISRAELI

The chain of wedlock is so heavy that it takes two to carry it, sometimes three. —ALEXANDRE DUMAS

Keep your eyes wide open before marriage, and half-shut afterwards. —BENJAMIN FRANKLIN

There is nothing stronger
and nobler than when man and wife
are of one heart and mind in a house,
A grief to their foes,
and to their friends great joy,
but their own hearts know it best. —HOMER

Many a man in love with a dimple makes the mistake of marrying the whole girl. —STEPHEN LEACOCK

The trouble with marriage is that while every woman is at heart a mother, every man is at heart a bachelor.

—E. V. LUCAS (*Reader's Digest*)

In modern wedlock, too many misplace the key.

—TOM MASSON

The great secret of successful marriage is to treat all disasters as incidents and none of the incidents as disasters.

—HAROLD NICOLSON

A husband is one who stands by you in troubles you wouldn't have had if you hadn't married him.

—READER'S DIGEST

In olden times sacrifices were made at the altar—a custom which is still continued. —HELEN ROWLAND

Matrimony was probably the first union to defy management. —CHARLES RUFFING

Why does "I do" turn into "I don't," "I won't," "I want"?

—MARILYN SCHUSTRIN

If we take matrimony at its lowest, we regard it as a sort of friendship recognized by the police.

—ROBERT LOUIS STEVENSON

Medicine
The trouble with being a hypochondriac these days is that antibiotics have cured all the good diseases.

—CASKIE STINNETT

Men
Boys will be boys, and so will a lot of middle-aged men.

—KIN HUBBARD

In relation to each other men are like irregular verbs in different languages; nearly all verbs are slightly irregular.

—SØREN KIERKEGAARD

Mind
It is well for people who think to change their minds occasionally in order to keep them clean.

—LUTHER BURBANK

Minds are like parachutes: they only function when open.

—THOMAS ROBERT DEWAR

Man's mind stretched to a new idea never goes back to its original dimensions.   —OLIVER WENDELL HOLMES

Mistakes
I can pardon everyone's mistakes except my own.

—MARCUS CATO

Moderation
I believe in moderation in all things including moderation.   —J. F. CARTER

I have not been afraid of excess: excess on occasion is exhilarating. It prevents moderation from acquiring the deadening effect of a habit.   —SOMERSET MAUGHAM

Money
Money often costs too much.

—RALPH WALDO EMERSON

The safest way to double your money is to fold it over once and put it in your pocket.   —KIN HUBBARD

I'm living so far beyond my income that we may almost be said to be living apart.   —H. H. MUNRO

When I was young I used to think that money was the most important thing in life; now that I am old, I know it is.   —OSCAR WILDE

Morals

What is moral is what you feel good after and what is immoral is what you feel bad after.

—ERNEST HEMINGWAY

A moral being is one who is capable of reflecting on his past actions and their motives—of approving of some and disapproving of others.   —CHARLES DARWIN

The state has no place in the bedrooms of the nation.

—PIERRE TRUDEAU

Motivation

The one sacred thing is the dissatisfaction of man with himself and his striving to be better than he is.

—MAXIM GORKY

The world is divided into people who do things and people who get the credit. Try, if you can, to belong to the first class. There's far less competition.

—DWIGHT MORROW

When I was a young man I observed that nine out of ten things I did were failures. I didn't want to be a failure, so I did ten times more work.

—GEORGE BERNARD SHAW

Movies

A wide screen just makes a bad film twice as bad.

—SAMUEL GOLDWYN

Music

Of all noises, I think music is the least disagreeable.

—SAMUEL JOHNSON

Wagner has beautiful moments but awful quarter hours.

—GIOACCHINO A. ROSSINI

How wonderful opera would be if there were no singers.
—GIOACCHINO A. ROSSINI

Nation

A nation can be only as great as its people want it to be.
A nation can be only as free as its people insist that it be.
A nation's laws are only as strong as its people's will to
see them enforced.   —RICHARD M. NIXON

Need

The entire sum of existence is the magic of being needed
by just one person.   —VII PUTNAM

Nerves

As nervous as a topless waitress at a candlelight dinner.
—BOB HOPE
As nervous as a tree on the Lassie program.
—FERRIS MACK

Neurotic

A person who, when you ask how she is, tells you.
—ELEANOR CLARAGE (*Reader's Digest*)

Nudity

I never expected to see the day when girls get sunburned
in the places they now do.   —WILL ROGERS

Obedience

One of the first things a man notices in a backward
country is that the children are still obeying their parents.
—CLAUDE CALLAN (*Reader's Digest*)

Obsolescence

The danger of personal obsolescence has never been
greater.   —LOUIS R. RADER

Opinion

He thinks by infection, catching an opinion like a cold.
—JOHN RUSKIN

He never chooses an opinion; he just wears whatever happens to be in style.   —LEO TOLSTOY

Opportunity

A wise man will make more opportunities than he finds.
—FRANCIS BACON

There is an hour in each man's life appointed to make his happiness, if then he seize it.
—BEAUMONT AND FLETCHER

Many are called but few get up.
—OLIVER HERFORD

Equality of opportunity is an equal opportunity to prove unequal talents.   —VISCOUNT SAMUEL

Optimism

I am an optimist. It does not seem too much use being anything else.   —WINSTON CHURCHILL

A pinch of probably is worth a pound of perhaps.
—JAMES THURBER

Parents

The two most difficult careers are entrusted to amateurs —citizenship and parenthood.
—ST. JOHN'S (Newfoundland) HERALD

Parties

Disarmament is like a party. Nobody wants to arrive until everyone else is there.   —CHANGING TIMES

Patience

Laziness is often mistaken for patience.
—FRENCH PROVERB

Patience is the art of hoping.   —VAUVENARGUES

Patriotism

"My country, right or wrong" is like saying, "My mother, drunk or sober".   —G. K. CHESTERTON

I venture to suggest that patriotism is not a short and frenzied outburst of emotion but the tranquil and steady dedication of a lifetime.   —ADLAI STEVENSON

People

There are two kinds of men who never amount to much: those who cannot do what they are told, and those who can do nothing else.   —Cyrus H. K. Curtis

God must have loved the plain people: He made so many of them.   —Abraham Lincoln

Everyone is a moon, and has a dark side which he never shows to anybody.   —Mark Twain

The two kinds of people on earth that I mean are the people who lift and the people who lean.

—Ella Wheeler Wilcox

Perfection

The nearest to perfection most people ever come is when filling out an employment application.   —Ken Kraft

Persistence

Consider the postage stamp: its usefulness consists in the ability to stick to one thing till it gets there.

—Josh Billings

Everything comes to him who hustles while he waits.

—Thomas A. Edison

Keep on going; I have never heard of anyone stumbling on anything sitting down.   —Charles Kettering

I must recommend to you what I endeavor to practice for myself, patience and perseverance.

—George Washington

Playboy

He had heard that one is permitted a certain latitude with widows, and went in for the whole 180 degrees.

—George Ade

Pleasure

The great pleasure in life is doing what people say you cannot do.   —Walter Bagehot

Poise

Always behave like a duck—keep calm and unruffled on the surface but paddle like the devil underneath.

—JACOB BRAUDE

Politicians

The world is weary of statesmen whom democracy has degraded into politicians.   —DISRAELI

Trouble is there are too many Democratic and Republican Senators and not enough United States Senators.

—SENATOR FORD

The mistake a lot of politicians make is in forgetting they've been appointed and thinking they've been anointed.

—MRS. CLAUDE PEPPER

Politicians and wives agree on one thing—if you postpone payment until some time in the future, it's not really spending.   —BILL VAUGHAN

Politics

Vote for the man who promises least; he'll be the least disappointing.   —BERNARD BARUCH

A politician is an animal who can sit on a fence and yet keep both ears to the ground.   —BEST QUOTATIONS

A politician thinks of the next election; a statesman, of the next generation.   —JAMES FREEMAN CLARKE

In politics, nothing is contemptible.   DISRAELI

Politics makes strange postmasters.   —KIN HUBBARD

The politicians were talking themselves red, white, and blue in the face.   —CLARE BOOTHE LUCE

Bad officials are elected by good citizens who do not vote.   —GEORGE JEAN NATHAN

Nothing is politically right which is morally wrong.

—DANIEL O'CONNELL

There is no more independence in politics than there is in jail.   —WILL ROGERS

Democracy substitutes election by the incompetent many for appointment by the corrupt few.

—GEORGE BERNARD SHAW

Every man who takes office in Washington either grows or swells.   —WOODROW WILSON

Pollution

Can pollution be a result of all that trash we've been burning in our TV sets?   —GOODMAN ACE

Industries seem to find it as hard to give up smoking as people do.   —BILL VAUGHAN

Poverty

For every talent that poverty has stimulated it has blighted a hundred.   —JOHN W. GARDNER

Power

Nearly all men can stand adversity, but if you want to test a man's character, give him power.

—ABRAHAM LINCOLN

In international affairs the weak can be rash, the powerful must be restrained.   —WILLIAM P. ROGERS

Praise

I praise loudly; I blame softly.

—CATHERINE II OF RUSSIA

Preaching

There is not the least use in preaching to anyone unless you chance to catch them ill.   —SYDNEY SMITH

Prejudice

The difference between a conviction and a prejudice is that you can explain a conviction without getting angry.

—READER'S DIGEST

President

When I was a boy I was told that anybody could become President; I'm beginning to believe it.

—CLARENCE DARROW

There's some folks standing behind the President that ought to get around where he can watch 'em.

—KIN HUBBARD

No man will ever bring out of the Presidency the reputation which carries him into it.   —THOMAS JEFFERSON

Problems

The best way out is always through.

—ROBERT FROST

Any man who is worth his salt has by the time he is 45 accumulated a crown of thorns, and the problem is to learn how to wear it over one ear.

—CHRISTOPHER MORLEY

Progress

No army can withstand the strength of an idea whose time has come.   —VICTOR HUGO

What we call progress is the exchange of one Nuisance for another Nuisance.   —HAVELOCK ELLIS

The longer I live the more keenly I feel that whatever was good enough for our fathers is not good enough for us.   —OSCAR WILDE

Psychoanalysis

Freud had it just backward. The task is not to make people conscious of their unconscious but to make them unconscious of their conscious.   —ROBERT M. HUTCHINS

Public Speaking

Accustomed as I am to public speaking, I know the futility of it.   —FRANKLIN PIERCE ADAMS

You can't usually tell whether a man is a finished speaker until he sits down.   —JACOB BRAUDE

A speaker who does not strike oil in ten minutes should stop boring.   —JACOB BRAUDE

Why doesn't the fellow who says, "I'm no speechmaker," let it go at that instead of giving a demonstration.

—FRANK MCKINNEY HUBBARD

Three things matter in a speech: who says it, how he says it, and what he says—and of the three, the last matters the least.   —JOHN MORLEY

Rhetoric is the art of ruling the minds of men.

—PLATO

Punctuality

The only way of catching a train I ever discovered is to miss the train before.　　—G. K. CHESTERTON

People who are late are often so much jollier than the people who have to wait for them.

—EDWARD VERRALL LUCAS

I am a believer in punctuality though it makes me very lonely.　　—EDWARD VERRALL LUCAS

I've been on a calendar, but never on time.

—MARILYN MONROE

Questions

No question is so difficult to answer as that to which the answer is obvious.　　—GEORGE BERNARD SHAW

Reading

Reading means borrowing.　　—G. C. LICHTENBERG

Knowing you'll have something good to read before bed is among the most pleasurable of sensations.

—VLADIMIR NABOKOV

Reason

It is the triumph of reason to get on well with those who possess none.　　—VOLTAIRE

Recognition

I don't recall your name, but your manners are familiar.

—OLIVER HERFORD

Regret

What cannot be repaired is not to be regretted.

—SAMUEL JOHNSON

Regret is an appalling waste of energy; you can't build on it; it's only good for wallowing in.

—KATHERINE MANSFIELD

Religion

If men are so wicked with religion, what would they be without it?　　—BENJAMIN FRANKLIN

God will forgive me; that's his business.

—HEINRICH HEINE

I feel that Simon and Garfunkel have done more to articulate a deep religious hunger in young people than Norman Vincent Peale, Billy Graham and Fulton Sheen all put together. —JOHN P. LEAHY

The half-baked sermon causes spiritual indigestion.

—AUSTIN O'MALLEY

There's too much churchianity and not enough christianity. —ADAM CLAYTON POWELL

My teachers used to say that for a Catholic I was pretty much of a Protestant. —PIERRE TRUDEAU

Research

When you take stuff from one writer, it's plagiarism; but when you take it from many writers, it's research.

—WILSON MIZNER

Reward

The reward of a thing well done is to have done it.

—RALPH WALDO EMERSON

Right

Always do right; this will gratify some people and astonish the rest. —MARK TWAIN

Rumor

Nobody believes a rumor here until it's officially denied.

—EDWARD CHEYFITZ

Nothing ever happens in a small town, but what you hear makes up for it. —VIRGINIA SAFFORD

Science

Science has promised us truth. It has never promised us either peace or happiness. —GUSTAVE LE BON

The most incomprehensible thing about the world is that it is comprehensible. —ALBERT EINSTEIN

Seeing

When indifferent, the eye takes still photographs; when interested, movies.   —AUTHOR UNKNOWN

Self-Esteem

No man can be happy unless he feels his life in some way important.   —BERTRAND RUSSELL

Silence

Blessed are they who have nothing to say, and who cannot be persuaded to say it.

—JAMES RUSSELL LOWELL

Sin

There are many people who think that Sunday is a sponge to wipe out all the sins of the week.

—HENRY WARD BEECHER

Pleasure's a sin, and sometimes sin's a pleasure.

—LORD BYRON

God may forgive your sins, but your nervous system won't.   —ALFRED KORZYBSKI

Singing

She was a town-and-country soprano of the kind often used for augmenting the grief at a funeral.

—GEORGE ADE

She was a singer who had to take any note above A with her eyebrows.   —MONTAGUE GLASS

Skill

A skill, like an appetite, demands to be used; once you have a skill you are absolutely energized.

—ERIC HOFFER

Sky

The sky is the daily bread of the eyes.

—RALPH WALDO EMERSON

Smile

They gave each other a smile with a future in it.
—RING LARDNER

Smiles

Wrinkles should merely indicate where smiles have been.
—MARK TWAIN

Smoking

Having read so much about the bad effects of smoking he decided to give up reading.   —JACOB BRAUDE

It is now proved beyond doubt that smoking is one of the leading causes of statistics.   —FLETCHER KNEBEL

What doctors seem to say in their reports on cigarette smoking is that Tobacco Road runs into a dead end.
—NATHAN NIELSEN

More than one cigar at a time is excessive smoking.
—MARK TWAIN

Snobbishness

He walks as if balancing the family tree on his nose.
—RAYMOND MOLEY

Solitude

Solitude is as needful to the imagination as society is wholesome for the character.
—JAMES RUSSELL LOWELL

Solutions

Some people think in terms of problems and some in terms of solutions.   —THEODORE KHEEL

Soul

Self is the only prison that can ever bind the soul.
—HENRY VAN DYKE

Speech

He talks like a watch which ticks away minutes, but never strikes the hour.   —SAMUEL JOHNSON

Nature, which gave us two eyes to see and two ears to hear, has given us but one tongue to speak.

—JONATHAN SWIFT

Noise proves nothing. Often a hen who has merely laid an egg cackles as if she laid an asteroid.

—MARK TWAIN

The reason there are so few good talkers in public is that there are so few thinkers in private.

—WOMAN'S HOME COMPANION

Speechmaker's Prayer

"Oh Lord," he says, "let my words be tender and sweet, for tomorrow I may have to eat them."

—NORMAN VINCENT PEALE

Statesmanship

In statesmanship, get the formalities right; never mind about the moralities.   —MARK TWAIN

Statistics

There are three kinds of lies; lies, damned lies, and statistics.   —DISRAELI

Study

He who devotes sixteen hours a day to hard study may become as wise at sixty as he thought himself at twenty.

—MARY WILSON LITTLE

Success

I had rather men should ask why no statue has been erected in my honor, than why one has.

—MARCUS PORCIUS CATO

The man who rests on his laurels is wearing them in the wrong place.   —HAROLD COFFIN

Everyone who got where he is had to begin where he was.   —ROBERT L. EVANS

Enthusiasm is the propelling force that is necessary for climbing the ladder of success.   —B. C. FORBES

The eminently successful man should beware of the tendency of wealth to chill and isolate.

—OTTO H. KAHN

The gent who wakes up and finds himself a success hasn't been asleep.   —WILSON MIZNER

The secret of business success is when you've got a lemon, make a lemonade out of it.

—JULIUS ROSENWALD

Superiority

I love being superior to myself better than [to] my equals.   —SAMUEL TAYLOR COLERIDGE

Superstition

Superstition is the religion of feeble minds.

—EDMUND BURKE

Suspicion

Suspicion is far more apt to be wrong than right; oftener unjust than just. It is no friend to virtue, and always an enemy to happiness. '   —HOSEA BALLOU

Tact

Tact consists of knowing how far we may go too far.

—JEAN COCTEAU

Without tact you can learn nothing.   —DISRAELI

To speak kindly does not hurt the tongue.

—FRENCH PROVERB

Talent

It took me fifteen years to discover I had no talent for writing, but I couldn't give it up because by that time I was too famous.   —ROBERT BENCHLEY

Natural gifts without education have more often attained to glory and virtue than education without natural gifts.

—CICERO

Every natural power exhilarates; a true talent delights the possessor first.   —RALPH WALDO EMERSON

Talk

Half the world is composed of people who have something to say and can't, and the other half who have nothing to say and keep on saying it.   —ROBERT FROST

Every time I read where some woman gave a short talk I wonder how she stopped.   —KIN HUBBARD

He can compress the most words into the smallest ideas of any man I ever met.   —ABRAHAM LINCOLN

Wise men talk because they have something to say; fools, because they have to say something.   —PLATO

His mouth works faster than his brain—he says things he hasn't thought of yet.   —READER'S DIGEST

Taste

There's no accounting for tastes, as the woman said when somebody told her her son was wanted by the police.
—FRANKLIN PIERCE ADAMS

Vulgarity is the garlic in the salad of taste.
—MARC CONNOLLY

My tastes are aristocratic; my actions democratic.
—VICTOR HUGO

Taxes

An income-tax form is like a laundry list—either way you lose your shirt.   —FRED ALLEN

The United States is the only country where it takes more brains to figure your tax than to earn the money to pay it.   —EDWARD J. GURNEY

Tears

The most effective water power in the world—women's tears.   —WILSON MIZNER

Tears are the silent language of grief.   —VOLTAIRE

Teaching

I had, out of my sixty teachers, a scant half dozen who couldn't have been supplanted by phonographs.
—DON HEROLD

Technology

The concern for man and his destiny must always be the chief interest of all technical effort.

—ALBERT EINSTEIN

Telephone

Average woman: One who can stay on the telephone longer than on a diet. —HUGH ALLEN

The telephone has been described by a sociologist as "the greatest nuisance among conveniences and the greatest convenience among nuisances." —ORTHODONTIPS

Temper

A perverse temper and fretful disposition will make any state of life whatsoever unhappy. —CICERO

We boil at different degrees.

—RALPH WALDO EMERSON

People who fly into a rage always make a bad landing.

—WILL ROGERS

Temptation

The devil's boots don't creak. —SCOTTISH PROVERB

I can resist everything except temptation.

—OSCAR WILDE

Thanks

As the cow said to the Maine farmer, "Thank you for a warm hand on a cold morning."

—THE KENNEDY WIT

Theater

A good musical comedy consists largely of disorderly conduct occasionally interrupted by talk.

—GEORGE ADE

It was one of those plays in which all the actors unfortunately enunciated very clearly.

—ROBERT BENCHLEY

Time

Americans have more timesaving devices and less time than any other group of people in the world.

—DUNCAN CALDWELL

I recommend you to take care of the minutes, for the hours will take care of themselves.

—LORD CHESTERFIELD

There is no time like the pleasant.

—OLIVER HERFORD

It's not the hours you put in; it's what you put in the hours.   —ELMER LETERMAN

Toasts

May you live all the days of your life.

—JONATHAN SWIFT

Transportation

Leisure time is no longer a problem; thanks to modern methods of transportation, you use it all up getting to and from work.   —FLETCHER KNEBEL

Travel

Tourists taking countries like vitamin pills—one a day.

—HELEN MACINNES

I dislike feeling at home when I'm abroad.

—GEORGE BERNARD SHAW

Troubles

Troubles, like babies, grow larger by nursing.

—LADY HOLLAND

Trust

Public office is a public trust.   —DAN S. LAMONT

Truth

As scarce as truth is, the supply has always been in excess of the demand.   —JOSH BILLINGS

The course of true anything never does run smooth.

—SAMUEL BUTLER

Men occasionally stumble over the truth, but most of them pick themselves up and hurry off as if nothing had happened.   —WINSTON CHURCHILL

The terrible thing about the quest for truth is that you find it.   —REMY DE GOURMONT

Pretty much all the honest truth-telling there is in the world is done by children.

—OLIVER WENDELL HOLMES

It is always the best policy to speak the truth, unless of course you are an exceptionally good liar.

—JEROME K. JEROME

He who is not very strong in memory should not meddle with lying.   —MONTAIGNE

Because I have confidence in the power of truth and of the spirit, I believe in the future of mankind.

—ALBERT SCHWEITZER

Ugliness

There are no ugly women; there are only women who do not know how to look pretty.

—JEAN DE LA BRUYÈRE

Better an ugly face than an ugly mind.

—JAMES ELLIS

Ugliness is a point of view: an ulcer is wonderful to a pathologist.   —AUSTIN O'MALLEY

Absolute and entire ugliness is rare.

—JOHN RUSKIN

Unselfishness

If I were a godfather wishing a gift on a child, it would be that he should always be more interested in other people than in himself. That's a real gift.

—COMPTON MACKENZIE

Real unselfishness consists in sharing the interests of others.   —GEORGE SANTAYANA

Vacation

No man needs a vacation so much as the person who has just had one.   —ELBERT HUBBARD

Value

I have received no more than one or two letters in my life that were worth the postage.

—HENRY DAVID THOREAU

Values

The longer one lives, the less importance one attaches to things, and also the less importance to importance.

—JEAN ROSTAND

Virtue

Recommend to your children virtue; that alone can make them happy, not gold.   —BEETHOVEN

The only reward of virtue is virtue.

—RALPH WALDO EMERSON

Only the young die good.   —OLIVER HERFORD

Men's virtues have their seasons even as fruits have.

—LA ROCHEFOUCAULD

I prefer an accommodation vice to an obstinate virtue.

—MOLIÈRE

Voice

Three things you can be judged by, your voice, your face and your disposition.   —IGNAS BERNSTEIN

Weather

If you don't like the weather in New England, just wait a few minutes.   —MARK TWAIN

Weight

He must have had a magnificent build before his stomach went in for a career of its own.

—MARGARET HALSEY

Welfare

You cannot help men permanently by doing for them what they could and should do for themselves.

—ABRAHAM LINCOLN

Wife

Of all the home remedies, a good wife is the best.

—KIN HUBBARD

Bigamy is having one wife too many. Monogamy is the same.   —H. L. MENCKEN

A loving wife will do anything for her husband except stop criticizing and trying to improve him.

—J. B. PRIESTLEY

Will

In her single person she managed to produce the effect of a majority.   —ELLEN GLASGOW

Where there's a will, there's a lawsuit.

—ADDISON MIZNER

Wisdom

It is easy to be wise after the event.

—ENGLISH PROVERB

Some are weather-wise, some are otherwise.

—BENJAMIN FRANKLIN

Gray hair is a sign of age, not of wisdom.

—GREEK PROVERB

The heart is wiser than the intellect.

—J. G. HOLLAND

Nine-tenths of wisdom consists in being wise in time.

—THEODORE ROOSEVELT

Wishing

A man will sometimes devote all his life to the development of one part of his body—the wishbone.

—ROBERT FROST

Wit

Sharp wits, like sharp knives, do often cut their owner's fingers.   —SINCLAIR LEWIS, *Arrowsmith*

A wise man will live as much within his wit as his income.   —LORD CHESTERFIELD

Wit is the salt of conversation, not the food.

—WILLIAM HAZLITT

Woman

Her features did not seem to know the value of team-work. —George Ade

I have never seen a pair of slacks that had very much slack in them. —Fred Allen

She never quite leaves her children at home, even when she doesn't take them along.

—Margaret Culkin Banning

She was a large woman who seemed not so much dressed as upholstered. —J. M. Barrie

My wife was too beautiful for words, but not for arguments. —John Barrymore

I wish Adam had died with all his ribs in his body.

—Dion Boucicault

Most women are not so young as they are painted.

—Max Beerbohm

With a man, a lie is a last resort; with women, it's First Aid. —Gelett Burgess

There are only three things in the world that women do not understand, and they are Liberty, Equality, and Fraternity. —G. K. Chesterton

A mother takes twenty years to make a man of her boy, and another woman makes a fool of him in twenty minutes.

—Robert Frost

Despite my 30 years of research into the feminine soul, I have not yet been able to answer . . . the great question that has never been answered: What does a woman want?

—Sigmund Freud

Every woman is wrong until she cries, and then she is right, instantly.

—Thomas Chandler Haliburton

A woman's mind is cleaner than a man's; she changes it more often. —Oliver Herford

Man has his will, but woman has her way.

—Oliver Wendell Holmes

Women are unpredictable. You never know how they are going to manage to get their own way.

—Franklin P. Jones

A perpetual emotion machine. —Frank Loesser

The only time a woman wishes she were a year older is when she is expecting a baby.   —MARY MARSH

A woman is never too old to yearn.

—ADDISON MIZNER

Your mind needs an uplift as well as your bust.

—CHRISTOPHER MORLEY

Why is the word "tongue" feminine in Greek, Latin, Italian, Spanish, French, and German?

—AUSTIN O'MALLEY

Every woman should have a three-way mirror in her life to see herself as others do.   —MITZI NEWHOUSE

Words

Man does not live by words alone, despite the fact that sometimes he has to eat them.   —ADLAI STEVENSON

The difference between the right word and the almost right word is the difference between lightning and the lightning bug.   —MARK TWAIN

Work

I always live by this code: You can't have bread—and loaf.   —LOUIS ARMSTRONG

I do most of my work sitting down; that's where I shine.   —ROBERT BENCHLEY

Doing a woman's work is like walking down a railroad track; the end seems in sight but never is.

—MARCELENE COX

The world is full of willing people; some willing to work, the rest willing to let them.   —ROBERT FROST

The brain is a wonderful organ; it starts working the moment you get up in the morning, and does not stop until you get into the office.   —ROBERT FROST

By working faithfully eight hours a day, you may eventually get to be a boss and work twelve hours a day.

—ROBERT FROST

I am a great believer in luck, and I find the harder I work the more I have of it.   —STEPHEN LEACOCK

My father taught me to work; he did not teach me to love it.   —ABRAHAM LINCOLN

The highest reward for man's toil is not what he gets for it but what he becomes by it.   —JOHN RUSKIN

The test of a vocation is the love of the drudgery it involves.   —LOGAN P. SMITH

Work keeps at bay three great evils: boredom, vice and need.   —VOLTAIRE

World

You'll never have a quiet world till you knock the patriotism out of the human race.

—GEORGE BERNARD SHAW

Worry

The reason why worry kills more people than work is that more people worry than work.   —ROBERT FROST

Worry is interest paid on trouble before it falls due.

—WILLIAM RALPH INGE

Life is too short for mean anxieties.

—CHARLES KINGSLEY

He who foresees calamities, suffers them twice over.

—PORTEUS

Writing

It has always been much like writing a check—it is easy to write a check if you have enough money in the bank, and writing comes more easily if you have something to say.   —SHOLEM ASCH

Sometimes it sounds like I walked out of the room and left the typewriter running.   —GENE FOWLER

With sixty staring me in the face, I have developed inflammation of the sentence structure and a definite hardening of the paragraph.   —JAMES THURBER

Youth

The young can bear solitude better than the old, for their passions occupy their thoughts.

—JEAN DE LA BRUYÈRE

In youth we learn; in age we understand.

—MARIE EBNER-ESCHENBACH

Adolescence: That period when a boy refuses to believe that someday he'll be as dumb as his father.

—HAWLEY R. EVERHART

The first years of man must make provision for the last.

—SAMUEL JOHNSON

All sorts of allowances are made for the illusions of youth; and none, or almost none, for the disenchantments of age.   —ROBERT LOUIS STEVENSON

Snow and adolescence are the only problems that disappear if you ignore them long enough.

—EARL WILSON

D. Suggested References

Excellent Inexpensive Paperbacks

FOR THE PUBLIC SPEAKER:

2500 Anecdotes for all Occasions—Fuller (Dolphin)
The Great Quotations—Seldes (Pocketbooks)
Best Quotations—Henry (Premier)
Viking Dictionary of Aphorisms
Dictionary of Humorous Quotations—Esar (Paperback)
Left Handed Dictionary—Levinson (Collier)
Reader's Digest Dictionary of Quotations

Periodicals: *Forbes Magazine,* "Thoughts on the Business of Life," monthly feature.
Vital Speeches of the Day (City News Publishing, Box 606, Southold, New York.)

FOR ADDING TO WORDROBES:

Dictionary of Synonyms and Antonyms—Devlin (Popular Special)
New Pocket Roget's Thesaurus (Washington Square Press)
Barron's Vocabulary Builder
30 Days to a Better Vocabulary—Funk & Lewis (Washington Square Press)

FOR PRONUNCIATION:

Pronunciation Dictionary of Troublesome Words—Colby (Apollo)

Better English (grammar, pronunciation, spelling)—Lewis (Dell)

Pronunciation Exercises in English—Clarey-Dixon (Regents)

Hard Cover

FOR SPEAKERS:

The International Dictionary of Thoughts (Doubleday)

Contemporary Quotations—Simpson (Crowell)

Speaker's Encyclopedia—Braude (Prentice-Hall)

Funk & Wagnall's Standard Encyclopedic Dictionary (See Quotation section)

The Complete Rhyming Dictionary—Wood (Garden City)

NBC Handbook of Pronunciation—Crowell (Crowell)

TEXTBOOKS FOR THE STUDENT:

Basic Principles of Speech—Sarett (Houghton-Mifflin)

Training the Speaking Voice—Anderson (Oxford)

Your Voice and Speech—Raubichek (Prentice-Hall)

Guide to Speech Training—Hibbitt-Norman (Ronald)

Index

The gal who asks all the right questions on the NBC-TV TODAY Show gives you her personal rules for conversational success.

How to talk with practically anybody about practically anything
by Barbara Walters

Would meeting a celebrity leave you speechless? Do you freeze with strangers at social gatherings? Is your conversation at dinner parties limited to requests for the salt? Are you unable to communicate with your boss, your secretary, your children, your mate?

Famous TV talk-star Barbara Walters reveals her personal rules for conversational success as she vividly describes her experiences on camera and off. Filled with delightfully candid stories of the great and near-great who have appeared with her on the TODAY Show, her book is both captivating reading and a guide that can dramatically enrich your conversation and your life.

"A guide to every kind of social situation, an etiquette book for the 70's . . . Excellent!"
—*Saturday Review*

A DELL BOOK $1.25